Popular Movements in Autocracies

This book presents a new explanation of the rise, development, and demise of popular movements and cycles of protest in autocracies, the conditions under which protest becomes rebellion, and the impact of protest and rebellion on democratization. Focusing on rural indigenous villages in Mexico's authoritarian regime, the book shows that the breakdown in local religious and political monopolies and the spread of competition for indigenous souls and votes empowered indigenous communities to fight for land redistribution and human rights. The expansion of electoral competition in some regions led opposition parties to eventually institutionalize protest. But the contraction of competition and the punitive implementation of neoliberal agricultural reforms in others led to the escalation of protest into rebellion and to the transformation of peasant demands into ethnic claims. The book analyzes why subnational indigenous rebellions led authoritarian elites to relinquish controls of electoral institutions and consent to free and fair national elections. Drawing on an original data set of indigenous collective action and on extensive fieldwork, the book tests its main theoretical claims through statistical analyses, natural experiments, case studies, and life histories.

Guillermo Trejo is Assistant Professor of Political Science at Duke University. He was previously on the faculty at the Centro de Investigación y Docencia Económicas (CIDE) in Mexico City. Trejo's research focuses on collective action and social movements, armed insurgencies and political violence, religion and politics, and ethnic identities. His work has been featured in the *American Political Science Review*, the *Journal of Latin American Studies*, and *Política y gobierno*. Trejo's doctoral dissertation received the 2006 Mancur Olson Award from the Political Economy Section of the American Political Science Association, and his research on religious competition and ethnic mobilization in Latin America received the 2011 Jack Walker Outstanding Article Award from the APSA Political Organizations and Parties Section.

D1595798

Cambridge Studies in Comparative Politics

General Editor
Margaret Levi, *University of Washington, Seattle*

Assistant General Editors
Kathleen Thelen, *Massachusetts Institute of Technology*
Erik Wibbels, *Duke University*

Associate Editors
Robert H. Bates, *Harvard University*
Stephen Hanson, *The College of William and Mary*
Torben Iversen, *Harvard University*
Stathis Kalyvas, *Yale University*
Peter Lange, *Duke University*
Helen Milner, *Princeton University*
Frances Rosenbluth, *Yale University*
Susan Stokes, *Yale University*

Other Books in the Series

David Austen-Smith, Jeffry A. Frieden, Miriam A. Golden, Karl Ove Moene, and Adam Przeworski, eds., *Selected Works of Michael Wallerstein: The Political Economy of Inequality Unions, and Social Democracy*

Andy Baker, *The Market and the Masses in Latin America: Policy Reform and Consumption in Liberalizing Economies*

Lisa Baldez, *Why Women Protest: Women's Movements in Chile*

Stefano Bartolini, *The Political Mobilization of the European Left, 1860–1980: The Class Cleavage*

Robert Bates, *When Things Fell Apart: State Failure in Late-Century Africa*

Mark Beissinger, *Nationalist Mobilization and the Collapse of the Soviet State*

Nancy Bermeo, ed., *Unemployment in the New Europe*

Carles Boix, *Democracy and Redistribution*

Carles Boix, *Political Parties, Growth, and Equality: Conservative and Social Democratic Economic Strategies in the World Economy*

Catherine Boone, *Merchant Capital and the Roots of State Power in Senegal, 1930–1985*

Catherine Boone, *Political Topographies of the African State: Territorial Authority and Institutional Change*

(*continued after Index*)

Popular Movements in Autocracies

Religion, Repression, and Indigenous Collective Action in Mexico

GUILLERMO TREJO

Duke University

CAMBRIDGE
UNIVERSITY PRESS

CAMBRIDGE
UNIVERSITY PRESS

32 Avenue of the Americas, New York NY 10013-2473, USA

Cambridge University Press is part of the University of Cambridge.

It furthers the University's mission by disseminating knowledge in the pursuit of education, learning and research at the highest international levels of excellence.

www.cambridge.org
Information on this title: www.cambridge.org/9781107680562

© Guillermo Trejo 2012

First published 2012
First paperback edition 2014

A catalogue record for this publication is available from the British Library

Library of Congress Cataloguing in Publication data
Trejo, Guillermo.
  Popular movements in autocracies : religion, repression, and indigenous
  collective action in Mexico / Guillermo Trejo.
    p.   cm. – (Cambridge studies in comparative politics)
  Includes bibliographical references and index.
  ISBN 978-0-521-19772-4 (hardback)
  1. Land reform – Mexico.   2. Social movements – Mexico.   3. Indians of
  Mexico.   4. Democratization – Mexico.   I. Title.
  HD1331.M6T74   2012
  333.3´172–dc23   2011047839

ISBN 978-0-521-19772-4 Hardback
ISBN 978-1-107-68056-2 Paperback

To Anne

Contents

List of Figures		*page* xi
List of Maps		xiii
List of Tables		xiv
Preface		xv
List of Acronyms		xix
	Introduction	1

PART I. THEORY

1.	A Theory of Popular Collective Action in Autocracies	29

PART II. PROTEST

2.	Accounting for Mexico's Cycle of Indigenous Protest: Quantitative Evidence	59
3.	Competing for Souls: Why the Catholic Church Became a Major Promoter of Indigenous Mobilization	85
4.	Competing for Votes: Why Electoral Competition Shaped Mexico's Cycle of Indigenous Protest	111

PART III. REBELLION

5.	A Call to Arms: Regime Reversion Threats and the Escalation of Protest into Rebellion	141
6.	From Social Movement to Armed Rebellion: Religious Networks and the Microdynamics of Rebel Recruitment	172

PART IV. THE POLITICIZATION OF ETHNICITY

7.	Politicizing Ethnicity: The Breakdown of Religious and Political Hegemonies and the Rise of Indigenous Identities	201

8. The Twilight of Ethnicity: Democratization as an Elite Strategy
    to Avert Mexico's Indigenous Insurgency   231
    Conclusion   254

Appendix A. Collecting Protest Event Data in Autocracies:
Indigenous Protest in Mexico   273
Appendix B. Additional Statistical Results   278
Appendix C. Criteria for Targeted Fieldwork and Ethnographic
Interviews   280
Appendix D. Questions from Public Opinion Surveys   285
References   289
Index   303

Figures

I.1. Mexico's cycle of indigenous protest, 1975–2000
(number of events)   *page* 4

I.2. International rights, neoliberal reforms, and indigenous
protest   6

I.3. Religious competition, electoral competition, and indigenous
protest   8

I.4. Land liberalization and the transformation of protest into
rebellion   11

I.5. International rights, neoliberal reforms, and the rise of ethnic
identities (proportion of indigenous protest events with
ethnic claims)   13

1.1. Traditional closed corporate communities   35

1.2. Structural dimensions of a typical ranked society in
Mesoamerica   51

2.1. Count of indigenous protest events by type, 1975–2000   62

2.2. Indigenous claims in protest events by category (relative
contribution)   64

2.3. (a) Total land area (hectares) and proportion of high-quality
land titled in Mexico. (b) Area of land (hectares) titled and
distributed in Chiapas   68

3.1. Decentralized and horizontal regional network with strong local
leaders and dense local associational networks   101

4.1. CIOAC networks in Chiapas, 1980s   114

4.2. Repression against indigenous populations by perpetrator
(relative contribution)   116

4.3. Centralized and hierarchical regional network with weak
local leaders and weak local associational networks   118

5.1. (a) Currency devaluation and rebellion. (b) Inflation
and rebellion. (c) International coffee price and rebellion.
(d) Neoliberal agricultural policy reform and rebellion   148

5.2. The impact of autocracy on the probability of rebellion
at different levels of protest   155

5.3. (a) Indigenous protest in Oaxaca and Chiapas. (b) Repression
against indigenous populations in Oaxaca and Chiapas   158

6.1. Social networks and rebel recruitment   192

7.1. Indigenous demands in protest events by category
(relative contribution)   206

7.2. Count of indigenous protest events with explicit ethnic
claims   212

7.3. Proportion of Zapatista actions with claims of ethnic
autonomy and self-determination   224

8.1. Coalition formation among leftist forces in Mexico:
(a) 1977–1993 and (b) 1994–1996   236

8.2. (a) Support for EZLN and (b) support for EZLN by
partisanship   238

8.3. Approval of Zapatista armed invasion of municipal
territories by partisanship   246

8.4. Sympathies for EZLN among leftist voters before
and after the 1997 midterm elections   247

Maps

2.1. Indigenous protest in Mexico, 1975–2000   *page* 63
5.1. Indigenous insurgent activity in Mexico, 1994–1997   146
6.1. Levels of Zapatista support by municipality in Chiapas,
     1992–1993   179
6.2. Geography of rebel support by village in Las Margaritas,
     Chiapas, 1992–1993   188

Tables

2.1. Negative Binomial Models of Intensity of Indigenous
Protest by Mexican Indigenous Municipality, 1975–2000   *page* 78

5.1. Views of Rural Population about Termination of Land
Reform Program and Liberalization of Land Tenure in
Mexico, November 1991   149

5.2. Ordered Probit and Probit Models of Levels of Indigenous
Rebel Activity by Mexican State for the 1994–1997 Period   153

5.3. Controlled Comparison of Two Mexican States, 1990   157

5.4. Penalties Associated with Different Forms of Collective
Action in Chiapas's Criminal Law, 1991   160

6.1. Ordered Probit Models of Levels of Community
Involvement in the EZLN across Indigenous
Municipalities in Chiapas, 1992–1993   184

7.1. Leading Zapatista Demands in Two Rounds of Peace
Negotiations   208

7.2. Negative Binomial Models of Intensity of Ethnic
Claim-Making by Mexican Indigenous Municipality,
1975–2000   216

7.3. Ordered Probit Regression Estimates of the Establishment
of a Zapatista Rebel Autonomous Municipality (MAREZ)
in Chiapas, 1996–2000   227

A.B.1. Negative Binomial Models of Intensity of Indigenous
Protest by Indigenous Municipality in Chiapas, 1987   278

A.B.2. OLS Regression Estimates of Extent of Indigenous
Rights by State in Mexico, 2000   279

A.C.1. List of Interviewees   283

Preface

This book is about popular movements in autocracies. It seeks to explain how the poor become organized, the conditions that enable them to take their claims to the streets and to the remote countryside, and the impact their collective action may have on the prospect of stability and change in authoritarian regimes. While most of our research in the social sciences focuses on the ways governments and international agencies can help the poor overcome economic adversity, the goal of this book is to explain how the poor take charge of their destiny themselves and collectively defy authoritarian rulers.

The book focuses on Latin America's indigenous populations – by some measures the population segment facing the harshest levels of economic, political, and social exclusion in the world today (Gurr, 1993). Although much has been written about the unprecedented wave of indigenous mobilization that took place in Latin America in the last quarter of the twentieth century, in this book I develop new theoretical propositions about the causes and consequences of indigenous mobilization in autocracies and test them against new quantitative and qualitative evidence. My goal is to remain as general as possible in theorizing about popular collective action in autocracies and to be as specific as possible in testing and explaining the microdynamics of popular mobilization in Mexico's rural indigenous villages. This book is necessarily multidisciplinary; it combines a variety of social science theories and methods, ranging from political science and economics to sociology, anthropology, and history, and from statistical methods to case studies and life histories.

The writing of this book went through many different stages. At every stage I benefited from support and feedback from prestigious institutions and generous colleagues and friends.

The book began as a dissertation project at the University of Chicago. Chicago's distinguished environment combining intellectual creativity and methodological rigor proved an ideal place to acquire the nuts and bolts of social science research. Witnessing faculty develop some of the pioneering and most influential cross-national and subnational data sets to answer vital questions about democracy and civil war was both illuminating and educational.

The scholarship, teaching, intellectual guidance, and mentorship of Susan Stokes were crucial in the conception, development, and completion of my dissertation. I owe much of my understanding of the social sciences and of comparative politics to David Laitin; his pioneering emphasis on the need for methodological triangulation has informed every step I have taken in my research. The intellectual feedback of John Padgett in the early stages of the dissertation was fundamental for launching my dissertation project, and the invaluable input of Carles Boix and Luis F. Medina were vital for its completion.

I conducted most of the data gathering and the initial quantitative analyses for this project as a member of the Department of Political Studies at CIDE in Mexico City. The scholarly commitment of the CIDE community to the development of original and systematic evidence for hypotheses testing was the ideal environment to launch a project that involved many years of data collection and analysis. I am grateful for the advice and intellectual support of Francisco Abundis, José Antonio Aguilar, Javier Aparicio, Jorge Buendía, María Amparo Casar, Alfonso Hernández, Matthew Kocher, Fabrice Lehoucq, Ignacio Marván, Gabriel Negretto, and Alain de Remes. The intellectual influence of colleagues from CIDE's Department of Historical Studies proved to be crucial in the transition from dissertation to book. My interest in life histories owes much to Luis Barrón, Gilles Bataillon, and Jean Meyer. I thank Carlos Elizondo and Blanca Heredia for their enthusiastic support during my years at CIDE. And I am grateful to my extraordinary CIDE students for helping me understand my vocation as a scholar and a teacher.

The transformation from dissertation to book took place after I moved from Mexico City to Durham, NC, and joined Duke in 2005, where, as our discipline was beginning to extensively use experimental methodologies, I became aware of the need to complement the statistical results of my research with new evidence. New social science research based on natural experiments and the experimental turn that some practitioners of case studies were taking became a persuasive invitation to rethink my use of quantitative and qualitative evidence and to go back to the field with new eyes and tools.

Duke's vibrant intellectual community was an ideal place to conduct these tasks and to complete this book. The advice I received from Karen Remmer and Erik Wibbels was crucial; feedback from Pablo Beramendi, William Keech, and David Soskice alerted me to new paths of research; and conversations with Donald Horowitz, Herbert Kitschelt, Timur Kuran, Abdeslam Maghraoui, and Margaret McKean helped me sharpen underdeveloped arguments and ideas. During my years at Duke, conversations with Pedro Lasch have been a constant reminder of the advantages of looking for creative answers in the most unexpected places. The collegial support of Alexander Downes and Ruth Grant was vitally important at critical times. My ongoing dialogue with Duke students has been fundamental for the evolution of my research. I am grateful for insightful discussions with those students who participated in my seminars on Collective Action and Social Movements, Political Violence, Religion and Politics, and Comparative Ethnic Politics.

The generous feedback I have received at workshop and seminar presentations over the past years has forced me to rethink my research in important ways. I have benefited from critical commentaries made by discussants and regular participants at presentations I have given at American University, Brown University, CIDE (Mexico), Columbia University, Cornell University, Duke University, Juan March Institute (Spain), Stanford University, the University of Chicago, the University of Florence (Italy), the University of North Carolina–Chapel Hill, the University of Notre Dame, the University of Texas–Austin, the University of Virginia, the Woodrow Wilson International Center for Scholars, and Yale University.

Insightful suggestions made by a number of remarkable colleagues and individuals led me to sharpen the main arguments of the book. I am grateful to Norma Alvarez, Jorge Bravo, Araceli Burguete, Matthew Cleary, Michael Coppedge, Cristina Corduneanu-Huci, Luis de la Calle, Alberto Diaz-Cayeros, Todd Eisenstadt, Rodrigo Elizarrarás, Federico Estévez, James Fearon, Marco Fernández, Edward Gibson, Eduardo Guerrero, Claudio Jones, Stathis Kalyvas, Robert Kaufman, Juan Antonio Leclercq, Claudio Lomnitz, Raul Madrid, Beatriz Magaloni, Scott Mainwaring, Shannan Mattiace, María Victoria Murillo, Julio Rios-Figueroa, Graeme Robertson, Ben Schneider, Lenka Siroki, Richard Snyder, Willibald Sonnleitner, Sidney Tarrow, and Daniel Treisman.

The generosity of a number of institutions and individuals facilitated data gathering and fieldwork for this project. I am grateful to the personnel of the Universidad Iberoamericana in Mexico City who provided me with thousands of newspapers over the course of eight months of intense data gathering. I owe a special word of gratitude to Mauro Monreal of Prodato (formerly SIPRO) for giving me access to his unparalleled collection of more than three million news clips stored at his home in Mexico City. I want to express my gratitude to the late Amado Avendaño and the late André Aubrey for opening the doors of their personal newspaper archives in San Cristóbal de Las Casas, Chiapas. Going through thousands of newspapers in the garage of the Avendaño family home while holding daily conversations with Don Amado – one of the most important journalists and social leaders in late-twentieth-century Chiapas – was the most valuable history lesson I have ever received. I am also grateful to researchers at CIACH for allowing me to spend several months of data gathering in their Chiapas office.

Rosalba Gómez and her family generously facilitated the logistics of my fieldwork in Chilón, Chiapas, and Ivania de la Cruz, Vicente de la Cruz, and Juan Pablo Morales facilitated my work in Oaxaca. But I am particularly indebted to all the interviewees who spent many hours sharing their life stories during in-depth interviews with me. I am grateful for their trust and for opening the doors of their offices, homes, places of worship, and lives to a researcher who simply knocked on their doors with no prior connections. As I explain in Appendix C, bypassing "academic brokers" and establishing direct contacts with interviewees who had been previously selected based on the statistical analysis was a crucial part of my fieldwork strategy.

Two grants from Duke's Center for Latin American and Caribbean Studies facilitated my fieldwork in Southern Mexico and the final stages of production of the book. I am grateful to Natalie Hartman and her teammates for their unconditional support and encouragement.

The hard work and commitment to excellence of a group of remarkable research assistants – some of whom are now themselves successful professionals – were crucial. I was fortunate to count on the full-time assistance of (in chronological order) Rosario Aguilar, Rolando Ochoa, Santiago Campero, Javier Madrid, Javier Márquez, and Sandra Ley. I also benefited from the efficient and enthusiastic part-time assistance of Nilbia Coyote, Marco Fernández, Sebastián Garrido, and Maralá Goode. In the final stages of preparation of this book, Sandra Ley, Sebastián Garrido, and Javier Márquez provided me with invaluable theoretical and methodological feedback. Working with this group of extraordinary research assistants was one of the most gratifying aspects of this long journey.

While writing this book, I have benefited from the editorial assistance of Margaret Schroeder. Margaret has been a tireless and thorough editor, and her invaluable professional input has helped me sharpen the language and content of this book in ways that go beyond usual editorial work.

Working with Cambridge University Press has been a privilege. I am grateful to Margaret Levi for her confidence in this project and to Lew Bateman and Anne Lovering-Rounds for the efficiency with which they took me through every stage of production of this manuscript. The generous intellectual feedback of Anthony Gill and a second reviewer forced me to rethink and helped me improve the final manuscript in fundamental ways. I am grateful for their timely input.

My nuclear and extended families have provided me with emotional support that has been vital for the research and writing of this book. I am grateful to my own Trejo Osorio clan for their unconditional friendship and to the Baxes for their continuous support. I want to express a special note of gratitude to Evita, my mother, whose extraordinary inner personal drive and tenacity to overcome adversity accompany me every day. I am thankful to Julian and Natalia who brighten every moment of my existence. I dedicate this book to Anne, who is my greatest source of personal and professional inspiration and my coauthor in life.

Acronyms

ANCIEZ	Alianza Nacional Campesina Independendiente Emiliano Zapata / Emiliano Zapata National Independent Alliance
ARIC-UU	Asociación Rural de Interés Colectivo-Unión de Uniones / Rural Collective Interest Association
CDHFBLC	Centro de Derechos Humanos Fray Bartolomé de Las Casas / Fray Bartolomé de Las Casas Human Rights Center
CDLI	Centro de Defensa de Las Libertades / Center for the Defense of Liberties
CEB	Comunidades Eclesiales de Base / Ecclesiastic Base Communities
CEC	Centro de Educación Campesina / Center for Peasant Education
CEDIPIO	Centro Diocesano de Pastoral Indígena de Oaxaca / Diocesan Indigenous Pastoral Center of Oaxaca
CIACH	Centro de Información y Análisis de Chiapas / Center of Information and Analysis of Chiapas
CIDE	Centro de Investigación y Docencia Económicas / Center for the Research and Teaching of Economics
CIOAC	Central Independiente de Obreros Agrícolas y Campesinos / Independent Central of Agricultural Workers and Peasants
CNC	Confederación Nacional Campesina / National Peasant Confederation
CNPA	Confederación Nacional Plan de Ayala / Plan de Ayala National Confederation
COCEI	Coalición Obrero-Campesino-Estudiantil del Istmo / Worker-Peasant-Student Coalition of the Isthmus
COCOPA	Comisión de Concordia y Pacificación / Commission for Peace and Reconciliation
CUC	Comité de Unidad Campesina / United Peasants Committee
DESMI	Desarrollo Económico y Social de los Mexicanos Indígenas / Center for the Social and Economic Development of Indigenous Mexicans

EPG	Ejército del Pueblo Guatemalteco / Guatemalan People's Army
EPR	Ejército Popular Revolucionario / Revolutionary Popular Army
EZLN	Ejército Zapatista de Liberación Nacional / Zapatista National Liberation Army
FECCAS	Federación Cristiana de Campesinos Salvadoreños / Christian Federation of Salvadoran Peasants
FSLN	Frente Sandinista de Liberación Nacional / Sandinista National Liberation Front
GATT	General Agreement on Tariffs and Trade
IFE	Instituto Federal Electoral / Federal Electoral Institute
ILO	International Labor Organization
MAREZ	Municipios Autónomos Rebeldes Zapatistas / Zapatista Rebel Autonomous Municipalities
MII	Mexican Indigenous Insurgency Database
MST	Movimento dos Trabalhadores Rurais Sem Terra / Landless Rural Workers Movement
NAFTA	North American Free Trade Agreement
OCEZ	Organización Campesina Emiliano Zapata / Emiliano Zapata Peasant Organization
PAN	Partido Acción Nacional / National Action Party
PCM	Partido Comunista Mexicano / Mexican Communist Party
PP	Poder Popular / Popular Power
PRD	Partido de la Revolución Democrática / Party of the Democratic Revolution
PRI	Partido Revolucionario Institucional / Institutional Revolutionary Party
PST	Partido Socialista de los Trabajadores / Workers' Socialist Party
PSUM	Partido Socialista Unificado de México / Unified Mexican Socialist Party
RAZ	Región Autónoma Zapatista / Zapatista Autonomous Region
SCLC	San Cristóbal de las Casas
SERAPAZ	Servicio para la Paz / Service for Peace
SERESURE	Seminario Regional del Sureste / Southeast Regional Seminary
SIL	Summer Institute of Linguistics
SIPRO	Servicio de Información Procesada / Service of Processed Information
TCO	Trabajo Común Organizado / Communal Organized Work
UCIRI	Union de Comunidades Indígenas de la Región del Istmo / Union of Indigenous Communities of the Isthmus

Introduction

THREE EXPERIENCES OF MICROLEVEL MOBILIZATION

Acquiescence

January 1, 1994 was an ordinary day in the lives of the Zoque Indians of Ocotepec – a poor, rural, predominantly indigenous municipality[1] in the western mountains of the southern Mexican state of Chiapas. As in most precapitalist agrarian societies, Zoque households consumed what they produced – coffee and corn. Two-thirds of Ocotepec's households were poor, and women followed traditional roles as mothers, housewives, and bearers of the Zoque culture. Two years earlier, when the Mexican government had ended a six-decade-old land reform program and amended the constitution to liberalize land tenure, Zoque Indians – like most rural households in Mexico – privately opposed the marketization of agricultural life but did not publicly contest it.[2] Nor did they publicly oppose the North American Free Trade Agreement (NAFTA), which went into effect on the first day of 1994.

Conspicuously absent from every cycle of rural indigenous mobilization that took place in Chiapas in the last quarter of the twentieth century (Lisbona, 2006), on the evening of January 1, Zoque households learned through national television that Tzeltal, Tzotzil, Chol, and Tojolabal Indians of the Zapatista National Liberation Army (EZLN) earlier that day had launched a major military offensive against the Mexican government and the army, gaining control over seven of Chiapas's indigenous municipalities in the central highlands and Lacandón jungle. Like most members of Mexico's sixty-two ethnolinguistic

---

[1] *Municipalidades* are second-level administrative regions within states; approximately equivalent to counties.

[2] A government-sponsored survey conducted one year before the reform showed that between two-thirds and three-quarters of Mexico's rural population opposed the end of land reform and the liberalization of land tenure. See Oficina de la Presidencia de la República (1991). For a more extensive discussion of this survey, see Chapter 5 and Appendix D.

indigenous groups, that evening, Zoque families heard for the first time the Zapatistas' appeal to all Mexican "progressive forces" to join them in removing Mexico's "neoliberal dictatorship." But they never joined.

Protest

January 1, 1994 was no ordinary day in the lives of Tzeltal villagers of the poor, rural, predominantly indigenous municipality of Tenejapa in the eastern part of the Chiapas highlands. Traditional male-dominated Tzeltal households, which grew corn, beans, coffee, and tropical fruits, had strongly and publicly opposed the liberalization of land tenure and NAFTA. Since the mid-1970s, Tzeltal villagers from Tenejapa had been important players in Chiapas's multiple cycles of rural indigenous mobilization. Over the course of two decades, they had created a dense associational network of economic and social cooperatives and strong local peasant and indigenous organizations that periodically engaged in peaceful demonstrations, demanding land redistribution, respect for human rights, and free and fair elections.

Even though the EZLN had not succeeded in recruiting combatants from Tenejapa, several Tzeltal communities in the municipality became sympathizers and were aware of the rebel plans to go to war. Seven days after the outbreak of conflict, Tenejapa became a battleground for Zapatista forces and the Mexican army, and Tenejapa villagers facilitated the rebels' retreat into the Lacandón jungle. In subsequent years, some of the municipality's most influential rural indigenous organizations followed the Zapatistas and other indigenous movements in transforming their collective claims for land and democracy into demands for autonomy and self-determination for indigenous peoples.

Rebellion

January 1, 1994 was an extraordinary day in the lives of Tzeltal villagers of the poor, predominantly rural, indigenous municipality of Altamirano in eastern Chiapas. After years of peaceful mobilization and land struggle, thousands of villagers from Altamirano had joined the EZLN and become a bastion of the rebel group. Assisted by their families, friends, and neighbors, on January 1, Zapatistas from Altamirano led the rebel occupation of the municipal palace of their hometown. It would be the first day of a long new journey that would lead many indigenous villagers from Altamirano and other municipalities in Chiapas into violent, fiercely fought territorial struggles against government security forces and paramilitary groups linked to the Institutional Revolutionary Party (PRI), the party that ruled Mexico from 1929 to 2000. Claiming legitimacy under Convention 169 of the International Labor Organization (ILO), which recognizes major ethno-territorial rights for indigenous peoples, the EZLN was able to establish de facto parallel municipal governments in up to one-third of Chiapas's municipalities, including Altamirano.

Ethnic Identification

Even though Zoque and Tzeltal villagers in Ocotepec, Tenejapa, and Altamirano spoke indigenous languages in their communities and indigenous customary practices remained important for everyday forms of local governance, for most of the twentieth century they did not articulate their public claims in ethnic terms. In the context of single-party hegemony, the government and the PRI dissuaded rural indigenous villagers from framing their public demands using ethnic identities and encouraged them instead to negotiate their claims on the state in terms of class (peasant) demands. Yet after two decades of peasant mobilization, independent rural indigenous movements in such places as Tenejapa and Altamirano transformed their claims for land and free and fair elections into demands for ethno-territorial controls and self-determination for indigenous peoples. The dramatic transformation of the EZLN from a peasant insurgency into a self-determination movement one year after the outbreak of war in Chiapas forced the government and party officials of an authoritarian regime that had fought for half a century to suppress ethnic forms of identification to negotiate rights to autonomy and self-determination for indigenous peoples.

QUESTIONS

Why do poor rural villagers living under similar economic and demographic conditions adopt such different strategies of collective action in response to major economic policy reforms they equally oppose? Why do the poor – like the Zoque of Ocotepec – so often not express their grievances publicly and de facto acquiesce to major reforms they privately oppose? What are the conditions under which poor rural villagers – like the Tzeltal of Altamirano and Tenejapa – succeed in creating autonomous organizations and join independent movements to peacefully express their grievances in the streets? What circumstances lead communities of independent movements to shift their struggles from the streets to the mountains and the jungles and to embrace the path of armed rebellion? What drives peasant movements and armed rebel groups to politicize demands and social identities previously stigmatized by authoritarian rulers like ethnicity?

Like most countries in Latin America, Mexico experienced a major wave of rural indigenous mobilization in the last quarter of the twentieth century. Based on a systematic review of eight Mexican national newspapers, Figure I.1 provides an empirical image of Mexico's cycle of indigenous protest. It shows the evolution of 3,553 acts of rural indigenous peaceful mobilization that took place in any of Mexico's 883 rural indigenous municipalities between 1975 and 2000.[3] Unlike the major urban demonstrations in capital cities around

---

[3] The Mexican federation has 31 states and 2,442 municipalities. Census authorities use linguistic criteria to identify indigenous populations. In this study Mexican municipalities with more than

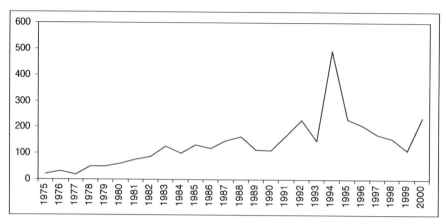

FIGURE 1.1. Mexico's cycle of indigenous protest, 1975–2000 (number of events).
Source: Mexican Indigenous Insurgency Dataset (MII). See Appendix A.

the world that typically capture the attention of the international media, these were tiny acts of micro mobilization that involved approximately 200 rural indigenous villagers who took their claims from the highlands or the lowlands into Mexico's state capitals and municipal seats. These were marches, sit-ins, and road blockades led by rural indigenous villagers like the Tzeltal of Altamirano and Tenejapa and that usually went unnoticed by the international press.

DOMINANT EXPLANATIONS

The canonical explanation of indigenous mobilization in Latin America suggests that the introduction of market-oriented neoliberal reforms and the expansion of capitalist markets into predominantly rural indigenous areas was the main motivation that triggered the wave of indigenous collective action.[4]

In Yashar's (2005) influential explanation, indigenous communities that survived under the façade of corporatist peasant unions built by populist authoritarian regimes and sustained through policies of land reform and agricultural subsidies led the mobilization against neoliberalism and capitalist penetration of their communities.[5] A crucial assumption in this explanation is that as members of state-controlled rural unions, indigenous villagers developed two identities: they acted as *peasants* in their negotiations with national state authorities but retained their *indigenous* identities in their villages. Beneath

10 percent of indigenous-language speakers at any time between 1970 and 2000 are classified as "indigenous" (N = 883).
[4] See Van Cott (1995, 2001 and 2008), Yashar (1998, 2005), and Brysk (2000) in the political science literature. For influential statements in anthropology see Bonfil (1987/1996) and Nash (2001), Gilly (1998) in history, and Rosero (1990) and Le Bot (1994) in sociology.
[5] This is Yashar's (1998, 2005) explanation of indigenous mobilization in the Andean highlands.

corporatist structures of state control, indigenous communities retained a space of local autonomy that enabled the survival of indigenous cultures and identities.[6]

In this account, the introduction of neoliberal agrarian reforms and the dismantling of traditional sources of peasant support eroded corporatist rural unions and became a major threat to indigenous local autonomy and cultural survival. This threat motivated indigenous communities to take to the streets and to the mountains to contest the destruction of their sphere of autonomy and cultural survival. In this struggle, the coporatist structures that had once served as mechanisms of state control ironically became the mobilizing vehicles for the articulation of indigenous villagers into regional and national movements against neoliberalism and for autonomy and self-determination.[7]

In the canonical explanation, democratization and the decline of state repression provided the political space for the expression of indigenous demands in the public arena, and the introduction of a new international regime of indigenous rights in the late 1980s provided the language and grammar for rural indigenous movements to justify their struggle against neoliberalism in terms of ethnocultural rights – the rights to autonomy and self-determination for indigenous peoples.[8]

Figure I.2 presents a visual description of the dominant explanation of indigenous mobilization based on empirical evidence from Mexico's cycle of indigenous protest. Three crucial events are identified: (1) the end of a six-decade-long program of land reform and the liberalization of land tenure in 1992 (neoliberal reforms); (2) Mexico's adoption of ILO Convention 169 in 1989 (international indigenous rights); and (3) the country's democratization in 2000 (democracy).

[6] This is an argument that echoes one of the most influential works in contemporary Latin American anthropology: Bonfil's *México profundo* (1987/1996). In "Deep Mexico," Bonfil argues that "appropriation" is a crucial mechanism for indigenous cultural survival (pp. 132–136). Appropriation is a process by which indigenous communities take control of foreign cultural elements and put them at the service of the group's own ends of cultural survival. In his words, through appropriation "[indigenous communities] create and re-create their culture, adjust it to changing pressures, and reinforce their own, private sphere of control. They take cultural elements and put them at their service; they critically perform the collective acts that are a way of expressing and renewing their own identity." (p. xvi)

[7] A second, related view suggests that in remote regions where states did not establish corporatist organizations, indigenous communities remained relatively isolated, continued practicing self-governance, and were able to retain ancient cultural norms and ethnic identities. Communities in these "regions of refuge" rejected outside influences and developed conservative traditional practices that withstood innovations imposed from outside. This is Yashar's (2005) explanation for indigenous mobilization in the Andean lowlands. It also echoes Bonfil's discussion of two other mechanisms of indigenous cultural survival: resistance to outside cultural imposition and to innovation from outside. In Bonfil's influential analysis resistance to outside imposition usually takes place in "regions of refuge" where indigenous communities live relatively isolated from the Mestizo and Ladino society (1987/1996: 131–135).

[8] See Brysk (2000) for the most elaborate analysis of the rise and impact of a new international regime for indigenous rights.

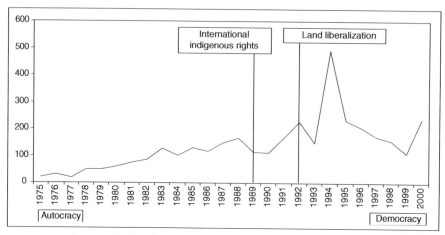

FIGURE I.2. International rights, neoliberal reforms, and indigenous protest.

This visual evidence suggests that any argument claiming that indigenous protest in Mexico resulted from the introduction of neoliberal agrarian reforms, the development of a new international regime of indigenous rights, or democratization would grossly underpredict the extent of indigenous mobilization – it would leave unexplained nearly a thousand protest events. As Figure I.2 shows, Mexico's cycle of indigenous protest began nearly two decades before the liberalization of land tenure and the introduction of a new international system of indigenous rights and a quarter of a century before the PRI lost presidential power in 2000.

While market-oriented reforms may have intensified and radicalized indigenous collective action and a new international regime of indigenous rights may have provided incentives for the politicization of ethnicity, the fact is that Mexico's cycle of indigenous protest was not initially triggered by the adoption of neoliberal agrarian reforms; it began under developmentalist economic systems when neoliberalism was not even part of the policy language of Latin American elites. This movement was not a post-transition phenomenon either; it began under autocracy and evolved as Mexico's authoritarian regime underwent significant transformations. In fact, as this book will show, indigenous mobilization had a major impact on the country's transition to democracy.

I take these empirical observations as an invitation to reframe and refine our initial questions about indigenous collective action. Rather than begin with markets and democracy, our inquiry should take us to the heart of authoritarian politics. We should try to understand how poor rural indigenous villagers created autonomous social organizations in autocracies and the conditions that enabled them to take their grievances to the streets despite repression. We should try to understand whether and why major policy transformations – such as the end of land reform and the liberalization of land tenure – and major changes in international institutions – such as the introduction of ILO

Convention 169 – may have stimulated the radicalization of indigenous collective action and the rise of ethnic identities. Finally, we should assess the long-term effect of protest and rebellion on the survival of authoritarian regimes.

A NEW EXPLANATION

This book develops an alternative sociopolitical explanation of indigenous mobilization centered on two of the most important transformations that took place in Latin America's indigenous world in the last quarter of the twentieth century: the breakdown of religious and political monopolies. In this book I argue that this dissolution of local religious and political monopolies and the spread of competition for souls and votes empowered indigenous communities to engage in large-scale movements for land redistribution and government agricultural support. When elites sought to implement neoliberal agrarian reforms through coercive means, eliminating basic civil rights and liberties, they contributed to indigenous radicalization – to the transformation of peaceful protest into armed rebellion and to the rise of movements for autonomy and self-determination for indigenous peoples.

Indigenous Protest

Competing for Indigenous Souls. In this book I suggest that a major wave of U.S. Protestant missionary activity in Mexico's poor rural indigenous regions in the last quarter of the twentieth century triggered an unprecedented process of religious competition between Catholic and Protestant churches; the rise of competition for indigenous souls in historically monopolistic Catholic religious markets, I argue, led to a major transformation of the internal power structures of rural indigenous communities and to the rise of new leaders, associational networks, and organizations that spearheaded or participated in ambitious movements for land redistribution and indigenous rights.[9]

Following a decentralized strategy of evangelizing, U.S. Protestant missionaries translated Bibles to indigenous languages, developed literacy programs and health clinics and established local community churches led by indigenous male villagers. In areas where the Catholic Church had been the only religious supplier and had underserved poor rural indigenous villagers for centuries, these novel proselytizing strategies attracted thousands of young indigenous villagers. Competition and the availability of an exit option empowered those who did not join the new churches to demand a major transformation of the Catholic Church to their ecclesiastic authorities or else defect.

Unable to decentralize ecclesiastic hierarchies to the extent that U.S. Protestant missionaries did, and facing a major reputation deficit for having sided with the rich and powerful for centuries, Catholic authorities in competitive districts

---

[9] I follow the political economy of religion (Iannaccone, 1996) and Gill's (1994, 1998) pioneering analysis on the political consequences of religious competition in Latin America.

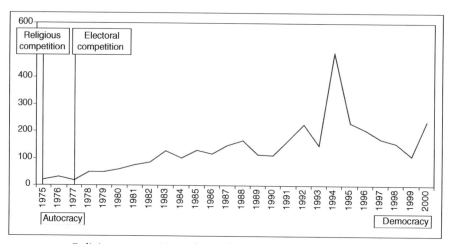

FIGURE I.3. Religious competition, electoral competition, and indigenous protest.

contributed to the creation of thousands of Bible study groups led by indigenous catechists and deacons and actively promoted and sponsored the creation of social and economic cooperatives and movements for land redistribution and indigenous rights.

To avoid a defection en masse to Protestantism, Catholic authorities in competitive districts contributed to the development of one of the most powerful social structures for collective action: decentralized regional associational networks with strong local leadership structures and dense communal associational networks. In this book I will show how the rise of these new associational networks transformed closed corporate indigenous communities, incapable of engaging in any meaningful form of collective action, into highly organized and connected communities capable of engaging in many different forms of collective dissent. In fact, the formation of these new associational structures empowered indigenous villagers in competitive districts to direct or to actively participate in Mexico's cycle of rural indigenous protest.

As Figure I.3 suggests, the spread of religious competition and the formation of new associational networks under autocracy is a crucial factor that explains the rise of Mexico's cycle of rural indigenous protest. As the book will show, religious competition is also a crucial factor that distinguishes poor rural indigenous villages that failed to engage in any type of independent collective action and to contest unpopular reforms –like the Zoque Catholic stronghold of Ocotepec – from poor rural indigenous villages that actively participated in multiple cycles of protest – like the religiously contested Tzeltal municipalities of Altamirano and Tenejapa.

Competing for Indigenous Votes. In this book I also argue that the introduction of government-controlled multiparty elections in Mexico's authoritarian regime and the spread of electoral competition across rural indigenous regions gave rise to socio-electoral coalitions and to the active participation of communist and socialist opposition parties in promoting social movements and protest.[10] Government-controlled elections motivated leftist opposition parties to sponsor the active mobilization of independent rural indigenous movements and in other cases to establish their own rural indigenous organizations for purely electoral purposes; authoritarian elections simultaneously activated the ballot box and the streets and contributed to the rise and development of a major cycle of peaceful indigenous protest.

As students of electoral autocracy have noted, partially free and unfair elections force opposition parties to compete for office while at the same time contesting the rules of competition.[11] To succeed in this double goal leftist opposition parties actively tried to recruit social zealots and risk takers with access to dense social connections – individuals capable of mobilizing opposition voters and leading major post-electoral rallies to contest fraud, such as the rural indigenous leaders and movements the Catholic Church contributed to create. In exchange for votes and antifraud mobilization, leftist opposition parties provided rural indigenous leaders and their movements with financial resources and support to mobilize for their own objectives outside election periods and offered them institutional protection in the event of government repression.

As part of their simultaneous struggles to establish an electoral core and fight fraud, opposition parties also developed their own social organizations populated by defectors from state-controlled corporatist organizations. Communist and socialist parties created their own peasant unions in rural indigenous regions. Whereas competition from U.S. Protestant missionaries (following a decentralized strategy of proselytizing) led the Catholic Church to develop decentralized regional associational networks with strong local leaders and dense community networks, competition from state-controlled corporatist unions led leftist opposition parties to develop centralized associational networks with strong central leaders and weak local associational networks. The book shows how the spread of electoral competition contributed to the transformation of closed corporate communities controlled by the PRI into hierarchically organized regional networks capable of actively participating in Mexico's cycle of rural indigenous protest.

As Figure I.3 visually suggests, the 1977 electoral reform, by which the Mexican government and the PRI legalized all opposition parties, including the Mexican Communist Party, and issued an amnesty for urban and rural guerrillas fighting in nonindigenous areas, made significant contributions to the rise of Mexico's cycle of rural indigenous protest. As the book will show, the spread of electoral competition was also an important factor that

[10] For insightful analyses of elections in autocracies, see Schedler (2002, 2006), Geddes (2003), Magaloni (2006, 2010), Gandhi and Przeworski (2007), and Greene (2007). For an important study of electoral competition and social protest in hybrid regimes, see Robertson (2010).

[11] This is what Schedler calls the "nested" nature of elections in autocracies.

distinguished municipalities that did not engage in any form of independent collective action – like the Zoque of Ocotepec, a PRI stronghold – from those who did – like the Tzeltal municipalities where leftist parties made their initial inroads in local politics in the 1980s.

Governing the Streets. The book shows that it was the continued spread of subnational electoral competition, rather than state coercion, what led to the eventual demise of Mexico's cycle of rural indigenous protest. As elections became increasingly free and fair, and as leftist parties became real power contenders for local positions of power, opposition party leaders and candidates increasingly discouraged radical mobilization and extremist demands to avoid alienating the median voter. As governors and mayors, leftist politicians actively sought to absorb leaders and activists of rural indigenous movements as government officials and brokers and tried to keep movements strategically demobilized through patronage.

In electoral autocracies, incumbent and opposition parties compete for control of independent social movements. Through policies of co-optation (carrots) and coercion (sticks), incumbents try to keep independent protest under control. Although opposition parties initially sponsor active participation by social movements in protest actions, once they become competitive or achieve office they also seek to co-opt social movement leaders and remove them from the streets. The book shows that the effect of co-optation and coercion on the dynamics of indigenous protest was conditional on the nature of social networks;[12] carrots and sticks were more effective in deterring protest when individuals and groups were immersed in centralized social networks – as the leftist secular unions were – and less effective when they belonged to decentralized regional networks with strong local leaders and dense community networks – as were the Catholic cooperatives and movements.

From Protest to Rebellion

Even though the introduction of neoliberal agrarian reforms did not trigger Mexico's cycle of indigenous protest, market-oriented reforms did intensify levels of mobilization and opened the way for the transformation of peaceful mobilization into armed insurgency. Figure I.4 provides visual evidence of the radicalizing effect that the end of land reform and the liberalization of land tenure had among rural indigenous protesters. Evidence from a major public opinion survey conducted by the Mexican government the year prior to the liberalization of land tenure shows that between two-thirds and three-fourths of Mexican rural households opposed market reforms; the survey unambiguously shows that market liberalization evoked a wide variety of

---

[12] Following different methodological approaches, Schock (2005) and Siegel (2011) persuasively show that the effect of government repression on social protest is conditional on social networks.

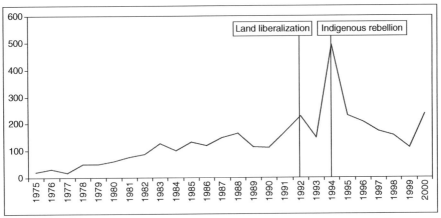

FIGURE I.4. Land liberalization and the transformation of protest into rebellion.

pre-revolutionary feelings ranging from grievances and relative deprivation to moral indignation.

Despite widespread grievances, not every rural household rebelled. Based on new indicators of indigenous rebellion in Mexico in the 1990s, the book shows that the escalation of protest into rebellion took place only in a few states; within these states, there was also widespread variation in levels of participation in rebel movements across municipalities and villages. As the brief vignettes of Ocotepec, Tenejapa and Altamirano suggest, attributing responsibility for the outbreak of indigenous rebellions solely to neoliberalism would over-predict the extent of revolutionary collective action in Chiapas and Mexico.

In this book I suggest that whether unpopular market-oriented reforms lead to revolutionary collective action depends on two factors: (1) the incumbent's governance strategies for implementation of reforms and (2) the conditions for rebel recruitment from social movements into armed rebel groups. When incumbents in electoral autocracies introduce major unpopular reforms in the midst of a cycle of peaceful mobilization, the critical question is how government authorities "manage"[13] those social movements that deeply oppose reforms and whether professionals in violence are able to recruit from within social movements when social activists give up on peaceful means of mobilization and consider the option of armed insurgency.

The book argues that when incumbents adopt compensatory measures to minimize the social costs of the policy shock and at the same time expand political and civic rights and liberties to allow dissident movements to continue expressing their grievances through the ballots or in the streets, protest may heighten but will likely remain peaceful. In contrast, when incumbents give up on compensatory measures and adopt repression as a dominant strategy

---

[13] I borrow this concept from Robertson (2010).

of governance, signaling a likely reversion to an authoritarian status quo ante, they will unintentionally give rise to a security dilemma for dissident communities. Under an imminent threat to their survival, communities will face meaningful incentives to preventively embrace violence before they are violently crushed by the state.[14]

Because governors were the gatekeepers of land redistribution in Mexico and because civilian police forces under the governors' command were responsible for repressing political dissent, to assess the political implementation of neoliberal agrarian reforms the book focuses on state-level politics. When governors assumed their challenger was a centralized and hierarchical peasant indigenous movement led by clerical and/or socialist external mestizo leaders (e.g. Chiapas in southern Mexico) and sought to crush them by suppressing civil rights and liberties and by decapitating the movement, they unwittingly provided the movement's rank-and-file with meaningful incentives for revolutionary collective action. But when governors assumed their challenger was a rural indigenous movement led by a multiplicity of interconnected local autochthonous leaders with access to deep communal roots, capable of responding to state repression through revolutionary means (e.g. Oaxaca in southern Mexico), they preventively adopted compensatory and democratizing policies to stimulate the prevalence of peaceful forms of collective action.

Within a statewide punitive context, as in Chiapas, not all rural indigenous villagers took up arms. The book shows that the mestizo leaders of the EZLN did not seek to recruit from (1) closed corporate indigenous communities like Ocotepec where they saw no returns for widespread recruitment and for the creation of a large social base for revolutionary action or from (2) communities connected through centralized and hierarchical socialist networks where leadership removal could easily trigger a network collapse and compromise any plan for guerrilla warfare.

Within a punitive context, rebel leaders actively sought to recruit a social base from the decentralized and horizontal regional networks the Catholic Church had built in response to the Protestant competition, where local village leaders (catechists) were both regionally connected to other villages through weak ties and internally connected to dense associational networks. This network structure facilitated underground recruitment because the multiplicity of local leaders and their strong local connections minimized the risks of information leaks and because access to one local leader led rebels to contact with a larger network of local leaders and communities. This network structure also provided organizational resilience against government repression because the removal of one leader did not compromise the group's ability to sustain radical mobilization or guerrilla warfare.

This book provides unambiguous evidence showing that the social networks built by the Catholic Church built in response to the Protestant competition

---

[14] In developing this argument, I build on earlier work by Della Porta and Tarrow (1986), Lichbach (1987), and Brockett (1991, 2005).

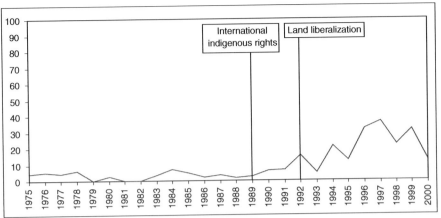

FIGURE I.5. International rights, neoliberal reforms, and the rise of ethnic identities (proportion of indigenous protest events with ethnic claims).

provided the social base for armed insurgency in Chiapas. It was rural indigenous villagers from networks in such municipalities as Altamirano and Tenejapa who took up arms to try to arrest what they saw as a likely reversion to an authoritarian status quo ante and to a repressive plantation economy like that from which their parents and grandparents had escaped. A crucial point the book makes is that the existence of Catholic progressive networks was not a sufficient condition for the outbreak of indigenous armed insurgency; in Chiapas's neighboring state of Oaxaca, a radical experience of Catholic progressive action did not give rise to a large-scale rebellion because the local political elite adopted a more compensatory program to implement neoliberal agrarian reforms.

Politicizing Ethnicity

The introduction of market-oriented agricultural reforms did not only provide incentives for the radicalization of rural indigenous collective action; it also provided meaningful incentives for the transformation of traditional peasant demands into claims for ethnic autonomy and self-determination for indigenous peoples. As Figure I.5 illustrates, ethnicity did not become an important public claim until two decades after the onset of Mexico's cycle of rural indigenous protest. Peasant indigenous movements publicly raised the ethnic banner only after the liberalization of land tenure and following the introduction of an international system of indigenous rights. As the literature has recognized, when market-oriented reforms disenfranchised rural indigenous populations as peasants, a new regime of international indigenous rights opened the way for the rise of ethnic claims (Brysk, 2000; Yashar, 2005).

Although these major policy changes predisposed rural indigenous peoples toward raising the ethnic banner, not all villagers made ethnic appeals in

Mexico's public plazas after the events of 1989–1992. Members of communities that resembled the structure of closed corporate communities under tight PRI control did not politicize their everyday indigenous ethnic practices. Ethnicity was politicized mainly in areas experiencing the most intense levels of religious and multiparty competition, where new leaders with access to regional associational networks used these channels of communication to coordinate their actions and facilitate the rise of new social identities.

The book argues that religious competition between Protestant and Catholic churches made important contributions to the revival of indigenous languages and ethnic identities. The Protestant strategy of translating Bibles to indigenous languages and the establishment of local Protestant churches served by indigenous autochthonous pastors led the Catholic Church to embrace indigenous languages and cultures as an integral part of their evangelizing mission. The competition for indigenous souls resulted in a new indigenous pride; native languages were no longer stigmatized but actively used as the language of God. Unable to decentralize hierarchies to native married indigenous couples, to avoid a defection en masse to the competition Catholic clergy opted for the "inculturation" of the Gospel – the interpretation of the Scriptures through indigenous histories and culture – and became major promoters of indigenous rights after 1989–1992.

The book also argues that the spread of electoral competition in Mexico's indigenous regions initially contributed to the rise of ethnic identities but eventually became an important motivation for the suppression of ethnic identification. As leftist opposition parties sought to create socio-electoral coalitions to establish core constituencies and fight fraud, they embraced a plethora of minority causes, including claims for indigenous ethnic rights. Their electoral goal was not to make broad programmatic appeals to attract the median voter but to make niche appeals to ideologically motivated groups. Because indigenous populations do not represent a majority in any of Mexico's states and because political parties are national political forces, once elections became relatively free and fair and opposition parties could appeal to the median voter to win office, leftist opposition party leaders and candidates incrementally gave up on radical minority demands, including ethnicity.

Whereas leftist opposition parties were only contingent supporters of the politicization of ethnicity, the EZLN became the most radical political supporter of ethnic identities. Scholars have identified the dramatic transformation of the EZLN from a peasant guerrilla movement (1994) into a self-determination movement (1995 onward) but have offered few persuasive explanations of this major change.

The book argues that the transition of the EZLN into a self-determination movement was a response to electoral fraud and relative political deprivation. Even though the Zapatista uprising motivated Mexico's ruling elite to introduce a major national electoral reform by which the government and the PRI surrendered their ability to manipulate electoral outcomes, allowing for a relatively clean presidential election in 1994, the Zapatista-supported leftist candidate to the governorship of Chiapas was defeated by fraud. At a time of national political liberalization, Zapatista communities confronted by fraud and paramilitary repression and authoritarian reversion opted to gain de facto territorial controls and establish parallel governments, claiming legitimacy under ILO Convention 169.

Indigenous Collective Action and Democratization

Whereas dominant explanations of Latin America's wave of indigenous mobilization frame indigenous collective action as a post-transition phenomenon, this book claims that Mexico's cycle of rural indigenous protest was a crucial factor for the country's transition from authoritarian rule to democracy. More specifically, I show that the two major electoral reforms of 1994 and 1996, by which the federal government and the PRI relinquished controls over the country's Federal Electoral Institute, established a Federal Electoral Tribunal and laid the foundation for subnational electoral reforms, were a direct response to the Zapatista uprising and its transformation into a self-determination movement.[15]

The book presents new evidence showing that Mexican elites consented to free and fair elections to avoid a major social insurrection. Reforms were aimed at marginalizing the EZLN and empowering the partisan Left to absorb the country's urban and rural movements into a path of electoral participation. PRI elites introduced the country's major electoral reforms to prevent the rise of a revolutionary coalition led by the EZLN at a time in which survey evidence showed the PRI would win in free and fair national elections. While the Mexican transition was ultimately a process in which the Mexican voter ousted the PRI from the presidency after seven decades in power, in the absence of a series of major electoral reforms that made elections free and fair, the transition might not have been completed. This book shows that two decades of indigenous mobilization and the outbreak of a large-scale rebellion in southern Mexico played a key historical role in the construction of the electoral institutions that guaranteed Mexican citizens that their vote would be fairly counted, even if they chose to vote against autocracy.

SCOPE AND METHODS

In this book, I am interested in theory building and testing as well as in the explanation of specific historical events. There is, in fact, a tension running throughout the book between general theoretical arguments, statistical testing, and micro-historical narratives. It is a tension that has always existed between social sciences and history. Whereas in the social sciences scholars use historical

---

[15] I follow the literature on "democratization from below." See Wood (2000) and Acemoglu and Robinson (2006). For important arguments about the impact of the 1994 Chiapas rebellion on the 1994 electoral reform see Becerra, Salazar and Woldeberg (2000) and Magaloni (2006; 2010).

data to test theory, historians use theory to explain historical realities. Whereas in the social sciences scholars classify empirical information into abstract categories and variables for hypothesis testing and seek to produce general causal claims free of proper names, historians are interested in explaining what people with names actually did. Theory and history need not be at odds, however; in this book they are not. Here, abstract concepts, variables, and people with proper names coexist with the dual purpose of theory testing and historical explanation.

Theory

This book develops a theory of popular mobilization in autocracies and tests its implications using extensive quantitative and qualitative information about three decades of rural indigenous mobilization in 20 Mexican states and 883 indigenous municipalities between 1975 and 2000. My goal is to explain how autonomous social networks and independent movements of poor rural villagers arise in autocracies and how these networks become politicized in the streets or in the mountains. I wish to understand what drives leaders, activists, and members of autonomous networks and popular movements to engage in peaceful cycles of mobilization and the conditions under which they may engage in revolutionary action. I also seek to account for the transformation of popular demands and identities through the course of protest and rebellion and to assess the impact of mobilization from below on the long-term stability of authoritarian rule and on the prospects for democratization.

Although the study of social movements, insurgencies, social identities, and regime change has evolved in separate trajectories, in this book I seek to integrate diverse specialized literatures into a single theoretical enterprise. My starting point is the study of social movements and cycles of peaceful protest in autocracies. I then assess how the governance of major economic shocks may lead to the radicalization of collective action and to the renegotiation of social identities. I finally analyze the conditions under which radical action may incite democratization.

Like most studies of collective action and social movements (McAdam, McCarthy and Zald, 1996; Tarrow, 1998), the book focuses throughout on three general factors that facilitate collective mobilization: (1) major external economic shocks that initially *motivate* group action; (2) the social networks and ideological resources that *enable* collective mobilization and group identification; and (3) the political processes and incentives that contribute to *translating* group mobilization into peaceful or violent collective action and to endogenously *transforming* group identities.[16]

---

[16] Although this framework is generally associated with the social movement synthesis of the 1990s, students of collective action in economics and analytical sociology use a similar framework of analysis. Hedstrom and Swedberg's (1998) macro-micro-macro model includes three types of mechanisms of collective action: motivating, enabling, and transformational.

Although I build on the canonical social movement framework, this book moves beyond the social movement literature in three significant ways. First, unlike classic studies of social movements that focus on advanced capitalist democracies, my theoretical focus is on authoritarian regimes, particularly on authoritarian systems in which national and subnational leaders are elected through government-controlled multiparty elections – that is, competitive or electoral autocracies.

The theory explains why the introduction of partially free and unfair multiparty elections changes the nature of authoritarian governance in significant ways and introduces opportunities and incentives for the rise of cycles of peaceful protest. As opposition parties try to simultaneously establish an electoral core and fight fraud, they become major promoters of social movements and social protest for purely electoral motives. Incumbents seek to keep protest under control and the opposition from expanding through the co-optation of social movement leaders or through targeted and moderate repression; this mixed strategy of governance stimulates, rather than depresses, peaceful protest.

By laying out the electoral incentives that lead political actors to either sponsor or tolerate social protest, my theory of popular mobilization in autocracies seeks to overcome the tautological nature that has afflicted political opportunity arguments in social movement theory since its inception.[17] The theory also provides an electoral rationale that helps explain why cycles of social protest are so prevalent in hybrid political regimes and why socio-electoral coalitions are so ubiquitous in electoral autocracies.

Second, unlike most studies of collective action and social movements that simply identify the different mobilizing structures that facilitate or hinder collective action, in this book I provide an explanation of how these mobilizing vehicles emerge and the impact they have in facilitating different forms of popular collective action, from peaceful protest to armed insurgency. Focusing on the breakdown of religious and political monopolies, I present an explanation of how the spread of competition for souls and votes in autocracies may lead to the rise of regional associational networks for independent collective action.

A crucial theoretical claim is that religious and secular competition may lead to the rise of different types of network structures: Whereas Protestant-Catholic competition may lead to the development of decentralized and horizontal networks, secular competition between a hegemonic populist party and a leftist opposition may give rise to centralized and hierarchical networks. These differences in network types have crucial consequences for the lifespan of social movements and cycles of protest and for the likely transformation of peaceful protest into more radical forms of collective action.

Third, unlike most of the social movement literature that analyzes political opportunities and mobilizing structures as two separate phenomena, my theory of popular mobilization suggests that the effect of governance on collective

---

[17] See Meyer (2004) for an important assessment of the political opportunity school.

action is conditional on social networks. Following recent advances in network theory, I argue that the autocrats' success in co-opting social movements or repressing independent mobilization is largely contingent on the types of social connections that leaders, activists, and members of popular movements are part of. The book suggests that while both centralized and hierarchical networks – developed by secular Leftist parties – and decentralized horizontal networks – sponsored by the Catholic Church – actively participated in cycles of peaceful protest, when autocrats sought to suppress movements through leadership co-optation or repression, the decentralized religious networks were more resilient than the centralized ones.

By accounting for the motivations that lead religious and secular actors to develop autonomous associational networks, the theory is able to identify the origins of different network types. To the extent that these different social structures make groups either more resistant or less resilient to co-optation or repression, we join scholars who have contributed to solving one of the most important puzzles in the study of governance and repression – repression can deter protest or stimulate it, depending on the social connections of dissident movements (Schock, 2005; Siegel, 2011). We suggest that religion generates more resilient social movements than secular politics because religious actors tend to build decentralized network structures with multiple local leaders, not because religion breeds more fundamentalist ideas than secular ideologies.

Explaining the conditions that give rise to the escalation of peaceful protest into armed insurgency is a major extension of my theory of popular mobilization in autocracies. The study of the escalation of protest into rebellion has not been a dominant concern in the social movement literature because this is a body of research dominated by the study of movements in advanced capitalist democracies, where armed insurgencies are nearly absent.[18] But the study of escalation has not been a relevant concern in the quantitative literature on armed insurgencies and civil wars either.

Dominated by structuralist accounts, scholars of insurgencies and civil war have explained the origins of political violence in terms of economic factors that render states incapable of policing criminal groups (low GDP per capita) and on conditions that facilitate rebel recruitment (poverty and mountainous and rural terrains).[19] Relying on time-invariant macrostructural factors, dominant explanations of insurgency have not properly addressed questions of agency, contingency and the strategic aspects associated with governance and collective action that are crucial to understand the outbreak of armed rebellions (Tarrow, 2007).

---

[18] For major exceptions see Della Porta and Tarrow (1986), Brockett (1991, 2005), Almeida (2003, 2008), and Hafez (2004).

[19] For classic statements in this literature, see Collier (2000), Fearon and Laitin (2003), and Collier et al. (2005).

Focusing on the different strategies authoritarian elites adopt to manage social protest when confronted by major exogenous economic shocks or when they adopt major unpopular reforms, this book seeks to introduce timing, agency and strategic interaction to our explanations of the origins of political violence. I explore how radical changes in governance by which elites withdraw limited rights and liberties granted in earlier periods of partial political liberalization, signaling a likely reversion to a punitive status quo ante, may provide incentives for the radicalization of peaceful movements. I consider two types of punitive measures of implementing unpopular reforms: major electoral fraud that effectively suppresses multiparty competition and the criminalization of protest.

Consistent with the idea that the effect of governance on collective action is conditional on social networks, I explore the social context that allows rural villagers confronted with security dilemmas to engage into violent action to contest change. Whereas dominant explanations of insurgency and civil war suggest that professionals in violence recruit rural villagers living in isolated mountainous terrain that serves as a sanctuary for recruitment, I argue that, regardless of terrain, rebel leaders recruit their social bases from specific social networks – decentralized and horizontal networks with multiple leadership structures tied to dense local associational networks.

Religion and progressive Catholicism have often produced the social bases for armed insurgencies in developing countries because clerics unwittingly contribute to creating the type of network structure that minimizes the risks associated with rebel recruitment while at the same time maximizing the extent of popular support for guerrilla warfare.

A major concern in the study of social movements is the long-term effects of popular mobilization – changes in social cleavages and identities, policy and institutions. Following the most recent literature on regime change that emphasizes how revolutionary threats from below can stimulate economic and political elites to consent to redistribution via democratization (Wood, 2000; Acemoglu and Robinson, 2006), in the final section of this book I assess the long-term impact of popular protest and rebellion on democratization. Unlike the literature that emphasizes the impact of workers and urban mobilization, I emphasize the effect of peasant mobilization and assess how different forms of rural collective action change elite perceptions, leading to regime change.

As the reader will note, some critical assumptions I make for theory building are informed by the social and political realities of Latin America and most specifically of rural indigenous communities. This choice limits my ability to make universal claims, but it nonetheless allows me to develop general propositions that can be tested with new data in Mexico and throughout Latin America. The study of indigenous politics has hitherto "used" and tested theoretical claims produced elsewhere based on the realities of advanced capitalist democracies; the present study is an exercise of theory building and testing using assumptions that reflect the realities of nondemocratic political regimes in developing countries.

Research Design

I use Mexico and Mexican subnational regions for hypotheses testing. Mexican Indigenous subnational jurisdictions provide a good sample for hypotheses testing because the country simultaneously experienced three major transformations in the last quarter of the twentieth century: (1) the transition from a state-led economy to a market economy; (2) the transition from single-party rule to electoral autocracy and to democracy; and (3) the transition from a religious monopoly to plurality. These parallel transformations allow us to assess the likely effect that the breakdown in local religious and political monopolies and the spread of the competition for souls and votes had on the dynamics of rural indigenous mobilization, while controlling for economic factors typically associated with different forms of collective action. The uneven spread of religious and electoral competition across Mexican indigenous regions and the uneven intensity of rural indigenous protest provide additional advantages for hypothesis testing.

I adopt a multilevel approach for hypothesis testing because the different components of the theory operate at different levels of analysis. Whereas the external shocks that motivate collective action (e.g., economic crises or major economic policy shifts) typically originate at the international or national level, governance is usually a national or subnational issue, and the social networks and mobilizing structures for popular collective action emerge at the local level of towns, villages, and hamlets. When individuals make decisions to engage in collective action, their choices are subject to external shocks, political opportunities, and the availability of vehicles for mobilization that operate at *different* geo-spatial levels.

The study of indigenous mobilization in Latin America has typically considered the international and the local dimensions, but in this book I make an explicit attempt to integrate multiple layers of analyses: global changes, national transformations, province-level governance, municipal politics, and community-level societal dynamics.[20]

EVIDENCE

In testing for the main theoretical claims made in this book, and in accounting for the historical evolution of Mexico's cycle of rural indigenous mobilization, I rely on quantitative and qualitative evidence, combining statistical analyses of event-count data with case studies and life histories. Following King and Powell (2008), my emphasis is on multiple sources of evidence rather than multiple methods. The statistical analyses, case studies, and life histories presented here are all informed by the logic of causal inference. What changes is the nature of the evidence I use to test the hypothesized causal associations. I combine quantitative and qualitative evidence to overcome the weaknesses of different sources of evidence and the different methods used.

---

[20] For the importance of political scale on political action, see Snyder (2001b) and Remmer (2010).

Quantitative Evidence

The quantitative analysis undertaken in this book is based on the Mexican Indigenous Insurgency Database (MII). MII contains information on 3,553 acts of rural indigenous protest, 5,120 claims, and 1,765 actions of government repression that took place in any Mexican municipality that at any time between 1970 and 2000 had at least 10 percent indigenous population (the national mean). Drawing on a detailed review of eight Mexican daily newspapers with national circulation, MII is the most extensive data bank on indigenous protest and repression from any Latin American country. These are micro-protest events that for the most part have gone unnoticed by the international press and are therefore absent from the main cross-national datasets used for the comparative study of conflict processes. Appendix A provides a detailed description of the main sources of information used to compile the MII dataset.

The panel structure of the MII dataset enables the temporal and spatial evolution of Mexico's protracted cycle of indigenous protest, from 1975 to 2000 and across 883 municipalities, to be analyzed. It allows us to test for the effect of religious and electoral competition and state repression on the evolution of protest and ethnic claims, while controlling for alternative explanations. For the study of the outbreak of insurgent collective action, systematic data on protest and government repression facilitate testing of two crucially omitted variables in the study of insurgencies and civil war. Focused mainly on the effect of structural and institutional variables, cross-national studies of political violence have failed to measure the effect of political processes on the outbreak of insurgencies and civil wars. Panel data on protest and repression allow us to explore directly whether rebellion grows out of nonviolent forms of direct political action and to establish not only where but when protest becomes rebellion.

However, any statistical analysis based on count data of protest events faces two major limitations that afflict all studies using *observational* and *aggregate* data: Results can only show ecological and statistical associations. Because statistical controls are weak and regression results do not tell enough about the specific actions of individuals involved in the mobilization processes, our ability to establish causal relationships solely on the basis of the statistical analyses is limited.

To improve our confidence in the causal effect of religious competition as a mechanism that empowered rural indigenous communities to mobilize, and the effect of electoral competition and state repression as mechanisms that shaped the nature of rural indigenous mobilization and demands, throughout the book I complement every significant statistical finding with qualitative evidence from life histories and case studies.

Qualitative Evidence

For the purposes of hypothesis testing, the book relies on ethnographic evidence that I present in the form of life histories and micro-comparative case studies.

Note, however, that the use of ethnographic evidence in this book departs in two fundamental ways from ethnographies developed by anthropologists.

First, case selection of rural indigenous villages and interview subjects was based on the statistical results.[21] I conducted extensive fieldwork in villages that I could identify on a regression line; that is, I traveled to places that I knew were "typical" (located along the regression line in the statistical output) or "atypical" (outliers). Before visiting any Mexican village or talking to any relevant actor, I had crucial ecological information about the history of religious and electoral competition in the village and about its likely association with different forms of collective action. Hence, the in-depth interviews I conducted did not resemble the open-ended format commonly used by anthropologists, but more closely resembled the structure of questionnaires used by survey analysts, where questions are informed by theoretical priors. Because the interviews were all framed in terms of life histories, each interviewee was invited to answer specific questions about social processes based on his or her own personal experience – in the singular, rather than in the plural. This provided a wealth of information about individual perceptions and choices made under different settings of competition and coercion.

Second, to compensate for the weaknesses associated with statistical controls in the quantitative analyses, the choice of cases and life histories was informed by the logic of natural experiments and of comparative case studies. My goal was to assess how nearly identical individuals whose exposure to different contexts might explain different experiences of engagement in collective action, or to assess nearly identical villages where one crucial difference accounts for different experiences of collective mobilization. Let me provide three brief examples.

Based on extensive interviews with Catholic clergy, in one case I assess the changing behavior of one influential Catholic bishop as he was transferred between Catholic jurisdictions with different levels of religious competition. By comparing the social and political behavior of a single individual in two contexts that share many similarities except for the level of religious plurality, I seek to show that this particular bishop became a major promoter of indigenous mobilization and ethnic identities only *after* he was transferred from a Catholic-dominated diocese to a diocese marked by rising levels of religious competition. The fact that the Vatican in the 1960s and 1970s transferred clergy between dioceses for efficiency and not for ideological reasons allows me to claim that this is a natural experiment – that is, the allocation of bishops to areas of high and low levels of competition was done "as if random." [22]

In another case, through the life histories of a group of indigenous leaders of the same age, all from one region in eastern Chiapas (Las Margaritas), one ethnic group (Tojolabales), and one organization (the Independent Central of

---

[21] See Lieberman (2005) and Seawright and Gerring (2008).

[22] I expand on this point in Chapter 3. For critical guidance on natural experiments, see Dunning (2008).

Agricultural Workers and Peasants – CIOAC), I analyze how the legalization of the Mexican Communist Party, the introduction of government-controlled multiparty elections, and the incremental rise of the Mexican Left to municipal power slowly transformed their mobilization strategies and demands. I show that the introduction of partially free and unfair elections led them to develop a meaningful coalition with Leftist parties, which enabled them to engage in an intense phase of mobilization. As the Left came to power, however, many of these leaders were demobilized and became either government officials or heads of clientelistic machines.

One crucial difference between these leaders was that some of them belonged to decentralized horizontal religious networks while others belonged to centralized hierarchical secular leftist organizations. I show that this significant difference made leaders from Catholic networks less vulnerable to co-optation and repression and members of secular Leftist networks more likely to give up on protest. This controlled comparison allows me to isolate as much as possible the effect of different types of networks on protest and rebel recruitment.

Building on statistical results on indigenous insurgent activity, I also conduct a series of matched comparisons of states, regions, municipalities, and villages that allow us to isolate the causal effect that differences in governance strategies had on the escalation (or not) of protest into rebellion and on the transformation (or not) of peasant demands into ethno-territorial claims. A comparison of two Catholic dioceses sharing similar histories of Catholic progressive practices in two neighboring states shows that catechists and members of social networks from the state where elites adopted compensatory policies to mitigate the negative effects of the liberalization of land tenure (Oaxaca) did not join any rebel group, whereas those from the state where elites repressively implemented the unpopular reforms (Chiapas) joined an armed rebel group.

ROADMAP

The book is divided into four major sections: Theory (Part I), Protest (Part II), Rebellion (Part III), and The Politicization of Ethnicity (Part IV).

Chapter 1, in Part I, develops a theory of popular collective action in autocracies and outlines a series of hypotheses about protest, rebellion and ethnic identification. The analytical focus is on the breakdown of local religious and political monopolies. I explain why the spread of competition for souls and votes in historically marginalized and isolated communities can empower the poor to build powerful movements for economic redistribution and social rights.

Part II focuses on Mexico's cycle of indigenous protest. Drawing on data about 3,553 protest events reported by the Mexican national press between 1975 and 2000, in Chapter 2 I present detailed statistical testing of my theory of popular protest and of alternative explanations. Controlling for economic and demographic factors typically associated with social protest, the chapter shows that indigenous municipalities experiencing the most intense processes of religious and electoral competition, rather than the most homogeneous, isolated, and cohesive municipalities, experienced the most intense levels of protest. Neoliberal reforms intensified protest but did not give rise to it.

By means of an examination of the life histories of four Catholic bishops, Chapter 3 seeks to isolate the causal impact of religious competition on the transformation of Catholic clergy into major promoters of the social infrastructure for rural indigenous mobilization. The study shows that Catholic bishops and their pastoral teams became major promoters of decentralizing and horizontal social networks for rural indigenous mobilization only *after* they were transferred from Catholic strongholds to dioceses under growing Protestant competition. Through interviews with indigenous catechists and deacons I establish how religious competition empowered villagers in competitive districts to build the social infrastructure that would enable them to actively participate in Mexico's cycle of indigenous protest.

Based on a comparison of the life histories of a group of Tojolabal leaders from the same region, ethnic group, and rural organization, Chapter 4 shows that the rise to power of a leftist party in a municipality historically dominated by the PRI was causally associated with the rise and demise of a powerful cycle of local rural indigenous protest. It shows that after the Mexican Communist Party was legalized, communist leaders developed strong socio-electoral coalitions with Catholic social networks and trained powerful secular local leaders, who became the vanguard of centralized and hierarchical communist peasant unions. Drawing on information from extensive interviews, I show that leaders deeply embedded in decentralized and horizontal Catholic social networks were more likely to defy government repression and co-optation than secular leaders embedded in centralized and hierarchical networks.

Part III focuses on the escalation of peaceful indigenous protest into armed insurgency. Chapter 5 shows that neoliberal agrarian reforms provided the initial motivation for the transformation of protest into rebellion. It explains why the political implementation of reforms distinguished states that experienced a large-scale rebellion from those who did not. Based on statistical analyses and on a paired comparison of two nearly identical regions of two neighboring states (Chiapas and Oaxaca), the chapter shows that in those states where governors adopted harsh repressive policies to politically implement the unpopular liberalization of land tenure, signaling a likely authoritarian reversion, protest became rebellion. Protest intensified as a result of neoliberal reforms but did not become rebellion where governors adopted compensatory measures.

Chapter 6 explains why within a context of statewide repression, only some municipalities and villages joined the EZLN and rebelled while others did not. Based on statistical analyses and case studies of municipalities and villages and on life histories, the chapter shows that rebel recruitment into Zapatism took place primarily through Catholic social networks. Peasant recruitment took place in the rural and mountainous terrains and jungles; but within these regions of rough terrain, recruitment took place almost exclusively through religious networks. Rebellion was the joint result of the punitive implementation of neoliberal reforms and of the availability of social networks for rebel recruitment.

Part IV focuses on the long-term impact of protest and rebellion on the transformation of indigenous collective identities and on the stability of Mexico's authoritarian regime.

Chapter 7 explains the transformation of peasant demands into claims for autonomy and self-determination. Based on quantitative and qualitative evidence it shows that neoliberal agrarian reforms and the introduction of an international regime for indigenous rights contributed to the rise of ethnic claims. Ethnicity, however, became a major demand mainly in municipalities experiencing the most intense levels of religious competition, where the Catholic Church became a major promoter of indigenous rights. Whereas Leftist parties initially embraced ethnic claims, electoral gains and the prospect of victory led Leftist leaders and candidates to give up on ethnicity. In regions where subnational elites arrested the spread of electoral competition through fraud and coercion, indigenous movements shifted from class and economic claims to radical demands for autonomy and self-determination for indigenous peoples. The surprising transformation of the EZLN from a peasant insurgency into a movement for autonomy and self-determination was the most emblematic example.

Chapter 8 analyzes the impact of indigenous protest, rebellion and the rise of radical demands for self-determination on the long-term stability of Mexico's authoritarian regime. Based on a detailed analysis of public opinion bi-weekly surveys conducted by the Office of the Presidency in Mexico – which served as input for decision-making by Mexican presidents – the chapter shows that the federal government and the PRI relinquished their ability to commit fraud and established autonomous electoral authorities to organize free and fair elections in response to the Zapatista rebellion (1994) and its transformation into a major movement that sought to renegotiate Mexico's federal structure along ethno-territorial cleavages.

The concluding chapter explores extensions of the key arguments outlined and tested in the book into other Latin American experiences of indigenous mobilization. Although I rely on secondary evidence, this information is a key source of external validity of my theoretical claims. In this concluding section I explore the implications of the book's findings to our understanding of indigenous collective action and the contributions of the book to the study of dynamics of contention in autocracies through the sociopolitical lens of religion and elections.

PART I

THEORY

I

A Theory of Popular Collective Action in Autocracies

This chapter develops a sociopolitical theory of independent collective action in autocracies, which will serve to outline the main hypotheses for testing throughout the book. My starting point is the theoretical synthesis that social movement scholars reached in the 1990s.[1] I assume that major economic crises or radical and unpopular economic policy shifts may provide the initial material motivations for social mobilization. Yet whether collective action actually happens and the form it takes mainly depend on the prior existence of (1) social networks and organizational structures that enable groups to express their claims in the streets; (2) ideological and cultural frameworks that justify collective action; and (3) political opportunities and constraints that define the benefits and costs associated with different forms of collective action.

Independent collective action is unusual in closed autocracies, because rulers adopt governance strategies that effectively deter the rise of autonomous organizations. Closed autocracies are regimes that do not hold elections for the selection of leaders and where societal claims are typically channeled through state-sponsored organizations. In the case of single-party autocracies, opposition parties are proscribed and independent civil organizations are repressed. The ruling party is the only mechanism available for attaining power and it is the privileged channel for the allocation of public goods and redistribution of public resources. The dominant strategy of governance in single-party autocracies is to reward loyalty and obedience and to use harsh and exemplary repression against those who seek public goods and redistribution through independent collective action.

How do autonomous social networks and independent movements ever emerge in autocracies? How do these networks become politicized in the streets? What are the conditions under which street protesters become radicalized and take their claims to the mountains or to the jungles and engage in armed insurgency? What drives independent movements to make public claims and embrace social identities traditionally suppressed by autocratic

---

[1] See McAdam, McCarthy, and Zald (1996) and Tarrow (1998).

institutions? How do protest, rebellion, and the rise of previously suppressed social identities affect the long-term stability of authoritarian regimes and the prospects for democratization?

The main proposition made in this chapter is that the introduction of limited forms of societal and political competition can generate conditions for the rise of autonomous organizations and cycles of independent mobilization in autocracies. Focusing on societies served by a single religious supplier and ruled by a single party, I suggest that the breakdown of religious and political monopolies and the spread of competition for souls and votes will empower previously marginalized and subjugated groups to develop popular movements for economic redistribution. The retraction of political competition in the midst of a major cycle of mobilization and the rise of major threats for group survival will generate incentives for radicalization – for the transformation of peaceful protest into armed rebellion and of demands for economic redistribution into claims for ethnic autonomy and self-determination.

In the first part of the chapter, I explain why autonomous social networks and independent social movements are absent in societies ruled by single-party monopolies and served by religious monopolies. I show how a dual religious and political monopoly in rural indigenous contexts such as those prevailing in twentieth-century Latin America created hierarchical, corporate, isolated indigenous communities linked to the national authoritarian structures but without autonomous leaders, associational networks, or independent movements. I show how the incentive systems created by religious and political monopolies gave rise to subjugated indigenous communities.

In the second part, I introduce religious plurality and develop a model of religious competition and collective action. The model shows that in a poor and unequal society served by a single religious supplier, the monopoly clergy will serve the interests of the state or of the rich. The entry of a new religious supplier, however, transforms the former monopoly clergy into an ally of the poor. Focusing on Latin American religious markets, the model explains why the spread of U.S. Protestant missionary action in rural indigenous regions would transform Catholic clergy into major promoters of indigenous movements for land redistribution and indigenous rights. It shows that as a member-retention strategy, Catholic clergy would contribute to the creation of new indigenous elites and intra and inter-community networks for a wide variety of dissident movements.

In the third part, I introduce limited political plurality and government-controlled elections and develop a model of electoral competition and collective action. The model explains why the "nested" nature of authoritarian elections, by which opposition parties compete for office while at the same time contesting the rules of competition, would motivate opposition parties to develop socio-electoral coalitions with independent social movements – such as the Catholic-sponsored movements – and become major promoters of social protest. It argues, however, that once elections become free and fair, opposition forces would seek to demobilize protest.

The electoral competition model explains why the introduction of government-controlled elections radically transforms authoritarian governance of independent movements. Seeking to avoid the development of socio-electoral opposition coalitions, incumbents respond with the partial satisfaction of dissident material demands and keep protest under control via moderate repression. The model shows that while this governance strategy activates the streets as a valid arena for policy negotiation and permits the rise of cycles of peaceful protest it does not stimulate armed rebellion.

An extension of the model shows that radical transformations of governance in times of crisis may stimulate radicalization from below – the escalation of protest into rebellion and the rise of demands for autonomy and self-determination of ethnic minorities.

Focusing on the governance of major economic crises or radical and unpopular shifts in economic policy in the midst of major cycles of peaceful protest, I explain that when elites give up on partial concessions and adopt strictly punitive strategies, signaling a likely reversion to an authoritarian status quo ante, they give rise to revolutionary feelings and to incentives for radical ethno-territorial struggles. The model suggests, however, that revolutionary fervor translates into revolutionary action only where conditions for rebel recruitment exist. I explain why participation in decentralized social networks with multiple local leaders and dense local associational networks facilitates rebel recruitment, and show that religion often provides the social base for revolutionary action because clergy typically develop this type of social network.

In the final section, I discuss the conditions under which revolutionary action and the threat of civil war may motivate authoritarian elites to consent to free and fair elections and democratization rather than repression.

COLLECTIVE ACTION IN CLOSED AUTOCRACIES

Political Hegemony under Single-Party Monopoly

Assume a poor, unequal multiethnic society ruled by a single party. In this closed autocracy, rulers maximize government revenue, personal profit, and societal compliance. Societal compliance, in turn, depends on real wages, government transfers, and repression. The government controls a large share of the economy.

Opposition parties are outlawed and independent social organizations and movements are severely restricted. Citizens are organized into government-controlled corporatist unions (e.g., workers, peasants, and professionals) or functional groups (e.g., women, youth, and seniors) linked to the ruling party. The poor are organized mainly under peasant and workers' unions.

The quintessential governance strategy in closed autocracies is to reward loyalists and repress independent citizens and movements. Patronage and government transfers are distributed mainly to party loyalists and the ruling party is the main institutional channel for the distribution of material rewards. In this system, independent citizens and organizations are harshly repressed and receive no government benefits.

The rules and incentives in closed autocracies discourage the existence of an autonomous civil society and independent collective mobilization. Citizens comply with the status quo and refrain from publicly expressing their views about the regime. This is particularly true of the poor, whose material subsistence is tightly linked to state patronage and subsidies. Cycles of independent protest are rare. When they do unexpectedly take place, however, they take the form of participation cascades and tides of protest that render governments dysfunctional and push them to the verge of collapse (Kuran, 1991, 1997; Beissinger, 2001).

Rulers in closed autocracies know that even under the most restrictive conditions, there is space for independent underground organization. Comparative historical experience shows that three social arenas have been particularly germane for the rise of independent/autonomous leaders and social networks in closed autocracies: religion, education, and the workplace. Let us concentrate on religion, which has traditionally served either as an institutional guarantor of authoritarian regimes or a major source for social and political transformation.

Social Hegemony under a Religious Monopoly

Assume this poor and unequal multiethnic society is served by a single religious supplier. The predominant religion is a universalizing creed, namely a proselytizing religion without significant barriers to entry. The monopoly clergy maximize membership, private monetary contributions, and state protection (Iannaccone, 1996; Gill, 1998). Membership includes rich and poor parishioners, and ethnic minorities are predominantly poor. The economic interests of the rich and the poor are inversely related. Although the poor are the largest group, the rich are the main contributors of private material resources to the monopoly clergy. State protection involves favorable legal provisions and government subsidies.

Under monopolistic conditions, membership is fixed and the utility of religious authorities depends primarily on state protection and private contributions. In the context of a state-sponsored religious monopoly, the monopoly clergy will serve the interests of state elites and will thus develop theological interpretations and pastoral practices that justify the political status quo. As Adam Smith (1776/1994) predicted long ago, this clergy will behave as a "lazy monopoly" and will grossly underserve its members (Iannaccone, 1996). Unless the state threatens religious authorities with withdrawal of its protection and patronage, the monopoly clergy will typically discourage parishioners from engaging in any type of dissident mobilization that may endanger the stability of autocratic rule (Gill, 1998).

In a monopolistic context marked by the strict separation of church and state, however, in which state protection and subsidies are unavailable, the monopoly clergy will rely on wealthy elites and develop theological interpretations and religious practices that justify the economic status quo. In Marx's famous formulation (1844/1994), religion will be "the opium of the people." Insofar as membership is fixed, the state does not threaten religious activities, and the rich maintain their patronage in favor of the monopoly church, clerical authorities will refrain from stimulating any type of poor people's movement for redistribution or indeed any movement that might endanger the status quo.

Under these conditions, religion is rarely a major source for independent mobilization and hence does not represent a major threat to authoritarian rulers. Even when the state is not a patron of the dominant religious supplier, insofar as the state does not become a threat to clerical activities, the monopoly clergy will not have any meaningful incentives to encourage poor parishioners to organize independently for material redistribution or regime change.

Political and Religious Monopolies in Indigenous Communities

Societies with dual political and religious monopolies generate few incentives for the rise of autonomous civil societies and independent collective action. For convenience, let us assess how the mechanics of control work in the micro context of poor, rural indigenous communities in twentieth-century Latin America, with special emphasis on Mesoamerica and Mexico.

Mesoamerican indigenous communities are groups larger than families but smaller than nation-states that (1) speak a shared pre-Hispanic language; (2) never became racially mixed with the Spanish conquistadores or with their mestizo descendants; (3) survived three centuries of colonial rule and two centuries of independent mestizo governments; and (4) developed communal governance practices and social and cultural norms (customary law and practices) distinct from all other members of the colonial and postcolonial societies.[2]

Since colonial times, the internal governance of indigenous communities rested mainly on civil-religious hierarchies associated with the "cargo system." Most males in the community were expected to contribute unpaid labor for the provision of public goods and the administration of civil and religious activities in their villages. Cargo duties ranged from agricultural work, to policing the community, to major local administrative and judicial decisions. Climbing the cargo ladder was a function of age, experience, and financial contribution, particularly to the annual festivity of the (Catholic) patron saint, when communities came together to celebrate their common bonds and to recognize the members of the cargo system. The most senior participants in the cargo system became *principales* and constituted the village elite – they played a prominent role in internal decision-making processes and functioned as liaisons with the nonindigenous national society and institutions.

---

[2] See Bonfil (1987/1996) for an extensive discussion of these features of indigenous communities.

Indigenous communities were corporate and hierarchical but not closed entities. During colonial times, the Catholic Church and the colonial state were the main external institutions with which indigenous communities negotiated their relative local autonomy and the terms of their subjugation to the larger colonial system. Throughout the twentieth century, the Catholic Church and the postrevolutionary state and the PRI were the dominant external institutions for indigenous communities. Even though postrevolutionary Mexico had a system of strict separation of religious and political spheres, at the micro level of municipalities, villages, and hamlets, a de facto dual monopoly of the Catholic Church and the PRI prevailed. Both the Church and the PRI exercised indirect controls over indigenous communities through the *principales*, who acted as the cultural and political brokers and negotiated the terms of incorporation of their communities into Catholicism and authoritarian rule.

Anthropological and historical accounts of Catholicism in rural indigenous regions suggest that Catholic monopoly clergy underserved rural indigenous communities for most of the twentieth century.[3] Delegating most ecclesiastic responsibilities onto the *principales*, Catholic authorities rarely visited rural indigenous communities, and when they did, they preached in Latin or Spanish and spread a religious message that legitimized the socioeconomic status quo dominated by landowners, *finca* owners, ranchers, and white and mestizo economic elites. In exchange for the support of the Catholic hierarchy and some relative autonomy to carry out pre-Hispanic religious practices in their communities, the *principales* guaranteed the Catholic hegemony in their villages. Even though everyone in these villages was officially Catholic, significant proportions of villagers practiced folk Catholicism known as *la costumbre* – "customary practice."

Anthropological and historical research shows that the communal structures and norms of reciprocity that had allowed communities to be cultural survivors became the bases for authoritarian control under the PRI (Rus, 1994). Postrevolutionary land reform programs and education policies for indigenous communities provided the patronage and public resources to control communities (Gutiérrez, 1999). When land plots were awarded to groups or indigenous families or communities, the new agrarian community authorities (commissars) became *principales*. As members of the PRI's rural unions, these commissars/*principales* were the main political liaisons between the centralized hierarchies of the ruling party and the communities. When young indigenous males were sent to state schools, they became indigenous teachers linked to state bureaucracies and PRI-affiliated unions. They also became *principales* in their communities and brokered the community's surrender to the PRI; they gave up ethnic independent claims and instead adopted class-based peasant identities tied to the hegemonic PRI.

Figure 1.1 illustrates the social landscape of rural indigenous regions under the dual monopoly of the PRI and the Catholic Church. Each triangle or

[3] Interviews with Fathers Ramón Castillo and Joel Padrón and with Bishop Emeritus Arturo Lona.

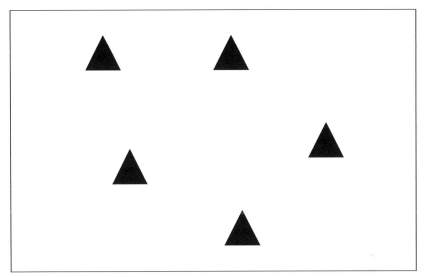

FIGURE 1.1. Traditional closed corporate communities.

pyramid represents a community or village. Even though indigenous customary practices included strict norms of reciprocity and individual contributions to the provision of public goods, community governance was structured through the hierarchical system of religious and civilian cargos described earlier. These were not horizontal but vertical relationships. Moreover, there were no associational networks but kinship ties and clientelistic linkages.

Although all communities in Figure 1.1 belonged to the same ethnolinguistic group, villagers were isolated from their "coethnics" living in neighboring villages; in fact, as the figure illustrates, there were no meaningful horizontal linkages between villages. Most existing connections linked the village to the centralized hierarchies of the Catholic Church or the PRI, and relations were mediated by the *principales*. Ethnolinguistic groups could be objectively identified on a map, but they were meaningless as a political category. Indigenous peoples nominally existed, but Indians were de facto organized as communities – the Institutional Revolutionary Community, in the effective language of Rus (1994).[4]

In the context of a dual religious and political monopoly, indigenous communities did not have independent community leaders, internal associational networks, cross-village connections, or access to external nongovernmental allies to engage in independent collective action to challenge the status quo or

---

[4] As Mattiace (2003) suggests, after the 1970s the model of closed corporate communities developed by Wolf (1957) did not reflect the reality of many peasant indigenous communities in Mexico. However, as she suggests drawing on Rus (1994), the closed corporate model did reflect important structural features of communities up until the 1950s and 1960s.

unpopular policies that endangered their lives. Most of them were subordinate clients.

The main claim of this book is that the entry of new religious and political actors into this hierarchical authoritarian equilibrium will create conditions for the rise of new community leaders, local associational networks, and movements for rural indigenous mobilization. Plurality and competition will transform both the internal structure of power and status in these communities and their articulation with the rest of society. Let us first explore the social consequences of the breakdown of religious monopolies and then the breakdown of secular controls.

A MODEL OF RELIGIOUS COMPETITION AND SOCIAL MOBILIZATION IN AUTOCRACIES

Assume the entry of new religious suppliers in the monopolistic society we have described thus far. The entry of new religious actors may result from a change in authoritarian restrictions on religious freedoms or from direct state sponsorship of a new religious supplier. Allowing or sponsoring the entry of religious challengers is a mechanism by which secular authorities may seek to weaken traditional religious monopolies. This is more likely to occur when secular authorities may need to withdraw economic resources from the monopoly clergy or when they may try to eliminate traditional clerical rights over specific policy domains (e.g., education) in which secular elites may want to establish controls (Gill, 2007).

Clerical Behavior in a Competitive Environment

The introduction of new religious suppliers into historically monopolistic markets will activate major social and ecclesiastic transformations. In a poor, unequal, ethnically diverse society, religious challengers will most likely target the religiously underserved and socially marginalized members of the community for conversion – the poor in general and ethnically discriminated minorities in particular.

In the context of strict separation of church and state, in which the monopoly church has no access to state protection, the entry of a new religious supplier will force the former monopoly clergy to compete for souls and respond to parishioners' demands that can no longer be ignored. The availability of an *exit* option (Hirschman, 1970) will indirectly empower parishioners of the (now) former monopoly church. Membership is no longer a constant but a variable, and as a result, the preferences of the "median" parishioner – in this case the poor – become a key component of the utility function of the former monopoly clergy. Competition enables parishioners in competitive districts to demand a new religious contract – a doctrinal reinterpretation of the scriptures and of pastoral practices now aimed at satisfying their preferences rather than the needs of the state or the rich.

Negotiating a New Religious Contract

Under this context of separation of church and state, the critical question, then, is what the former monopoly church can offer to its members under increasingly competitive conditions (the supply-side question), and what poor parishioners themselves, now empowered by competition, will demand – short of defecting en masse (the demand-side question).

Let us first consider demand. Assume that parishioners seek to maximize worldly rewards (w) and spiritual or otherworldly rewards (s) (Azzi and Ehrenberg, 1975). Worldly religious rewards include material goods and social services (w_m) that most religious suppliers offer to their members (e.g., education and basic health care), and ecclesiastic rewards (w_e) mainly involve decentralization of clerical authority to the laity (e.g., entrusting clerical functions to parishioners and allowing native community members to run their own churches from the bottom up). Whereas w_m can be an important source of economic mobilization for parishioners, w_e can be a major source of social status differentiation. Otherworldly or spiritual rewards involve answers to existential questions about the soul and the afterlife (Stark and Finke, 2000).

The main issues involved in the renegotiation of a new religious contract between poor parishioners of the former monopoly religion and their clerical authorities will critically depend on the proselytizing strategies of the market's most successful incoming challenger. In this model, the leading challenger is, in fact, the agenda setter of the game – the single actor who defines the issues that will dominate the new religious market and the terms of negotiation of a new religious contract.

This assumption takes us back to the supply side of the story. By construction, the conversion strategy of new religious challengers may focus on improving the supply of material or spiritual rewards. Which factor challengers favor is a question of doctrine and strategy. But because challengers proselytizing in poor, unequal multiethnic societies are more likely to target the "unchurched" and underserved members of the monopoly religion, incoming missionaries are most likely to concentrate their actions in poor regions, including ethnic-minority areas. Challengers will therefore face strong incentives to devise proselytizing strategies that emphasize material rewards.

Why the Catholic Church Becomes a Major Promoter of Popular Movements

For convenience, assume the challenger in this society is a U.S. mainline Protestant church and the monopolist is the Roman Catholic Church – as was the case in many indigenous regions in twentieth-century Latin America. Following the quintessential Protestant evangelizing strategy, Protestant missionaries will (1) translate Bibles to native languages to facilitate an "unmediated" relationship between new believers and God; (2) establish *decentralized* local autochthonous churches led by newly trained native clergy; and (3) provide basic

social services to converts, including literacy and basic health care. Bible translations will channel competition into the linguistic and ethnocultural arena;
building decentralized ecclesiastic hierarchies into the institutional structure of
churches; and social service provision into parishioners' material living conditions. This strategy will, in fact, narrow the negotiating agenda of a new religious contract between Catholic parishioners and their authorities to cultural
(w_c), ecclesiastic (w_e), and material (w_m) worldly rewards.

Empowered by competition, poor Catholic parishioners in competitive districts will condition their allegiance to Rome to the clergy's capacity to credibly supply them with a future stream of worldly rewards that is greater than
that received by the Protestant converts. But the ability of Catholic authorities to surpass the competition may be limited by the Church's own doctrinal
and institutional constraints and the extent of its reputation deficit for having
served the interests of the rich and powerful for centuries.[5]

Improving on the Protestant decentralization of ecclesiastic rewards is a
major challenge for a centralized, hierarchical organization like the Catholic
Church. A multinational, multilayered corporation, Roman Catholicism is
institutionally structured into national episcopates which are, in turn, subdi-
vided into subnational dioceses and local parishes. Within these multiple layers,
dioceses are the most important ecclesiastic jurisdictions and bishops are the
most influential actors in the everyday operation of Catholicism (Camp, 1997).
Bishops enjoy a great degree of relative autonomy and centralized power in
their local churches. But they are accountable to the Pope, who appoints and
removes them at will. Decentralization of diocesan ecclesiastic hierarchies is
unlikely, because bishops would face few incentives to give up power to parish
priests and would be institutionally hindered from doing so unless the entire
"industrial organization" of Roman Catholicism were changed.

Unable to even closely match the Protestant provision of ecclesiastic rewards,
Catholic authorities in competitive districts would need to oversupply material rewards to retain Catholic parishioners. In a context of strict separation of
church and state, Catholic authorities would be incapable of extracting public
resources from the state to finance social services for the Indian poor. And in
an unequal rural society, it would be highly unlikely that Catholic authorities
could transform economic elites and landowners into long-term sponsors of
sufficient financial resources to satisfy the material needs of thousands of poor
parishioners.[6]

Given the financial inability of the Catholic clergy to become a long-term
provider of social services to the poor and to credibly surpass the Protestant supply of material and ecclesiastic rewards, the promotion of community self-help
groups for the provision of social services would become an attractive option.

[5] For the pioneering argument on why a history of complicity with economic and political elites
created major reputation problems for the Catholic Church, see Gill (1998).
[6] Sokoloff and Zolt (2008) show that in highly unequal societies, states are less able to tax the
rich.

However, two problems make the "self-help" strategy an unlikely long-term solution to preventing massive defection to Protestantism. One is that it would not ensure a strictly greater provision of material rewards than that offered by the challengers. Given that Protestant missionaries also offer material rewards, simply matching or barely surpassing the Protestant stream of social services would not be enough to persuade poor Catholic parishioners to remain in the fold. Another problem is that the creation of self-help groups would not solve the reputation deficit that afflicts Catholic authorities; there is simply no credible guarantee that this would not be a short-term opportunistic strategy undertaken to hold back the formation of a critical mass of defectors.

A more radical and credible member-retention strategy would be to create, promote, and directly sponsor the organizational and ideological infrastructure for rural indigenous villagers to directly demand public policies of material redistribution from the state. In the context of a highly unequal poor rural society, this would mean that the Catholic clergy would become a major institutional promoter of rural indigenous associational networks and movements for material (land) redistribution. While Protestant challengers would offer education and health care services, Catholic authorities could match this offer through self-help groups but would better it by promoting and sponsoring the social bases for struggles for material redistribution. Siding with poor rural indigenous movements demanding a radical transformation of rural economic structures, even in the event of state repression or a violent reaction by the rich, would be a powerful and credible signal of a long-term Catholic commitment to the material well-being of poor parishioners. Put more succinctly, we should expect that:

H.1a. The spread of Protestant competition in rural indigenous regions will motivate Catholic bishops and priests to become major promoters of community associational networks and social movements for material redistribution.

H.1b. Villages with higher levels of religious competition between Catholic and mainline Protestant churches should experience greater levels of secular social mobilization.

The rise of new local lay leaders and the development of new community associational networks and trans-community connections would transform the social landscape of closed corporate communities and indigenous regions in radical ways. At the village level, this new elite of lay local leaders with extensive connections to local Bible study groups, social and economic cooperatives, and secular movements for material redistribution would upset the communities' traditional balance of power. With their dual functions as religious and secular leaders, these new Catholic lay leaders would be empowered to rival traditional local elites linked to the corporatist structure of the ruling party and to compete with a rising native Protestant clergy. At the regional level, the social ties these local lay leaders would forge with other villages in the development of regional associational networks and movements for land redistribution would connect once isolated communities and transform them into powerful regional players.

In the conceptual language of network theory, in responding to the decentralized evangelizing strategy followed by U.S. Protestant missionaries as they expanded into rural indigenous regions, Catholic clergy would create decentralized regional networks of multiple local lay leaders with access to dense community associational networks and loose inter-village connections. They would create network structures that approximate the "village" or "clique" structure described by Siegel (2009, 2011).

As network theorists suggest, this type of social network can serve as the organizational basis for the rise of a wide variety of powerful movements for independent collective action.[7] This is a powerful organizational structure because it combines dense intra-village connections that provide the advantages of small groups in solving collective action problems (Olson, 1966) with loose inter-village connections that provide the advantages of weak ties for the articulation of group action (Granovetter, 1973). As Siegel (2011) suggests, following recent advances in network theory, these are resilient movements because the removal of one leader or the elimination of one village does not bring about a general failure in the collective action capacity of the group.

Why the Catholic Church Becomes a Major Sponsor of Ethnic Identities

The emphasis of Protestant missionary activity on the use of autochthonous languages can have important and unexpected consequences in terms of ethnic revival. In authoritarian regimes in which ethnic minorities and their languages are traditionally suppressed, translating Bibles to local languages and training native clergy to preach in their own languages is a revolutionary action. The rise of a native clergy from ethnic minority groups historically marginalized from any clerical position dramatically transforms the racial composition of churches, and the translation of Bibles to historically stigmatized minority languages can lead to a linguistic revival. Because both race and language are key components of ethnicity, these two major ecclesiastic and pastoral transformations may lead to the rise of a new ethnic pride.

Unable to decentralize ecclesiastic hierarchies to the extent that Protestant missionaries typically do or to allow married indigenous males to be ordained as members of the Catholic clergy, Catholic authorities in competitive districts would be compelled to focus on providing major cultural rewards in the religious and secular realms.

Promoting the revitalization of indigenous languages, cultures, and ethnic identities would be a second powerful member-retention strategy Catholic clergy could follow. If Protestants translated Bibles into local minority languages and native pastors used these new Bibles for preaching in their own language, Catholic clergy could go a step further, embracing indigenous cultures

---

[7] On the power of decentralized horizontal network structures for resilient collective action, see Schock (2005) and Siegel (2011).

and reinterpreting the Christian gospel in terms of indigenous cultures, histories, and prevailing socioeconomic circumstances. The conclusions of the Second Vatican Council, a historic meeting of all of the world's cardinals and bishops in Rome, where the clergy called for the opening of Catholicism to non-Western cultures, provided the institutional space for the "inculturation" of the Gospel. Hence, defending indigenous cultures in the secular sphere and becoming a major promoter of movements for indigenous rights would be another powerful member-retention strategy.

While the quintessential Protestant strategy of translating Bibles to local native languages in Latin America – like the early translations of the Bible to European vernacular languages during the Reformation – would contribute to an indigenous linguistic revival, the Catholic (more encompassing) reaction of embracing indigenous cultures would contribute to the mobilization of a public ethnic consciousness. Building on the decentralized Catholic networks, Catholic authorities would have powerful incentives to contribute to recreate ethnolinguistic identities repressed and denigrated by the Spanish conquest and to encourage villages of coethnics to begin imagining themselves as peoples – in the same way that the translation of Bibles and secular narratives allowed disconnected European villagers to begin imagining themselves as nations (Anderson, 1991). It follows that:

H.2a. The spread of Protestant competition and the translation of Bibles to indigenous languages will motivate Catholic bishops and priests to embrace indigenous cultures and become major promoters of ethnic identities.

H.2b. Villages with histories of more intense Catholic-Protestant competition will be more likely to experience ethnic mobilization.

The Limits of Religion as an Explanatory Factor of Collective Action

Religion can be a major source for the development of autonomous local leadership structures, networks, and organizations for the mobilization of poor parishioners in authoritarian regimes. We have suggested that the rise in competitive pressures in traditionally monopolistic religious markets can become a major incentive for traditionalist clergy to step into the secular realm and promote and sponsor autonomous social mobilization. Yet religion is neither the only source for the development of independent movements in authoritarian regimes nor a sufficient factor to explain the strategies of mobilization embraced by independent leaders and movements.

As a whole generation of social movement scholars from Tilly (1978) to McAdam (1982/1999), Kitschelt (1986), and Tarrow (1998) have suggested, we need to go beyond organizational resources and ideologies to explain strategies of social mobilization and collective action; we need to explore the political institutions and incentives that independent leaders and organizations face when they take their grievances to the streets. Rather than identify the dimensions of politics that provide opportunities for social protest in democracies and apply them to non-democratic conditions – as most students of social movements do – here we identify the logic of governance in autocracies and seek to understand the opportunities and costs associated with protest.

A MODEL OF ELECTORAL COMPETITION AND SOCIAL MOBILIZATION IN AUTOCRACIES

Assume authoritarian elites introduce government-controlled multiparty elections in response to a major external economic shock that threatens the stability of the regime. As students of autocracies have shown, authoritarian elites introduce power-sharing agreements to avoid coups or revolutions (Geddes, 2003; Gandhi and Przeworski, 2007; Magaloni, 2008). They partially decentralize power to avoid a systemic collapse, giving up some control to remain in power. Following Schedler (2006) and Magaloni (2006), I characterize authoritarian regimes that select their leaders through government-controlled multiparty elections as electoral autocracies.

Governance and Independent Mobilization in Electoral Autocracies

The introduction of government-controlled elections entails major institutional changes that affect the dynamics of governance and independent collective action in fundamental ways. Even though elections are neither entirely free nor completely fair, the new rules of authoritarian competition introduce new actors and political practices and new opportunities for independent collective action.

Opposition parties are a new major actor. The main goal of opposition leaders is to win elections and assume office, but their most immediate task is to make sure their vote share is fairly counted. At the initial stages in the life of electoral autocracies, opposition party leaders play a "nested game;" they have to compete for office while at the same time contesting the rules of competition (Schedler, 2002; Mainwaring, 2003). This institutional constraint will motivate opposition parties to establish close relationships with independent social movements and seek to influence the dynamics of social protest.

Voters are a second major actor. Whereas in closed autocracies, citizens' policy preferences are publicly repressed, in electoral autocracies citizens can express their preferences through the ballot box. Even if authoritarian rulers can distort the voice of the median voter through electoral manipulation (Schedler, 2006), voters have the ability to partially express their preferences by voting, abstaining, or spoiling their ballots. This institutional possibility transforms incentives for governance and social protest in important ways.

Social movements are a third major actor. When autocrats consent to government-controlled multiparty elections, they typically consent to granting basic civic rights and liberties, including the right to petition, organize, and demonstrate peacefully. These rights provide autonomous organizations and movements – such as the Catholic associational networks described in the previous section – with legitimate access to the streets. Leaders and activists of independent organizations and social movements are individuals with strong policy preferences on specific policy issues; they maximize the probability of achieving their policy goals and minimize the odds of repression (Lichbach, 1987). The introduction of government-controlled elections and the emergence of new political actors will shape their strategies of social protest in fundamental ways.

Why Opposition Parties Become Major Promoters of Independent Movements

After a long period of single-party rule, creating a core constituency of voters from scratch is one of the main challenges faced by opposition parties once authoritarian incumbents have introduced government-controlled multiparty elections. With no access to office and patronage, opposition parties have few immediate material rewards to offer voters. Hence, at the initial stages of multiparty competition, opposition parties in electoral autocracies become niche parties (Greene, 2007). Opposition leaders appeal to voters on the basis of ideological principles and moral duty; they become a source of expressive behavior for independent citizens with strong policy preferences. In the early stages of competition, the net benefit of casting a vote for opposition parties is associated with uncertain benefits and likely (moderate) costs of repression. But even if voters are not repressed, the problem remains that their vote may not be fairly counted. Voting for the opposition is a risky venture in electoral autocracies.[8]

To overcome the challenges associated with the early stages of government-controlled electoral competition, opposition party leaders actively seek to develop socio-electoral coalitions with independent social movements and actively try to recruit leaders and activists who were able to create extensive autonomous associational networks under closed authoritarian rule – such as the lay leaders and Catholic social networks described in the first part of this chapter. Social leaders and activists are crucial for early opposition-party development because they possess the social characteristics to fulfill the chief electoral goals of opposition parties: they are highly motivated, issue-oriented, risk-acceptant individuals with access to dense local networks and an invaluable cross-regional organizational infrastructure.

Social leaders and activists have access to social networks and to potential opposition voters who are likely to accept the risks involved in casting a vote against the ruling party. They can play key electoral roles during rough election campaigns, including mobilizing their social constituencies to participate in campaign rallies, canvassing on the day of the election, and serving as watchdogs at polling stations. Leaders and activists of independent networks

---

[8] There is a substantial body of literature on how perceptions of risk shape political behavior in electoral autocracies. See Buendía (1997) for the pioneering statement.

and movements can also play an important role in postelection mobilization to contest fraud. These are particularly important and risky electoral tasks in poor, remote rural regions, where clientelism, vote buying, and coercion are widespread.[9]

In exchange for this crucial electoral support, opposition parties can offer significant financial and institutional resources to leaders and activists of independent organizations and social movements. Opposition parties can become important sponsors of the financial and logistic resources that facilitate independent peaceful mobilization during elections and, most crucially, in nonelection years. They can also become major institutional defenders of the human rights of social movement leaders and activists and their social constituencies. These sources of support and protection become more effective when opposition parties gain access to legislative chambers or subnational office, where they have access to financial resources to sponsor their own activities and those of their allies and where they gain an institutional position that enables them to more formally denounce government repression. From a position of subnational power, opposition party leaders can also serve as an institutional voice for the movements' main policy claims.

But these strategic socio-electoral partnerships may undergo significant transformations once opposition parties become real power contenders or win office at subnational levels. To the extent that electoral victories often entail the adoption of moderate multi-class and multiethnic political compromises (Przeworki and Sprague, 1988), partisan leaders will at some point face powerful incentives to moderate the actions of their social movement allies and their niche demands (Greene, 2007), discourage public demonstrations, and drop from their platforms radical demands and identities that may alienate the median voter. These electoral incentives will eventually turn opposition parties into an important force for demobilization and institutionalization of protracted cycles of independent protest. Access to patronage, candidacies, and public resources will be a powerful incentive for social movement leaders and activists to follow party leaders in institutionalizing protest.

In summary, the rise, growth, and consolidation of opposition parties in electoral autocracies will shape the rise, development, and demise of cycles of independent mobilization in significant ways. To put it more precisely:

H.3a. The introduction of government-controlled elections in authoritarian regimes will motivate opposition party leaders to become major promoters of independent social mobilization. But once elections are relatively free and fair and opposition parties become major power contenders, partisan leaders will face incentives to discourage social mobilization and radical demands.

H.3b. At the initial stages of multiparty autocracy, villages with higher levels of competition will experience more intense levels of peaceful mobilization. But once opposition parties become likely contenders for office, greater competition will be associated with declining levels of independent protest.

[9] See Lehoucq (2003) and Eisenstadt (2004).

Although opposition parties have strong incentives to establish socio-electoral coalitions with most independent movements, they also actively seek to sponsor the development of their own social organizations, including workers' and peasant unions. As the literature on authoritarian politics suggests, opposition growth is typically associated with elite defections from the ruling party in times of economic crisis (Greene, 2007). Here I want to highlight defections of local activists from state-corporatist organizations who, in search for leadership positions that are not easily attainable within the ruling party, may spearhead the formation of dissident unions linked to the opposition. Joining an opposition party is a long-term investment that young members of state-corporatist unions make in search of alternative sources of power and resources made available by the introduction of multiparty elections.

Given that opposition parties compete against state-corporatist organizations controlled by strong centralized leadership structures, to make defection attractive they establish societal organizations with strong centralized leadership positions. They seek to develop organizations led by charismatic leaders who develop multiple connections with local villagers but who do not necessarily become involved in the formation of dense local networks. Whereas the Protestant strategy of ecclesiastic decentralization motivates the Catholic Church to develop decentralized social networks, competition against state-corporatist organizations channels opposition forces into establishing centralized network structures that resemble the "opinion leader" networks discussed by Siegel (2009, 2011) – organizational structures in which a leader has multiple connections to all his followers but followers themselves are sparsely connected. In the language of European socialism, this is a description of "democratic centralism."

As network theorists suggest, although these are powerful network structures for collective action, they are structurally vulnerable to targeted attacks against leaders. Unlike the decentralized religious networks where the removal of a leader does not lead to the collapse of group action, the removal of leaders from centralized organizations cuts off villages and compromises the ability of the group to act collectively.

Governing the Streets

Knowing that independent leaders, grassroots organizations, and social movements represent a crucial constituency for the initial growth of opposition parties, incumbents in electoral autocracies will try to prevent the formation of a strategic partnership between opposition parties and independent social movements. Whereas under closed autocracy, authoritarian elites keep independent movements under control via harsh systematic repression, under electoral autocracy, incumbents face limited, albeit potentially significant, electoral constraints that prevent them from freely and brutally suppressing dissent. Instead of crushing independent movements, government authorities in multiparty autocracies typically seek to actively co-opt independent social movements or at least insulate them from the reach of opposition parties.

To prevent the formation of socio-electoral coalitions of independent movements and opposition parties, incumbents in electoral autocracies adopt a new governance strategy: They respond to protest by independent movements with partial satisfaction of their material claims (in the hope of co-opting their leaders) and try to keep demands under control via targeted nonlethal repression (in case co-optation fails). This combination of (partial) carrots and (moderate) sticks is the quintessential governance strategy in electoral autocracies; it is a strategy by which autocrats accept the streets as a legitimate venue for policy negotiation with independent movements – a strategy by which autocrats try to "manage" dissent (Robertson, 2010).

The partial satisfaction of independent movements' material claims and the use of moderate forms of repression to keep protesters from pressing additional demands can sometimes result in the co-opting of leaders and activists but can also become a stimulant for greater mobilization. Social networks play a crucial role here. Following Siegel (2009, 2011), I suggest that leaders and activists from hierarchical centralized social organizations with weak communal networks will be more easily co-opted through selective government incentives and will more rapidly refrain from continuous mobilization when confronted with repression. In contrast, leaders and activists from decentralized organizations with strong local leadership structures and dense communal networks will more likely react to attempts at government co-optation or repression with renewed mobilization.

Government co-optation is more likely to succeed in the case of hierarchical organizations with centralized leadership structures and weak local networks because leaders are not constrained by effective checks and balances and because communities cannot effectively keep their leaders accountable. Government repression in these organizations is more effective because the removal (e.g., imprisonment) of leaders leaves weakly knit communities without the centralized structure that facilitates collective action in the first place (Siegel, 2011). This structural weakness prevents communities from effectively contesting the removal of their central leaders.

Government co-optation will be less effective in horizontal decentralized organizations where multiple local leaders are more accountable to densely organized local networks. The geographic and structural proximity of leaders to organized communities prevents defection. Moreover, government repression in these organizations is less likely to deter group collective action, because leaders who are removed are easily replaced by other leaders (Siegel, 2011), and because closely knit communities and their neighbors are more likely to contest the removal of their leaders in the streets.

Access to dense social networks empowers social leaders and activists. In fact, the history of social interaction and reciprocity that sustains such networks allows leaders and members to work with longer time horizons and to become more risk-accepting than they would otherwise be.[10] With a longer time

---

[10] For a detailed discussion on how preferences for time and risk define social power, see Knight (1992).

horizon, they can afford to wait for a future stream of additional government material concessions in response to independent mobilization and are empowered to reject the short-term benefits associated with co-optation. Dense social networks also serve as a ring of protection that helps safeguard leaders and activists against state repression and helps them discount nonlethal repression as a *sunk cost* they need to pay to have the partial benefits offered by government authorities extended into the future.

We should therefore expect that the effect of co-optation and coercion on independent social protest will be conditional on the structure of social networks. Thus:

H.4a. Partial material concessions and/or targeted government repression will discourage social movement leaders and activists that belong to hierarchical centralized organizations from constantly taking their grievances to the streets, but will be a stimulant for further mobilization for leaders and activists from decentralized organizations with dense local social networks.

H.4b. Villages where governments respond to opposition claims with partial material concessions and targeted repression will experience lower levels of protest when communities are organized in weak networks and participate in hierarchical centralized organizations. But the same strategy will stimulate protest in villages with dense social networks in which communities and local leaders belong to decentralized horizontal organizations.

Note that in our discussion it is religious actors, rather than secular actors, who spearhead the development of the most powerful social networks for sustained collective action, namely decentralized regional networks of multiple local leaders with access to strong community associational webs. We are not suggesting that religious ideas and beliefs make Catholic lay leaders less co-optable and more resilient than secular socialist leaders. Instead, my key theoretical claim is that the decentralized network structures Catholic clergy develop in response to the Protestant competition accounts for the tremendous resilience of movements associated with these social structures; the fundamental theoretical point is about organizational capacity rather than ideology.

Governing the Streets in Times of Crisis: Why Regime Reversion Threats Promote the Escalation of Protest into Rebellion

As students of conflict escalation have argued for more than two decades, a sudden radical change in governance in the midst of a cycle of peaceful protest can stimulate the transformation of collective action from nonviolence to violence (Lichbach 1987; Brockett, 1991, 2005; Hafez, 2004; Sambanis and Zinn, 2006). In the context of electoral autocracies, the governance strategies that incumbents choose to "manage" cycles of peaceful protest in times of major economic crises, or when elites themselves adopt major universally opposed economic reforms, is a crucial determinant of whether social movement leaders and activists will turn into rebel combatants and whether peaceful protest escalates into armed rebellion (Almeida, 2003).

Incumbents can attempt to prevent the radicalization of protest by means of partial material concessions and moderate repression to independent movements – the quintessential governance strategy in electoral autocracies. Elites could try to compensate what social movements of aggrieved populations lose in one policy domain with new resources in an alternative policy domain. For example, if the liberalization of land tenure eliminates basic privileges Indian peasants enjoyed as peasants, elites may try to compensate them by introducing new cultural rewards that recognize them as Indians or by extending citizen rights to increase their limited ability to shape subnational electoral outcomes through electoral participation. But incumbents may very well choose to prevent radicalization through strictly punitive means; they may adopt harsh repression as a dominant short-term strategy to avoid revolutionary action.

Assume that elites choose their preferred governance strategies in a world of imperfect information.[11] If rulers believe social protest is a spontaneous phenomenon without a strong social base for sustained collective action – that is, without social networks – they might seek to bring mobilization to an end by means of indiscriminate violence. If incumbents believe there is a network base behind the cycle of social protest but that this network is centrally dominated by outside leaders and communities do not have the capacity to act collectively on their own, they may seek to abort any revolutionary threat through policies of targeted repression against leaders – a major wave of leadership removal through unlawful arrests. Alternatively, if elites believe aggrieved populations are part of decentralized networks with multiple local leaders and powerful local associational networks, capable of opposing reforms through revolutionary means, they may opt for compensatory measures.

I have argued in the previous section that when incumbents in electoral autocracies seek to manage independent mobilization through a combination of partial material concessions and moderate and targeted repression, they generate cycles of peaceful protest but not armed rebellion. However, if in response to a major external shock, government elites abruptly stop dispensing partial material concessions to independents, withdraw basic rights and liberties granted in the liberalization phase, and adopt harsh repression as the dominant response to rising independent mobilization, this new governance strategy will radicalize leaders, activists, and members of grassroots organizations and social movements. The sudden retraction of rights and resources that resulted from the rise of limited electoral competition will most likely lead to radicalization of independent movements already accustomed to negotiating policy concessions and material resources in the streets.

To the extent that members of independent movements and their leaders perceive the government's new actions as a credible signal of a likely reversion to a punitive authoritarian status quo ante, in which previously won rights (e.g., economic, political, or cultural) will be permanently withdrawn, and where

---

[11] For an insightful analysis of governance and dissident mobilization in a context of information asymmetries see Pierskalla (2010).

their lives will be under constant threat, they will face meaningful incentives to give up on street protest, move to the mountains, and engage in revolutionary action. That is, confronted by a security dilemma, social leaders and activists will seek to preventively take up arms to assure their own self-preservation. Hence:

H.5. When incumbents in electoral autocracies seek to manage major negative economic shocks by withdrawing basic rights and liberties previously awarded during a phase of political liberalization and adopt harsh repression as their dominant governance strategy, social movement leaders and activists are likely to embrace revolutionary violence if they believe this new governance strategy is a credible signal of a reversion to an authoritarian status quo ante.

While punitive governance of major economic crises or radical and unpopular economic policy shifts may stimulate revolutionary feelings among peaceful protesters, whether they actually join armed insurgent groups and take up arms crucially depends on the conditions for rebel recruitment; revolutionary feelings will translate into revolutionary action only if rebel recruitment is possible. Unlike dominant explanations of insurgency and civil war that emphasize economic factors (e.g., poverty or class structures) or geography (e.g. mountains) to explain rebel recruitment, I follow Gould (1995) and Petersen (2001) in emphasizing the importance of social networks for recruitment into groups engaged in guerrilla warfare. Because recruitment into guerrilla insurgencies typically takes place at the micro level of villages and hamlets, where insurgent groups seek to build strong social bases of support and recruit combatants, Petersen (2001) suggests that community networks of friends, neighbors, and coreligionists often serve as the most effective vehicles for rebel recruitment.

Building on our previous discussion about different social network structures, here I suggest that recruitment from communal associational networks and social movements into guerrilla groups is more likely when social movements are structured as decentralized horizontal networks with multiple local leaders and dense community networks than when they are organized as hierarchical centralized organizations with weak local leaders and weak communal networks or as closed corporate communities.

Rebels do not recruit their social base from closed corporate communities because these villages are dominated by clientelistic politics and lack any type of independent leadership and politicized associational networks. Moreover, because these communities are isolated from coethnic neighboring villages, they do not provide many opportunities to build extensive regional networks of support for rebel groups.

Rebels are unlikely to recruit their social bases from social movements structured as centralized hierarchies because the risks associated with recruitment of leaders are high: Not only are these leaders highly visible, but if they are caught and eliminated by state security forces, the network collapses and rebels are deprived of a social base. These social structures are also not conducive to rebel recruitment because communities that participate in these movements do not have strong local leaders and dense community structures that facilitate recruitment, nor do they have the dense local networks that are crucial for any guerrilla group that needs a place to hide after mounting surprise attacks against their enemies.

Rebel recruitment is most likely in social movements built on a base of decentralized regional networks with strong local leaders and dense community associational networks because recruitment is both safer and more effective. Access to one local leader provides access to dense community networks and to other leaders with similar dense community connections. This provides the secrecy and trust that is vital for underground recruitment. If one leader is caught and removed, the network does not collapse and other leaders and their communities may sustain the structural foundation for the rebel group. It follows that:

H.6. In the context of a major regime reversion threat, rebel recruitment is more likely to take place through social movements that are structured as decentralized organizations of interconnected strong local leaders with access to strong community networks than through centralized hierarchical organizations.

Note that in this chapter we have argued that the associational networks and the leadership structures built by Catholic religious authorities in response to the Protestant competition can be conducive both to *peaceful* social protest and to *armed* insurgencies. Yet the key factor that explains the different paths that lay leaders and communities espousing the same religious beliefs and ideas may take us outside of the religious realm; what distinguishes these communities is their exposure to different governance strategies taken by authoritarian elites to "manage" independent protest: Whereas policies of partial material concessions (carrots) and moderate repression (sticks) produce cycles of peaceful social mobilization, regime reversion threats and the adoption of purely punitive (stick) strategies stimulate the transformation of networks for peaceful mobilization into networks for preventive violence.

Renegotiating Social Identities in Times of Crisis

As a whole generation of constructivist theorists of nationalism and social identities have argued, states make nations and shape social identities rather than the other way around.[12] By means of policy incentives and coercion, states seek to shape the dominant social cleavages and identity markers in society. In the case of authoritarian regimes, through policies of state-building nationalism elites seek to favor some social identities while suppressing others (Laitin, 1986; Posner, 2005).

From Latin America to North Africa and the Middle East, twentieth-century authoritarian regimes typically opted to suppress religious or ethnic identities and embraced class as the master cleavage for governance

---

[12] See Laitin (1986), Przeworski and Sprague (1988), Kalyvas (1996), and Hechter (2000).

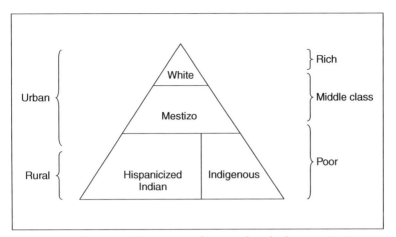

FIGURE 1.2. Structural dimensions of a typical ranked society in Mesoamerica.

(Stavenhagen, 1992; Rosefsky Wickham, 2002). Through a wide range of policies, including conscription, education and agriculture, autocrats tried to eliminate potentially dangerous social identities and sought to establish class as the dominant cleaveage of politics; in exchange for access to land, for example, peasants were expected to give up on mobilizing along ethnic or religious identities. As long as states could provide the material bases to sustain class identities, and insofar as they had the coercive means to punish dissenters, class remained the equilibrium identity. However, when major economic crises or radical economic policy shifts render states incapable of sponsoring a master cleavage of governance, societies enter into a period of renegotiation of social identities.

Consider the case of rural indigenous populations in Latin America. In these poor unequal, multiethnic societies, class, ethnicity, and place of residence correlate in important ways. In the conceptual language of Horowitz (1985), these are ranked societies. Figure 1.2 is a stylized society similar to many Latin American countries in the twentieth century. It shows that at one extreme, lighter-skinned people were richer and more urban, while darker-skinned and predominantly rural indigenous populations were at the bottom of the social scale. In between these two extremes were Mestizos (racially mixed persons of white and indigenous descent) and Hispanicized Indians (racially indigenous persons who have been culturally Hispanicized). The probability of having a wealthy or upper-middle-class indigenous person or a poor white individual is close to zero.[13]

In this society, indigenous persons have two identity choices: to organize on the basis of ethnicity (indigeneity) or on the basis of class (poor peasants). Authoritarian regimes in Latin America, like most closed authoritarian

[13] See Villarreal (2010).

regimes in the twentieth century, followed policies of state-building nationalism that sought to eliminate race and ethnicity as major cleavages of mobilization and resorted to class as a master cleavage for authoritarian politics. Through policies of land reform and agricultural subsidies, authoritarian elites contrived to mobilize indigenous populations into peasant unions linked to the ruling party. Authoritarian land reform programs and the development of ambitious agricultural subsidy systems were aimed at avoiding major insurrections in the countryside but also at reshaping identities – turning Indians into peasants.

Following the literature on ethnic mobilization in Latin America (Yashar, 2005) and on religious revivals in the Muslim world (Rosefsky-Wickham, 2002), I suggest that when authoritarian rulers engage in major policy shifts that undermine the material bases that sustain social identities traditionally sponsored by the regime – such as class – the relative benefits associated with previously suppressed forms of identification – such as ethnicity or religion – tend to increase. For example, the sudden elimination of land reform policies or generalized subsidies to education should provide incentives for major social identity shifts. In the context of globalization, the emergence of international regimes in favor of religious freedoms and ethnic minorities – such as the ILO Convention 169 for Indigenous Peoples – contribute in significant ways to increasing the relative worth of previously suppressed social identities. Hence we should expect that in the context of the global resurgence of rights for minorities,

H.7. The dismantling of major economic policies that had historically sustained class forms of identification and suppressed ethnic identities should be associated with the rise of ethnic forms of mobilization.

Whether ethnicity becomes politicized and whether it becomes a major cleavage for politics depends on the existence of ethnic coalitions and on electoral incentives for parties. Contrary to explanations that emphasize the survival of ethnic or religious identities underneath class structures and their politicization after the state is no longer able to suppress these forms of identification, here we take a strictly constructivist view and suggest that social identities do not automatically reawaken but need to be actively mobilized. Hence, we should not expect closed corporate communities to lead the politicization of ethnicity.

We suggested in earlier sections that the Protestant strategy of creating native churches and translating Bibles into indigenous languages would lead to a linguistic revival and the rise of a new ethnic pride (H.2a and 2b). We should hence expect that in competitive districts, the Catholic Church should be a powerful ally for the mobilization of ethnicity. To the extent that the provision of cultural rewards increases the chance of member retention, Catholic clergy should be active long-term supporters of indigenous identities and rights.

Whereas social actors may play an important role in creating the social base for ethnic mobilization, the role that governments and opposition political parties play is more crucial in defining whether social identities are politicized in electoral campaigns and in the distribution of public resources. Hypotheses H.3a and 3b suggested that at the initial stages of competition in electoral autocracies, opposition parties would face incentives to establish socio-electoral coalitions and support independent social mobilization but would discourage mobilization once elections were relatively free and the opposition became serious contenders for power.

Building on the partisan logic developed in H.3a and 3b, we may also suggest that at the initial stages of competition, when opposition forces behave as niche parties, we may expect leftist parties to embrace ethnic claims. But once power is within their reach and they need to establish pluralistic cross-class coalitions, they will most likely discourage their candidates and leaders from embracing ethnic forms of identification. In societies like those depicted in Figure 1.2, in which indigenous populations are a minority, opposition parties are likely to be short-term opportunistic supporters of ethnic identities, until elections have become free and fair.

Our theoretical suggestion is that the spread of competition and the democratization of elections in electoral autocracies should provide incentives for moderation of movement-parties. Access to candidacies, patronage, and resources from holding subnational office should provide strong incentives to leaders of rural indigenous movements to moderate their ethnic claims. Redistribution under democracy should provide a powerful institutional base for them to try to achieve as citizens what they may have lost as peasants. As Bakke and Wibbels (2006) suggest, the existence of national parties that integrate ethnic minorities and make them co-partisans in terms of access to power and resources should lead to moderate actions and to embrace more universalistic demands associated with class rather than to their embracing ethno-territorial claims.

Whereas the expansion of electoral competition and inclusion of social movements into national parties may invite moderation, exclusion from the likely benefits of democratic redistribution should encourage rural indigenous movements and rebel groups to make radical ethno-territorial claims and seek to achieve as indigenous peoples what they lost as peasants and what they could not get as citizens. That is, when ruling elites seek to govern major policy shocks through fraud, suppress electoral competition, and repress ethnic minorities, rural indigenous movements will face powerful incentives to make radical ethno-territorial demands and develop programmatic agendas for ethnic autonomy and self-determination. We should expect that:

H.8. The spread of electoral competition and the electoral victory of leftist opposition parties at the subnational level should lead to the erosion of ethnic claims, but the suppression of electoral competition should contribute to the rise of radical ethno-territorial demands and identities.

Insurgent Identities and Regime Change

In this chapter we have analyzed how the introduction of government-controlled elections in authoritarian regimes can give rise to cycles of peaceful protest. We have also analyzed how the inconsistent handling of protest in times of crisis may give rise to radicalization – to the outbreak of armed insurgencies and to the mobilization of previously suppressed social identities. The final question we need to ask is about the effect of armed rebellion and of demands for ethno-territorial claims on the stability of authoritarian regimes. Although these are subnational movements that start at the micro level of hamlets and villages, they are likely to have important macro political consequences.

Following theorists of democratization from below (Wood, 2000; Acemoglu and Robinson, 2006), we suggest that the outbreak of rebellion and the rise of self-determination movements will lead to democratization if three conditions are fulfilled: (1) Elites believe these subnational movements are likely to lead to a generalized civil war that will put the system into severe threat of survival; (2) elites know that under free and fair elections the ruling party is likely to win or remain a key power player; and (3) elites believe that the distribution of power resulting from free and fair elections will not lead to major economic redistribution in favor of the poor nor to major institutional changes that will radically transform the current status quo. If these conditions hold, elites will consent to free and fair elections and try to institutionalize rebels and ethno-territorial movements through democratic institutions. It follows that in electoral autocracies:

H.9. The outbreak of subnational armed insurgency will lead to democratization if elites believe that the introduction of free and fair elections will prevent the escalation from insurgency to civil war and expect that the ruling party will remain a key power player in a new democratic system.

CONCLUSION

Building on theories of collective action and social movements, in this chapter I have developed a sociopolitical theory of collective action in autocracies. Focusing on poor, unequal multiethnic societies, I have tried to integrate different forms of popular collective action that are typically analyzed as separate phenomena: the rise of autonomous networks and movements in autocracies, the development of cycles of peaceful protest, the conditions under which peaceful protest gives way to armed insurgency and the circumstances under which revolutionary action motivates elites to democratize.

To assess these different forms of popular collective action in autocracies, I have suggested that major exogenous economic shocks provide the initial motivation for independent mobilization. Following the canonical model of social movement theory, I have argued that whether aggrieved populations mobilize or not and how they do so largely depends, however, on the availability of (1) social networks and organizational vehicles; (2) ideological resources to justify group action; and (3) political opportunities and threats that define the likely benefits and costs associated with the politicization of group collective action.

To explain how the organizational infrastructure and political opportunities and constraints for popular collective action arise in autocracies, I have focused on a single social mechanism: competition. Focusing on the breakdown of religious and political monopolies, I have developed a theoretical rationale that explains why the spread of competition for souls and votes in poor, unequal multiethnic societies can empower poor rural villagers and ethnic minorities to engage in movements for economic redistribution and ethno-cultural rights. I have also developed a theoretical justification to explain why the retraction of basic rights and liberties when elites seek to impose radical and unpopular reforms may give rise to the radicalization of peaceful movements.

In the remainder of the book, I subject the propositions developed in this chapter to multiple empirical tests, using quantitative and qualitative evidence from Mexico's protracted cycle of rural indigenous mobilization spanning 20 states and 883 indigenous municipalities, and covering the last quarter of the twentieth century. The focus of the next section is on the rise and demise of Mexico's influential cycle of peasant indigenous protest. Controlling for basic economic, demographic and geographic factors typically associated with the rise and development of cycles of peaceful protest, we will seek to understand whether the breakdown of religious and political monopolies and the spread of competition for souls and votes empowered rural indigenous Mexican villagers to enter into a major cycle of peaceful protest.

PART II

PROTEST

2

Accounting for Mexico's Cycle of Indigenous Protest

Quantitative Evidence

Like most countries in Latin America, Mexico experienced a prolonged cycle of rural indigenous protest in the last quarter of the twentieth century. Dominant explanations of indigenous mobilization in Latin America suggest that the introduction of neoliberal agrarian reforms and the disenfranchisement of Indians as peasants provided the initial motivation for mobilization. Indigenous communities that survived under the façade of rural corporatist unions built by authoritarian rulers used these financially weakened corporatist structures as the mobilizing vehicles to contest the marketization of agricultural life in public demonstrations. Isolated communities that remained untouched by corporatist structures drew on their cultural autonomy to contest the marketization of their lands. In this narrative, the civil rights and political liberties that became effective in post-authoritarian contexts provided the opportunities for active indigenous mobilization.

In Chapter 1, we developed an alternative explanation of rural indigenous collective action in which cohesive and homogenous communities of cultural survivors and corporatist organizational structures are not the main actors and vehicles for mobilization. We suggested, rather, that communities experiencing the most intense processes of cultural and political diversification would be at the forefront of cycles of protest in favor of economic redistribution and political and ethnic rights.

Focusing on religion, we developed a religious competition model in which the successful spread of U.S. Protestant missionary activity and the *competition for indigenous souls* motivates the Catholic Church to become a major sponsor of the leadership structures and the associational networks supporting the struggles for land redistribution and indigenous rights. Focusing on elections in authoritarian regimes, we developed a model in which the introduction of government-controlled elections and the *competition for indigenous votes* motivates opposition parties to develop socio-electoral coalitions with independent movements and become major sponsors of peaceful social protest.

In this alternative account, in which the renegotiation of religious affiliations and political allegiances empowers indigenous communities and generates incentives for direct political action, government repression does not quell cycles of independent protest. Moderate and targeted forms of repression associated with electoral autocracies may not deter protest but stimulate it, particularly among communities linked to decentralized social networks with multiple local leaders – like the Catholic networks. We conjectured that cycles of independent protest would, instead, come to an end as a result of electoral competition. When elections were no longer fraudulent and opposition parties stood a chance to win, party leaders would discourage intense mobilization by their movement allies to avoid marginalizing the median voter and jeopardizing their chances of electoral victory.

Drawing on the MII Dataset – a new data collection that reports information about 3,553 indigenous protest events that took place in any of Mexico's 883 indigenous municipalities between 1974 and 2000 – in this chapter I put to test my sociopolitical theory of popular collective action outlined in Chapter 1 alongside dominant explanations of indigenous mobilization in Latin America. This is one of the first attempts at empirically testing rival hypotheses of indigenous mobilization using micro data on indigenous protest events from national sources and covering a national sample throughout the entire life of a cycle of mobilization.[1] Given that dominant explanations of indigenous mobilization rely on social movement theory, by testing extant accounts of indigenous collective action in Latin America we are also testing dominant theories of social movement in political science and sociology.

In the first part of this chapter, I present an empirical portrait of Mexico's cycle of peasant indigenous protest and discuss some of its main features. By analyzing the temporal evolution of protest, we are able to show that the cycle began nearly two decades before the adoption of neoliberal agrarian reforms. The evidence shows that the onset of the cycle was intimately associated with a radical change in rural authoritarian governance.

In the second part, I explain why this change in rural governance facilitated the rise of a powerful cycle of protest. After the 1968 student massacre, seeking to avoid a major social insurrection of students and peasants Mexican authorities launched a massive wave of land reform that for the first time in five decades benefited both PRI and non-PRI affiliates. Because the land was titled but not necessarily distributed and because the land that was actually distributed was of poor quality or in possession of other claimants, the reform generated a widespread sense of relative deprivation. I suggest that the desire to close this gap between titled land and land plots actually distributed motivated independent peasants to engage in direct political action. I also suggest that the political liberalization of 1977, aimed at aborting the potential for social insurrection that populist measures did not completely eliminate, activated the streets as a legitimate site for policy bargaining.

---

[1] For pioneering studies of indigenous protest aimed at theory testing using original quantitative data, see Brockett (2005), Inclán (2008), Trejo (2009), and Arce and Rice (2009).

The third and most extensive part of the chapter discusses the results of negative binomial models testing for the temporal and spatial evolution of indigenous protest. The results show an unambiguous and strong relationship between religious competition and the intensity of indigenous protest. This evidence suggests that the indigenous lay leaders and social networks that emerged from the dynamics of religious competition between Catholic and Protestant churches played a key role in Mexico's cycle of indigenous protest. The results also show a strong relationship between electoral competition and the frequency of indigenous protest. The evidence shows that opposition parties became major promoters of indigenous protest on their way to local power but contributed to demobilization of protest after a threshold of competition was passed. Local democratization, rather than repression, contributed to slowdown protest and to the eventual demise of the cycle.

Although neoliberal reforms did not trigger Mexico's cycle of indigenous protest, statistical evidence reveals that protest substantially intensified when elites introduced market-oriented reforms. We have no evidence to suggest, however, that the most culturally cohesive communities spearheaded the cycle of indigenous protest or that corporatism served as the main vehicle for indigenous mobilization. Rather, results consistently show that local leaders and communities from the most culturally and political diverse communities led Mexico's cycle of indigenous protest.

In the final section, the chapter discusses the implications of these findings for our understanding of indigenous mobilization in Latin America and for theories of social protest in autocracies.

MEXICO'S CYCLE OF INDIGENOUS PROTEST

The MII dataset records 3,553 acts of peasant indigenous protest reported for any Mexican municipality that at any time between 1970 and 2000 had at least 10 percent indigenous population (N = 883). As shown in Figure 2.1, acts of protest included public accusations, marches, demonstrations, sit-ins, hunger strikes, road blockades, land invasions, occupation of government buildings, destruction of government buildings, and kidnapping and lynching of government authorities. Public accusations, marches, sit-ins, road blockades, and occupation of government buildings were the most common acts of peasant indigenous mobilization in Mexico.

Unlike large urban demonstrations, which often comprise thousands of protesters in a country's capital and are reported by international news sources, these acts of nearly invisible peasant indigenous protest involved, on average, 200 participants. These participants were Indian peasants who traveled for days from their hamlets and villages in the mountains or jungles to state capitals to express their grievances and demands. Under exceptional circumstances, they took their claims to Mexico City, as rural indigenous villagers from all over the country did in 1992 to protest the Quincentenary of the Conquest of the Americas, and Zapatista commanders and rank-and-file members did in

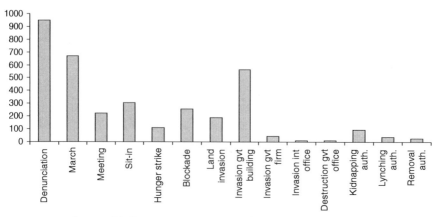

FIGURE 2.1. Count of indigenous protest events by type, 1975–2000.

1996, 1999, and 2001 to press for successful completion of peace negotiations with the federal government. Solving the logistics and overcoming the difficulties of launching a major demonstration from the deep jungles or the highlands all the way to Mexico City was seen by participants as a major sign of organizational maturity and power.[2]

Mexico's cycle of indigenous protest was a protracted one; it grew steadily from the mid-1970s to the early 1990s, experienced a dramatic increase between 1992 and 1994, and then slowed down at the end of the transition to democracy, particularly after 2001.[3] The cycle experienced first moderate and then more dramatic peaks in presidential election years: 1976, 1982, 1988, 1994, and 2000. Although the cycle began nearly two decades before the introduction of Mexico's preeminent neoliberal agrarian reforms (the end of land reform and the liberalization of land tenure in 1992), protest nearly doubled in the post-1992 period.

Mexico's cycle of indigenous protest was a synthesis of various subnational cycles of indigenous protest. Whereas states such as Chiapas, Oaxaca, and Veracruz experienced protracted cycles that lasted for the entire period of the transition from authoritarian rule to democracy, others such as Michoacán, Hidalgo, and Tabasco experienced the most intense levels of mobilization in the 1980s and their cycles slowly faded during the 1990s. Despite moderate peaks of protest in 1992 and 1994, the most intense instances of rural indigenous mobilization in these states took place in the late 1970s and 1980s. At the same time, other states such as Yucatán, Puebla, and Campeche experienced no cycle of indigenous mobilization at all.

Within the states, rural indigenous protest was concentrated in a small number of municipalities. As shown in Map 2.1, only 8.9 percent of municipalities

---

[2] Interviews with social activists from Chilón and Las Margaritas, Chiapas.
[3] See Figure I.1 in the Introduction.

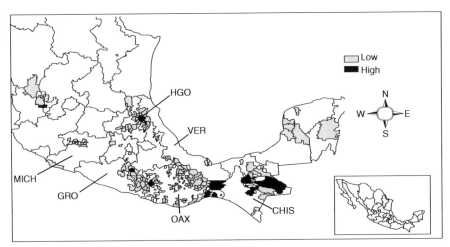

MAP 2.1. Indigenous protest in Mexico, 1975–2000.

saw high levels of protest; 15.1 percent registered moderate levels and the remaining 76 percent experienced low levels or no protest at all. This shows that indigenous mobilization was primarily led by fewer than 100 municipalities. The power of indigenous organizations from these municipalities rested mainly in their geographic scope; they operated in three geographic regions: Chiapas, Guerrero, and Oaxaca (Pacific South); Michoacán and Hidalgo (Central); and Tabasco and Veracruz (Gulf of Mexico). Within these states, municipal protestors concentrated on specific subregions that served as epicenters of protest. For example, the state of Chiapas had five regional epicenters of protest, involving at least four different Mayan ethnolinguistic groups; Oaxaca had three major epicenters of protest, involving four different indigenous groups; and Guerrero had one epicenter of protest, involving two indigenous ethnolinguistic groups. The central state of Puebla and the southeastern states of Campeche and Yucatán experienced very low levels of protest.

Beyond the temporal and spatial evolution of rural indigenous protest, it is worthwhile highlighting five key features that illustrate the peaceful, methodic, and strategic nature of peasant indigenous collective action.

First, Mexico's cycle of rural indigenous protest was predominantly peaceful. Sixty-three percent of all acts of protest involved no violence at all (public accusations, marches, public meetings, and sit-ins) and 30 percent involved low levels of violence (land invasions and occupation of government buildings). This evidence suggests that in the cases where Mexican rural indigenous villagers solved collective action problems and were able to mobilize, violence was not their first or preferred option. As I show in Part III of the book, the escalation of peaceful protest into armed rebellion only took place as a reaction to changing government strategies in dealing with independent rural protest.

Second, the cycle involved organized acts rather than spontaneous responses. Sixty percent of all acts of protest were led by established rural indigenous

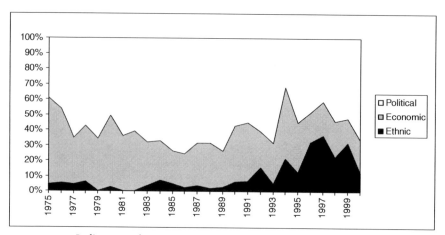

FIGURE 2.2. Indigenous claims in protest events by category (relative contribution).

organizations and the remaining 40 percent by informal community networks. These proportions varied between decades, however. Whereas in the 1970s and early 1980s, community and village-level leaders and members of informal social networks were at the forefront of rural indigenous protest, by the late 1980s formal peasant and indigenous organizations were the major carriers of protest. Although a few *national* peasant indigenous movements were active throughout the cycle, most organizations were *subnational* and no single organization ever dominated national or state-level dynamics of mobilization. The MII records the existence of more than 650 different peasant indigenous organizations between 1975 and 2000. After the Zapatista uprising and the expansion of the Left in electoral politics, many organizations split into what were termed "official" and "independent" factions.

Third, indigenous demands and identities were not fixed but malleable, changing endogenously throughout the period. I take this to be a strong indication that primordial identities never existed; whatever social identities indigenous movements adopted were the corollary of strategic choices. Figure 2.2 illustrates the evolution of peasant indigenous claims throughout the cycle of mobilization. MII identifies 5,120 protest demands made in 3,553 protest events. I grouped forty-two different types of claims into three main categories: economic, political, and ethnic. At the early stages of the cycle in the mid-1970s, economic demands for land redistribution were dominant and ethnic demands practically nonexistent. As the cycle progressed, political demands for free and fair elections and against human rights violations became dominant, but ethnic demands remained absent. Ethnic demands for rights to autonomy and self-determination for indigenous peoples appeared for the first time in the early 1990s and by 1997 had become nearly as frequent as political demands, while economic demands for land redistribution gradually faded.

Fourth, the target audiences of protest acts were selected strategically. When indigenous protesters chose to block state roads rather than federal highways, their actions were based strategically on the goal of provoking the attention of state governors rather than federal authorities. Information from the MII shows that most demands were targeted at subnational authorities. Despite Mexico's highly centralized political system, governors were the main institutional target of peasant indigenous protest. Fifty-three percent of all indigenous contentious collective actions targeted state governments, 29 percent federal authorities, and 18 percent municipal governments. As I discuss in greater detail in subsequent chapters, the frequent involvement of state-level police forces in repressing indigenous protest was the main reason why state governments were the key target of indigenous collective action. However, in the 1990s, the federal government became an important target of indigenous dissent when President Carlos Salinas passed a constitutional reform to liberalize land tenure in 1992 and when President Ernesto Zedillo and the EZLN discussed constitutional reforms to grant indigenous peoples the right to autonomy and self-determination in 1996–1998.

Finally, it is worth noting that Mexico's cycle of indigenous protest was not the only cycle of social mobilization that took place as Mexico transitioned from authoritarian rule to democracy. Industrial workers and university students were at the vanguard of social mobilization in the 1970s, and elementary school teachers, urban residents, peasants, and university students led mobilization in the 1980s. Peasant indigenous movements only became the vanguard of Mexico's multiple waves of social mobilization in the 1990s, particularly after the Zapatista uprising in 1994.

ACCOUNTING FOR THE ONSET OF THE CYCLE OF INDIGENOUS PROTEST

Information from the MII dataset clearly reveals that the introduction of neoliberal agrarian reforms in 1992 did not trigger Mexico's cycle of indigenous protest. Even if we take 1982 – the year of Mexico's debt crisis – as the starting point of market-oriented reforms, the fact remains that the cycle began many years before the rise of neoliberalism. In fact, the cycle began as Mexican elites adopted a program of economic populism and introduced major political transformations to avoid a major civil war after the 1968 student massacre. In this section, I provide historical evidence showing that a radical change in rural governance to avoid a major civil war in the 1970s provided the motivation and presented the opportunities for the rise of Mexico's cycle of rural indigenous protest.

Cracks in Mexico's Authoritarian Regime: 1968

A few days before the inauguration of the 1968 Olympic Games in Mexico City, Mexican federal authorities brutally crushed a rising wave of student protest. Convinced that Mexican students were being manipulated by international communist forces who wanted to embarrass the Mexican government and the PRI internationally by preventing the Olympics, military and paramilitary forces under the command of federal officials gunned down approximately 300 unarmed students during a demonstration in downtown Mexico City. Although the Olympic Games did take place, the massacre sparked a severe political crisis for the regime. Autocrats reacted with a combination of force and reform. Within the next decade, Mexican presidents introduced major transformations to traditional authoritarian governance practices, which changed the incentives for independent mobilization, particularly in the countryside.

As hundreds of university students moved to the countryside to recruit rural villagers into guerrilla groups to launch a major social insurrection, authoritarian elites preventively embarked on the most ambitious wave of land redistribution since the 1930s. Although government authorities awarded thousands of land titles without immediately distributing the land plots, and even though most titles went to PRI loyalists, members of independent rural organizations also benefited. For the first time since the inception of the land reform program in the 1930s, government authorities were showing a willingness to distribute land to independent non-PRI affiliates and to engage in policy negotiation with them. This major transformation in rural governance provided the initial motivation for independent indigenous protest. Because this change would have a long-lasting effect in Mexico's rural indigenous landscape, let me expand on the logic of land redistribution under the PRI before and after the 1968 student massacre.

Changes in Land Redistribution Criteria *after* 1968

Like many other authoritarian regimes in the twentieth century, Mexican authoritarian elites introduced a major program of land redistribution to mitigate rural violence and establish a strong rural base of electoral support for the ruling party. Although the political bases for land reform had been laid out during the 1917 constitutional convention – when delegates drafted the influential Article 27 on agrarian property and land redistribution to placate Emiliano Zapata's revolutionary army – an extensive land reform program did not begin until the mid-1930s under the administration of President Lázaro Cárdenas. The postrevolutionary program of land redistribution operated under the principles outlined in Article 27 of the Constitution and within the legal framework of the 1938 and 1972 Laws of Agrarian Reform, and lasted until 1992 when it was ended as part of the major constitutional reforms adopted by the Mexican government in preparation for entry into NAFTA. Nearly half of Mexico's arable land was distributed during the twentieth century, but it was not distributed following efficiency or equity criteria.

Land redistribution in Mexico operated under a clientelistic system by which presidents, governors, and PRI agrarian leagues reaped the electoral and material benefits of limited, piecemeal redistribution (Hardy, 1984). Agrarian laws provided the institutional basis for clientelistic redistribution. According to the 1972 Agrarian Law, applications for land restitution and redistribution were initially to be made to a subnational agrarian commission controlled by state governors and local PRI agrarian leagues. If the application was approved, subnational authorities would send the land request to Mexico City, where the president was the only official with the authority to issue a decree to assign the titles. Once the president granted a land title to the petitioner(s), the actual allocation of land plots fell under the jurisdiction of subnational authorities. Governors and local agrarian leagues were the gatekeepers of agrarian redistribution and key players in the struggle for land by independent organizations and movements. In theory, the whole process took somewhat more than a year; in practice, it took, on average, up to a decade.

The president's incentives for land redistribution were not the same as those of state and local authorities, and he readily granted land titles. Governors and local agrarian authorities, however, took much longer to actually distribute the land. The gap between land titled through presidential decrees and land plots actually distributed came to be known in the Mexican agrarian lexicon as the *rezago agrario*, or land distribution backlog.

While all presidents since Cárdenas titled more land than was actually distributed, it was during the administrations of presidents Gustavo Díaz Ordaz (1964–1970) and Luis Echeverría (1970–1976) that federal authorities issued the greatest number of land titles in contemporary Mexican history. Fearing a revolutionary uprising led by repressed university students moving to the countryside after the 1968 massacre, for the first time since the beginning of the land reform program, PRI authorities included non-PRI affiliates as potential beneficiaries.

Although most of the land titles went to PRI members, independent rural households and communities were also awarded titles to significant shares of land. Yet as shown in Figure 2.3a, during these years, presidents granted land plots that had been already allocated to other communities or simply land of very poor quality. Moreover, many independent applicants were receiving titles but not land. Based on information from Chiapas, Figure 2.3b shows that it was in these years that the land redistribution backlog reached its highest levels since the start of the program.

Given the generalized agricultural slowdown and unusually high rates of population growth in the 1960s and 1970s, the distribution of poor land and the unprecedented growth of the land redistribution backlog gave rise to a widespread feel of relative deprivation – rural indigenous communities felt they were not receiving the land the state had already conceded. This sense of injustice became a powerful motivation for independent rural organizations to engage in direct political action.

Whereas PRI affiliates could rely on their clientelistic networks to speed up the land allocation process, independent rural households and communities had access to few means to exert effective political pressure. In the early

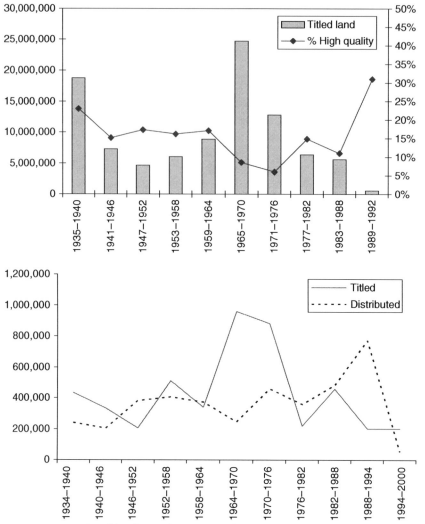

FIGURE 2.3. (a) Total land area (hectares) and proportion of high-quality land titled in Mexico. (b) Area of land (hectares) titled and distributed in Chiapas.

Sources: SRA (1992) and Villafuerte et al. (1999).

1970s, elections in a de facto single-party regime were a sterile mechanism for accountability, and the Dirty War was suppressing demands made by rebel groups. Direct peaceful mobilization for land redistribution seemed to be the only option available to non-PRI affiliates. As evidence reported in Figure 2.2 shows, Mexico's cycle of indigenous protest began as a *peasant* movement for land redistribution.

But independent rural villagers and communities needed legal advice to navigate the complicated bureaucratic process of land petition and allocation, as well as access to social networks and organizational resources to exert direct political pressure on governors and subnational agrarian authorities. Catholic religious authorities and members of the (then outlawed) Mexican Communist Party were among the first external actors to offer technical advice and social support to independent land claimants.

Most historians and rural villagers I interviewed situate the onset of Mexico's cycle of rural indigenous protest in the government-sponsored Chiapas Indigenous Congress of 1974. A close associate of President Echeverría, Governor Manuel Velasco, asked Bishop Samuel Ruiz, head of the Diocese of San Cristóbal de Las Casas, to organize a major town hall meeting with all of the state's independent rural indigenous households to learn about their most pressing needs. Velasco convened this meeting a few months after the Mexican army had discovered a rebel training camp in the heart of the Lacandón jungle and killed the urban leaders of the rebel group. Bishop Ruiz mobilized the extensive networks of rural indigenous communities and cooperatives his pastoral team had contributed to building in the previous decade in response to the rapid spread of U.S. Protestant missionary activity in the state (see Chapter 3).

This historic three-day meeting of rural indigenous villagers in San Cristóbal de Las Casas became the single organizational event that gave rise to Chiapas's three-decade-long cycle of rural indigenous protest and Mexico's cycle of peasant indigenous mobilization. Deacon Eduardo López, a Tojolabal Indian from Las Margaritas, Chiapas, and a participant in this historic meeting, put it succinctly: "It all began there."[4]

Changes in Rural Governance *after* 1977

Despite a new wave of land redistribution and in spite of widespread subsidies to public universities, the inconsistent use of concessions and repression against rural villagers and university students led to a major wave of insurgencies in the urban and (nonindigenous) rural countryside in the 1970s. The federal government's initial reaction was to combine economic populism and a progressive foreign policy with harsh anti-insurgent activity. While the government and the PRI opened Mexico's doors to thousands of refugees fleeing South American dictatorships, Mexican authoritarian elites adopted anti-insurgency strategies that resembled the Dirty Wars of the Southern Cone. Although thousands of students and rural villagers were assassinated, tortured and disappeared, the revolutionary potential was not completely wiped out (Sierra, 2003).

Conscious of the threat of a real possibility of a major social insurrection, Mexican authoritarian elites introduced a series of major political reforms to avoid regime breakdown. In 1977, the incoming administration of President José López Portillo (1976–1982) legalized all political parties, including the Mexican Communist Party (PCM), which had been proscribed from competition since 1940. It also introduced a proportional representation (PR)

---

[4] Interview with Deacon Eduardo López.

mechanism for the election of one-third of national congressional seats and promulgated an amnesty law that applied to participants of the urban and rural guerrilla movements that had spread throughout central and northern states during the 1960s and 1970s.

These major political reforms transformed Mexico from a de facto single-party autocracy to a multiparty electoral autocracy.[5] This transition, in turn, introduced three major changes in authoritarian governance practices that were crucially important for rural indigenous independent mobilization.

First, lifting the ban on extremist opposition parties and the introduction of PR established opposition parties as major institutional players and gave former rebel leaders and members an incentive to express their grievances and demands by electoral means. Although the federal government retained de jure and de facto powers to manipulate electoral outcomes and engineer electoral victories, the PR system allowed extremist parties such as the PCM to become minority forces in legislative chambers. These small pockets of representation gave opposition parties a voice and access to institutional resources. A subsequent reform in 1983 extended the PR system to the selection of municipal authorities. Opposition parties soon shifted their political resources to the periphery and began the long journey of building core constituencies of subnational supporters at the state and municipal levels, from which they would eventually launch their own bids for national power.

Second, the activation of limited forms of multiparty competition and the amnesty for rebels transformed the strategies, tactics, and targets of government repression. Fernando Gutiérrez Barrios, chief of Mexico's powerful secret police during the country's Dirty War and Secretary of the Interior in the 1980s, eloquently expressed the difference in governance strategies under single-party rule and multiparty autocracy. As head of the secret police in the 1960s and 1970s, "Don" Fernando – as he was known in Mexican political circles – consistently encouraged government officials to answer dissident collective action with brutal force. But his advice changed after the political liberalization of 1977. When asked by PRI governors how to deal with dissident social movements in the 1980s, Don Fernando was fond of saying, "Buy them off! It's cheaper [than repressing them]."[6]

Although repression certainly did not disappear from the governance menu of Mexican presidents and governors, throughout the 1980s and 1990s it was transformed in significant ways. One visible change was that the army was replaced by subnational police forces as the first resort called on by ruling elites to repress independent movements.[7] Another important change was that

[5] Although small pro-regime leftist parties and the right-wing National Action Party were allowed to compete for office in Mexico's authoritarian regime, the exclusion of the Communist Party from competition between 1940 and 1977 left rural indigenous municipalities without access to a meaningful opposition force. Prior to 1977 Mexico's rural indigenous regions lived in a de facto situation of single-party autocracy.
[6] "¡Cómpralos! – es más barato." See Aguayo (2001).
[7] This changed after the outbreak of the Zapatista rebellion in 1994, when the army was called out of the barracks again.

repression was no longer lethal and random, as in the 1960s and 1970s, but nonlethal and targeted. Unlawful arrests and physical violence replaced assassination and torture as the modal forms of repression.

A third major transformation in governance was that policies of material redistribution to independent communities and movements – as Don Fernando's maxim suggests – became more common than in the past. Whereas under de facto single-party autocracy, the dominant strategy of governance had been to systematically and lethally repress dissident groups, after 1977, under multiparty autocracy, governors combined partial material concessions to independents with nonlethal repression.

The transformations in authoritarian governance that Mexico experienced after 1977 opened a new era for independent collective action. Although the PRI's electoral hegemony remained uncontested, one of the major implications of the 1977 reform was that the streets were activated as a legitimate arena for policy negotiation for independent movements. If the wave of land redistribution of the late 1960s and early 1970s provided the initial motivation for rural indigenous independent protest, the 1977 reform institutionalized the opportunities for direct political action as an effective mechanism to agitate for material redistribution.

TEMPORAL AND SPATIAL VARIATION WITHIN THE CYCLE OF INDIGENOUS PROTEST

Who took advantage of the new opportunities for independent mobilization that resulted from Mexico's major transformation of rural governance of the 1970s? Using information from the MII dataset, our goal in this section is to test whether the breakdown of local religious and political monopolies and the spread of competition for indigenous souls and votes empowered indigenous communities to seize these opportunities and engage in major waves of mobilization for land and for political and cultural rights.

The Dependent Variable

The *intensity of indigenous protest* is the dependent variable used for statistical testing. I use the annual number of protest events undertaken by indigenous populations from any of Mexico's 883 indigenous municipalities between 1975 and 2000 as indicator of the intensity of indigenous protest. To avoid biases associated with a protest count based simply on the geographic location of events, I distinguish between the site of protest and the place of residence of protesters. A protest event is assigned to a municipality every time indigenous villagers or groups from that municipality participated in a protest event, regardless of where the event took place. Hence, although MII contains data on 3,553 protest events, I use as the measure of the dependent variable the number of municipalities represented per protest event (N = 5,570).

The count P_{it} expresses the intensity of indigenous protest in municipality *i* in year *t*. This panel includes 22,958 observations, of which only 8.5 percent are nonzero counts. As in most data sets on protest counts, the data on indigenous protest presents a problem of overdispersion: the standard deviation of protest is three times higher than the mean. As I explain below, we adopt the appropriate statistical techniques to overcome this problem.

Explanatory Factors

Religious Competition. One of the central theoretical claims made in Chapter 1 was that religion can play a major role in the creation of the social networks and ideological resources for independent social mobilization in authoritarian regimes. In the context of Latin American indigenous regions, the chapter hypothesized that the spread of Protestant competition in historically hegemonic Catholic districts would empower rural indigenous Catholic parishioners to call for institutional support from their clerical authorities to build a social base for mobilization for land redistribution. Our expectation was that villages with higher levels of religious competition between Catholic and mainline Protestant churches would experience greater levels of social protest (see H.1b).

I use the effective number of religions (ENR) as an indicator of *Religious competition*. ENR is defined as $1/\sum r_i^2$ where r_i represents the proportion of a municipal population that adheres to religion *i* as reported by the Mexican population censuses of 1970, 1980, 1990, and 2000. Mexican census information groups religious affiliation into six categories: Catholic, Protestant, Jewish, Other, None, and No Response.[8] The Protestant category includes all non-Catholic Christian creeds. In indigenous municipalities, the Jewish category is generally empty, but the latter three categories are unusually high and in some places represent up to 30 percent of responses. Garma (1998) suggests that these residual categories may be a good proxy for *la costumbre* – a syncretic mix of Catholic and pre-Hispanic indigenous religious practices. I consider *la costumbre* as a religious affiliation distinct from Catholicism and in calculating ENR take the sum of the residual categories as a proxy for *la costumbre*. In the absence of competition, when membership was not an issue, the Catholic Church learned to "tolerate" *costumbristas*; however, as soon as the Protestant expansion rendered membership relevant, Catholic clergy in competitive districts actively sought to win *costumbristas* back into the church.[9]

The average ENR for the entire sample is 1.3. This is clearly a monopoly situation. Even though religious competition experienced an unprecedented growth of nearly 40 percent between 1960 and 1990, ENR remained at around 1.4 for the rest of the cycle. The most relevant point, however, is that Mexico

---

[8] Starting in 2000, the Mexican census distinguished between different non-Catholic Christian churches. Because prior census information does not include this important distinction, I am forced to group all of these churches into a single category.

[9] I interpolate using the census data of 1970, 1980, 1990, and 2000 to estimate the annual level of religious competition using the formula $V_t = V_{t-1}(1 + r)$, where $r = [V_f / V_i]^{1/10} - 1$; f is the value of the final census year (e.g., 1980) and i stands for the value of the initial census year (e.g., 1970).

experienced different subnational patterns of religious competition. If we disaggregate the national numbers, we observe that at one standard deviation from the mean, the ENR value is 1.7 – a semi-competitive situation. If we take a longitudinal view, we can observe significant changes over time: whereas 7.3 percent of Mexico's indigenous municipalities had a semi-competitive religious market in 1980, 20 percent had more than 1.67 effective religions by 2000. Likewise, focusing on a lower level of geographic units reveals considerable variation between regions: whereas at one extreme, the average indigenous municipality in Chiapas was already experiencing a semi-competitive situation in 1980 (ENR = 1.7) and was fully competitive by 2000 (ENR = 2.1), at the other extreme, Puebla remained a Catholic monopoly throughout the entire period (ENR = 1.2). And within each state, plurality varied; for example, the Tzeltal municipalities in eastern Chiapas experienced far more competition than the Zoque municipalities in the western part of the state.

Electoral Competition. One of the key theoretical claims of the electoral competition model discussed in Chapter 1 was that the partial liberalization of authoritarian power structures and the introduction of government-controlled multiparty elections would transform patterns of independent dissent. In their attempt to fight fraud and build a critical electoral mass, we argued, opposition party leaders and activists would have powerful electoral incentives to forge political coalitions with independent communities and social movements and sponsor their protest activity in exchange for electoral support and for their participation in postelection rallies to contest fraud. Once opposition parties became real contenders for power, however, the prediction was that party leaders would discourage radical demands and mobilization to avoid alienating the median voter. In the Latin American context in which leftist parties have been contingent allies of rural indigenous movements, the expectation was that at the initial stages of multiparty competition, leftist parties would encourage rural indigenous mobilization but would discourage mobilization after a threshold of competition (see H.3b).

I use the effective number of parties (ENP) as an indicator of *Electoral competition.* ENP is defined as $1/\sum v_i^2$ where v_i represents the proportion of a municipal population that votes for party *i* as recorded in the Banamex (2001), CIDAC (2009), and de Remes (2000) data sets.[10] Because municipal elections in Mexico are held every three years, I calculate ENP for the years in which elections take place and extrapolate this number between election years. To test for a nonlinear relationship between electoral competition and indigenous protest, I test for ENP and ENP^2.

---

[10] Official records of municipal elections in Mexico were systematically collected but never made publicly available by the Secretariat of the Interior. In the late 1990s, various think tanks and scholars had access to government records from the 1970s to the late 1990s and painstakingly cleaned the data and made them publicly available. See de Remes (2000), Banamex (2001) and the CIDAC Web site.

The PRI and a host of leftist parties that underwent significant transformations over the course of the transition to democracy were the most influential political parties in Mexico's rural indigenous regions. One group of leftist parties included communists, socialists, and Trotskyists, which eventually coalesced with PRI defectors to create the Party of the Democratic Revolution (PRD) – Mexico's preeminent leftist electoral force in the 1990s. Another group of leftist parties included a group of socialist parties formed by PRI defectors in the 1950s, most notably the Workers' Socialist Party (PST), which was influential in the 1970s and 1980s but was eventually absorbed by the PRD in the 1990s.

The average ENP for the entire sample is 1.4. This is, as in the case of religious markets, a quasi-monopoly situation. Yet unlike religious markets, which after three decades of Protestant expansion remained at 1.4 effective religions, the effective number of parties underwent a dramatic rise in the 1990s and reached virtual bipartisanship between the PRI and the Left by 2000. Within the period between the 1988 presidential election and the 1994 Zapatista uprising, the Left experienced its first sizeable expansion in rural indigenous municipalities, and average levels of competition reached 1.5 effective parties. But after the Zapatista uprising, and in the context of the major macroeconomic crisis of 1994–1995, rural indigenous municipalities, like urban municipalities, experienced a rapid transition to bipartisanship.

If we disaggregate the average level of ENP, we can observe sources of considerable additional variation in the early phases of Mexico's multiparty autocracy. At one standard deviation from the mean, the average indigenous municipality shows an ENP of 2. If we take a closer geographic focus, we can observe uneven patterns of electoral competition and leftist presence: Whereas on average rural indigenous municipalities in states such as Guerrero or Michoacán had already reached a bipartisan competition scenario by the late 1980s, states such as Chiapas were under tight PRI control and would only become bipartisan after the Zapatista rebellion of 1995.

Material Concessions and Repression. In Chapter 1, we argued that the introduction of government-controlled multiparty elections in authoritarian regimes is likely to transform traditional governance practices. One of the key goals of governance for incumbents in electoral autocracies is to prevent independent social movements from forging electoral alliances with opposition parties. To this end, we argued, incumbents are likely to provide partial material concessions to independent movements and try to keep demands from growing exponentially via moderate repression. The prediction was that villages in which social movement leaders and activists had greater access to dense social networks would be more likely to resist government attempts at co-optation and would respond to both partial material concessions and repression with greater mobilization (see H.4b).

Testing for this conditional hypothesis in the context of Mexico's rural indigenous regions would require data on material concessions, government repression, and social networks for 883 municipalities from 1975 to 2000. Because I have access to systematic data only on material concessions and government repression, I will postpone the test of the conditional effect of governance on social networks to the qualitative chapters (see Chapter 4). All I can do here is test for the individual effects of material concessions and repression on the intensity of protest.

To test for the effect of partial material concessions, I use the *proportion of land plots* allocated to independent rural indigenous movements by subnational governments in a given year. Information on land redistribution by group affiliation is not available for all states and municipalities in the sample, so I rely on information reported by local Chiapan agrarian authorities on land recipients from the Agrarian Rehabilitation Program for 1984. One of the advantages of using these data is that government authorities reported the amount of land plots distributed by group affiliation, distinguishing between PRI and non-PRI affiliates. Because of the limited nature of the data, however, I can only test for the effect of land redistribution on the intensity of indigenous protest for Chiapas's fifty-eight indigenous municipalities for 1984.

A prominent example of rural governance under electoral autocracy, the Agrarian Rehabilitation Program was devised by Governor Absalón Castellanos and operated in Chiapas between 1984 and 1987. Through this program, the Chiapas government either bought land from private landowners to distribute among poor rural households or granted households access to land that had previously been held under federal protection. The program benefited more than 10,000 rural households. Official statistics report that one-quarter of the land plots were granted to PRI affiliates and the rest went either to rural households with no affiliation or to affiliates of non-PRI organizations. Although General Castellanos has been widely viewed as one of the most repressive governors in Chiapas contemporary history and the governor who singly issued the greatest number of executive decrees to shield large landholdings from becoming targets of agrarian reform, the statistical record shows that alongside his repressive and pro-rich actions, Castellanos was also one of the most active land-reforming governors in the state, allocating land to both PRI and non-PRI petitioners.

However, governance in liberalizing autocracies, we have argued, is not only about the distribution of carrots; it also involves the use of the stick. To test for the effect of repression on the intensity of protest, I use the count of all events involving acts of *Repression* per municipality for the 1975–2000 period. The MII records 2,180 acts of repression against indigenous populations. These are highly concentrated in a few states and municipalities. The mean level of repression is 0.095, with a standard deviation of 0.681. The frequency of repression is greater in municipalities within the southern states of Chiapas and Oaxaca and the central states of Hidalgo and Veracruz. Repression is relatively low to nonexistent in states such as Campeche and Yucatán.

I also test for the *severity of repression*. Acts of repression ranged from low levels of violence (physical harassment) to moderate (physical aggression, invasion of property, eviction), high (unlawful arrest, abduction, population displacement), and severe (rape, torture, assassination). Physical aggression (moderate) and unlawful arrest (high) were the most common acts of repression. A wide range of state and non-state actors were involved as perpetrators of human rights violations. Subnational police forces under the jurisdiction of governors and mayors committed 60 percent of all acts of repression; the army was responsible for 15 percent of cases; and private guards of landowners and PRI-affiliated indigenous villagers and groups were responsible for the remaining 25 percent.

Economic Crises and Policy Shifts. One of the key assumptions in the theoretical framework developed in Chapter 1 is that major economic crises or radical policy shifts in traditional economic policy serve as triggers for initial mobilization; these exogenous shocks provide the initial motivation for collective action. The literature on indigenous mobilization in Latin America suggests that major economic crises associated with the unraveling of import substitution industrialization policies and the neoliberal policy shift motivated indigenous collective action (Van Cott, 2000; Yashar, 2005). I test for the effect of stagflation and currency collapses and create a dummy variable (*Economic crises*) for the years 1976, 1982, 1983, 1985, 1986, 1987, and 1995. I also test for major *Economic policy shifts* and create a dummy variable for the years when Mexico entered the General Agreement on Tariffs and Trade (GATT – 1986) and NAFTA (1994), and when the government ended the country's six-decade-old program of land reform and liberalized land tenure (1992).[11]

Alternative Explanations and Controls

Cultural Survivors. One of the dominant explanations of Latin America's influential wave of indigenous mobilization is that it was those municipalities where indigenous communities were able to resist three centuries of Spanish colonial rule and two centuries of mestizo assimilationist policies that collectively defied the penetration of capitalist markets into traditional indigenous territories. Communities that retained indigenous customary laws, norms, and practices were more effectively equipped with the emotional and ideological resources that motivated communal action against the marketization of agricultural life. I take the proportion of indigenous-language-speaking population, *Indigenous pop. (%)*, as a proxy for cultural survival and communal autonomy.

Corporatism. Another influential argument suggests that state-sponsored rural corporatist unions became the organizational bases for indigenous

[11] Dummy variables for economic crises and policy shifts only vary across time. Results remain unchanged if we use data on GDP growth, inflation, and currency devaluations. I nonetheless report the dummy variables to allow for comparisons between economic crises and policy shifts.

mobilization. Le Bot (1994) and Yashar (2005) argue that when states lost their financial ability to sustain traditional corporatist loyalties, underfunded corporatist rural unions became the main organizational vehicle for dissident indigenous mobilization. Yashar (2005) argues that where state corporatism did not destroy indigenous communal autonomy, and served as a façade enabling the survival of indigenous languages, cultures, and political institutions, local peasant indigenous leaders used formerly corporatist organizational structures to engage in independent protest. In her influential account, these communities provided the cultural and ideological frames for the politicization of ethnicity and unions served as the main vehicles for mobilization.

I use a multiplicative variable that combines turnout and vote share for the PRI in municipal elections as an indicator of *Corporatism*. My assumption is that municipalities in which all eligible rural indigenous voters participated and all cast their vote in favor of the PRI were cases of strong corporatism, whereas those with low turnout and low PRI support were instances of weak corporatism.

Other Controls. I include four additional controls: *Poverty* (measured as the arithmetic average of the municipal proportion of illiterate population and households earning less than one minimum wage), *Indigenous pop. (ln)*, a one-year lag of the dependent variable to control for the path-dependent nature of protest, *Protest*$_{t-1}$, and a dummy variable for the *South* (Chiapas, Guerrero, and Oaxaca).[12]

Statistical Modeling

I test for random effects (RE) and fixed effects (FE) negative binomial (NB) regression models. NB models are the most appropriate estimation technique because Mexico's cycle of indigenous protest – like most cycles of collective action elsewhere – presents a problem of overdispersion, and because protest events are not independent (Scott, 1997; Cameron and Trivedi, 1998). To check robustness and specifically to address the potential for bias owing to the large number of zero counts, I distinguish between those municipalities with zero and positive protest counts, and run a logit model with a dichotomous (0, 1) dependent variable where 1 indicates a municipality with a nonzero count. I subsequently run NB models only with those cases that have positive counts (the number of protest events ranged from 1 to 36).

Statistical Results

Table 2.1 presents regression models of the total frequency of protest by indigenous municipality for the period from January 1975 to December 2000. For

---

[12] I draw information for the poverty index and demographic variables from Mexican censuses, 1970–2000, and interpolate the data using the formula described earlier. See DGE (1972) and INEGI (1985, 1991a and 2001).

TABLE 2.1. *Negative Binomial Models of Intensity of Indigenous Protest by Mexican Indigenous Municipality, 1975–2000*

Indep. Var.	Model 1			Model 2 (Logit)		Model 3 (Counts > 0)	
	RE	IRR	FE	RE	FE	RE	FE
Religious	0.599***	1.821	0.652***	0.951***	2.437***	0.147***	0.587***
competition	(0.090)		(0.105)	(0.137)	(0.290)	(0.047)	(0.136)
Electoral	0.962***	2.618	1.235***	1.577***	1.614***	−0.032	−0.095
competition	(0.183)		(0.192)	(0.269)	(0.281)	(0.126)	(0.148)
Electoral	−0.198***	0.820	−0.247***	−0.311***	−0.318***	−0.006	0.005
competition²	(0.041)		(0.047)	(0.067)	(0.069)	(0.030)	(0.034)
Repression	0.081***	1.085	0.099***	0.777***	0.686***	0.071***	0.077***
	(0.007)		(0.006)	(0.055)	(0.054)	(0.005)	(0.005)
Economic	−0.056	0.945	0.014	0.011	0.102	−0.043	0.031
crises	(0.045)		(0.045)	(0.066)	(0.066)	(0.035)	(0.038)
Economic	0.795***	2.214	0.773***	0.731***	0.699***	0.481***	0.494***
policy shifts	(0.044)		(0.045)	(0.077)	(0.078)	(0.033)	(0.035)
Controls							
Indigenous	−1.258***	0.284	−0.480**	−1.766***	2.484***	−0.158	−0.383
pop. (%)	(0.167)		(0.214)	(0.225)	(0.878)	(0.101)	(0.434)
Indigenous	0.921***	2.512	0.690***	1.135***	0.961***	0.149***	0.289***
pop. (ln)	(0.041)		(0.054)	(0.056)	(0.224)	(0.022)	(0.159)
Corporatism	−0.533***	0.586	−0.492***	−0.561***	−0.432***	−0.115	−0.193*
	(0.122)		(0.127)	(0.173)	(0.187)	(0.099)	(0.116)
Poverty	0.958***	2.608	−0.232	1.658***	0.024	0.456**	−0.138
	(0.314)		(0.354)	(0.439)	(0.652)	(0.201)	(0.483)
Protest$_{t-1}$	0.044***	1.045		0.880***		0.045***	
	(0.005)			(0.071)		(0.004)	
South	0.029	1.030		0.444***		0.185***	
	(0.086)			(0.121)		(0.045)	
Constant	−10.281***		−8.453***	−15.098***		0.825***	−0.587
	(0.411)		(0.499)	(0.595)		(0.303)	(1.274)
T × N	21,576		11,569	21,576	11,543	2,328	2,227
Log Like.	−8,387		−6,672	−4,664	−3,369	−4,206	−3,189
Wald chi²	1,994.82		1,385.92	1,453.28	1,057.94	897.83	459.56

***Significant at the 0.01 level; ** Significant at the 0.05 level; * Significant at the 0.1 level.
Entry cells are unstandardized coefficients; standard errors are in parentheses.
RE = random effects; FE = fixed effects; IRR = incidence rate ratios.

purposes of substantive interpretation, I rely on Model 1. Models 2 and 3 are robustness checks. RE and FE regressions yield similar results. *Indigenous pop. (%)* and *Poverty* are the only variables for which the FE results are different from RE. Note, however, that in most cases, it is the RE coefficients that remain statistically significant. The inconsistencies in the results associated with these two variables can be partly explained by the fact that both change very slowly over time. This renders the use of FE less appropriate. It is for this reason that for purposes of interpretation, I emphasize cross-sectional variation over temporal change and rely on RE models. To facilitate the substantive interpretation of the statistical output, I transform coefficients of RE models into incidence rate ratios (IRR) using the SPost program (Long and Freese, 2001).

Religious Competition. Results across models show that religious competition is a strong predictor of indigenous protest. Model 1 suggests that all else being equal, for every additional effective religion that entered Mexico's indigenous municipalities, indigenous protest would increase by 82 percent (IRR = 1.82). This means that relative to a Catholic monopoly, protest would nearly double in a municipality under a Christian duopoly (with Protestants controlling one-half the market and Catholics the other half). Another way to understand the substantive effect of religious competition on indigenous protest is to compare a situation with a perfect Catholic monopoly (ENR = 1) with the average level of religious competition for the whole sample (ENR = 1.32). A shift from 1 to 1.32 (an increase of one standard deviation) would imply a 26.2 percent increase in the intensity of protest.

As an illustration, consider the Mayan Tzeltal municipality of Chilón in eastern Chiapas and the Zoque municipality of Ocotepec in western Chiapas. Between 1970 and 2000, the two municipalities shared many socioeconomic and electoral features but differed notably in one: the level of religious competition. Chilón was one of the most successful U.S. Protestant missionary fields in twentieth-century Mexico and in 1976 had 1.53 effective religions. The same year, Ocotepec had 1.27 effective religions. Model 1 predicts that protest in Ocotepec in 1976 would have been 21.3 percent more intense had the municipality experienced Chilón's level of religious competition. If we take a longitudinal view and examine both municipalities two decades later, by 1996, Chilón had 2.24 effective religions, but Ocotepec had experienced little change. Model 1 predicts that protest in Ocotepec in 1996 would have been 70 percent greater had the municipality experienced the same level of religious competition as Chilón did. Over the course of three decades, whereas Chilón experienced eighty-five protest events and became an epicenter of protest in Chiapas and a recruitment site for the EZLN, Ocotepec did not take part in any of the multiple cycles of mobilization in Chiapas.[13]

Electoral Competition. Results from Models 1 and 2 show that electoral competition is a strong predictor of the intensity of indigenous protest. The regression coefficient of the quadratic term confirms the hypothesis that the relationship between electoral competition and the intensity of protest is curvilinear. If we take PRI hegemony (ENP = 1) as our starting point, a

---

[13] Is it possible that Protestant missionaries were attracted to Mexican municipalities experiencing higher levels of protest and thus protest explains religious competition? The historical record shows that the main missionary activity that sowed the seed for the expansion of Protestantism took place between 1930 and 1970 when there was practically no indigenous protest. As I explain in Chapter 3, Protestant missionaries were mainly attracted to areas where the Catholic Church was grossly underserving indigenous populations. Hence the causal association should run from religious competition to indigenous protest and not the reverse.

one-unit increase in ENP would increase the intensity of protest by 76 percent (IRR = 1.761).[14] However, the effect of electoral competition on protest grows at decreasing rates until ENP reaches a maximum value at 2.4 parties (where IRR = 1.0) and then declines. Beyond this level, the expansion of electoral competition would contribute to the *demobilization* of protest and to the *institutionalization* of dissident movements.[15] If we fix the level of ENP at 3.0, a one-unit increase of ENP would decrease protest by 21 percent (IRR = 0.797).[16]

As an illustration, consider again the Tzeltal municipality of Chilón in eastern Chiapas. In 1982, the PRI had full hegemonic control both in Chilón and in the state of Chiapas in general. By 1995, however, the ENP for Chilón was 1.8. According to Model 1, the rise of bipartisan competition in Chilón would yield a net increase in protest of nearly 76 percent. The historical record confirms that social protest in Chilón increased together with the rise of the Left. In fact, leftist parties became important promoters of the social networks and movements that sprung up in Chilón throughout the 1980s under the sponsorship of the Jesuit Mission of Bachajón. Yet after the PRD became a real power contender in 1994 and won the municipal presidency in 1996, party leaders discouraged radical mobilizaton. Although the PRD mayor was intimately linked to the Catholic associational networks that had been instrumental in his rise to power, he discouraged mobilization. As a point of comparison, consider the case of Chapultenango, a Zoque municipality that experienced no meaningful electoral competition and remained under PRI control for the entire period. As in most Zoque municipalities, there was almost no protest at all in Chapultenango.[17]

Material Concessions and Repression. For a first assessment of the effect of partial material concessions and moderate repression on protest, let us look

[14] Because this is a nonlinear relationship, we cannot interpret the substantive effect of electoral competition on protest from the individual IRRs associated with ENP and ENP^2. To calculate the substantive effect, I solved for the first derivative of the equation y = −10.281 + 0.962 ENP − 0.198 ENP^2. When ENP = 1, dy/dENP = 0.566, and this value is exponentiated (e ^ 0.566) to obtain IRR = 1.761.

[15] To calculate the maximum, I solved for the first derivative of the equation 0.962 ENP − 0.198 ENP^2 = 0.

[16] I followed the same procedure as in note 12 but assumed a level of ENP = 3.0.

[17] Is it possible that the causal relationship between electoral competition and protest goes from protest to electoral competition rather than the other way around? Is it possible that indigenous peoples and movements took to the streets because they wanted to win elections? Although it is certainly true that protest may have had an effect on subnational democratization, as far as indigenous movement participants' preferences are concerned, democracy was not their initial driver. As information on indigenous claims reported in this chapter shows, Indian peasants in Mexico initially took to the streets to demand land, not democracy. Later in the cycle, as they were repressed, democracy became a major indigenous demand. But their main objective was not gaining office; it was winning respect for their human rights. In contrast, winning office was the main objective of opposition parties and they promoted indigenous independent mobilization for purely electoral reasons. Hence the causal association should run from electoral competition to indigenous protest and not the reverse.

at the results shown in Appendix B, Table A.B.1. Recall that because of data limitations, I restrict the statistical testing to fifty-seven rural indigenous municipalities in Chiapas. Results in Model 1 show that both the redistributive and coercive actions of the Chiapas state government had a statistically significant positive effect on the intensity of indigenous protest. For every additional percentage point of land distributed to non-PRI affiliates in 1984–1985 through the Agrarian Rehabilitation Program, protest more than doubled in 1987. Results also suggest that for every additional act of repression in 1986, protest increased by 8.9 percent in 1987.

For a more comprehensive assessment of the effect of repression on the intensity of protest using the national sample, let us return to Table 2.1. The results of Model 1 confirm that state repression stimulated rather than restrained indigenous protest in Mexico. For every additional act of state repression, protest increased by approximately 8.5 percent in the national sample. In models not shown, I ran additional tests distinguishing between levels of repressive violence. Results show that more violent forms of repression did not deter, but rather stimulated protest: Every additional unlawful arrest yielded a 10.8 percent net increase in protest and every additional assassination generated an 11 percent increase.

For purposes of substantive interpretation, consider the Tzeltal municipality of Palenque in eastern Chiapas and the Tzotzil village of Huixtán in the southern part of the state. Both municipalities share many similarities along the economic, political, and cultural dimensions but have different histories of land reform and government repression: Whereas Palenque experienced both partial concessions and active state repression in the 1980s, Huixtán experienced few concessions and significantly less repression. As part of the Agrarian Rehabilitation Program, 75 percent of the land distributed in Palenque between 1984 and 1985 was awarded to non-PRI affiliates, whereas no land was distributed to independents in Huixtán. Results from Model 1 in Appendix B using the Chiapas sample predict that this difference in land redistribution to independents would yield levels of protest three times greater in Palenque than in Huixtán. Model 2 using the national sample predicts that simply based on the difference in repression events, protest would be nearly 20 percent higher in Palenque than in Huixtán. Information from the MII shows that in 1987, protest in Palenque was greater than in Huixtán – much greater, in fact, than what the model predicts.

External Shocks. Results across models suggest that economic policy shifts, rather than economic crises, were the main external shocks motivating indigenous mobilization. The results show that the liberalization of land tenure and the negotiation of various trade agreements were important stimuli for rural indigenous protest. On average, in years of major neoliberal policy shifts, protest grew by 121.4 percent. But neoliberal reforms also had long-lasting effects. Additional tests using a dummy variable that distinguishes the years before and after the end of land reform and the liberalization of land tenure (1992) show that protest was likely to be more than 30 percent greater in the post-1992 period than before. Both results confirm that, as elsewhere in Latin America (Arce and Bellinger 2007; Roberts, 2008), the adoption of neoliberal policies in Mexico did have short- and long-term effects as a stimulus of peaceful rural indigenous protest. Yet, although neoliberal policies did stimulate a significant rise in rural indigenous protest, neoliberalism did not trigger Mexico's cycle of indigenous mobilization.

Alternative Explanations and Controls. Results across models show that indigenous protest was more intense in municipalities with relatively weaker corporatist controls and less intense where corporatism remained strong. It is unclear from these results whether weak corporatist peasant unions served as mobilizing structures for independent indigenous mobilization, or if the erosion of corporatist controls simply lifted an important barrier to independent mobilization. Given that the National Peasant Confederation (CNC), the PRI's preeminent rural corporatist federation, survived the 1992 liberalization of land tenure, the 1994 Zapatista uprising, and the defeat of the PRI in the 2000 presidential elections, it would be misleading to view the Mexican case in the same way as other cases such as Ecuador and Bolivia, where rural state corporatism did indeed collapse and indigenous movements were allegedly built on the ashes of old corporatist structures. Even though some leaders of Mexico's rural indigenous movements may have come from the ranks of state corporatist structures, there is little historical evidence of the widespread use of the PRI's rural corporatist structures for independent mobilization.

What the statistical results make clear, however, is that more culturally autonomous and homogenous communities did not serve as mobilizing structures for protest. The negative sign associated with the proportion of indigenous-language-speakers would in principle cast some doubt on the argument that "cultural survivors" led the cycle of protest. In fact, a closer inspection of the overall results shows that smaller municipalities with greater proportion of indigenous-language-speakers and more homogenous religious and political structures were *less*, not more, likely to engage in protest. In contrast, larger and more heterogeneous municipalities experiencing greater linguistic, religious, and political diversity were more likely to mobilize. This does not mean that external agents mobilized otherwise passive indigenous communities; rather, as I show in the qualitative sections of this book (Chapters 3 and 4), it means that the penetration of new religious and political actors into the indigenous world led to the renegotiation of traditional local hegemonies. The new local leaders, social networks, organizations, and ideological frames that emerged from this process facilitated indigenous mobilization.

CONCLUSIONS

The statistical results reported in this chapter have important implications for the study of rural indigenous protest in Latin America and for the study of cycles of social protest in authoritarian regimes. These results are an invitation to rethink extant theories of popular protest in non-democratic settings.

We have presented extensive evidence that questions the widespread belief that neoliberal reforms triggered Mexico's cycle of rural indigenous protest; we showed that protest began at a time when authoritarian elites adopted populist redistributive policies and a new rural governance regime to abort a major social insurrection. Although we provide evidence that the introduction of neoliberal agrarian reforms did heighten protest, the fact remains that market-oriented reforms did not give rise to the cycle of indigenous collective action.

We have also presented extensive evidence showing that the most culturally cohesive and homogenous indigenous communities did not participate in Mexico's cycle of indigenous protest; rather, the evidence systematically and consistently suggests that heterogenous communities experiencing the most intense processes of cultural and political differentiation were the central actor of this cycle of protest. Results reveal that these communities did not use corporatist structures as vehicles for mobilization; the evidence unambiguously shows that the organizational infrastructure and resources associated with processes of religious and electoral competition served as the mobilizing vehicles for indigenous protest.

Even though we identify the importance of economic motives of relative deprivation, the basic finding of the statistical analysis is that the most critical factors that distinguish those communities that engaged in major struggles for land redistribution and political and cultural rights from those that did not are sociopolitical rather than economic variables – the competition for indigenous souls and votes.

Results reported in this chapter question some of the basic propositions of the school of political opportunity structures (POS) in social movement theory. Classic POS theory suggests that democratization and electoral competition should increase social protest because repression under democratic regimes tends to be lower than in closed and repressive autocracies (McAdam, McCarthy, and Zald, 1996; Tarrow, 1998; Meyer, 2004). The quintessential POS prediction is that democratization stimulates protest and repression depresses it.

Focusing on electoral competition as an indicator of democratization, the evidence reported in this chapter shows that the relationship between democratization and protest is not positive but curvilinear. While it is possible that post-authoritarian structures may facilitate the rise of new social movements, our focus on the evolution of social movements from autocracy to electoral autocracy to democracy shows that the social movements that engaged in socio-electoral coalitions tend to fade with democratization. This result highlights the importance of electoral competition as a mechanism that explains the rise and demise of cycles of protest in hybrid regimes.

By decoupling repression from elections we are able to show that repression does not depress protest but stimulates it. Note, however, that our theoretical argument in Chapter 1 was a conditional one; we conjectured that the effect of repression on protest is conditional on social networks. In Chapters 3 and 4, I will provide qualitative evidence of this conditional relationship and show that members of decentralized religious networks with multiple local leaders and dense local community associational networks were the dissidents who were most resilient to government repression; they were capable of responding to repression with renewed mobilization.

The statistical results reported in this chapter are a first step in establishing a causal association between the spread of religious and electoral competition and peaceful indigenous protest. Controlling for a host of factors typically associated with protest, we have shown that the competition for souls and votes is a significantly relevant and substantively important predictor of indigenous collective action. Yet these associations are limited in two respects: Statistical controls are weak and the association between structural factors and events provides us with little information about how the breakdown of religious and political monopolies and the spread of competition transformed indigenous communities' internal structures of power, producing incentives for mobilization. In the next two chapters we turn to natural experiments and case studies of individual behavior to investigate beyond the limitations of the statistical analysis. Let us start by explaining how the competition for souls empowered indigenous communities to engage in major struggles for economic redistribution and cultural and political rights.

3

Competing for Souls

Why the Catholic Church Became a Major Promoter of Indigenous Mobilization

One of the most consistent and surprising findings in the social sciences in more recent years is the religious origins of some of the most powerful *secular* social and political movements of our times (Kalyvas, 1996). We now know that religion has been a particularly influential sphere for the incubation of the leadership and development of the social networks and ideological narratives for powerful dissident movements in *autocracies* (Smith, 1996). The nineteenth-century consensus that viewed religion as the opium of the masses has been superseded by a new agreement: Religion can be a source of obedience with the status quo or a progressive force for social and political transformation (Philpott, 2007). Yet, the conditions under which clergy and religious communities go one way or the other remain relatively unknown.

The dominant explanation of the potentially progressive role of religion relies on religious ideas. Take the example of the progressive religious practices that Catholic clergy in Latin America have adopted in recent decades. Although dominant accounts of indigenous mobilization in Latin America have not considered religion to be a crucial explanatory factor, authors have nearly unanimously agreed that under the influence of the progressive teachings of the Second Vatican Council and two major Latin American bishops' conferences, Catholic bishops and priests embraced the cause of the poor and most marginalized members of Latin America's societies and became influential promoters of indigenous mobilization (Cleary and Steigenga, 2004; Van Cott, 2000; Yashar, 2005).

One of the main flaws of explanations based primarily on ideas is that they often fail to explain variation: In the post-Vatican II era, some Catholic clergy in Latin America's poor indigenous regions adopted progressive practices and sided with the poor, but many others living under similar conditions continued to side with the rich (Mainwaring and Wilde, 1989; Smith, 1996; Gill, 1998).

Following the influential work of Gill (1998) and the economics of religion, in Chapter 1 we developed an alternative explanation based on the structure of religious markets. Under conditions of monopoly, we conjectured, Catholic clergy in poor and unequal societies would side with the state or the rich. But under competitive pressures, they would face strong incentives to side with the poor. Focusing on the spread of U.S. Protestant missionary activity, we suggested that the inability of Catholic clergy in competitive districts to decentralize ecclesiastic hierarchies to native indigenous villagers as Protestants did, and the reputation deficit for having had sided with the rich and powerful for centuries led them to step into the secular realm and become major promoters of the organizational infrastructure for the rise of powerful movements for land redistribution and indigenous rights.

Building on the statistical results from Chapter 2, which showed the existence of a strong association between religious competition and indigenous protest, in this chapter I seek to provide qualitative evidence showing that this is a *causal* relationship. To do this, we need to show that controlling for almost every factor possible, the rise of religious competition explains why Catholic religious authorities became major promoters of the mobilizing structures and ideological resources for rural indigenous mobilization (see H.1a).

I rely on the logic of natural experiments and on life histories. Focusing on the lives of four Mexican bishops, I assess changes in their clerical and social behavior as the Vatican transferred these four bishops between nearly identical Catholic dioceses with different structures of religious competition. Based on extensive fieldwork and in-depth interviews, I analyze the actions of these clerics *before* and *after* they were exposed to different levels of religious competition. My intention is to isolate as much as possible the effect of religious competition on the changes in the clerical and social behavior of individual bishops and their pastoral teams and show that they became major promoters of poor people's movements in response to Protestant competition.

I first analyze the story of Bishop Samuel Ruiz, head of the Diocese of San Cristóbal de Las Casas (SCLC), Chiapas, from 1960 to 2000, and one of the most influential defenders of indigenous rights in Latin America. Bishop Ruiz and SCLC represent the Mexican region with the single highest level of religious competition and the most intense experience of indigenous mobilization. I explain the dramatic transformation of Ruiz from a conservative clergyman at the beginning of his tenure into a passionate advocate of rural indigenous causes *after* he learned firsthand about the dramatic inroads U.S. Protestant churches had made into the diocese where he had just been transferred.

Based on extensive interviews with Catholic authorities and parishioners from the Diocese of SCLC, I show that in response to the Protestant competition, Catholic clergy contributed to the creation of decentralized and horizontal regional networks with powerful local leadership structures led by catechists and nurtured by dense community ties. These powerful lay leaders and networks played a crucial role in the rise and development of Chiapas's cycle of rural indigenous protest. I also show the critical role that the pastoral team of the Diocese of SCLC played in creating the ideas and identities that contributed to sustaining the cycle.

The chapter also analyzes the sudden transformation of Cardinal Ernesto Corripio from a socially progressive to a conservative bishop *after* the Vatican transferred him from the Archdiocese of Oaxaca (1970–1976), an ecclesiastic jurisdiction facing growing Protestant competition in the 1970s, to the Archdiocese of Puebla (1976–1977), a traditional Catholic stronghold. This is followed by the experience of Bishop Arturo Lona who abandoned traditional pro-rich pastoral practices and embraced a pro-poor, pro-indigenous approach *after* he was transferred from Huejutla, Hidalgo, an archdiocese marked by low levels of religious competition in the 1960s, to the Isthmus of Tehuantepec, Oaxaca, a diocese that experienced a significant wave of Catholic defection to Protestantism between 1950 and 1980.

The chapter finally analyzes an outlier: Catholic authorities who do not adopt progressive practices despite facing high levels of religious competition. The experience of Manuel Castro, Archbishop of Yucatán from 1980 until 2000, illustrates a case in which Catholic clerical authorities responded to competition by developing Catholic Charismatic Renewal movements focused on charismatic religion, spiritual healing, and personal self-improvement rather than sponsoring social movements for material redistribution or indigenous rights. This case highlights an important point: When challengers emphasize spiritual rewards and charismatic practices (as Pentecostals do), rather than material rewards (as mainline Protestant denominations do), the renegotiation of a religious contract triggered by competition may lead to conservative social outcomes.

FOUR LIFE HISTORIES

Bishop Ruiz

On a cold, misty Sunday afternoon in January 1960, in a ceremony that resembled the crowning of a medieval prince, Samuel Ruiz was ordained bishop of San Cristóbal de Las Casas in the heavily indigenous highlands of Chiapas (Benítez, 1967; Fazio, 1994). As a young, conservative mestizo Catholic clergyman from the central state of Guanajuato who had trained at the prestigious Gregorian University in Rome, Ruiz was candid in his first encounter with the press about his plans for the predominantly Catholic diocese: to civilize the Mayan Indians, fight communism, check the secularizing tendencies of the PRI, and combat Protestantism (Benítez, 1967).

Forty years later, the civilizing intentions of the young conservative bishop had been entirely transformed. On January 25, 2000, in a colorful religious folk ceremony that combined Catholic and pre-Hispanic symbols and rites, Tzeltal, Tzotzil, Chol, and Tojolabal Indians took center stage in Ruiz's farewell mass as he entered retirement. In his last sermon, the bishop spoke eloquently on the ethical superiority of Mayan cultures and ways of life and of the historical responsibility of the Catholic Church to contribute to the empowerment and liberation of indigenous peoples.[1]

Over the course of four decades, Ruiz had undergone a dramatic transformation from a socially conservative, paternalistic anticommunist cleric to the most influential promoter of indigenous theologies in Latin America (Fazio, 1994; Meyer, 2000; Ríos, 2005). At the same time, most pastoral members of the diocese of SCLC became major institutional promoters of rural indigenous movements and of the rights to autonomy and self-determination for indigenous peoples. With Bishop Ruiz's full endorsement and sponsorship, these networks came to serve as the organizational infrastructure for the most powerful subnational cycle of rural indigenous protest in Mexico. Although without Ruiz's consent, some of these organizational networks became the social base of the EZLN.

Cardinal Corripio

After serving as bishop in his northern home state of Tamaulipas for almost a decade, in 1967, Ernesto Corripio was named Archbishop of Antequera in the heavily indigenous southern state of Oaxaca. A traditional, conservative cleric educated at the Gregorian University, Corripio experienced a personal transformation in Oaxaca, embraced the cause of the Indian poor, developed an incipient indigenous theology, and became one of the founders of the Diocesan Indigenous Pastoral Center of Oaxaca (CEDIPIO), the state's influential pastoral center for training catechists in progressive religious, social, and cultural practices (Hernández Díaz, 2001; Norget, 2004).

But when Pope Paul VI transferred him to the central state of Puebla in 1976 and then promoted him to Archbishop of Mexico City, Cardinal, and Primate of Mexico, Corripio soon returned to his traditional conservative identity. During his brief stay in Puebla, a state with a significant rural indigenous population, he did not develop any indigenous theology, and in Mexico City he did not promote progressive practices. It stands as a great irony that in Puebla – the host state of the 1979 Latin American Bishops' Conference, in which Latin American Catholic authorities famously affirmed their "preferential option for the poor" – neither Corripio nor any of his successors ever opted for the Indian poor and never encouraged social movements for land redistribution or indigenous rights.

Bishop Lona

A native of the conservative Catholic stronghold of Aguascalientes in northern Mexico where he received his priestly training before joining the Jesuit

---

[1] Author's personal recollection from Samuel Ruiz's sermon, San Cristóbal de Las Casas, Chiapas, January 25, 2000.

seminary in Montezuma, New Mexico, Lona was appointed in 1958 to serve as priest and dean of the Divinity School of Huejutla in the Nahua highlands of the central state of Hidalgo. Together with the diocesan team, Lona adopted traditional theological and pastoral practices, sided with rich landowners, and even bought a ranch in the region for himself.[2]

Yet after Pope Paul VI appointed him bishop of the predominantly indigenous Diocese of Tehuantepec in southeastern Oaxaca, Lona underwent a dramatic transformation and became a major institutional promoter of rural indigenous causes. Over the course of the next three decades, the communal leaders and social networks Lona's pastoral team helped build became the organizational base for the rise and development of a powerful cycle of rural indigenous mobilization in the region.

Archbishop Castro

A traditionalist cleric from the western state of Michoacán, Manuel Castro trained under the influence of conservative clergy from his home state and neighboring Guanajuato, and then attended the Pontifical Pio Latin American College and the Gregorian University in Rome. Pope Paul VI appointed Castro archbishop of the heavily Mayan southeastern state of Yucatán in 1969. A practitioner of Catholic conservative orthodoxy among middle- and upper-class Yucatecos, in the late 1970s, Bishop Castro became an enthusiastic supporter of charismatic and spiritual religious practices among poor urban and rural Mayans. Even though he promoted the translation of the Bible to Yucatec Mayan, Castro never embraced liberation or indigenous theologies but worked to suppress them. Economically and socially conservative, Castro encouraged the adoption of heterogeneous practices for the Mayan poor, including charismatic preaching, spiritual healing, and psychological self-improvement, rather than organizing economic cooperatives or indigenous movements (Garma, 1994; Várguez, 2008).

In the remainder of the chapter, I will show that exposure to different levels of religious competition explains the radical transformation these bishops experienced from conservative to progressive practices. These life histories represent limited forms of natural experiments. The cases of Bishop Ruiz and Archbishop Castro are instances in which individuals suddenly adopt radically different religious and social practices in their ecclesiastic jurisdictions *after* learning firsthand about the widespread existence or rapid expansion of non-Catholic Christian faiths. No other factor changed in these clerics' individual histories or in their social context apart from the spread of competition.

[2] Immediately after Lona bought the *Rancho Oxtomal*, Nahua peasants claiming ancestral rights to the land ambushed the bishop and threatened to kill him if he did not give up his title to the property. Before leaving Huejutla, Lona transferred his property to the community and claims to have sowed the seeds for the rural struggles for land redistribution that marked this region in the 1970s and 1980s. Interview with Bishop Emeritus Arturo Lona.

The cases of Bishop Lona and Archbishop Corripio are examples of clerics who are transferred between fairly similar jurisdictions and adopt radically different religious and social practices *following* their exposure to different levels of religious competition. In all cases, we can assume that clerics were randomly assigned – their personal ideology played no significant role in their appointment.

BISHOP RUIZ AND CHIAPAS: PROTESTANT COMPETITION AND INDIGENOUS MOBILIZATION

Luther Goes to Indian Mexico

Since the mid-twentieth century, the indigenous regions of Chiapas have been among the most dynamic religious marketplaces in Mexico. Although at the turn of the twenty-first century, neo-Pentecostals, Jehovah's Witnesses, and Latter-Day Saints (Mormons) are among the fastest growing denominations in the state, for most of the twentieth century, mainline U.S. Protestant churches were the leading challengers to the Catholic monopoly.[3] Presbyterianism once was the second-largest Christian denomination in the Diocese of SCLC, and some of the most fundamental transformations that took place in the diocese were a direct response to five decades of successful Presbyterian proselytizing.[4]

U.S. mainline Protestant churches began their international missionary activity in Mexico in the first quarter of the twentieth century. Discouraged from working in Asia by political instability (Gill, 1998), they targeted Latin America. As historians of Mexican Protestantism remind us, the U.S. Northern Presbyterian Church was charged with proselytizing in southern Mexico (Esponda, 1986). U.S. Presbyterian missionaries first unsuccessfully targeted Catholics in Mexico's urban centers, but soon shifted their strategy to evangelize the most marginalized and underserved Catholic group, namely rural indigenous populations. Without much missionary experience, Presbyterians turned to other churches and NGOs with expertise in missions to indigenous peoples, particularly the Reformed Church in America (with Native Americans in the United States) and the Summer Institute of Linguistics, or SIL (with Mayan Indians in Guatemala).

The SIL was particularly influential in shaping the evangelizing strategies of U.S. Protestant missionaries in Latin America. The largest NGO specializing in the study of minority languages in the world today, the SIL was founded in 1934 by William Townsend. The SIL was created as a network of U.S. Protestant missionaries and professional linguists who traveled all over the world to study minority languages, translate Bibles, and establish Protestant missionary fields

---

[3] See Rivera Farfán et al. (2005).
[4] The perception of Catholic clergy and catechists confirmed this point. Interviews with Father Felipe J. Ali Modad, SJ; Father Ramón Castillo; and former catechist Límbano Vázquez.

(Rus and Wasserstrom, 1984; Hartch, 2006). The SIL first flourished in Mexico under the sponsorship and political protection of the Mexican presidents of the day, who actively invited Protestant and SIL missionaries to counter the power of the Catholic Church, particularly after the *Cristero* War between Catholic militias and the Mexican postrevolutionary government in the 1920s.

John Kempers, a Reformed missionary from Iowa, led the first U.S. Protestant missionary groups into Chiapas in the 1930s. Protestant missionaries entered Mexico in the midst of the *Cristero* War and the coercive attempt of the Mexican postrevolutionary elites to enforce the anticlerical 1917 constitution. The timing of Kempers's missionary expansion into the Mexican religious marketplace left long-term legacies. Because the constitution banned foreign-born clergy from clerical activity (Camp, 1997), U.S. Protestant missionaries were institutionally limited to training native clergy and setting up predominantly local churches. Because the constitution suppressed all civil and political rights of clerics (Camp, 1997), U.S. missionaries and their native trainees were compelled to adopt an unusually low political profile. Moreover, the strategic partnership established by William Townsend and the SIL with every president from Lázaro Cárdenas (1934–1940) to Carlos Salinas (1988–1994) discouraged Protestant missionaries from becoming promoters of an independent critical civil society as their counterparts did elsewhere (Hartch, 2006).

The pastoral conversion strategy that Kempers and other mainline Protestant missionaries followed in Chiapas and Mexico's indigenous regions was built on a scheme of decentralized evangelization based on studying the Bible (Esponda, 1986). Missionaries first learned and translated Bibles to indigenous languages, then established Bible study and literacy groups, trained a local indigenous clergy, built houses of worship and local health clinics, and established workshops for training agricultural labor. After a decade of missionary work, they would move on to another community. Their work was aimed at creating Protestant *native* focal points – groups of indigenous ministers and pastors who then became local missionaries and evangelized others of their own ethnolinguistic group.

This strategy of decentralized evangelizing introduced three major transformations into Chiapas's quasi-medieval religious landscape. First, unlike white or mestizo Catholic priests, who lived and worshiped in the municipality's cathedral that stood in the downtown area of the municipal seat alongside the centers of economic and political power, U.S. missionaries were compelled to live in the impoverished rural peripheries in remote indigenous villages in the highlands or the jungle, where they resided for years or decades. In the context of mid-twentieth-century Chiapas, in which villages were located one-half to a full day's walking distance from the municipal seat, few religious or secular authorities had ever ventured into the remote Tzeltal, Tzotzil, or Tojolabal villages where most Indians lived. Traveling and establishing residence in these deserted territories awarded U.S. Protestant missionaries, such as SIL linguist Marianna Slocum and her missionary partner, nurse Florence Gerdel, a

mythical status among generations of Protestant indigenous communities from
Tzeltal and Tojolabal villages in the Lacandón jungle.[5]

Second, in contrast to the majestic Catholic cathedrals, which operated as
houses of worship for the rich, the small, humble Protestant churches mushroomed among the poor indigenous huts in the periphery of indigenous municipalities in the 1950s and 1960s. In the context of plantation economies such
as those prevailing in mid-twentieth-century Chiapas, in which social relations
between the poor Indian peons and white or mestizo landowners were zero-
sum, both the geographic location and the physical size of Protestant churches
emphatically created an image of Protestantism as the church of the poor and
underprivileged in contrast with Catholicism, seen as the church of the rich
and powerful.[6]

Third, whereas white or mestizo elitist priests from outside Chiapas were
in charge of Catholic cathedrals and churches in predominantly indigenous
regions, Protestant churches were headed by native Mayan pastors. The creation of a native Protestant clergy and the translation and use of indigenous
languages for evangelization introduced into the minds of indigenous communities in the Chiapas highlands and the Lacandón jungle the appealing idea of
Tzeltal, Tzotzil, or Tojolabal churches. While the Catholic white or mestizo
priest preached in Latin with his back to the people, newly trained Protestant
indigenous pastors faced and engaged the members of their congregations in
their own indigenous languages.

Young Indian males living in poor, overpopulated areas, facing shortages
of land and largely unattended by Catholic authorities were the first to join
Protestantism (Garma, 1994). On material grounds, conversion to Protestantism
entailed attractive economic rewards: access to informal education (literacy)
and basic health care, and economic savings that came along with the social
norms and lifestyle changes Protestant converts were expected to adopt (e.g.,
giving up alcohol and refraining from contributing to the annual festival honoring the local Catholic patron saint). On cultural grounds, the use of native
languages and translation of the Bible contributed to creating a new linguistic
pride among natives whose languages had been stigmatized as backward "dia-
lects" doomed to disappear. On social grounds, by encouraging the creation of
a native clergy and establishing indigenous churches, Protestantism introduced
a powerful source of status differentiation, simply because Indians had been de
facto excluded from the Catholic priesthood.

The Protestant provision of economic, cultural, and ecclesiastic rewards
to communities that had been historically marginalized both by the Mexican
state and the Catholic Church had dramatic consequences. Between 1940 and
1990, growth rates of Protestant membership increased by double and triple
digits in many indigenous municipalities. Protestant conversion rates reached

[5] Interviews with members of Presbyterian churches from various Chiapan regions: Carlos (Las
Margaritas), Elías (Chenalhó), and Sr. Gutiérrez (Ocosingo). See also De Vos (2002).
[6] Interview with Father Ramón Castillo.

their highest levels in Tzeltal, Chol, and Tojolabal municipalities in eastern and northern Chiapas, where U.S. Protestant missionaries had developed the most successful missionary sites; conversions were also sizeable in the Tzotzil region in the highlands and in Mam municipalities in the southeastern part of the state. In contrast, the Zoque region in the western part of the state experienced few conversions.

The Catholic Church Reacts

As Benítez's interview with the recently appointed bishop makes clear (1967), Samuel Ruiz had initially deemed communism and the "uncivilized" ways of indigenous lifestyles as the main challenges to his church. But after visiting every township in the state, he realized membership retention was by far his greatest challenge. Not only was Protestantism spreading rapidly in indigenous regions, but *la costumbre* – pre-Hispanic religious practices – was more entrenched than he had initially realized. Ruiz's personal radical transformation and the reconstitution of his diocese's theological, pastoral, and social practices began here.[7]

Once he had internalized the extent of the Protestant challenge, Bishop Ruiz reacted like a talented entrepreneur. Like his Presbyterian challengers, Ruiz favored specialization, and in 1964 he persuaded Vatican authorities to let him redraw the state's ecclesiastic geography so that the indigenous population of Chiapas would be served under a single diocese (SCLC).[8] By institutional design, Ruiz forced himself and his team to serve the Indians, who represented two-thirds of his new diocese and the single most important population segment under Protestant "threat." Furthermore, within his own diocese, in 1967 Ruiz introduced a new ecclesiastic geography by which six new pastoral regions were created, some along ethnic lines. This geographic reorganization laid the administrative base for the creation of the Tzeltal, Tzotzil, Chol, and Tojolabal "churches."

Like his Presbyterian challengers, who had subcontracted SIL and Reformed missionaries for proselytizing, Ruiz subcontracted three religious orders to help him defend the Catholic hegemony and strategically placed them in areas of rapid Protestant growth: the Society of Jesus (which had been initially invited by Ruiz's predecessor in 1957) in the Tzeltal/Chol region,[9] the Dominican

---

[7] Interview with Father Ramón Castillo. See also Ríos (2005).

[8] The state of Chiapas is divided into three Catholic dioceses: SCLC, Tapachula, and Tuxtla Gutiérrez. SCLC is a predominantly indigenous diocese, and the latter two are predominantly mestizo.

[9] Members of the Jesuit Mission of Bachajón openly admit that they were called to Chiapas's Tzeltal region by Jesuit Bishop Lucio Torre Blanca in the 1950s to arrest the rapid growth of Protestantism in the areas where Marianna Slocum had successfully proselytized for more than a decade. Although initial Jesuit plans were to launch a major missionary site in Oaxaca, Torre Blanca persuaded the Mexican Province that the Tzeltal region was the single Mexican indigenous area under greatest Protestant threat. Interview with Father Carlos Camarena, SJ. See also De Vos (2002) and Misión Jesuita de Bachajón (2010).

Order in Tzotzil and Tzeltal municipalities (where the order had had a strong presence since Colonial times and up to the late nineteenth century), and the Little Brothers of Mary (or Marists) in Tojolabal, Tzeltal, and Mam regions. Ruiz's diocesan team was multinational, including Mexican diocesan priests and missionaries from Argentina, Belgium, France, Spain, and the United States (Meyer, 2000).

Like the U.S. Protestant missionaries, who had founded Bible institutes to train native pastors, in 1962 Bishop Ruiz opened three schools for indigenous catechists; one in the city of SCLC under the leadership of Marist Brothers, another in Bachajón under the Jesuit Mission, and a third in Comitán under direct diocesan control. These schools were created at the request of indigenous community leaders and principals in unchurched areas where SIL and Presbyterian missionaries were successfully proselytizing.[10]

Indigenous individuals chosen by the diocesan team would spend between three and six months learning basic theological and pastoral principles and participating in a variety of workshops including literacy, nursing and basic health care, farming, carpentry and shoemaking. Approximately 700 catechists were trained in these schools during the 1960s (Iribarren, 1985). Catechists were expected to return to their communities to start and lead Bible study groups and share their newly acquired skills with their peers, starting community self-help cooperatives. As native missionaries preaching in their own language, catechists were expected to curb the success of the Protestant strategy of proselytizing in indigenous languages. To this end, and following the dictums of Vatican II, Ruiz dropped Latin as the liturgical language of his diocese and encouraged his team members to learn and use the indigenous languages of their pastoral areas.

Although these ecclesiastic and pastoral transformations entailed important changes from traditional Catholic practices in the region, it seemed to parishioners that Catholic authorities fell short of even matching what Protestant missionaries offered to converts. In terms of material rewards, Ruiz and his diocese did not offer communities more than their Protestant competitors were already providing: basic education and health care services. In the area of ecclesiastic rewards, however, Ruiz and his pastoral team's policies did not even rival the Protestant offer. Whereas by the 1960s, U.S. missionaries had established Tzeltal, Chol, and Tzotzil presbyteries under native control, there were no equivalent autochthonous Catholic churches. And whereas Tzeltal, Chol, and Tzotzil Indians had been trained and ordained as Protestant ministers and were part of a rising clerical indigenous local elite, Catholic Indians could only aspire to be catechists – that is, lay assistants to the mestizo and white clergy. Finally, in terms of cultural rewards, whereas U.S. SIL and Protestant missionaries had nearly finished translating the New Testament to the Tzeltal, Tzotzil, Chol, and Tojolabal languages, Ruiz and his team members were only in the process of becoming acquainted with indigenous languages.

---

[10] Interviews with Fathers Carlos Camarena SJ and Ramón Castillo.

Catholic Parishioners Demand a New Religious Contract

A decade after Samuel Ruiz had been ordained bishop of SCLC, catechists and indigenous Catholic loyalists in religiously competitive areas were not entirely satisfied with the bishop's initial wave of ambitious theological and pastoral transformations. Throughout the 1970s, catechists voiced their concerns to the bishop and demanded more radical and credible transformations, threatening to leave the Catholic Church otherwise.

Belgian historian Jan De Vos, a former Jesuit missionary who served in the Bachajón Mission in the Tzeltal region in the 1970s, and Pablo Iribarren, a Spanish Dominican friar who served in the Ocosingo-Altamirano Tzeltal Mission in the 1970s and 1980s, provide detailed accounts of the intense negotiations that took place between the catechists and Bishop Ruiz as parishioners tried to renegotiate a new "religious contract." The content of these negotiations was profoundly influenced by the proselytizing strategy and worldly rewards that Presbyterian and other mainline Protestant missionaries offered to converts to their creed.

Material redistribution and the diocese's long-term commitment to the Indian cause were at the top of the agenda. By the late 1960s, indigenous catechists had become convinced that their material situation could not be dramatically improved in the absence of more radical action beyond the promotion of economic self-help cooperatives. Thus they confronted Bishop Ruiz and the diocesan team in 1968: "The Church and the gospel have told us how to save our souls, but we don't know how to save our flesh; while we work for the salvation of our souls [...] we are victims of hunger, illness, poverty and death" (Iribarren, 1985; De Vos, 2002).

Ecclesiastic decentralization was another major concern. Catechists sensed that Protestant converts were getting a better deal than they were. Presbyterian converts were not religious instructors (catechists), but ministers (pastors); they were no longer part of the laity but heads of churches. A Presbytery had been founded as a Tzeltal institution and it was run by Tzeltal Indians, not mestizo or white clergy. In a heated debate, a group of catechists from the Chilón region led by Domingo Gómez – where SIL missionary Marianna Slocum had developed one of the most successful Protestant missionary sites in southern Mexico – confronted Bishop Ruiz in 1972 and demanded both full ecclesiastic decentralization and transformation of the Catholic gospel to the Tzeltal culture: "If the Church does not turn Tzeltal here, we don't understand how it can be Catholic at all" (Iribarren, 1985; De Vos, 2002)

These radical critiques by catechists empowered by competition moved Ruiz and his diocesan team to adopt a new religious contract with the Indians. In the view of Ruiz and the leading members of his diocesan team, the single most important idea that would guide the making of this new religious contract was that the Catholic Church in SCLC would no longer be part of the system of economic and cultural exploitation that had subjugated Indians for centuries and would instead become an autochthonous institution that would work for the economic and cultural emancipation of poor and rural indigenous parishioners.[11]

In this new interpretation, the Catholic Church would no longer be associated with majestic cathedrals but with small community shrines (Misión Jesuita de Bachajón, 2010) built in the rural indigenous periphery where Protestant churches were rapidly spreading. Moreover, white or mestizo priests would not be the heads of these new shrines; instead, a new generation of indigenous catechists would take on a leadership role in their communities and spearhead the creation of community-based autochthonous churches.

To properly train the new generation of indigenous catechists, Ruiz and his diocesan team expanded enrollment in the catechist training houses and introduced major curriculum innovations. Following Paulo Freire's (1970) influential *Pedagogy of the Oppressed*, the Jesuit, Marist, and diocesan missionary teams developed three-month workshops that continued to offer courses on Bible study, literacy, carpentry, farming, shoemaking, and baking, but this time all these courses would be part of a larger group reflection based on the historical and cultural context of indigenous participants. In the words of Father Ramón Castillo, director of *La Castalia*, the diocesan school for catechists located in the southeastern city of Comitán, the ultimate goal of these workshops was to contribute to the "cognitive liberation" of thousands of indigenous men and women who had been selected by their communities to become catechists.

By developing a Biblical and social scientific perspective on the *finca* (plantation) system that had dominated economic life in Chiapas up to the 1960s and early 1970s, these workshops sought to provide a cognitive framework that would facilitate catechists' understanding of the economic and cultural structural exploitation that had prevailed in the state's indigenous regions for most of the twentieth century. By providing them with the linguistic skills (Spanish) and education previously reserved for whites and mestizo landowners and their descendents, these workshops sought to teach Indian peasants that they were perfectly capable of doing what their bosses did and that they could use these skills to reverse their structural situation of economic and cultural exploitation.[12]

During the first half of the 1970s, catechists trained in these new schools returned to their communities and engaged in missionary work in their home regions. Under the supervision of missionary agents, who no longer lodged in the houses of landowners but in the community chapels, catechists became facilitators of inter-community religious dialogues based on their family histories in the *fincas* and their personal struggles for land redistribution, and their

---

[11] For information on the diocesan view, I rely on interviews with Fathers Joel Padrón and Ramón Castillo. For the view of Dominican friars, see Iribarren (1985), and for the Jesuits' view, see Misión Jesuita de Bachajón (2010).

[12] Interview with Father Ramón Castillo.

communities' needs for basic public goods and services, including roads, public transportation, health clinics, and schools. In a context where large *fincas* and ranches were still the dominant economic units in the Chol, Tzeltal, and Tojolabal region and in Chiapas's central valleys and the northern Tzotzil municipalities, and where young catechists and their families were engaged in requesting land redistribution, land tenure became a central theme of inter-community religious dialogues.[13]

Under the guidance of Dominican friars, catechists and communities in the Lacandón jungle of eastern Chiapas developed a powerful narrative of their historical struggles for land redistribution based on the Book of Exodus. Drawing analogies from the Old Testament, Dominican friars and communities portrayed the migrant Tzeltal, Tzotzil, and Tojolabal communities that had escaped from the *fincas* and settled in the Lacandón jungle in search for land as the Mayan equivalent of the Jewish people escaping Egyptian rule in search of the Promised Land.[14] Missionaries and communities went a step further and merged indigenous religious cosmologies built around land and motherhood with Christian theology. These narratives became the intellectual basis for the development of a *Theology of Land* – a compelling religious justification for indigenous land struggles that would no longer view land redistribution as a gift from the postrevolutionary state to landless peasants, but a gift from God to the Mayan people.

Demands for land redistribution and indigenous empowerment took on a political dimension during the 1974 Indigenous Congress – a gathering of Chiapan indigenous communities convened by the state government and orga-nized by Bishop Ruiz's diocesan team to celebrate the 500th anniversary of the birth of Dominican Friar Bartolomé de Las Casas, a passionate defender of the Indians in the early years of Spanish Colonial rule, and to enable indigenous communities to express their grievances to government authorities. Dominated by catechists from the Tzeltal, Tzotzil, Chol, and Tojolabal regions, the lead-ing demands of the Congress involved land redistribution, government subsi-dies for agricultural production and marketing, and educational and health services.

Beyond specific policy demands, the most powerful message of the three-day congress was the unanimous claim that the fulfillment of indigenous demands could only be possible if villagers took this process into their own hands. In the closing plenary session of the congress, a catechist asked his peers: "Who will be the new Bartolomé [de Las Casas] now? Will there be one? No, brothers, it is *we* now who must become the new [de Las Casas]; it is our communities coming together that will make us strong" (Morales, 1995). As a participant in the Congress later expressed it to me, "It all began there."[15]

---

[13] Interview with Deacon Eduardo López and former catechist Límbano Vázquez.

[14] See De Vos (2002), Iribarren (1985), and Leyva (1995).

[15] Interview with Deacon Eduardo López.

Building the Organizational Infrastructure for Peasant Indigenous Mobilization

In the face of persistent threats that community leaders might defect to the Protestant Missions, following the 1974 Indigenous Congress, Ruiz introduced a series of radical transformations to increase ecclesiastic and material rewards to Catholic loyalists in competitive regions.

On the ecclesiastic front, Ruiz initiated an ambitious program to promote hundreds of catechists to permanent deacons, that is, low-ranking clerical members with some sacramental rights, including the right to celebrate baptisms and marriages. Together with the religious orders, Ruiz also began a radical process of "inculturation" of the gospel, which went beyond the translation of Bibles to indigenous languages and included reinterpretation of the Holy Scriptures through the lens of indigenous peoples' own cultures and histories, and the nominal creation of what Ruiz termed the Tzeltal, Tzotzil, Chol, and Tojolabal "churches." For all practical purposes, however, even though deacons had been upgraded to members of the clergy, they remained in a subordinate position vis-à-vis the mestizo and white priests. And despite the nominal existence of local indigenous churches, decision-making power remained in the hands of the bishop.

If Bishop Ruiz and his pastoral team were unable (or unwilling) to decentralize ecclesiastic power as U.S. Protestant missionaries had done, they were left with the possibility of responding with major innovations on the material and cultural fronts. In the realm of economic rewards, Ruiz responded to the unified demand expressed at the Indigenous Congress to encourage the politicization of communal associational networks, and from 1975 on, his diocese became a major promoter and sponsor of economic cooperatives and rural indigenous movements for land redistribution.

The Diocese of SCLC promoted community cooperatives in all economic and social activities in which indigenous communities were either dependent on landowners or on government brokers (*coyotes*). To end peasant dependence on the *fincas*' infamous company stores (*tiendas de raya*), where rural workers were forced to buy staple goods at monopoly prices, catechists led the formation of communal shops. To prevent peasants from owing debts to landowners – the financial basis of peasant servitude up to the 1970s – pastoral agents encouraged the creation of communal saving banks. To give indigenous communities increased access to larger markets in the municipal seat, catechists also led the creation of cooperatives for communal transportation to link their hamlets to villages and towns, particularly the municipal seat. And to bypass *coyotes* and other government middlemen who brokered the trade of agricultural goods between communities and consumers in major urban centers, pastoral agents and catechists created inter-community cooperatives to market their own agricultural commodities.

In the aftermath of the Indigenous Congress, Bishop Ruiz and his diocesan team invited political activists to assist catechists, Bible study groups, and cooperatives in constructing rural organizations and movements to petition and press for land redistribution. In other cases, catechists and communities joined already constituted rural organizations sponsored by leftist parties. The fight for land redistribution over the next two decades combined legal petitions with peaceful forms of mass protest and land invasions.

Catechists and deacons played a leading role in the creation and development of three of the most powerful trans-community organizations in eastern Chiapas. These organizations López sprung up in precisely the municipalities experiencing the highest levels of religious competition in the 1970s: Quiptic-ta-Lecubtesel in Ocosingo (ENR= 1.8), Altamirano (ENR = 2.1) and Las Margaritas (ENR= 2.0); Lucha Campesina in Altamirano and Las Margaritas; and Union de Ejidos Tierra y Libertad in Las Margaritas.[16] These three organizations would merge in the 1980s and become the Rural Collective Interest Association (ARIC-UU), the most powerful network of rural indigenous organizations in eastern Chiapas. When members of these organizations splintered into a reformist wing, which negotiated with government officials for agricultural subsidies, and a more radical wing favoring land redistribution, Ruiz's diocesan team sided with the radical faction. As we discuss in Chapter 6, many of these communities would eventually become the social base for the EZLN.

Where leftist secular organizations were already leading the struggle for land, catechists and Bible study groups established strategic alliances with them. This was the case of CIOAC, the communist-sponsored peasant organization, which was particularly influential in the valleys of Las Margaritas (ENR = 2.0) and in the northern Tzotzil region of Simojovel (ENR = 1.6), El Bosque (ENR = 1.9), and Huituipán (ENR = 1.7). CIOAC became one of the most powerful peasant indigenous organizational networks in Chiapas in the 1980s and 1990s. After a brief period focusing on rural workers' rights in *fincas* and ranches, CIOAC embraced the struggle for land redistribution through mass mobilization and land invasions and contributed to developing cooperatives for communal transportation to connect remote indigenous villages to their municipal seats. Most Catholic Indian peasants and catechists from the valleys in Las Margaritas and several communities from the jungle became CIOAC members[17] and practically all catechists and members of Catholic social networks in Simojovel joined CIOAC.[18]

The repressive reaction against Catholic-sponsored movements and their allies by landowners, Indian villagers affiliated with PRI agrarian leagues, and the state police opened a unique window of opportunity for Ruiz and his diocesan team to show their long-term commitment to the struggles of their faithful

[16] Interview with Deacon Eduardo López, member of Lucha Campesina and cofounder of Tierra y Libertad. For concise histories of these organizations, see Iribarren (1985), Legorreta (1997), Leyva (1995), and Mattiace (2003).

[17] Interviews with Deacon Eduardo López, former catechist and former CIOAC member Límbano Vázquez, and Father Ramón Castillo.

[18] Interviews with catechist and former CIOAC member Andrés Díaz and Father Joel Padrón.

parishioners in competitive districts. Siding with rural indigenous villagers against government authorities and landowners in matters of human rights violations would go a long way to dispelling the church's historical reputation deficit as an ally of the rich and the powerful.

Throughout the 1980s and 1990s, the Diocese of SCLC developed an influential network of internationally recognized human rights NGOs in Chiapas. With the aid of Dominican friars, in 1988, Ruiz opened the influential Fray Bartolomé de Las Casas Human Rights Center (CDHFBLC) to denounce the wide range of repressive actions against his parishioners. At the same time, Jesuits from the Bachajón Mission encouraged the creation of two major social organizations, the Center for the Defense of Liberties (CDLI) and Xi-Nich, to combat human rights violations in the northern Tzeltal and Chol region, and later started their own local human rights NGO in Chilón. In the aftermath of the Zapatista rebellion, Dominican friars started a human rights NGO in Ocosingo. This dense network of NGOs provided an influential institutional infrastructure to connect the indigenous regions of Chiapas, disseminate news about government repression, and serve as an effective means of communicating with the international community.

Throughout the 1980s and 1990s, catechists and Bible study groups held numerous conversations about the religious meaning of government repression, leading to the development of a Theology of Resistance. Continuing the analogies between the Jewish people in their search for the Promised Land and the repressive actions of Egyptian Pharaohs, and drawing on Pontius Pilate's persecution of Jesus, Ruiz's diocesan team developed influential religious narratives to stimulate the resilience of villagers, communities, and social movements against the repressive reaction of state and non-state actors.

Transforming Social Networks and Rebuilding Regional Power

Religious competition transformed people like Bishop Ruiz in radical ways, but the actions of Catholic clergy in competitive districts transformed the distribution of social power in fundamental ways. The member-retention strategies Ruiz and his pastoral team adopted led to the rise of a new local elite and powerful social structures that served as the social base for a wide variety of powerful social movements. Religious competition transformed closed corporate and isolated communities into reinvigorated communities that were part of decentralized and horizontal regional networks, as shown in Figure 3.1 These new social connections transformed the internal power structure of communities and the inter-village connections gave rise to new forms of regional social power.[19]

[19] The social network structure illustrated in Figure 3.1 is a graphic representation of the network connections described to me by Father Ramón Castillo and some of the most influential catechists and deacons in Las Margaritas, Chiapas. Following the principle of snowball sampling, I reconstructed these network ties by following the connections of my own interviewees,

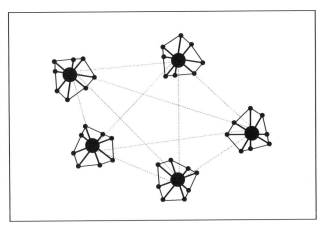

FIGURE 3.1. Decentralized and horizontal regional network with strong local leaders and dense local associational networks.

The first major transformation involves changes in the internal structure of power and status in traditionally hierarchical communities. Whereas rural indigenous villages were traditionally structured as corporate and hierarchical entities, the spread of religious competition spearheaded the creation of new local elites tied to new dense village-level associational networks. The thick black dots in Figure 3.1 identify these lay community leaders – the catechists – who were strategically situated at the intersection of several local organizations, including Bible study groups and a host of economic and social cooperatives. Centrality within local associational networks gave catechists a tremendous degree of power. As religious and secular leaders, catechists would not only compete with Protestant native pastors, but as leaders of peasant indigenous movements they would challenge the traditional power of *principales* linked to the PRI.

The second major transformation involved the creation of trans-community linkages that connected coethnic villagers through flexible network ties. Whereas closed corporate communities were purposefully isolated from their neighbors by the government and the PRI, in their struggle to prevent the spread of Protestant competition across the region Catholic clergy encouraged the articulation of inter-village ties, as shown in Figure 3.1. Under the lead of diocesan pastoral teams, these linkages would connect lay community leaders (catechists) and their local networks with other community leaders and their

particularly those of Father Castillo, Deacon Eduardo López and former catechist Límbano Vázquez. Several conversations with the pastoral teams of Bachajón, Chilón, Simojovel, El Bosque and San Andrés Larraínzar confirmed the existence of these decentralized and horizontal regional network structures beyond Las Margaritas. Conversations elsewhere with Bishop Emeritus Lona and his pastoral team confirmed that this network structure captures the social connections Catholic clergy built in response to the spread of Protestant missionary activity.

networks. These loose regional connections became effective preferred channels for trans-local information sharing and for group coordination. As the key
actors connecting several villages for religious and secular purposes, catechists
became powerful regional players.

As we argued in Chapter 1, this type of decentralized horizontal regional
network structure connecting multiple local leaders with access to their own
community associational networks, can serve as the organizational infrastructure for the rise of a wide variety of powerful autonomous movements for
independent collective action. As we show in Chapter 4, this network structure
proved to be highly resilient to government repression and co-optation and, as
we show in Chapter 6, it became the most effective vehicle for recruitment of
many lay local leaders and communities into the Zapatista National Liberation
Army (EZLN).

CARDINAL CORRIPIO: FROM PROGRESSIVE (IN OAXACA) TO CONSERVATIVE (IN PUEBLA)

By the time the young conservative Ernesto Corripio was named archbishop
of the Diocese of Antequera in the southern state of Oaxaca, the diocese's
vast rural indigenous regions had already experienced a first significant wave
of Catholic defection to mainline Protestantism (Marroquín, 2007). Since at
least the 1950s, SIL linguists and U.S. missionaries from Baptist, Nazarene,
Methodist, Presbyterian, and Pentecostal churches had successfully proselytized in some of Oaxaca's most remote rural indigenous regions (Gross, 2003).
As in Chiapas, Protestant missionaries in Oaxaca (1) translated portions of
the Bible into the state's main indigenous languages (Zapotec, Mixtec, and
Mixe); (2) established local churches led by native pastors; (3) promoted the
creation of hundreds of Bible study groups and two influential clerical training
institutes; (4) sponsored local health clinics and literacy programs; (5) banned
alcohol consumption among their converts; and (6) tried to free their members
from the obligation to participate financially in the annual festival of the local
village or municipal (Catholic) patron saint.

The ecclesiastic, cultural, and material rewards that accompanied these
actions attracted young Indians in unprecedented numbers. Conversions
to Protestant churches were particularly high across villages in the Zapotec
Central Valleys, the northwestern Mixtec highlands, the northeastern Zapotec
and Chinantec mountains, and in the Mazatec northern tip along the border of
Oaxaca with Veracruz.

In responding to competition, Corripio adopted similar strategies to those
that Bishop Ruiz had initially employed in Chiapas. Because the spread of
Protestantism was affecting other dioceses in Oaxaca, together with the state's
clerical authorities, Corripio redrew the ecclesiastic boundaries of the state to
allow for greater specialization, particularly in those indigenous regions where
the Catholic Church was facing the greatest challenges either as a result of conversions to Protestantism or because *la costumbre* (folk Catholicism) remained

deeply rooted. Before Corripio's tenure, the Vatican had created a prelature (a special zone) in the northern Mixe region and had placed it under the jurisdiction of the Italian Salesian Order. In 1972, Corripio promoted the creation of the prelature of Huautla and the Vatican placed it under the missionary watch of the Italian Order of Saint Joseph (Josefinos). In 1979, the Vatican created the Diocese of Tuxtepec in the northeastern part of the state and invited the Italian Combonian missionaries to assist the new bishop.

Whereas Ruiz had attracted some of the most powerful Catholic multinational orders to assist him in responding to the Protestant challenge, Corripio and the Oaxacan clergy drew their main clerical capital from the Southeast Regional Seminary (SERESURE), a diocesan seminary for training Mexican priests in theological and pastoral work for rural indigenous regions. Although members of small Italian orders were posted strategically in specific regions, Corripio and his successors worked mainly with SERESURE-trained parish priests. Like Ruiz, Corripio also promoted the creation of a first generation of catechists, initially hand-picked by the bishop and his pastoral team, who soon became the main foot soldiers in the fight to stem defections from the Catholic Church.

To continuously update his pastoral team in new "integral evangelization" methods in rural indigenous regions, and to train a new generation of young indigenous catechists, Corripio led the creation of CEDIPIO, a theological and pastoral center that, over time, became the institutional focal point for the coordination of indigenous pastoral actions in Oaxaca and for the development of Indigenous Theologies (Norget, 2004). Under Corripio's tenure, the diocese's pastoral team and newly trained catechists led the creation of hundreds of Bible study groups that would be planted throughout Antequera in the following decades. Most senior parish priests and pastoral agents were encouraged to drop Latin and instead embrace the diocese's multiple indigenous languages. Corripio's team gradually began reinterpreting the Gospel based on rural indigenous economic and cultural realities. During these early years, CEDIPIO offered workshops on agrarian law to assist rural indigenous communities in their attempts to petition for land redistribution, and on cultural anthropology to begin discussions on ways to implement the "inculturation" of the Gospel (Hernández Díaz, 2001).

But Corripio would not have a chance to lead the implementation of the changes he introduced. In 1976, Pope Paul VI transferred him to head the Archdiocese of Puebla, and then promoted him to the highest ecclesiastic post in Mexico City.

Corripio underwent a rapid transformation once in Puebla. He gave up the important, albeit incipient, progressive theological and pastoral practices he had adopted in Oaxaca and rapidly adopted the traditional conservative Catholic practices that had prevailed in Puebla since colonial times. Although SIL missionaries had penetrated the northern indigenous highlands of the state in the 1950s and succeeded in converting a few Catholic indigenous villagers, the Catholic monopoly was never seriously challenged in Puebla's indigenous regions (Garma, 1994). By the time Corripio was transferred to Puebla in 1976, the monopolistic structure of his new diocese provided him with little incentive to implement the teachings of Vatican II, let alone to introduce the progressive indigenous practices he had initiated in Oaxaca. In fact, Puebla's traditional religious market structure turned Corripio and his successors into traditionalist conservative bishops and provided them with no motive to embrace the Indian cause or promote the creation of peasant indigenous movements for land redistribution and indigenous rights.

Had Corripio stayed in Oaxaca, he might have become a champion of indigenous causes, as his immediate successor did. A conservative bishop in the predominantly indigenous diocese of Huejutla in the central state of Hidalgo, Bartolomé Carrasco underwent a dramatic transformation as soon as he replaced Corripio in Antequera, Oaxaca, and over the course of the next two decades became one of the most influential promoters of indigenous causes in Latin America. Had Corripio stayed in Oaxaca, he would be remembered today as a father of the Indians and not as a mainstream, conservative cleric.

BISHOP LONA: FROM CONSERVATIVE (IN HIDALGO) TO PROGRESSIVE (IN OAXACA)

A young conservative Arturo Lona – who had adopted conservative and pro-rich theological practices while serving in the predominantly rural indigenous diocese of Huejutla, Hidalgo – experienced a dramatic personal transformation when Pope Paul VI appointed him to serve as bishop of the predominantly indigenous Diocese of Tehuantepec in southeastern Oaxaca in 1971. By the time of Lona's appointment, SIL linguists and U.S. missionaries from mainline Protestant churches had made significant inroads into the Isthmus of Tehuantepec, and new U.S. missionary teams were arriving in the region, particularly Seventh-Day Adventists, Jehovah's Witnesses, and Mormons. Although Seventh-Day Adventists were beginning to shift the region's religious marketplace toward the provision of spiritual rewards, when Lona arrived in Tehuantepec, the same provision of ecclesiastic, material, and cultural rewards that was attracting young Indian souls away from the Catholic Church in Chiapas was also emptying Catholic pulpits in Tehuantepec.

Although Lona initially embraced the incipient progressive theological and pastoral practices that Archbishop Corripio was practicing in Antequera, and developed a first generation of catechists, Bible study groups, and economic cooperatives to counter the Protestant expansion, by the mid-1970s a group of dynamic young catechists were loudly demanding a more radical Catholic commitment to rural indigenous causes. More than the new liberationist theological winds blowing throughout Latin America, pressure from below alerted Lona and his colleagues in Oaxaca to the need to step into the secular realm and mobilize for social change.

During the annual National Catechists' Convention held in Oaxaca City in the summer of 1976, a group of ninety-five indigenous Oaxacan catechists raised their voices and demanded changes in Catholic religious and social practices. In the plenary session of the convention, catechists listed their communities' main problems: (1) low prices on their agricultural commodities; (2) high levels of alcohol consumption by male heads of households; and (3) political oppression. In the same plenary session, echoing the claims of the 1974 Indigenous Congress in Chiapas, catechists proposed solutions to their fellow participants: "To work as a community because it is we who are responsible for the progress of our people; to create social organizations and pressure government authorities for solutions to our problems; and to take charge of evangelizing our own people, so we can all work together toward our liberation" (Esparza, 2004).

Unable to decentralize ecclesiastic hierarchies to the same extent as non-Catholic churches or to the degree that catechists were already calling for, Oaxaca's clergy responded to this clear appeal for ecclesiastic and political empowerment by stepping into the secular realm. The conclusions of an inter-diocesan meeting that brought together all of the state's bishops suggested that the Catholic Church should assist parishioners and communities "in their struggles against rural caciques and landowners and against judicial and economic injustices" (Esparza, 2004). Liberationist clergy also interpreted the call of indigenous catechists to take the evangelization of their peoples into their own hands as a demand for the incorporation of indigenous cultures into Catholic evangelizing.

With the aid of a legion of SERESURE priests and hundreds of nuns from various religious orders, throughout the 1970s and 1980s Lona and his pastoral team trained a new generation of indigenous catechists who led the development of dense community networks and cooperatives for the provision of social services, support for agricultural production and marketing, and for the promotion of human and indigenous rights and native cultures.[20] Catechists soon became natural community leaders and were at the forefront of a dramatic expansion of Bible study groups in municipalities facing the highest levels of religious competition in the diocese.[21]

Catechists and other members of Lona's pastoral teams received their training in CEDIPIO in Oaxaca City, and in various centers developed by Lona and his pastoral team during his tenure. The focus of pastoral training during the 1980s and early 1990s was on eco-agricultural issues, indigenous customary practices, non-Catholic Christian religions, and civil and political rights and liberties. CEDIPIO's main courses included workshops on (1) economic and political analysis; (2) neoliberalism and economic crisis; (3) natural/indigenous medicine; (4) marketing agricultural crops, particularly coffee; (5) folk religiosity; and (6) Protestantism.[22]

With the full involvement of catechists, Lona and his pastoral team developed various centers for social service provision and economic training. The

---

[20] Interview with Bishop Emeritus Arturo Lona.
[21] Interview with Father Marcelino Rivera.
[22] See Hernández Díaz (2001) and Norget (1999, 2004).

pastoral team opened a health clinic, where they provided basic health services to indigenous communities in the region. Physicians and nurses at the clinic also promoted alternative indigenous medicine. In addition, the diocesan team developed a Center for Peasant Education (CEC) where the children of rural indigenous villagers lived for several months in a community center outside of the city of Tehuantepec and received formal training in the basic techniques of organic agriculture and on the intimate relationship between indigenous cultural traditions and the principles of organic agriculture. Communities that participated in CEC programs were connected through radio transmission systems sponsored by the diocese. Finally, Lona's diocesan team ran a Communal Organized Work (TCO) center charged with promoting economic and social cooperatives in rural indigenous regions.[23]

To respond to the catechists' call for assistance in developing the organizational infrastructure to pressure government authorities in their campaign for land and agricultural support programs, Lona encouraged catechists, communities, and cooperatives either to establish strategic political coalitions with already existing rural indigenous secular organizations or to join cooperatives together into regional secular movements. In the late 1970s and throughout the 1980s, Lona and his team established a strategic coalition with the Worker-Peasant-Student Coalition of the Isthmus (COCEI), the leading social organization in Juchitán and the Tehuantepec Isthmus.[24] A coalition of rural workers, students, and indigenous communities, COCEI led land invasions in the region in the mid-1970s and then turned to electoral politics. Facing harsh repression first from landowners and the military and then from the state police, COCEI soon became a nationally and internationally renowned focal point of grassroots mobilization for free and fair elections and respect for human rights (Rubin, 1997). A large segment of COCEI membership and mid-level leadership came from Bible study groups led by Lona's pastoral team.

Lona himself and his pastoral team also sponsored the creation of rural organizations to fight for land redistribution. In the Chimalapas jungle in the eastern part of the Isthmus, the diocesan team sponsored the development of Bible study groups and economic and social cooperatives and provided legal advice for Chinantec and Zoque Indians in their fight to legalize land they had received in the 1960s, which was under fierce dispute with ranchers and landowners from the neighboring state of Chiapas. This is a region to which Lona was personally attached throughout his four decades in the Isthmus. It is here that his pastoral journey began in the diocese and where he still spends most of his time since his retirement.[25] It is also a region where Catholicism faces considerable challenges. From the early 1970s throughout the subsequent two decades, the Chimalapas region was a focal point of defection from

---

[23] See Norget (1999, 2004) for extensive discussions of these centers.
[24] Interviews with Leopoldo De Gyves and Héctor Sánchez.
[25] Interview with Bishop Emeritus Arturo Lona.

Catholicism and of *costumbrismo*: municipal ENR reached 2.1 in Santa María Chimalapa in 1990 and 1.9 in San Miguel Chimalapa, the two major municipalities in the Chimalapas jungle.

But the most important organizational project sponsored by the diocese took place in the Zapotec-Mixe highlands. Building on the organizational infrastructure of Bible study groups under the advice of Dutch missionary Frans Vanderhoff and the active participation of Father Ramón Raygosa, the diocesan parish priest of Santa María Guienagati, a group of Zapotec and Mixe catechists led the creation of the Union of Indigenous Communities of the Isthmus (UCIRI) in 1983.

A large, dense network of unions of cooperatives devoted primarily, albeit not exclusively, to the production and export of organic coffee, UCIRI has been internationally recognized as one of the pioneers in the fair trade movement and one of the most successful organic coffee cooperatives in the developing world. Throughout the 1990s, UCIRI expanded its scope to health, education, transportation, and to the promotion of communal stores for provision of subsidized staple goods. It also became a major promoter of Biblical reflection on the relationship between Christianity, pre-Hispanic religions, and organic agriculture. UCIRI emerged mainly in municipalities experiencing the most intense levels of religious competition and Catholic defection in the Diocese of Tehuantepec, particularly Santiago Lachiguiri (ENR = 2.8), Gueva de Humboldt (ENR = 2.4), Santa María Guienagati (ENR = 2.4), Santa María Coatlán, Santo Domingo Petapa (ENR = 1.9), and San Juan Guichicovi (ENR = 2.1). Neighboring municipalities where the spread of Protestantism was relatively weak did not participate in UCIRI.

As in Chiapas, to show the diocese's long-term commitment to the indigenous struggle for land, agricultural production, and indigenous rights, Lona and his team became major institutional promoters of human rights and indigenous rights. When COCEI, UCIRI, villagers in the Chimalapas regions, and several other social organizations and movements faced harsh repression, Lona spoke out strongly against human rights violations. In 1992, the Diocese of Tehuantepec opened the Tepeyac Human Rights Center, which rapidly became one of the three leading human rights NGOs in the state. In the years leading to the Quincentenary of the Conquest of the Americas in 1992, and in the aftermath of the Zapatista rebellion in 1994, the center became a focal point for the promotion of indigenous rights.

As the life history of Bishop Lona shows, it was his transfer from a Catholic stronghold to a region in which the traditional monopoly of the Catholic Church was unraveling that explains his radical transformation from a conservative clergyman to a major promoter of the social base for rural indigenous collective action in the Diocese of Tehuantepec. In response to competition, Lona and his pastoral team developed a vast network of community leaders, social networks and organizations, and ideas and identities that served as mobilizing vehicles for three decades of rural indigenous mobilization in southeastern Oaxaca.

ARCHBISHOP CASTRO IN YUCATÁN: PENTECOSTALISM AND
THE RISE OF CATHOLIC CHARISMATIC PRACTICES

One decade into his tenure as archbishop of Yucatán, a conservative Manuel Castro, whose diocese's main constituency had been middle- and upper-class Yucatecs, experienced a significant personal transformation that led him to shift the focus of his diocese toward urban and poor rural indigenous villagers. However, unlike Bishops Ruiz and Lona – whose transformations led them to become major promoters of peasant indigenous movements for land and material redistribution – Archbishop Castro developed charismatic theological and pastoral practices that encouraged poor Mayan Catholic parishioners to face their everyday problems and marginalization through a spiritual religious approach as part of the Movement of Catholic Charismatic Renewal in the Holy Spirit (Garma, 1994; Várguez, 2008).

Although SIL linguists and U.S. mainline Protestant missionaries had tried to develop influential missionary sites in Yucatán in the 1950s and 1960s, it was not until the spread of U.S. neo-Pentecostal and charismatic churches in the 1970s that Catholic authorities came to perceive a true challenge to the formerly uncontested Catholic hegemony in the region. In a long interview held in the 1980s, Castro and his pastoral team clearly identified these churches as the leading challengers in Yucatán's religious landscape (Guzmán, 1989). Based on proselytizing strategies that emphasized charismatic practices, speaking in tongues, and spiritual healing – rather than Bible literacy, the use of autochthonous languages, or the provision of social services and material rewards – the rapid spread of U.S. Pentecostalism among poor urban and rural indigenous villagers set the agenda for the negotiation of a new religious contract on a spiritual rather than material basis.

In responding to the neo-Pentecostal "threat" in Yucatán, concerns about charismatic renewal and spirituality outweighed material concerns for land redistribution or indigenous rights. With the support of the powerful Legion of Christ, Archbishop Castro developed theological ideas and pastoral practices that did not challenge the economic status quo in Yucatán. No major independent peasant or indigenous movement emerged in Yucatán, partly because neo-Pentecostal churches centered the arena of competition on spiritual concerns.[26]

The life history of Archbishop Castro reveals the relevance that theological ideas and pastoral practices may have for secular mobilization: Whereas the U.S. mainline Protestant proselytizing emphasis on indigenous languages and social service provision set the agenda for the renegotiation of a new religious contract between Catholic parishioners and their authorities on cultural and material rewards, the emphasis neo-Pentecostals gave to charisma and

---

[26] The strong grip of the PRI's rural corporatist structures and the absence of leftist parties also explain the absence of independent indigenous mobilization in Yucatán. See Mattiace (2009).

spirituality led to a new religious contract based on spiritual rewards.[27] Hence, despite facing high levels of religious competition, Archbishop Castro did not develop movements for material redistribution, but focused his response on the provision of spiritual rewards and favoring the economic status quo.

CONCLUSIONS

In an influential essay published a few months before 9/11, Alfred Stepan (2000) argued that no single religious tradition can be associated with a specific form of secular politics. Because the world's major religious traditions are multivocal, he argued, the same set of religious doctrines have served at different times and in different contexts to justify obedience or revolt, nonviolent or violent collective action, apathy or social transformation. Although Stepan helps us rule out religious doctrine as the chief driver for secular action, his argument does not explain under what conditions clerical authorities would adopt one or another type of religious practices.

Focusing on Catholicism in poor rural indigenous regions in Latin America, in Chapter 1 we identified the spread of Protestant competition as a potentially important explanatory mechanism for the transformation of Catholic clergy from conservatism to social activism. Building on the statistical findings of Chapter 2, in this chapter I have developed case study evidence that seeks to isolate the causal effect of religious competition on progressive Catholic behavior.

The life histories discussed in this chapter have shown that Catholic bishops became major promoters of the organizational infrastructure and ideological resources for rural indigenous mobilization *in response to* the spread of U.S. Protestant churches. In the absence of Protestant competitive pressures, Catholic clergy did not embrace the cause of poor rural indigenous villagers and did not become major promoters of the organizational vehicles for social mobilization. As the experience of Cardinal Corripio in Puebla shows, even those clerics who attended Vatican II – and endorsed its powerful message in favor of impoverished and culturally marginalized peoples – failed to become major promoters of indigenous struggles for material redistribution and ethnocultural rights when they headed dioceses where Catholicism reigned unchallenged. Consistent with Gill (1994, 1998), we found that the effect of religious market structures trumped the effect of religious ideas on clerical behavior; clergy did not become progressive for ideological convictions but to avoid the emptying of their pews.

In this chapter, I have also provided important historical evidence showing how the competition for indigenous souls transformed the internal organization of indigenous communities in radical ways, leading to the rise of

---

[27] For the pioneering statement on the rise of the Catholic Charismatic movement in Latin America, see Chesnut (2003).

new communal leadership structures, associational networks, and ideas and identities for collective action. The chapter showed that in response to the decentralized evangelization strategy followed by U.S. Protestant missionaries, Catholic clergy contributed to developing decentralized regional network structures with multiple local lay leaders and dense communal networks. The chapter also showed that Catholic clergy contributed to the development of powerful religious narratives that helped indigenous parishioners in the process of cognitive liberation and creation of the social norms and identities for persistent collective action. I have given extensive evidence showing that these local leaders, networks, ideas, and norms provided the organizational infrastructure and cognitive and normative motivation for the construction of important rural indigenous movements for land redistribution and cultural recognition. These movements were at the forefront of Mexico's protracted cycle of peasant indigenous protest.

After centuries of associating religion with social apathy and political oppression, scholars in the social sciences have now come to acknowledge the potential of religion for progressive social transformation (Smith, 1996). Whereas the emphasis in the literature has been placed on the power of religious ideas and beliefs in stimulating radical collective action (Cleary and Steigenga, 2004), the evidence from this chapter suggests an alternative explanation: Religion contributes to the creation of the organizational bases for powerful dissident movements when religious authorities develop decentralized regional networks of powerful local leaders and dense local associational groups. In Latin America, Catholic clergy contributed to the creation of these powerful decentralized social networks for secular action in response to the successful Protestant strategy of decentralized evangelizing.

Although our goal in this chapter has been to show that religious competition can be a causal factor that motivates traditionalist clergy to become major promoters of the social basis for indigenous collective action, we know that neither religion nor social networks on their own can account for the type and intensity of collective action. As we maintain throughout the book, what community leaders and their networks and movements do or fail to do is largely shaped by the political context and the response of political actors to the rise of new independent leaders and associational networks and their claims. It is to these secular processes that we now turn our attention – to the competition for indigenous votes.

4

Competing for Votes

Why Electoral Competition Shaped Mexico's Cycle of Indigenous Protest

Social leaders and grassroots organizations do not operate in a political vacuum. As three decades of research in social movements have shown, whether grassroots organizations engage in sustained actions of protest and become social movements or whether they fail to take their claims to the streets largely depends on the structure of political opportunities and threats available to them (McAdam, McCarthy, and Zald, 1996; Tarrow, 1998). Building on the experience of advanced capitalist democracies, the canonical explanation in social movement theory suggests that open democratic environments marked by electoral competition and human rights respect facilitate the development of cycles of peaceful protest, whereas closed autocracies, ruled by an iron-fist, give rise to acquiescence.

Although social movement theory has succeeded in establishing the importance of political regimes and institutions in defining the opportunities and constraints for peaceful protest, the effect of electoral competition and government repression on protest remains controversial (Davenport, 2000, 2005; Meyer, 2004). Take the contradictory findings in the extensive literature on indigenous mobilization in Latin America: Whereas some studies find that the spread of electoral competition and the decline of government repression in Latin America's new democracies opened up opportunities for peaceful indigenous mobilization (Yashar, 2005), others suggest that it was the absence of competition under Latin America's repressive authoritarian regimes that stimulated peaceful indigenous protest (Rivera, 1986; Mejía and Sarmiento, 1987).

Given that most cycles of indigenous mobilization in Latin America began under authoritarian rule, in Chapter 1 I suggested that a way to judge between these contradictory findings is to analytically redefine the opportunities and threats for social mobilization under autocracies and generate new theoretical predictions for testing. Rather than simply "use" the list of opportunities that social movement scholars have identified in advanced capitalist democracies to explain dynamics of protest in autocracies, we set out to rethink how the logic of governance in authoritarian regimes defines opportunities and threats for mobilization.

In Chapter 1 we developed a new explanation of the rise, development and demise of cycles of independent protest in autocracies. We suggested that the introduction of government-controlled multiparty elections in autocracies gives rise to socio-electoral coalitions between opposition parties and independent grassroots organizations. Seeking social allies to fight fraud and establish a core electoral base, we conjectured, opposition parties recruit leaders and activists of grassroots organizations and in exchange become major sponsors of social protest in non-electoral times. As elections become relatively free and fair, and opposition forces stand a reasonable chance of victory, party leaders have no clear motivations to encourage protest; to avoid marginalizing the median voter, they become a major force of institutionalization of social mobilization.

In this explanation government repression or co-optation does not necessarily bring cycles of protest to an end. Because autocrats can no longer randomly and brutally repress dissent, they adopt new governance strategies by which they try to deter protest through targeted co-optation and repression of social leaders and activists. Because the effect of repression and co-optation on social protest is conditional on the existence of social networks, we suggested that targeted forms of repression or co-optation are more likely to work when social movements are structured as centralized networks dominated by a few powerful leaders rather than as decentralized and horizontal structures.

Chapter 2 provided extensive quantitative evidence showing that the initial spread of leftist electoral competition in Mexican indigenous municipalities was strongly associated with the rise of rural indigenous protest. It also presented evidence showing that government attempts to prevent the consolidation of a coalition of leftist parties with rural indigenous movements using carrot-and-stick policies did not discourage but invigorated indigenous mobilization. Although repression did not deter protest, statistical results showed that protest began to decline only after the Left became a major power contender for municipal office.

In this chapter we provide extensive micro-historical information that enables us to test in a relatively controlled environment the effect that the introduction of government-controlled elections and the spread of multiparty competition had on the political behavior of six male indigenous leaders, as Mexico transitioned from autocracy to multiparty democracy (see H.3a).

Given that my goal is to isolate as much as possible the effect of changes in electoral competition and governance on the dynamics of micro-mobilization through the course of a protracted cycle of protest, I selected six Tojolabal indigenous leaders from Las Margaritas, Chiapas, who share many socioeconomic and demographic characteristics that may be relevant for explaining collective action: they are all from the same age cohort, ethnolinguistic group, and municipality; they all belong to families of peons who escaped from the region's *fincas*; they all have vivid memories of the exploitation that their parents and grandparents suffered in the *fincas*; they were all born in communal ejido villages and at an early age became involved in struggles for land extension and redistribution; and they all participated in these struggles as members of the CIOAC – the leading rural organization in the region.

Because we seek to test the conditional effect of coercion and co-optation on independent protest, I selected leaders who, despite belonging to the same organization (CIOAC), were part of different social networks. One significant difference between these six leaders is that three of them were part of the extensive decentralized social networks constructed by the Diocese of San Cristóbal de Las Casas in the 1970s and 1980s (see Chapter 3), while the others were part of centralized social networks constructed by Leftist parties.

The analysis shows that the initial expansion and the road to municipal power of leftist opposition parties in Margaritas had a major effect in shaping the mobilization strategies of CIOAC leaders. The chapter provides extensive evidence of the rise and development of an important strategic coalition between Catholic social networks, CIOAC, and leftist parties *after* the introduction of government-controlled multiparty elections. It shows how CIOAC leaders slowly transformed their struggle for land into a struggle for human rights respect and free and fair elections and how leftist parties embraced radical demands for land and ethnic rights. It also shows the surprising transformation of the CIOAC from an independent social movement into a leftist electoral machine *after* the Left won municipal power in Margaritas and shows how the Left in power actively contributed to the demise of a long cycle of indigenous protest.

A systematic comparison of these leaders' political choices shows that those embedded in the dense Catholic social networks were more likely to resist cooptation attempts by PRI government authorities and were also more likely to carry on their protest despite government repression. It also reveals that leaders from secular networks – but not those embedded in Catholic networks – became key players in the leftist electoral machines after the Left won executive power in Margaritas.

The chapter is divided into three sections. I first relate the life histories of the six CIOAC leaders from Margaritas. For purposes of exposition, the narrative focuses on the life of Antonio Hernández, a secular socialist leader with close connections to Catholic social networks, but I add the voices of other leaders along the way. At critical junctures, however, I distinguish the behavior of leaders with access to religious networks from those with secular connections. In the second part, I assess how the spread of electoral competition shaped indigenous protest in other states and municipalities beyond Margaritas. In the concluding section, I discuss the relevance of this chapter's findings for our understanding of cycles of peaceful protest in autocracies.

THE RISE AND DEMISE OF RURAL INDIGENOUS PROTEST: A LIFE HISTORY OF CIOAC LEADERS IN LAS MARGARITAS, CHIAPAS

Founded by leaders of the Mexican Communist Party (PCM) as a union of rural indigenous wage workers in the 1970s, the CIOAC in Chiapas rapidly

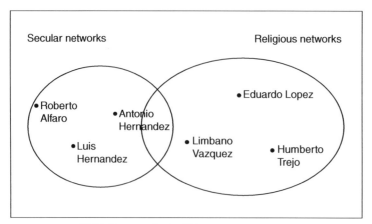

FIGURE 4.1. CIOAC networks in Chiapas, 1980s.

evolved into one of the state's leading organization for land redistribution in the 1980s and 1990s.[1] As shown in Figure 4.1, the CIOAC was built on a base of two major indigenous networks: bilingual teachers serving in rural indigenous communities and Catholic catechists and their extensive associational networks of Bible study groups and economic and social cooperatives. Whereas the teachers had been socialized through state institutions and secular leftist politics, the catechists and their communities were part of the progressive networks built by Bishop Samuel Ruiz and the Diocese of San Cristóbal de Las Casas. Secularists with access to religious networks, like Antonio Hernández, were the most powerful CIOAC leaders.

Figure 4.1 identifies six CIOAC leaders. My goal is to compare the political choices these leaders made as electoral conditions changed in Margaritas. Throughout the chapter, I draw mainly from extensive interviews conducted with Roberto Alfaro, Antonio Hernández, Límbano Vázquez, and Eduardo López. References to Luis Hernández are based on information provided by his colleagues. I do not discuss the case of Humberto Trejo in this chapter, but will return to it in Chapter 6 when I discuss the mechanics of recruitment from social movements to rebel groups, in which Trejo played a crucial role recruiting indigenous leaders and communities into the Zapatista National Liberation Army (EZLN). I include in Appendix C a brief biographical note of the occupation and status of these leaders at the time of the interview.

Demanding Land Redistribution under Autocracy

As it was for every CIOAC leader of his generation, for Antonio Hernández, his grandparents' experience as peons in the *finca* system that prevailed in

---

[1] For important information and insightful narratives of the CIOAC, see Harvey (1998), Sonnleitner (2001), Mattiace (2003), and Saavedra (2008).

Las Margaritas until the 1970s lingers heavily in his personal memory.[2] After Antonio's grandmother was sexually assaulted by the son of the owner of the San Mateo *finca* and his grandfather tortured for denouncing the assault, together with other peons, the Hernández family petitioned the federal government for access to ejido land and left San Mateo when agrarian authorities awarded them the Ejido Veracruz as part of Mexico's post-Revolutionary program of agrarian reform.[3]

The small plot that the Hernández family had been given to use soon proved insufficient for a family of fourteen. By the 1960s, together with other families, the Hernández began a cumbersome and complicated bureaucratic process to apply for more land. Because government authorities either (1) did not approve the petition for land, (2) gave out land titles but the land was never actually awarded, (3) awarded insufficient land, or (4) awarded land of very poor quality, Antonio's generation became involved in agrarian politics from an early age. As Eduardo López from nearby Ejido Tabasco put it, social leaders of their cohort initially got involved in agrarian struggles "to guarantee their children's generation access to land."[4]

Under Mexico's closed authoritarian regime of the 1960s and 1970s, landowners and their private guards often succeeded in hijacking the land redistribution process. When landowners found out their peons were demanding of subnational state authorities that the small land plots they leased from the *finca* for their family's sustenance be transformed into ejidos or that they be given access to land plots in the periphery of the *finca*, they first tried to coercively intimidate the peons and their families to make them desist from filing their petitions.[5]

If intimidation did not work, and the petition was received by local officials, landowners would then try to buy off the agrarian engineers responsible for surveying the boundaries of the land plots. If co-optation of local authorities did not work, landowners resorted to coercive violence. Communal leaders behind the land-petitioning process were tortured or assassinated by the landowners' private guards. As Eduardo López recalls, when the owners of the El Medellín *finca* learned that some of their peons had joined communal leaders of the Ejido Tabasco to apply for land, they ordered their private guards to execute the ejido commissar of Tabasco.[6] As the peon group had no social or political allies to assist them in their struggles, the murder of the Tabasco ejido commissar went unpunished and derailed the process of petitioning for land for many years.

---

[2] Hernández was fifty-six years old at the time of the interview.
[3] Unless otherwise indicated, all the information about Hernández's history comes from three in-depth interviews I conducted with him in Las Margaritas and Comitán, July and August 2010.
[4] Interview with Eduardo López.
[5] Interviews with Eduardo López and Límbano Vázquez. Andrés Díaz from Simojovel tells a similar story.
[6] Ibid.

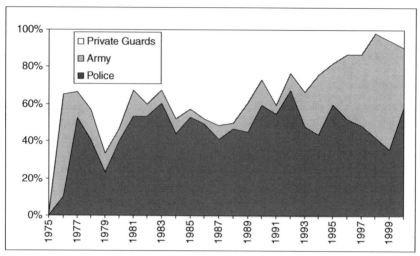

FIGURE 4.2. Repression against indigenous populations by perpetrator (relative contribution).

Information from the MII Dataset reported in Figure 4.2 shows that in the 1970s, landowners and their private guards were indeed the most active agents involved in repressing rural indigenous villagers and grassroots organizations. Reports from the MII and from the CIOAC's own records show that when private guards faced any opposition from indigenous villagers, the Mexican army typically assisted them in suppressing dissent, as was the case in the brutal murder of the Ejido Tabasco commissar.

Demanding Land Redistribution under *Electoral* Autocracy

Unlike the struggles of the 1960s and 1970s, in which independent rural indigenous communities petitioned for land without institutional assistance from any external institutional actors, in the late 1970s the Catholic Church and the Mexican Communist Party became major institutional promoters and sponsors of rural indigenous movements in such places as Margaritas. Clerics, party leaders, and activists had a significant influence in the transformation of land petitioning from individual endeavors into powerful collective movements for land redistribution.

Religious Allies. As discussed in Chapter 3, in reaction to the spread of U.S. SIL and Presbyterian missionaries, in the late 1970s the Catholic Church in the Comitán/Margaritas region became a major institutional promoter of the leadership and organizational infrastructure assisting Catholic Tojolabal communities in their struggle for land redistribution. *La Castalia*, the influential diocesan center for catechists in the Tojolabal region, was the school where many of the communal leaders that spearheaded the struggles for land redistribution in Margaritas were trained.

As Father Ramón Castillo – director of *La Castalia* in the 1970s and again in the 2000s – recalls, a young Antonio Hernández was a precocious participant in the three-month workshops his pastoral team offered. Although at the end of the course Antonio did not go back to his home village to proselytize and spread the knowledge and skills he had acquired in the workshops – as most participants did – and would distance himself from religion, his training at *La Castalia* helped him establish important links with catechists and Catholic communal leaders from across Margaritas, many of whom eventually joined the CIOAC and brought their communal networks into the movement. Trained under progressive Theologies of Land and Theologies of Resistance, these community members were ideologically prepared to fight for the Promised Land.

Political Allies. The Catholic Church was not the only important institutional ally for Tojolabal communities in their struggles for land in Margaritas. The partial liberalization of Mexico's closed authoritarian regime in 1977, by which all political parties were legalized and allowed to compete for office under government-controlled elections, had brought leftist opposition parties seeking to recruit young risk-taking leaders with access to independent communities and grassroots organizations to such places as Margaritas.

Antonio Hernández recalls his recruitment by the national leaders of the PCM and CIOAC – then the party's peasant branch – during a public speaking contest the PCM organized in San Cristóbal de Las Casas. After he left *La Castalia*, Antonio lived in state-sponsored group homes for indigenous teenagers enrolled in middle school in Zinacantán, a highland municipality adjacent to the city of San Cristóbal de Las Casas. In Zinacantán, Antonio established strong links with a whole generation of future indigenous bilingual teachers, some of whom were eventually recruited into the CIOAC through such events as the contest that had enabled PCM and CIOAC leaders to recruit Antonio in the first place. Direct access to rural indigenous teachers and Catholic catechists would position Antonio at the center of many inter-communal associational networks and provide him with a strong social base to become one of the most powerful social leaders in the state.

The PCM, the PSUM and other leftist opposition parties did not only seek to establish socio-electoral coalitions with independent social networks such as the Catholic social bases, but they also actively sought to create their own social organizations, including peasant and teachers' unions. Through a careful strategy of recruiting of bilingual indigenous teachers trained by the state, and local leaders working with reformist state institutions such as the National Indigenous Institute (INI), leftist parties developed new organizational structures built around strong charismatic young secular leaders they carefully selected and trained by sending them to Mexico City and abroad, including such places as Cuba, Nicaragua, and the former Soviet Union.

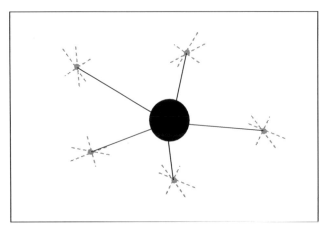

FIGURE 4.3. Centralized and hierarchical regional network with weak local leaders and weak local associational networks.

Figure 4.3 shows the network structures fostered by leftist opposition parties: centralized regional structures with strong and charismatic leaders connected to weakly organized village networks.[7] Building on principles of "democratic centralism," leftist party leaders adopted these centralized structures because they were recruiting defectors from state-run programs or state-trained young elites, who, by joining the Left, were giving up on the possibility of becoming leaders of PRI-sponsored corporatist structures. To attract the most talented leaders, they had to appeal to young leaders, like Antonio Hernández, with long time horizons, and offer them leadership positions in social organizations in which they would be at the center of power.

Unlike the decentralized and horizontal Catholic social networks described in Chapter 3, in which multiple local lay leaders with access to dense local associational networks became the focal points of the network, here a handful of powerful regional secular leaders dominated the network. Villages were connected to each other through these leaders and the primary effort of leftist parties was to train powerful regional leaders rather than promote the rise of dense local associational structures. Sometimes centralized leftist secular networks came together with decentralized Catholic networks for the creation of powerful peasant organizations. In fact, as we discussed in reference to Figure 4.1, the CIOAC was the juxtaposition of centralized secular structures and

---

[7] The social network structure illustrated in Figure 4.3 is the result of extensive in-depth interviews with a few of the core CIOAC historical leaders in Margaritas, particularly Professor Roberto Alfaro and Antonio Hernández. Additional conversations with Límbano Vázquez, Eduardo López and residents from Ejido Tabasco and Ejido Veracruz in Margaritas helped me complete this picture. In-depth interviews with COCEI leaders in Oaxaca persuaded me that this centralized structure was part of a more general phenomenon of leftist secular social organizing.

decentralized Catholic social networks, in which secular leaders were at the forefront of the organization.

The State's Response: Repression and Concessions. In the 1960s, land redistribution was limited to PRI loyalists, and demands for land redistribution from independent organizations were answered with severe repression by landowners and their private guards. But after the partial liberalization of Mexico's authoritarian regime in 1977, and throughout the next decade, independents were met by a different government response. Repression remained the most important tool for governance, but the nature, intensity, and targets of government coercion were transformed. Moreover, and perhaps more importantly for the purposes of independent mobilization, Chiapas's subnational authorities developed ad-hoc land redistribution programs in which a small proportion of beneficiaries included members of independent grassroots movements. As indigenous leaders and Catholic clergy nearly unanimously reported in several interviews, even Governor Absalón Castellanos (1982–1988) – an army general from a traditional family of landowners from the Comitán/Margaritas region and one of the most repressive political figures in contemporary Mexico – consistently relied on "carrots and sticks" to negotiate with independent organizations and movements.

Repression. Even though a considerable number of rural indigenous leaders were assassinated under the Castellanos government, and young leaders such as Antonio Hernández survived various assassination attempts, unlawful arrest of leaders and activists became the most common act of government repression against independent movements in the Chiapas of the 1980s. And despite Castellanos's multiple connections with the military and the state's landholding class, during his term in office, subnational *civilian* police forces and PRI-affiliated rural indigenous villagers linked to the National Peasant Confederation (CNC) slowly replaced the army and the landowners' private guards as the main institutional actors of government repression in Chiapas.[8] This was a national trend: After a decade of active participation in Mexico's Dirty War in the early 1970s, the federal government moved the military into the barracks and subnational police corporations became the new repressive arm of the state – now under the jurisdiction of state governors (see Figure 4.2).

As Eduardo López of Ejido Tabasco explains, state police agents in Chiapas would arbitrarily arrest rural indigenous leaders and activists without arrest warrants after they had engaged in public demonstrations or land invasions. Unlawful arrests were accompanied by physical aggression, destruction of property, and some kind of torture once in prison. After serving short sentences,

---

[8] The army took control of internal security in Chiapas following the 1994 Zapatista rebellion. Nonetheless, police corporations under the command of the state governor and vigilante groups associated with the local PRI remained the two crucial actors in the everyday practices of state repression.

however, most political prisoners would leave jail alive. During the 1980s, Chiapas's prisons – rather than the state's cemeteries – became overpopulated with grassroots indigenous leaders and activists and a few of their mestizo associates, including journalists, pastoral agents, and leftist party leaders and activists.[9]

Despite the repressive practices of Governor Castellanos and his associates, when comparing the perils associated with agrarian struggles in Chiapas in the latter four decades of the twentieth century, Eduardo López identifies a clear difference between the 1960s and 1970s vis-à-vis the 1980s:

In the past, landowners and their private guards, sometimes assisted by the army, killed peasants demanding land redistribution – just as they did with the commissar of Ejido Tabasco, when we got serious about our petitions for land extension. But the 1980s were different. By then, we were organized and the landowners didn't dare continue the same repressive actions they had adopted in previous years. Under Castellanos, it was the state judicial police that incarcerated rural activists.

Concessions. Although Castellanos granted an unprecedented number of certificates that exempted *fincas* from becoming targets of land redistribution in Chiapas, his government also distributed an unprecedented amount of land to PRI-affiliated peasants and to independent organizations and movements. Professor Roberto Alfaro, a Tojolabal leader from Margaritas, summarized it aptly: "Castellanos was a tough son of a bitch, but he was open to negotiations." Whereas under closed autocracy, PRI governments rarely awarded material concessions to independent movements, Castellanos did. Through the Agrarian Rehabilitation Program – the flagship agrarian program of his administration – Castellanos bought thousands of hectares under dispute from landowners and granted them primarily to PRI-affiliated peasants but also to independent movements such as the CIOAC.

Castellanos's goal was to either co-opt independent peasant indigenous leaders into the PRI via policies of selective and partial material redistribution, or to keep a reasonable number of protesters in the streets negotiating land redistribution with government authorities instead of working with opposition parties to oust the PRI or moving to the mountains to launch a revolution. As CIOAC leaders put it in several interviews, the government activated the streets and public plazas for limited policy negotiation with independent movements as an "escape valve" to avoid more radical acts. In the conceptual language of Robertson (2010), his goal was to "manage" independent protest – to co-opt it or control it.

When Did Coercion and Concessions Deter Protest? *The prisoner's dilemma.* Cerro Hueco – Chiapas's infamous state prison – became a second home for many CIOAC leaders and activists of Antonio Hernández's generation. When judicial police forces under the direct command of Governor Castellanos

---

[9] Interview with Amado Avendaño.

arrested CIOAC leaders and activists, they would typically offer the new convicts a deal: If they agreed to sign a contract by which they committed to no longer participate in land invasions, street blockades, or public demonstrations, the government would immediately release them from prison. Otherwise, judicial authorities would press charges and keep them in Cerro Hueco for several years.[10]

As reported by Antonio Hernández and his former CIOAC colleagues, through physical and psychological coercion, government authorities actively tried to force indigenous leaders and activists into signing these informal contracts. Judicial authorities worked hard to persuade CIOAC convicts that their peers had betrayed them and were no longer in the streets pressuring authorities for their release.[11] If psychological persuasion did not work, police guards subjected CIOAC convicts to "moderate" torture to increase the costs of imprisonment and weaken their resolve.[12]

In the language of game theory, Chiapan prison authorities presented the CIOAC and other social movement leaders and activists with a one-shot Prisoner's Dilemma and tried through psychological pressure and torture to persuade them to save their lives and avoid becoming the "suckers" – that is, those players who decline to cooperate with their captors and remain loyal to the movement without knowing that their comrades have already betrayed them.

As reported by most CIOAC leaders and human rights activists, dissident indigenous leaders embedded in dense communal associational networks were less likely to accept the government's deal than those with weak network connections. Professor Roberto Alfaro, a longtime CIOAC leader and retired teacher, recalled that catechists with strong connections to the dense Catholic liberationist networks and secular socialist leaders with strong connections to the Catholic-sponsored networks were the CIOAC members least likely to cut deals with judicial authorities in Cerro Hueco. Leaders and activists connected to weak communal network structures – such as indigenous dissident teachers – were more likely to abandon dissent. This does not mean that all Tojolabal dissident teachers betrayed the CIOAC base and made deals with government authorities, or that no catechist linked to Catholic liberationist networks ever gave up the contentious struggle for land; it only means that, all else being equal, those with strongest network ties to Catholic communities were more likely to resist.

---

[10] Interview with Professor Roberto Alfaro.
[11] This is confirmed by catechist Andrés Díaz of Simojovel, Chiapas, another CIOAC stronghold.
[12] The three most common types of torture in Cerro Hueco in the 1980s included the "*Corcholata*" (prisoners were made to kneel on a wooden table carpeted by bottle caps for several hours); the "*Bartolina*" (prisoners were locked in a tiny room in a vertical position while a drop of water fell on their heads every few seconds for long periods of time); and the "*Tambo*" (the prisoner's head was repeatedly immersed in a toilet until he nearly drowned). Interviews with Alfaro, Hernández, and López.

Solving the prisoner's dilemma. Dense social networks, particularly those associated with Catholic Bible study groups and economic and social cooperatives, served as a ring of protection for Antonio Hernández and many other CIOAC leaders and activists who suffered unlawful arrests in the 1980s. These networks empowered leaders and activists in Cerro Hueco to resist government co-optation and coercion attempts for three fundamental reasons.

Access to dense associational networks provided valuable information that allowed captured CIOAC leaders and activists to resist co-optation attempts. Even if they could not establish communication with the rank and file of the movement, the communities' social norms and prior histories of interaction served as guidance for action and resistance; they helped them create firm expectations that CIOAC militants would remain mobilized in the streets until achieving their release. Even if leaders and activists could not verify whether CIOAC militants were marching or camping out in downtown Tuxtla Gutiérrez – the state's capital – those with strong bonds to Catholic networks and with histories of interaction with the rank and file knew they could count on CIOAC members and other movement allies to actively pressure authorities in the streets for their release. As Eduardo López put it, "We knew and they knew that we simply could not let the government incarcerate our leaders."

Social networks also helped leaders and activists transform their attitudes toward risk. Knowing that communities would not leave them helped independent leaders and activists become more risk acceptant when facing repression and its consequences. As a human rights activist working in Chilón, Chiapas, suggested, "When facing dangerous situations, leaders know communities will protect them because they elected them."[13] This social norm allowed leaders and activists to transform the uncertainty associated with arbitrary detentions into a calculated risk – one that was reasonable to accept in the context of an electoral autocracy.

Lastly, social networks extended the time horizon of CIOAC leaders and allowed them to be patient while in prison. Prior experiences when leaders and activists had been released became important victories that showed them that even iron-fist governors like General Castellanos could not afford to arbitrarily keep social leaders in prison indefinitely. As Eduardo López recalls, "The release of our leaders from Cerro Hueco was a partial victory that stimulated great conversations within the community Bible study groups and these conversations, in turn, led to a greater impetus to carry on with the struggle."

By providing social leaders and activists with valuable information, helping them lower the risks associated with arbitrary detention, and extending their time horizons while in prison, social networks empowered them to transform a one-shot Prisoner's Dilemma into an iterated game – that is, a coordination game.[14] In this new context, choosing to defy the authorities at Cerro Hueco was not an irrational option but a rational equilibrium strategy.

---

[13] Interview with Father Oscar González, SJ.

[14] Chong (1991) makes a strong claim that social incentives contribute to transforming collective action from a PD game to a coordination game. For the importance of communities and social

Resilience paid off for leaders and communities. Defying the government's co-optation attempts in Cerro Hueco and returning to the struggle for land (and by then for human rights and free and fair elections) guaranteed leaders and activists a badge of social honor.[15] Resilience provided leaders and activists with a special community and social status that would last for the rest of their lives; in fact, resilience in the face of repression became a leadership-building strategy. But resilience was also a mechanism that strengthened intra-group social norms of reciprocity, which strengthened both social networks (e.g., Catholic Bible study groups) and formal organizations (CIOAC).

Selective incentives. Unable to systematically and lethally repress independent communities and movements making claims for land, PRI governors in the 1980s sought to manage independent protest through a policy of partial material concessions to independent movements. As Professor Roberto Alfaro recalls: "Serving time in prison was indeed costly, but benefits for CIOAC-affiliate communities would typically follow; land, roads, schools, etc." In fact, Antonio Hernández and other CIOAC leaders and Catholic clergy suggest that the Agrarian Rehabilitation Program was the direct response by Governor Castellanos to the epic one-month march that CIOAC led from Tuxtla Gutierrez to Mexico City in 1983 to denounce a wave of state repression and incarceration against CIOAC leaders in Chiapas.

However, a policy of selective incentives in favor of independent leaders and activists and CIOAC communities did not always work. Statistical results in Chapter 2 showed that municipalities where independent rural indigenous movements received the greatest share of land from the Agrarian Rehabilitation Program were more likely to continue protesting than those who did not become beneficiaries. CIOAC leaders considered that in many cases, receiving land from the program was another partial victory that stimulated communities to continue protesting.[16] Nevertheless, they bitterly pointed out, there were also instances in which co-optation via the distribution of selective incentives actually worked.

Once again, the connection network of leaders and activists seemed to have played a critical role in distinguishing those who accepted the benefits and carried on with the struggle from those who did not. Leaders and activists

norms in solving collective action problems, see Taylor (1982), Hardin (1995), Lichbach (1996), and Wood (2003). For the pioneering work that explicitly links the structure of social networks with the social norms that facilitate the solution of coordination dilemmas, see Petersen (2001). For an influential formulation based on computational methods, see Siegel (2011).

[15] This is widely recognized by most indigenous leaders I interviewed. In their narratives, they appeared to be *ex ante* cognizant that resilience would provide deeply networked social leaders with a special status in their organizations. Interviews with Antonio Hernández (Las Margaritas, Chiapas), Hector Sánchez (Juchitán, Oaxaca), and Manuel Gómez (Chilón, Chiapas). For an elaborate discussion of how leaders' decision to return to the streets after serving time in prison earned them a badge of honor in the context of the U.S. civil rights movement, see Chong (1991).

[16] Interviews with Antonio Hernández, Límbano Vázquez, Roberto Alfaro, and Eduardo López (Margaritas), as well as Andrés Díaz (Simojovel) and Father Joel Padrón.

embedded in decentralized and horizontal regional networks with dense local associational ties were more likely to resist government co-optation attempts than other villagers for three reasons.

First, dense Catholic social networks provided leaders and activists with a social safety net and a stream of informal social services that empowered them to resist the temptation to capitulate in the struggle for land when some of them received access to small land plots or other material kickbacks. As we discussed in Chapter 3, as a member-retention strategy, the Diocese of San Cristóbal had developed a dense network of economic and social cooperatives that made life more affordable and production more efficient for Catholic parishioners in Margaritas and other eastern municipalities. Hence, the material opportunity cost of protest was lower for them than for non-networked dissidents.

Second, Catholic social networks provided members with a rationale that justified patience. As members of Catholic liberationist networks, most CIOAC members had been trained under the ideological precepts of theologies of land and resistance, which drew analogies between indigenous struggles for land and the search of the Jewish people for a Promised Land. One of the key theological messages in Bible study groups was patience and resistance. The struggle for the Promised Land was seen as a life-long project that entailed tremendous personal and family sacrifices. Tojolabal peasants were indeed prepared to wait. This conviction notwithstanding, any small land plot that resulted from the struggle or any leader released from jail became a treasured partial victory that encouraged the CIOAC rank and file to continue with the struggle.[17]

Finally, Bishop Ruiz, parish priests, members of the diocesan pastoral team, and the communities themselves represented important controls that would monitor members and censure deviations from the example of solidarity set by catechists and other grassroots leaders. Father Joel Padrón, a parish priest in the Comitán/Margaritas region and then in Simojovel, and a close associate of the CIOAC, personally confronted former catechists who moved on to positions of leadership within CIOAC when he and his pastoral agents perceived they were becoming too close politically to the position of PRI authorities and landowners.[18] In the case of Simojovel's secular CIOAC leaders, Padrón and his pastoral team were not able to prevent co-optation.[19] Secular CIOAC leaders with weak communal connections were not subject to the same checks and balances as former catechists and hence were easier targets for co-optation.

If PRI government authorities were unable to co-opt or deter the actions of CIOAC leaders and activists, particularly those with deep connections to dense Catholic social networks, the question then is what kind of relationship opposition parties developed with grassroots movements and the CIOAC, and in what ways this relationship shaped the indigenous struggle for land redistribution.

---

[17] Interview with Eduardo López.
[18] Interview with Father Joel Padrón.
[19] Interviews with Andrés Díaz and Antonio Hernández.

Why the Initial Electoral Expansion of the Left Stimulated Indigenous Mobilization. Despite government attempts to keep rural indigenous movements away from opposition parties, the electoral strategies of leftist parties and the spread of electoral competition in Margaritas played a key role in the decisions of Antonio Hernández and other CIOAC leaders of his generation to mobilize. By the mid-1980s, most catechists in Margaritas had become CIOAC members and most CIOAC members had enrolled in the parties that succeeded the Mexican Communist Party: first the Unified Mexican Socialist Party (PSUM) and eventually the PRD. The boundaries between peasant movements and leftist opposition parties were tenuous, and the local PSUM and then the PRD became party-movements.[20] The momentums of electoral competition and social mobilization converged in the 1980s, Catholic-sponsored grassroots movements, CIOAC, and the partisan left becoming three overlapping networks and three interchangeable social identities.

The development of a socio-electoral coalition between Catholics and the CIOAC began shortly after the 1974 Indigenous Congress in Chiapas, when the Diocese of San Cristóbal de Las Casas decided to organize the "power of the people" to assist catechists and their communities in their struggle for land redistribution. CIOAC was one of the most influential groups to approach the Tojolabal/Margaritas region, offering their professional expertise to the nascent grassroots movement.

Father Joel Padrón, who served as parish priest in Comitán (next to Margaritas) and was then transferred to Simojovel in the highlands, reports that the local clergy played a key role in brokering the entry of the CIOAC in the region. Even though Catholic liberationist clergy and communist leaders had huge disagreements on the status of religion (opium versus liberation) and on issues of public health (the concept of the family, reproduction, contraception, and abortion), they did share a crucial goal: their interest in capturing indigenous souls (Catholics) and votes (communists).

The Catholic-CIOAC-Leftist coalition was a contingent strategic partnership that depended on specific exchanges and rewards. Shortly after a few PSUM members were elected to the Chiapas state legislature in the early 1980s, leftist leaders provided specific rewards to their predominantly Catholic CIOAC base.

To assist Catholic clergy and catechists in their campaign against U.S. Presbyterian missionaries linked to the SIL, communist and socialist parties had since the 1970s become a major voice demanding the expulsion of the SIL from Mexico. Although communist elites cared little about religion, they played a key role in publicly denouncing U.S. Protestant missionaries as agents of U.S. imperialism and of the Central Intelligence Agency.[21]

---

[20] See Kitschelt (2003) for an extensive discussion of the relationship between social movements and political parties in the Western European experience.

[21] These were not only ideological battles. In the mid-1980s, a series of violent evictions of Protestant and Pentecostal families from their communities took place in Margaritas. Catholic and CIOAC

Leftist elected politicians embraced the cause of rural indigenous villagers – first and foremost their struggle for land, and eventually their claims for indigenous autonomy and self-determination. Even though these were radical demands that might have alienated the median voter both in Margaritas and in the larger districts in the jungle and the state, leftist parties initially embraced these demands in the 1980s and sponsored peasant mobilization.[22] Leftist parties provided financial and logistic resources for peasant mobilization, particularly means of transportation and shelter in Tuxtla Gutiérrez and in Mexico City to facilitate the participation of Tojolabal CIOAC villagers in marches and sit-ins to demand land redistribution or the release of their leaders from jail.

Finally, leftist elected politicians became important institutional players in defending the human rights of CIOAC leaders and activists when they were imprisoned in Cerro Hueco. As Araceli Burguete, a chief adviser of the CIOAC in the 1980s, reports, "liberating a leader from jail was always easier and more expedient when a leftist legislator helped us broker the release."[23]

In exchange for the ideological, organizational and institutional support provided by leftist parties and politicians to Catholic CIOAC members and its leaders, Catholic communities and the CIOAC became loyal voters for PSUM and PRD candidates in Chiapas and participated in post-electoral rallies denouncing fraud. The electoral involvement of Catholic communities and the CIOAC became more evident when Tojolabal CIOAC leaders such as Antonio Hernández became candidates for legislative and executive municipal positions. Antonio Hernández first ran as a candidate of a leftist coalition for the municipal presidency of Margaritas in 1988. In the aftermath of the Zapatista rebellion in 1994, he was elected federal deputy for the district of Ocosingo, which encompassed the entire Lacandón jungle and its nearby townships under a PRD-CIOAC-Zapatista coalition.

CIOAC communities, leaders, and activists played a key role at all stages of elections: in campaign rallies, canvassing and mobilizing voters on election day, serving as party representatives in electoral precincts, defending the ballots, and then leading postelection demonstrations to denounce fraud.[24] The CIOAC social base was critical in mobilizing opposition anti-PRI votes in the two CIOAC regional strongholds: Margaritas/Comitán in southeastern Chiapas and Simojovel in the northern highland region. But the CIOAC was also heavily involved in gubernatorial races in 1994 and 2000.

---

local leaders played a key role in some of these events. In fact Ejido Veracruz, the hometown of Antonio Vázquez and other key leaders of CIOAC, was a hotspot of anti-Protestant violence by Catholic community members. (Anonymous interview with a Seventh-Day Adventist from Ejido Veracruz, 2010). For a thorough examination of dynamics of religious violence in Chiapas, see Rivera Farfán et al. (2005).

[22] Interviews with Antonio Hernández and Límbano Vázquez. See also Sánchez (1999) and Mattiace (2003).

[23] Interview with Araceli Burguete, 2009.

[24] Chapter 6 deals extensively with the motivations that led some CIOAC leaders and members of Catholic-sponsored rural indigenous cooperatives and movements to join the EZLN.

The 1994 Zapatista rebellion had a major effect in redefining socio-electoral coalition-making strategy across Mexico's indigenous regions. The political impact of the EZLN was even greater in Margaritas because Tojolabal communities from the eastern part of the municipality had become a bastion of Zapatism and the headquarters of the rebel group. After a first unsuccessful round of peace negotiations between the federal government and the EZLN, the Zapatistas decided to support the candidacy of Amado Avendaño to the governorship of Chiapas in 1994. A respected journalist and a life-long friend and collaborator of Bishop Samuel Ruiz, Avendaño received the support of a PRD-Zapatista coalition backed by the state's major rural indigenous movements, the CIOAC included. Despite Avendaño's personal charisma and the tremendous social support he received from organized communal organizations and movements, he lost the election amid major allegations of vote buying, voter intimidation, and fraud.[25]

After the fraudulent 1994 gubernatorial election, the EZLN adopted three major decisions that forced rural indigenous movements, including the CIOAC, to decide between the revolutionary and the reformist paths: (1) Zapatista commanders called on Chiapan social movements and civil society to boycott every single election in the state thereafter; (2) they called on their sympathizers and militant bases to establish de facto autonomous municipalities and regions and create parallel de facto governments backed by Convention 169 of the ILO; and (3) they called on EZLN participants and sympathizers to enter a phase of civil disobedience and reject participation in any government program.

These three initiatives triggered major splits within the CIOAC and led to divergent routes of social mobilization and political participation. The first major split was based partly on the question of electoral participation. The CIOAC splintered into two groups: (1) CIOAC-Independiente, a pro-EZLN network led by Antonio Hernández and Límbano Vázquez, one of the most influential catechists of the Lacandón jungle region; and (2) CIOAC-Histórico, a group that distanced itself from the EZLN, led by Luis Hernández, Antonio's brother, and Professor Roberto Alfaro.

Whereas Antonio Hernández and his colleagues from CIOAC-Independiente became a major force in favor of indigenous peoples' rights to autonomy and self-determination and threw their support behind the construction of de facto autonomous regions and municipalities, his brother Luis Hernández and his colleagues from CIOAC-Histórico decided to participate in the 1995 municipal election, despite the Zapatista veto. Falling only 550 votes short of victory in 1995, a candidate from the CIOAC-Histórico group ran again unsuccessfully in 1998, and finally won municipal office in 2001. This group remained in power until 2010.

Participation in two major government-sponsored programs for land redistribution was another issue of bitter contention. In the aftermath of the Zapatista rebellion, Chiapas experienced a dramatic wave of land invasions. In

---

[25] Interview with Amado Avendaño, 2000. I analyze this event in greater detail in Chapter 8.

Margaritas, peasants linked to the PRI, CIOAC, the EZLN, and a myriad other social movements engaged in a massive wave of land invasions. Between 1994 and 1997, federal and state governments launched two programs to regularize land tenure, bought invaded land property from private landholders, and granted titles to those who had occupied the land (Reyes, 1998).

While the EZLN urged most of its combatant bases and sympathizers not to enter into any agreement with the government, CIOAC-Histórico leaders encouraged their social base to accept the land and sign the agreements with the government. This strategic decision brought many of the CIOAC communities who had become Zapatistas and enrolled in CIOAC-Independiente back to CIOAC-Histórico. CIOAC members were among the major beneficiaries of these ad-hoc land reform programs propelled by the Zapatista rebellion. CIOAC-Histórico leaders framed this as the culmination of two decades of mobilization in the region and capitalized on these waves of redistribution in subsequent municipal elections from 2000 to 2007.

In summary, the historical evidence shows that the rise of the partisan Left to electoral power was closely associated with the rise of rural indigenous mobilization. Catholic communities and rural indigenous movements such as the CIOAC helped leftist parties develop a strong electoral base in Margaritas and fight fraud, and in exchange the parties embraced rural indigenous causes and provided institutional resources for continuous mobilization and for defending the human rights of CIOAC leaders and activists. The electoral growth of the partisan left in Margaritas directly contributed to encouraging greater indigenous mobilization, and this greater mobilization, in turn, facilitated local democratization.

Why the Rise to Power of Leftist Parties Led to Social Demobilization. Even though the CIOAC had participated in leftist electoral campaigns since the early 1980s, it was only in the aftermath of the 1994 Zapatista rebellion that the CIOAC-PRD alliance became a highly competitive electoral option (Sonnleitner, 2001). At the same time that Antonio Hernández and CIOAC-Independiente were embracing the more radical option presented by Zapatism and renouncing involvement in elections, Luis Hernández and other CIOAC-Histórico leaders embraced the electoral route and became increasingly moderate in their demands, discouraging radical forms of mobilization associated with Zapatism.

Antonio Vázquez, the CIOAC-PRD candidate for municipal power in Margaritas in 1995, had previously been sworn in as president of the de facto Zapatista municipality of San Pedro Michoacán in late 1994. After CIOAC-Histórico broke with Zapatism and a potential electoral victory in the municipality became a reality, Vázquez set aside radical ethnic demands during his campaign and emphasized a more peasant-farmer-oriented, class-based discourse in favor of land redistribution.

A few years later, during the 2001 election, CIOAC-Histórico leaders established a strategic alliance with the local business community and under a more moderate multi-class ticket won municipal power in Margaritas. A year earlier, a multiparty coalition had displaced the PRI from power in the governorship of Chiapas. By 2001, a leftist candidate had become governor of Chiapas in Tuxtla Gutiérrez and a CIOAC-supported PRD candidate had become mayor of Margaritas.

The shift toward moderate demobilization and deradicalization that had started in 1996 became even more evident after 2001. In fact, over the course of the first decade of the twenty-first century, the CIOAC in Margaritas became a political machine that served successive PRD administrations to maintain their position in power until 2010. Under the direct control of Luis Hernández and his colleagues, the CIOAC became a preferred channel for the distribution of private goods, particularly housing and home-improvement benefits. In less than a decade, the political culture of CIOAC was completely transformed from one of radical leaders and activists struggling for land redistribution and democracy to one in which CIOAC members demanded and engaged in clientelistic arrangements.

Ten years after the changeover of power at the state and municipal levels and after nearly a decade of CIOAC/PRD rule, peasant indigenous mobilization had come to an end in Margaritas. The CIOAC had become a fragmented political machine, the historical leaders of the movement were bitterly divided, and several of them faced accusations of corruption. In the 2010 election, the CIOAC-Histórico PRD candidate, Professor Alberto Alfaro, lost to the candidate of the Green Party (a historical ally of the PRI), who was supported by former CIOAC-Independiente leaders Antonio Hernández and Límbano Vázquez. A few months before the 2010 election, these rivalries escalated to physical violence between the two CIOAC factions. In a major historical irony, CIOAC leaders had contributed to the victory of a candidate closely associated with the PRI in Margaritas.

At the end of a long interview, in which he chronicled his personal life and the historical evolution of CIOAC, Professor Alfaro closed his recollections with a bitter observation. Thinking about the CIOAC leadership as a collectivity, he was sober in his judgment: "Everyone became corrupt." Antonio Hernández, Alfaro's political nemesis, ended a sequence of three long interviews on a similar note of disillusionment: "There are no more social movements in Margaritas, there are only political machines. Democracy has become a business of clientelistic exchanges of votes for private goods." In his nostalgic closing words, Hernández reflected on how the years of unity, programmatic politics, and independent mobilization against the PRI were lost in the past; social movements had faded after the Left and CIOAC came to power. Indeed, for him, the transition from single-party PRI hegemony to multiparty democracy had caused the transformation of "radicals into clients."[26]

Not every radical in Margaritas became a client, however. Deacon Eduardo López gave up political activism altogether after his family won a land plot in

---

[26] I borrow this phrase from Stokes (1995).

the new Ejido Tabasco 2000. As his former peers were moving into municipal power, he climbed to the top of the ecclesiastic ladder available to laymen by becoming one of the most influential Catholic deacons in Margaritas. Together with one of his sons – one of the first Tojolabal seminarians in the Diocese of San Cristóbal de Las Casas – López is engaged in further exploring the "inculturation" of the Tojolabal tradition and the memory of their own struggle for land into the Christian Gospel.

Some of López's catechist peers from nearby Ejido Tabasco went on to participate in powerful socioeconomic cooperatives devoted to the export of organic coffee to the United States and Western Europe. Still others remain active in Zapatism, as they try to keep the autonomous municipality of San Pedro Michoacán alive. With profound respect, López referred to the latter group as the "brothers in resistance."

THE POLITICS OF INDIGENOUS PROTEST *BEYOND* LAS MARGARITAS

The introduction of limited multiparty competition in Mexico's authoritarian regime changed the incentives for governance and dissent across rural indigenous regions beyond Margaritas. Although the rise of the Left in rural indigenous regions often resulted in the transformation of independent movements into clientelistic political machines, we have other cases in which movements splintered but became successful economic cooperatives focused on organic agriculture. In still other cases where leftist parties did not become major local actors, social movements either became NGOs focused on indigenous rights, or continued their struggles for indigenous rights in the streets. Social networks played a key mediating role.

From Social Movements to Leftist Electoral Machines

COCEI in Oaxaca. The story of the COCEI, one of the most successful rural indigenous movements of the 1970s and 1980s, is a near–mirror image of the life cycle of the CIOAC in Chiapas.[27] A Zapotec movement with a secular socialist leadership and a dense base of activists and communities linked to Catholic liberationist movements, the COCEI's initial demands for land redistribution in the 1970s were met with harsh repression. But after the 1977 reform that legalized all political parties and transformed the Mexican regime into an electoral autocracy, local governments slowly moved into "silver and lead" policies, combining coercion and concessions to "manage" collective dissent.[28]

As in Margaritas, COCEI leaders and activists responded to partial material concessions of land redistribution and harsh episodes of military and police repression with increased mobilization. Extensive interviews with Héctor

---

[27] For an insightful in-depth study of the COCEI, see Rubin (1997).
[28] Interview with Héctor Sánchez.

Sánchez and Leopoldo DeGyves, two of the original COCEI leaders, and with Bishop Emeritus Arturo Lona, a close ally of the COCEI in the 1980s, provide rich evidence that Catholic Bible study groups and social networks served as a ring of protection allowing the leaders to carry on their protest despite unlawful incarceration and assassination attempts. Social networks empowered the leaders to defy repression in the early 1980s when a communist coalition led by the COCEI and DeGyves won the municipal presidency of Juchitán in 1983 but was removed from office. The COCEI returned to power in 1989 and was in and out of office during the following twenty years.

The spread of electoral competition and the rise of the partisan left to local power was a critical factor in defining the life cycle of COCEI mobilization. Like the CIOAC in Margaritas, COCEI established a strategic coalition with progressive Catholics in opposition to U.S. SIL and Protestant missionaries and with leftist parties trying to make inroads in Oaxaca. The conflictive rise of the Left to local power in Juchitán – the political and cultural center of the Isthmus of Tehuantepec – was associated with a steep rise in social mobilization led by the COCEI.

But after Héctor Sánchez won office and the government and the PRI did not prevent him from becoming the lawful mayor of Juchitán in 1989, the COCEI movement entered a period of gradual deradicalization, demobilization, and internal fragmentation. Facing a PRI-dominated state governorship, Sánchez and other COCEI-PRD mayors initially discouraged the total demobilization of their social base and sponsored episodic mobilizations mainly as part of their negotiations with state PRI authorities for government transfers.[29]

Over time, like the CIOAC in Margaritas, the COCEI slowly transformed itself into a powerful clientelistic machine that became a critical actor in the electoral victory of every PRD candidate in Juchitán and a key organization for governance and policy making. Like the CIOAC, the COCEI splintered into rival factions, COCEI-Oficial and COCEI-Histórica, led by two of its original leaders. Like the CIOAC leaders, all major COCEI leaders have faced serious accusations of corruption. And as in Margaritas, in the 2010 election, the rivalry between the two COCEI factions enabled the return of the PRI to power in Juchitán.[30]

From Social Movements to Capitalist Enterprises and NGOs

Not all rural indigenous movements in Mexico became political machines as electoral competition absorbed social protest. The experience of rural indigenous movements with Catholic leadership and a Catholic social base show that

[29] This is part of a more general phenomenon of state-sponsored mobilization. Robertson (2007 and 2010) shows that in negotiating federal transfers to the regions, Russian governors with weak connections to Moscow sponsored societal mobilization to pressure federal authorities for more generous transfers. For a similar argument on urban protest in Mexico, see Bruhn (2008).

[30] The rise to power of the Left in the city of Juchitán transformed most of the COCEI's Catholic base into a powerful clientelistic machine, but Catholic grassroots organizations elsewhere in the Diocese of Tehuantepec followed a different path. See discussion later in the text.

after the Left came to power and the movements splintered, progressive Catholic priests and catechists were able to guide the transformation of some of these movements into powerful agricultural cooperatives and influential NGOs for indigenous rights. Rather than follow the path of clientelistic machine politics, these movements became successful capitalist social enterprises or professional interest groups.

Yomlej in Chilón. One paradigmatic case in this category is a network of social organizations that emerged in northeastern Chiapas. Sponsored by the Jesuit Mission of Bachajón, Chilón, a series of grassroots organizations agitating for land redistribution and the defense and promotion of human rights and indigenous rights emerged in northeastern Chiapas in the second half of the 1980s. CDLI, Xi-Nich, and Yomlej soon gave rise to one of the most powerful social movements in Chiapas denouncing the 1992 liberalization of land tenure, the Quincentenary of the Conquest of the Americas, and the repressive actions adopted by the Chiapas government to implement the unpopular 1992 reform.

In the municipality of Chilón, Manuel Gómez, the son of one of the first catechists of the Jesuit Mission and one of the leading figures of the Jesuit education system of private middle and high schools for Tzeltal rural villagers, worked hard to establish a strategic alliance between Yomlej and the PRD.[31] As a veterinary student at the National University in Mexico City in the 1980s, Gómez had established political links with leftist parties in Mexico City. As part of this alliance, Yomlej became a major promoter of the PRD in the 1991 and 1994 elections in Chiapas, and the PRD in Chiapas embraced Yomlej causes.

With the support of Yomlej and the vast Catholic social network, Gómez became the PRD candidate for the municipal presidency of Chilón for the 1995 election. Although he won the popular vote, he faced a local insurrection by the Chinchulines, a group of Tzeltal peasants affiliated with the PRI who launched a major attack to prevent Gómez and the PRD from taking office. After setting Gómez's house on fire and forcing his family into exile in Mexico City, and in the midst of similar actions by other PRI-affiliated groups who were fighting against the expansion of Zapatista-sponsored de facto autonomous municipalities, Yomlej and the Catholic-sponsored networks served as a protective shield that enabled Gómez to transform fear into opportunity. Even though the national PRD leadership advised him to stay in Mexico City, and the PRI governor of Chiapas warned him that he had no control over the Chinchulines, Gómez returned to Chilón and took office amid major mobilization.

[31] This section is based on in-depth interviews with Manuel Gómez and his family and with members of the pastoral team of the Jesuit Mission of Bachajón, particularly with Fathers Oscar González, SJ and Felipe J. Ali Modad, SJ, and catechists Gilberto Moreno and Don Manuel. For the Jesuits' own narrative of this process, see Misión Jesuita de Bachajón (2010). Chávez (2005) provides an insightful analysis of the work of Manuel Gómez and the Jesuit mission in the provision of private secondary education in the region and of how these projects served Gómez as a social platform to become one of the most influential social and political leaders in Chilón.

Once in office, like Sánchez and COCEI in Juchitán, Oaxaca, Gómez did not encourage Yomlej to demobilize completely because he faced a hostile PRI governor. Although Gómez did not recruit his municipal cabinet from within Yomlej, the organizational infrastructure of the Jesuit Mission and Yomlej served as institutional channels for the distribution of public goods and services during his term in office. As the PRI and the PRD alternated in power in Chilón during the late 1990s and throughout the 2000s, successive leftist government authorities incrementally discouraged Yomlej from mobilizing and fighting for radical (ethnic) causes associated with the EZLN, particularly after 2000, when the PRI lost gubernatorial power. Yomlej slowly became a political machine and some of its leaders faced similar charges of corruption and clientelism to those in Margaritas. Chilón's cycle of mobilization gradually faded throughout the 2000s.

Yomlej eventually dissolved, but the social base behind the movement served as the social infrastructure for the construction of two other social enterprises: rural cooperatives involved in organic agriculture (particularly export coffee through networks associated with the fair trade movement) and NGOs for the promotion of indigenous ethnic rights. Whereas the CIOAC and COCEI experienced a dramatic transformation from radical rural indigenous movements to clientelistic leftist electoral machines, Yomlej became a successful capitalist social enterprise and a network of indigenous-rights NGOs that began to operate as (social) interest groups rather than social movements. Unlike CIOAC and COCEI leaders who eventually faced numerous charges of corruption or who joined the PRI, Gómez went back to civilian life and continued to participate in the Jesuit Mission's education system.

The Jesuit Mission and the powerful network of Bible study groups, cooperatives and communal organizations in Chilón played a key role in preventing Yomlej from becoming a clientelistic political machine like the CIOAC and COCEI. In fact, the Jesuit Mission served as a powerful force for horizontal accountability and the dense Catholic communal networks served as an effective means of vertical accountability for leaders like Gómez and other catechists and deacons who had been actively involved in the cycles of social protest of the 1980s and 1990s. These informal mechanisms of societal accountability raised the costs for Yomlej leaders of becoming absorbed into local clientelistic politics.

When Social Movements Prevail

UCIRI in Oaxaca. The UCIRI, one of the most influential social cooperatives for the export of organic coffee in the developing world, represents a paradigmatic case of rural movements that remain active despite the rise and fall of cycles of mobilization elsewhere in the country.[32] A network of

---

[32] For this section I rely mainly on interviews with Bishop Emeritus Lona and on the work by Hernández Díaz (2001) and Norget (2004).

cooperatives spearheaded in the 1980s by the pastoral team of Bishop Arturo Lona from the Diocese of Tehuantepec in the Zapotec/Mixe highlands, the UCIRI transformed itself from a movement for land redistribution to a dense network of coffee cooperatives and NGOs focused on organic agriculture and the promotion of indigenous rights and cultures.

For the past three decades, the UCIRI has been a key participant in Oaxaca's cycles of social mobilization, fighting for land redistribution, indigenous rights, and respect for human rights. Unlike one of its longtime social and political allies, the COCEI, in the neighboring municipality of Juchitán, the UCIRI did not become a clientelistic political machine but remained a powerful independent force for active mobilization in the Tehuantepec region.

Two factors account for the persistence of the UCIRI as a social movement. First, unlike the valley of Juchitán, the PRD did not become a major political force in the Zapotec/Mixe highlands, home of the UCIRI. The adoption in 1995 of an indigenous customary law system for the selection of municipal presidents in these Mixe municipalities, by which all political parties were banned from participating in the selection of municipal authorities, who were elected by indigenous customary practices, prevented the consolidation of the Left in the Zapotec/Mixe highlands region. In the absence of multiparty competition for the selection of mayors, the UCIRI was not drawn into partisan politics and remained a major social and political force for local governance.

A second factor is that as in the case of Yomlej in Chilón where the Jesuit Mission and the Catholic social networks served as mechanisms of accountability for social leaders, in the case of the UCIRI and the Mixe/Zapotec municipalities, the pastoral team of the Diocese of Tehuantepec, the Catholic Bible study groups and the dense associational networks in the region became a powerful force for societal accountability. This social monitoring kept UCIRI leaders and activists from involvement in clientelism and corruption.

Single-Party Hegemony and the Absence of Social Movements

To most indigenous activists from the highlands and eastern Chiapas, the Zoque of western Chiapas represent a mystery.[33] Even though they are part of one of the most contentious states in Mexico, the Zoque of Chiapas did not take part in any of the major cycles of mobilization in the state. They did not attend the 1974 Indigenous Congress; they did not participate in the major statewide demonstrations to condemn the 500th anniversary of the Conquest of the Americas in 1992; they did not protest against the end of land reform and the liberalization of land tenure in 1992; and they were not part of the EZLN uprising in 1994 or of the major negotiations for indigenous rights of autonomy and self-determination in 1995 and 1996 (Lisbona, 2006).

Geography, demography, and the absence of competition offer a solution to the enigma. The Zoque were cut off from all other indigenous ethnic groups

[33] See interviews with Andrés Díaz (Simojovel) and Deacons Gómez (Chilón) and López (Margaritas).

in Chiapas when Bishop Samuel Ruiz redrew Chiapas's ecclesiastic boundaries in 1963 and left them outside of the Diocese of San Cristóbal de Las Casas – Chiapas's foremost indigenous ecclesiastic jurisdiction. Because the western mountains were relatively inaccessible from San Cristóbal de Las Casas, and because Zoque municipalities were not experiencing similar levels of religious competition to those where other indigenous ethnic groups lived, Ruiz assigned the Zoque to the Diocese of Tuxtla Gutiérrez, where they became a minority group in a predominantly mestizo jurisdiction.

Faced with Pentecostal competition, the Diocese of Tuxtla became charismatic. For the most part unattended by the Tuxtla clergy, the only pastoral actions in favor of the Zoque region involved charitable donations brought by Catholic charismatic preachers when they traveled through the region to spread the gospel of spiritual healing. Unlike most other indigenous ethnic groups in Chiapas, Zoque Indians did not have the organizational resources to protest major policy shocks in the streets.

But the electoral geography of the state also politically marginalized the Zoque region. Federal electoral boundaries grouped Zoque villages with predominantly mestizo municipalities. For leftist opposition parties active in eastern and northern Chiapas, crossing the western mountains into the Zoque region was particularly costly. With few networks and leadership structures to build on and high logistic and transportation costs, the PCM, PSUM, and later the PRD did not make any significant inroads into the Zoque region. Zoque Indians had neither the organizational networks that resulted from dynamics of religious competition nor the institutional resources that resulted from multiparty competition and facilitated independent mobilization elsewhere in Chiapas.

The story of the CIOAC is relevant here. The CIOAC became a major actor in the Zoque region five years after the demise of the state's protracted cycle of rural indigenous protest when CIOAC militants expanded into the Zoque region with the full support of the PRD state government. As part of a reform of the state's federal districts, in 2005 half of the Zoque municipalities were grouped together with the Tzotzil highlands where the CIOAC had been a major actor of independent mobilization and had become a major political machine. It was only after this reform that the CIOAC entered the Zoque region and established one of the first social organizations in the area. Had the reform taken place in the 1970s or 1980s, leftist parties and the CIOAC or other organizations might have penetrated into the region and the Zoque municipalities would have not remained entirely on the sidelines of the state's history.

CONCLUSION

Although students of social movements in advanced capitalist democracies have assumed for a long time that social protest tends to monotonically increase as countries transition from authoritarian rule to democracy, in recent years the study of social protest in nondemocratic contexts has forced us to rethink the canonical political opportunity hypothesis. Scholars have found that government repression may stimulate rather than deter social protest, while the spread of electoral competition may deter rather than stimulate protest.

In Chapter 1 we developed a theory of social protest in autocracies centered on the effect of electoral competition. Our key argument was that social protest was endogenous to electoral competition – limited competition under electoral fraud stimulated street protest and higher levels of competition in relatively free and fair elections contributed to demobilization. Rather than a positive linear relationship, we outlined an electoral rationale to support the inverted-U hypothesis first discussed by Tocqueville (1858/1983) and more recently by Eisinger (1973).

The life stories related in this chapter provide important evidence showing that the introduction of multiparty elections in autocracies indeed provides powerful incentives for the rise of socio-electoral coalitions between independent grassroots movements and nascent opposition parties. Together with the statistical results discussed in Chapter 2, the evidence in this chapter strongly suggests that the growth of leftist opposition parties and the competition for indigenous votes did have a causal effect on the rise and fall of Mexico's cycle of indigenous mobilization.

At the initial stages of state-controlled multiparty elections, electoral incentives drove leftist parties to build political coalitions with rural indigenous movements and to become major promoters of peasant indigenous mobilization. Once the Left became a competitive force, however, electoral incentives transformed leftist party leaders and candidates into a major force for the de-radicalization and institutionalization of rural indigenous movements. As the life stories recounted here showed, social movement leaders and activists were not passive observers of this process, but leading actors of the transformation of social mobilization and local democratization.

We have seen how incumbent authorities in electoral autocracies did not remain passive as opposition parties try to establish political coalitions with social movements to oust the ruling party from power. As the life stories in this chapter reveal, governors tried to co-opt independent leaders and activists through policies of partial material concessions and sought to keep protest under control via nonlethal repression.

One of the most perplexing questions in the study of social movements is the recurrent finding that repression sometimes deters but others stimulate social protest (Davenport, 2000 and 2005). The life histories reported in this chapter showed that the autocrats' success in co-opting social leaders and activists or deterring their dissident actions was contingent on the network connections of the targets. The stories from Margaritas demonstrated that leaders and activists with strong connections to decentralized Catholic social networks were more likely to defy government repression and to resist the temptations of co-optation – by the PRI or by opposition parties once in power. But leaders and activists that were part of centralized secular networks were more likely to give up their protest when facing unlawful arrest or when they were offered material selective incentives.

The findings of this chapter provide new evidence showing that the effect of government repression and co-optation is contingent on the nature of social networks. As Siegel (2011) has shown, the same act of government repression can have contradictory effects, depending on the network connections of the target population. Let me be clear about one point: I do not interpret the greater resilience of leaders connected to Catholic social networks to be an indication that the religious message of Jesus creates greater commitment to social protest than, say, the secular message of Marx; rather, my point is that dissidents who are part of decentralized associational networks are more likely to have the social assets that empower individuals to defy co-optation or deterrent attempts.

Because Catholic networks provided leaders with access to denser associational networks than did centralized networks, religion in this case provided rural indigenous leaders and activists with a safety shield to resist government co-optation and a protective ring to defy government repression. In the case of co-optation into leftist political parties and opposition governments, these same Catholic social networks and the clergy associated with them served as important sources of vertical and horizontal accountability that prevented the transformation of radicals into clients.

Although in this chapter I have shown that the advent of multiparty competition and the rise of opposition parties to power contributed to the ascent and demise of Mexico's cycle of indigenous protest, we need to assess two major developments that took place before the cycle came to a close: In the ascending phase of the cycle, protest became rebellion and demands for land redistribution became claims for ethno-territorial rights. We now turn to an explanation of the surprising transformation of peaceful indigenous protest into armed rebellion.

PART III

REBELLION

5

A Call to Arms

Regime Reversion Threats and the Escalation of Protest into Rebellion

Our understanding of the outbreak of insurgencies and civil wars has undergone an intellectual revolution in the past decade. Based on new cross-national datasets of domestic armed conflict, a predominantly quantitative literature has reached a new consensus: Poor countries ruled by failed states and with extensive natural resource-wealth are at greater risk of the onset of political violence than any other society in the world. This is a story about greed and poor governance; in these societies criminal groups recruit young unemployed men from poor rural villages in remote and mountainous areas, where the state has no presence or control, to plunder natural resources and remove those in power through guerrilla warfare.[1]

Although this influential account helps us distinguish countries at risk of insurgent collective action from those that are not, its main causal claims lose explanatory power as we try to account for the microdynamics of rebellions. Whereas GDP per capita, rurality or mountainous terrains are macro factors that help us explain why Guatemala but not Belgium experienced a major civil war in the second half of the twentieth century, these factors are less helpful in explaining why rural indigenous villagers living under practically identical economic and geographic conditions followed such different paths of collective action in Guatemala – some villagers joined the rebels, others became counter-insurgents, and others sought to remain neutral. Explanations based on time-invariant factors such as mountains and natural resources, moreover, are of little use to explain a fundamental aspect of rebellions: the timing of outbreak.

From a micro subnational perspective, dominant explanations of insurgency and civil war both over-predict and under-explain the extent of political violence. Because armed insurgencies and guerrilla warfare are phenomena in which micro village-level dynamics of recruitment and control are absolutely crucial (Kalyvas, 2006; Weinstein, 2006), these are not minor issues.

In Chapter 1 we developed an alternative explanation of the outbreak of insurgencies centered on the conditions that give rise to the transformation of

[1] See Collier (2000), Fearon and Laitin (2003), and Collier, et al. (2005).

social movements into armed insurgencies and to the escalation of peaceful protest into armed rebellion. Our goal was to add time, dynamics, agency and strategic interaction to the study of outbreaks of armed insurgencies. Building on the crucial finding in the cross-national quantitative literature that insurgencies are more likely in hybrid political regimes than in closed autocracies and established democracies, our focus was on the governance strategies that incumbents in electoral autocracies adopt to "manage" dissent in times of major economic crises or when governments adopt radical and unpopular economic policy shifts.

We argued that when incumbents adopt compensatory measures in the midst of major cycles of peaceful protest to offset the losses from exogenous economic shocks, protest intensifies but does not lead to rebellion. But when incumbents give up on concessions, adopt punitive strategies, and withdraw some of the limited political rights and liberties awarded in an earlier phase of liberalization, signaling a likely reversion to a closed autocracy, they will provide meaningful incentives to leaders and activists of social movements toward revolutionary action (see H.5)

In this argument the adoption of compensatory or punitive strategies depends on elite information and beliefs: they adopt punitive strategies only when they have information that leads them to believe that the aggrieved group is vulnerable to repression and would be easily demobilized through punitive measures. Yet in a context marked by information asymmetries, if elites repress, and the targeted group has the ability to resist, the elite response would unwittingly lead to revolutionary action.

The end of six decades of land reform and the liberalization of land tenure in the midst of a major cycle of rural indigenous mobilization in Mexico provide us with a unique opportunity for theory testing. My goal in this chapter is to test whether the adoption of this major neoliberal agrarian reform was indeed widely unpopular – as is generally assumed – and whether the governance strategies that Mexican authorities adopted to politically implement this radical reform contributed to the radicalization of peaceful indigenous protest.

Drawing on information from a national survey of rural residents conducted by the Mexican government one year before the approval of a major constitutional reform in 1992 that put an end to six decades of land reform and laid the legal basis for the liberalization of land tenure, in the first section of this chapter I show that the reform generated widespread grievances, frustration, and moral indignation in Mexico's rural countryside. I argue that this deep dissatisfaction explains the *timing* of indigenous rebellions in the 1990s, but does not explain the geographic spread of rebel activity; equally angry, frustrated, and morally outraged Indian peasants followed different strategies in response to the reform: most acquiesced, others took their grievances to the streets, and only a few took up arms.

Because governors, rather than national executives, were the gatekeepers of land reform, and because civilian police forces under their command were responsible for political repression in Mexico, the appropriate units of analysis for hypothesis testing are the states. To explain cross-regional variation, the chapter analyzes how governors dealt politically with the social challenges associated with a universally unpopular reform of traditional agricultural policies. I rely on statistical analysis and case studies.

Statistical results reported in the second part of the chapter show that, controlling for poverty, inequality, and rough terrain, indigenous rebel activity in the 1990s was most intense in Mexico's most authoritarian states with the worst records of human rights violations, particularly where governors adopted more repressive practices to keep subnational cycles of peasant indigenous protest under control. The analysis confirms the conditional nature of the theoretical argument: Autocratic states with no protest and states with protest but democratic structures experienced no rebellion; rebellion took place primarily in states where elites repressed powerful rural indigenous movements and utilized fraud to block any option for contestation through electoral means.

To overcome some of the limitations of the statistical analysis and to more effectively isolate the hypothesized causal effect of governance on the escalation of peaceful protest into armed rebellion, in the third section I present a paired comparison of the political strategies that the governors of the neighboring states of Chiapas and Oaxaca followed to implement the end of land reform and the liberalization of land tenure. I focus on two regions within these states that share many economic, demographic, ethnic, and geological features typically associated with insurgency. Furthermore, both share similar histories of social organization and both had progressive bishops following radical social practices in response to the spread of Protestant competition.

By isolating the political responses that elites in the two states adopted to implement agrarian neoliberal reforms in the Diocese of Tehuantepec (Oaxaca) and in the Diocese of San Cristóbal de Las Casas (Chiapas), I am able to show that the limited multicultural reforms the Oaxaca elite introduced and their recognition of major opposition electoral victories in municipal contests contributed to the prevalence of peaceful mobilization as the dominant strategy for expressing group social grievances in Tehuantepec. In contrast, the criminalization of protest and the elimination of electoral competition via blatant fraud and coercion led to the radicalization of peasant indigenous movements in Chiapas.

MEXICO'S INDIGENOUS INSURGENCY

Two decades after the partial liberalization of authoritarian rule, Mexico experienced a major wave of insurgent collective action. Unlike previous waves in the 1970s, in which university students had led urban insurrections and (non-indigenous) rural villagers had declared war on the Mexican state, this wave in the 1990s was predominantly rural and primarily indigenous. Although the Zapatista National Liberation Army (EZLN) was undisputedly the most prominent rebel group of this wave, a host of other less visible groups were active across southern and central states. The most important of these was the Popular Revolutionary Army (EPR).

EZLN

Founded in 1983 by northern Mexican middle-class university professors and students who had participated in rebel activities in the 1970s, the EZLN spread from its headquarters in the Lacandón jungle in eastern Chiapas to several indigenous municipalities across the state. Recruitment into the EZLN was slow from 1983 to 1988, but between 1989 and 1992 Zapatism became a mass movement in Chiapas. By the time the Zapatistas launched their first attack on the Mexican government and the army in 1994, they had a base that was estimated to include 2,500 to 5,000 full-time combatants and a dense network of community supporters throughout the state's foremost indigenous regions.

Even though open combat between the EZLN and the Mexican army lasted only twelve days, the conflict continued until 2001. As two rounds of peace negotiations took place between 1994 and 1997, the Zapatistas gained de facto control of small regions across one-third of Chiapas's municipalities, where they established parallel autonomous governments. Between 1996 and 2000, the EZLN battled an anti-insurgency campaign led by local paramilitary groups. These were poor, Mayan villagers with links to the PRI who battled their Zapatista neighbors for land and territorial control. By 2001, the EZLN controlled no more than one-tenth of the state's territory, organized under regional and local rebel autonomous governments.

Human rights NGOs and information from the MII Dataset estimate that 750 to 1,000 people died between 1994 and 2001 in conflicts associated with the Zapatista uprising. Most victims were members of the EZLN, but casualties also included members of the Mexican army, Indian peasants linked to the PRI, and social movement leaders. Approximately 500 people died in the first days of open combat and the rest were killed over the following seven years, including the infamous massacre of Chenalhó, in which 42 Zapatista sympathizers were assassinated by heavily armed Indian peasants, some of whom have been identified by survivors as members of local paramilitary groups linked to the local PRI. Between 1994 and 2000, approximately 20,000 people were displaced from their homes to other parts of the state as a result of the conflict.

EPR

A second rural indigenous uprising took place in the southern state of Guerrero, where the EPR, a predominantly rural army, declared war on the Mexican government and armed forces in 1996. After its first public appearance, in which EPR commanders read a communiqué in Spanish and Nahua to denounce a history of repression in the state of Guerrero, over the course of the next two years, EPR forces launched a scattered series of attacks against military and police stations and planted bombs in urban areas in the southern states of

Guerrero and Oaxaca. Less visible acts took place in the central states, including Michoacán, Morelos, Mexico State, and the Huasteca region of Hidalgo and Veracruz.

Little is known about the leadership structure of the EPR, but there is strong evidence suggesting that the founders were survivors, relatives, and associates of members of the Army of the Poor – an army of rural teachers and peasants from the southern state of Guerrero that fought a popular war against the Mexican government in the 1970s (Sierra, 2003). The community base of the EPR was sparse, but the group developed alliances with radical communal indigenous groups and movements that had suffered some of the harshest repression in the previous two decades, particularly in the Guerrero highlands, southern and western Oaxaca, central Chiapas, and the Huasteca region of Hidalgo and Veracruz. This was a secular, leftist base, which did not join the EZLN in 1994.

In 1998, the EPR underwent a significant series of splits. Information from the Mexican national press documents fewer than 100 combat-related casualties in attacks led by the EPR and related guerrilla groups. Unlike the Zapatistas, EPR forces did not establish any meaningful territorial control. EPR forces remained active beyond 2001.

MEASURING INDIGENOUS INSURGENT COLLECTIVE ACTION

I define indigenous rebellions as sustained acts of social contestation undertaken by organized *armed indigenous groups* whose aim is to overthrow a political regime, change the structure of property rights, or transform the political and territorial geography of a country by means of violent action (De Nardo, 1985). Because indigenous armed rebel groups have always been militarily weaker than their opponents, they resort to the military strategy of the weak: guerrilla warfare.

Note that I do not define an indigenous rebellion in terms of ethnic goals, but in terms of the ethnic affiliation of its participants. An indigenous guerrilla group must be wholly or principally constituted of members of indigenous ethnic groups, but indigenous rebel groups may or may not make demands for ethnic autonomy and self-determination. Under this definition, I typify a predominantly indigenous guerrilla group fighting for peasant demands under a class-based Marxist-Leninist program as an indigenous rebellion if rebels belong to or operate in an indigenous region (like the EPR), even if they do not make ethnic claims (like the EZLN prior to 1995). I assume that the politicization of ethnicity by insurgent groups is endogenous to the process of mobilization.[2]

To operationalize indigenous rebellions, I follow Gurr and Moore (1997) and use a seven-point scale of rebel activity: 0 – none; 1 – rebels spread propaganda among villagers; 2 – rebels engage in sporadic robbery, kidnapping, or

---

[2] This will be the subject of Part IV of this book.

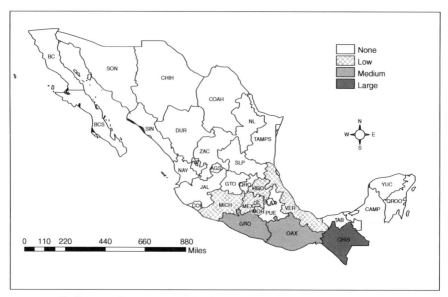

MAP 5.1. Indigenous insurgent activity in Mexico, 1994–1997.

destruction of private property; 3 – rebel groups of fewer than 100 combatants engage in sporadic attacks on security forces and government buildings; 4 – rebel groups of more than 100 but fewer than 500 combatants engage in frequent attacks in several localities; 5 – rebel groups of more than 500 but fewer than 1,000 combatants engage in frequent attacks in several regions; 6 – rebel groups of more than 1,000 but fewer than 5,000 combatants engage in frequent attacks and gain territorial control of several localities within a region; and 7 – rebel groups with more than 5,000 combatants engage in frequent attacks and gain territorial control over several regions within a country.

I use three criteria to decide whether any of these actions would qualify as "indigenous": (1) the action must take place in a municipality that at any time between 1970 and 2000 had at least 10 percent indigenous population (the national mean); (2) there must be some indication that members of indigenous groups participated in the rebel action; and (3) there must be some indication that the rebel group enjoys some degree of support among indigenous communities and municipalities.

Drawing on information from eight Mexican daily national newspapers on activities by the EZLN, the EPR, and EPR-related guerrilla groups, I created a seven-point scale of indigenous guerrilla activity in Mexico for the 1994–1997 period. Map 5.1 shows the geography of rural indigenous insurgency by Mexican state. Guerrilla activity was clustered in and near the southern and central states, particularly the poorest, most rural, and most unequal states in the country.

Because of the EZLN, Chiapas scored large-scale violence (Level 6), but it was the only state to do so, and the EZLN had no military presence outside of Chiapas. The EPR, in contrast, operated mainly in the neighboring states of Guerrero and Oaxaca, but it was only able to undertake sporadic, albeit deadly, attacks (Level 3) between 1996 and 1997. EPR and former EPR forces had a less visible presence (Levels 1 and 2) in central states, including the Huasteca region in Hidalgo and Veracruz, and in the central states of Morelos, Mexico, and Michoacán.

ACCOUNTING FOR THE TIMING OF REBELLION: ECONOMIC CRISES OR POLICY SHIFTS?

Whereas the economics literature on insurgencies and civil wars suggests that major economic crises and major commodity price shocks may stimulate rebellions, a significant number of studies in anthropology and sociology suggest that radical policy shifts, often associated with economic globalization and market-oriented reforms, provide incentives for insurgent collective action. To assess whether economic crises or commodity price shocks triggered Mexico's wave of indigenous insurgency in the 1990s, I graphically analyze the likely effect of inflation, currency devaluations, and fluctuations in the international price of coffee on the timing of rebellion.

Figures 5.1a and 5.1b plot the evolution of rural indigenous rebellions alongside the evolution of major macroeconomic indicators. A simple visual analysis shows that the peaks of currency devaluation and inflation of the 1980s were *not* associated with the outbreak of rebellion and that the major macroeconomic collapse of 1995 followed, rather than preceded, the Zapatista uprising.

Figure 5.1c plots changes in the international price of coffee. A visual inspection shows that the outbreak of rural indigenous rebellions took place soon after a dramatic collapse in the price of coffee. Although it remains to be tested whether coffee-producing regions were more likely to rebel, of the three variables associated with economic "crises," the coffee price collapse could be the closest to a trigger of rebellion.

To assess the effect of major policy shifts on the onset of Mexico's indigenous insurgency, Figure 5.1d shows two vertical lines on the time series of rebellion, which identify the policy reforms that entailed the most radical transformation in Mexican agricultural life in the last quarter of the twentieth century – the 1992 constitutional reform that put an end to six decades of land reform and established the legal basis for the liberalization of land tenure and the coming into effect of NAFTA in 1994. The Quincentenary of the Conquest of the Americas made 1992 a highly symbolic year for indigenous peoples. Because most Mexican Indians still lived in rural areas in 1990, 1992 became a critical year for discussions of peasant and ethnic identities – the "two eyes" of indigenous peoples, as Mattiace's (2003) book reminds us.

A simple visual inspection shows that the wave of rural indigenous rebellions of the 1990s began one year after the 1992 reforms, when the Mexican

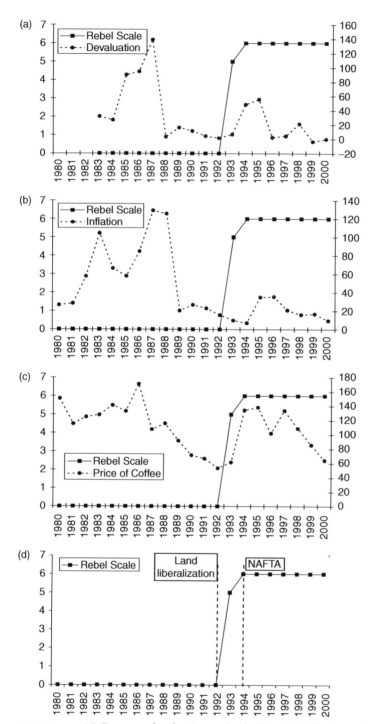

FIGURE 5.1. (a) Currency devaluation and rebellion. (b) Inflation and rebellion.
(c) International coffee price and rebellion. (d) Neoliberal agricultural policy reform
and rebellion.

TABLE 5.1. *Views of Rural Population about Termination of Land Reform Program and Liberalization of Land Tenure in Mexico, November 1991*

	Total	Gvt. buys product	Others	Statistical significance
Believes land redistribution should continue (%)	78.3	81.3	76.9	*
Opposes peasants enjoying the right to sell their land plots to private buyers (%)	63.6	74.7	58.2	***
Believes rich will buy most land from poor (%)	69.5	76.9	66.0	***
Believes reform betrays principles of Mexican Revolution (%)	75.8	75.0	75.9	

*** Significant at the 0.01 level; **Significant at the 0.05 level; * Significant at the 0.1 level
Source: Oficina de la Presidencia, "Ejido: Reforma al artículo 27 constitucional", November 1991.

army discovered a Zapatista training camp and the two forces engaged in open conflict. The fact that 1992 was a major stimulus for rural indigenous mobilization is not new in the narrative of this book. Recall that the statistical analyses in Chapter 2 showed that a dummy variable identifying the years following the 1992 reform was a powerful predictor of the intensity of peaceful indigenous protest. What is new in this part of the narrative, however, is that the reform may have also triggered a wave of violent mobilization.

A series of national surveys conducted by the Office of the President in Mexico in the years prior to the constitutional reform provide the most compelling evidence of the importance of the 1992 agrarian reforms for understanding the radicalization of rural collective action in Mexico. Table 5.1 summarizes results from a representative national survey of rural villagers of their views about the end of the country's six-decade-long program of land redistribution and the liberalization of land tenure.

The evidence reveals that the Mexican peasantry nearly universally opposed the reform. As shown in the first column (total), more than three-quarters of Mexico's rural residents believed that land redistribution should continue and two-thirds opposed the liberalization of land tenure and believed that the reform would enable the rich to buy the land from the poor. Finally, more than three-quarters of Mexican rural residents believed that the reform betrayed the main principles of the Mexican Revolution.

These views hold constant regardless of differences in access to land, income level, partisanship affiliations, and place of residence. It is revealing, however, that the only statistically significant difference among rural residents is between villagers whose agricultural products were bought at subsidized prices by the government and those whose were not. As the comparison between the second and the third columns shows, people in rural households who were more closely tied to government agencies for marketing of their products were more likely to oppose the reforms. This shows that Mexican rural dwellers were perfectly aware that the end of land reform and the liberalization of land tenure entailed the withdrawal of federal subsidies and the end of the postrevolutionary pact between the Mexican (PRI) state and the peasantry.

The survey evidence unambiguously shows that Mexico's major neoliberal agricultural reform was a deeply unpopular measure among Mexico's rural residents. It was a major source of *relative deprivation* because rural villagers felt the reform had not achieved its goals and therefore should continue. It was a source of *economic insecurity* because most people believed that the reform allowed the rich to get their land back and would therefore undo the achievements of six decades of land reform. It was also a major source of *moral indignation* because most rural villagers believed the reform betrayed the historical basis on which the ejido system had been built – Emiliano Zapata's revolutionary slogan that "land belongs to those who work it."[3]

The deep-rooted emotions evoked by the end of land reform and the liberalization of land tenure among Mexico's rural residents is a powerful indicator of the likely triggering effect the neoliberal agrarian reforms had on the outbreak of rural indigenous insurgent collective action in the 1990s. Yet although these deep negative emotions were almost universally shared by the Mexican peasantry, the geography of insurgency discussed in Map 5.1 shows that rebel activity took place only in a few regions. This fact crucially indicates that the effect of grievances and moral indignation on the escalation of protest into rebellion must have been conditional on other factors. To identify these conditions, we first need to assess through regression analyses the economic and political determinants of the spatial distribution of rebel activity across Mexican states.

ACCOUNTING FOR CROSS-REGIONAL VARIATION:
STATE-LEVEL REBELLIOUS ACTIVITY

The Dependent Variable

Rebellion. The *level of indigenous rebel activity*, 1994–1997, is the dependent variable under analysis in this section. The index of rebel activity shows that 74 percent of Mexico's thirty-one states experienced no rebel activity at all and that Chiapas was the only state where large-scale rebellion took place (Level 6). Two other southern states, Guerrero and Oaxaca, experienced moderate levels of violence (Level 3), and in five other cases in central Mexico, rebels had a weak presence (Level 1). Note that even though the index defines seven different categories, rebel activity clustered around these three levels.

Explanatory Factors

Because my argument about the escalation of protest into rebellion focuses on the various governance strategies that incumbent authorities follow to deal

---

[3] "La tierra es de quien la trabaja."

with peaceful social mobilization and on the institutional means for social contestation available to social movement participants, I test for two different explanatory factors: the state history of rural indigenous protest and the state level of autocracy/democracy. I test for the independent and joint effects of these variables, but the interaction of autocracy and protest more accurately captures the nature of the argument: a punitive strategy of governing rural indigenous protest may provide incentives for the escalation of peaceful mobilization into violence.

A History of Protest. Drawing on information from MII, I use the count of indigenous protest events per state as an indicator of *Protest*. This includes all collective actions from petitions to marches and sit-ins to land invasion and the occupation of government buildings. Even though some of these events may include some level of violence, I do not count them as rebel actions because it was social movements rather than armed rebel groups that led mobilization. To capture the history of protest, I use the cumulative count of protest for the 1975–1992 period. Rebel groups that build on the basis of community bonds and social capital (Weinstein, 2006) typically seek to recruit their combatant bases from among the most experienced social movement and grassroots leaders and activists. When leaders and activists join rebel groups, it is usually after long periods of peaceful mobilization. To adjust for the size of indigenous population, I test for the per capita history of protest. As discussed in Chapter 2, the southern states of Chiapas and Oaxaca experienced the most intense cycles of rural indigenous mobilization, followed by the central states of Hidalgo and Michoacán and the states of Tabasco and Veracruz in the Gulf of Mexico.

Authoritarian Governance. I use Hernández's (2000) composite index of subnational autocracy/democracy as an indicator of authoritarian governance, *Autocracy*. Hernández uses electoral and human rights indicators to measure subnational regimes: (1) electoral competition in state legislatures (1989–1997); (2) opposition seats in state legislatures (1989–1997); (3) alternation in gubernatorial office (1989–1997); (4) human rights violations per 1,000 inhabitants as measured by independent NGOs (1995); and (5) complaints on state-level human rights violations issued by the National Human Rights Commission (1990–1996). Using principal component analysis, Hernández's index of subnational autocracy/democracy in Mexico was calculated for the 1989–1997 period. The index captures two dimensions of critical importance to my argument: the unconstrained and punitive powers of governors and the absence of electoral channels for independent political action. The index shows that states where governors followed the most autocratic practices were clustered in the southern and central parts of the country and the least autocratic in northern regions. Until the mid-1990s, Chiapas was the most autocratic Mexican state.

I test for the interaction of a state's history of protest and authoritarian governance, *Protest* x *Autocracy*; this interaction term tests for the effect of protest on insurgency conditional on the unconstrained and repressive behavior of subnational elites (see H.5).

Controls

Following the quantitative literature on insurgencies and civil war, I use state GDP per capita to test for the effect of *Economic Development* on rebel activity and a Gini index of inequality to test for the effect of *Income Inequality* (Hernández, 2000). I use mean elevation per state as a proxy for mountainous terrain (*Mountains*) and the proportion of indigenous population (*Indigenous %*) to control for a state's ethnolinguistic structure. Finally, I include a lagged rebel action variable to assess whether rebellion is path-dependent (*Rebel activity 1970s*). We have strong historical evidence of the leadership continuity between the wave of urban and rural insurgencies of the 1960s and 1970s and the indigenous wave of the 1990s. I create a seven-point scale of guerrilla activity by state for the 1965–1977 period based on information from Castellanos (2007).

Statistical Model

Given the ordinal nature of the dependent variable, I use ordered probit models. I test for the outbreak of rebellion by running a cross-sectional model using the index of state-level rebellion for the 1994–1997 period – the time when the EZLN, the EPR, and related forces first appeared. It is important to note that the small size of the sample (N=31) and the skewed nature of the distribution of rebel action across states (70 percent zero scores and only one state with a high level of violence) introduce considerable statistical challenges. To partially overcome these problems, I tested for different specifications of the dependent variable. I first ran one set of models using the actual scores of the six-point scale. I then recoded all states into a three-point scale: none, low, and medium/high rebel activity. Finally, I tested for a binary scale: no rebellion or some rebellion activity.

Although results are consistent across models, given the high levels of uncertainty associated with point predictions in the models using the six-point scale, I only present and discuss models using the three-point and binary scales. An additional challenge is that many of the economic and political factors are correlated. To partially account for this problem I ran separate models with different economic variables and estimated robust standard errors. Despite these partial solutions to the statistical problems, results should be taken with caution.

Results

Table 5.2 summarizes the results. Models 1 and 2 test for the standard *economic structures* and geographic variables used in cross-national studies of insurgency and civil war, excluding sociopolitical processes. If one is only

TABLE 5.2. *Ordered Probit and Probit Models of Levels of Indigenous Rebel Activity by Mexican State for the 1994–1997 Period*

	Model 1 (3-point scale)	Model 2 (3-point scale)	Model 3 (3-point scale)	Model 4 (3-point scale)	Model 5 (binary scale)	Model 6 (binary scale)
Economic structures						
Economic development (ln GDP/capita)	-3.296**		1.256	1.719	2.414	2.947
	(1.407)		(1.914)	(2.276)	(2.045)	(2.149)
Income inequality (Gini index)		15.669**				
		(6.889)				
Sociopolitical processes						
Protest, 1975–1992			0.419	0.233	0.577**	0.455*
			(0.264)	(0.200)	(0.273)	(0.246)
Autocracy, 1989–1997			2.866***	0.899	2.461**	0.854
			(1.027)	(0.881)	(0.993)	(1.104)
Protest × Autocracy				0.768**		0.615**
				(0.322)		(0.274)
Controls						
Indigenous (%)	8.501***	7.349**				
	(2.739)	(3.459)				
Mountains (ln altitude)	0.531*	0.408**	0.759**	1.121**	1.037**	1.391***
	(0.309)	(0.161)	(0.381)	(0.445)	(0.424)	(0.514)
Rebel activity, 1970s	0.593**	0.601***	0.364***	0.518***	0.012	0.079
	(0.234)	(0.182)	(0.128)	(0.149)	(0.134)	(0.116)
Cut 1	-20.985	12.530	19.126	25.243		
Cut 2	-18.740	15.009	21.849	28.784		
Constant					-30.532	-37.185*
					(19.454)	(20.983)
N	31	31	31	31	31	31
Log-Likelihood	-9.495	-9.677	-5.959	-4.994	-4.812	-4.289
Chi-squared	15.87	18.58	13.49	17.85	13.53	18.03
Significance	0.0032	0.001	0.019	0.006	0.018	0.006
Pseudo R^2	0.587	0.579	0.748	0.782	0.728	0.757
BIC	-66.859	-66.494	-70.497	-68.994	-76.224	-73.837

***Significant at the 0.01 level; ** Significant at the 0.05 level; * Significant at the 0.1 level. Robust standard errors in parentheses.

controlling for (1) prior levels of rebellion, (2) the state's mountainous terrain, and (3) the state's ethnic structure, then per capita GDP would seem to be a good predictor of rural indigenous insurgent activity: Insurgencies were more likely in less economically developed states than in wealthier regions. Using the same controls, income inequality also seems to be a strong predictor of indigenous insurgent collective action: Rebel activity was more likely in the most unequal states. A prior history of guerrilla activity and mountainous terrain are good predictors of insurgency.

The inclusion of sociopolitical variables associated with a state's history of rural indigenous protest and the autocracy/democracy index in Models 3 and 4 transforms the regression outcomes in significant ways. One of the most important transformations is that all variables associated with the states' economic structures drop out of statistical significance. At the same time, Models 3 and 4 gain in overall explanatory capacity. In Model 3 autocratic governance becomes the strongest predictor of levels of insurgent violence. Model 4 shows that the effect of protest on rebellion is conditional on autocratic governance. Using a different specification of the dependent variable, Model 5 provides additional evidence showing that protest and autocratic governance are important determinants of rebellion. Model 6 confirms that the autocratic handling of indigenous protest is associated with higher levels of rebel activity.

A simple statistical simulation based on Model 5 and using Clarify (Tomz, et al., 2003) shows that keeping all other variables at their mean values, democratizing states like San Luis Potosí (North) and Tabasco (Gulf) were less than 20 percent likely to experience any type of rebel activity. In contrast, autocratic states like Chiapas were more than 75 percent likely to experience insurgent collective action. Uncertainty associated with point predictions, however, should lead us to an important cautionary note. Confidence intervals are narrow at low levels of autocracy but wide at high levels of autocracy. Based on these results, we can confidently say that if Chiapas had the same levels of electoral competition and human rights respect experienced in the mid-1990s as San Luis Potosí or Tabasco, the state would have only experienced a mild rebellion or no rebellion at all. Yet we cannot say that if San Luis Potosí or Tabasco had experienced the same level of autocracy as Chiapas, they would have experienced a major indigenous uprising. In fact, our ability to conclude anything about governance at high levels of autocracy is limited.

Based on Model 6, Figure 5.2 shows the effect of autocracy on the probability of rebellion at different levels of indigenous protest. It can be observed that protest had practically no effect on the probability of rebellion at low levels of autocracy. These would be states such as San Luis Potosí, Tabasco, or Michoacán, with small but vibrant indigenous populations, where despite major government attempts at blocking opposition growth via fraud, leftist parties and other local political forces became viable political actors in the state's municipalities and state legislatures in the 1990s. The growth of leftist opposition parties in local elections provided rural indigenous villagers and movements with an institutional mechanism to contest neoliberal reforms

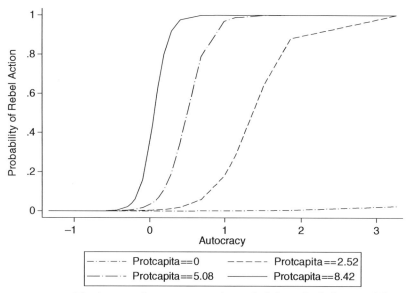

FIGURE 5.2. The impact of autocracy on the probability of rebellion at different levels of protest.

and to renegotiate new sources of public support for the loss of traditional agrarian supports.

Figure 5.2 also indicates that in the absence of protest, autocracy had practically no effect on the probability of rebellion. As Che Guevara tragically learned in the mountains of Bolivia, in the absence of organizational networks and access to peasant movements, the most autocratic state may not provoke the rise of armed insurgency. The southeastern Mexican state of Campeche is a good example. The state was a PRI stronghold where rural corporatist organizations effectively suppressed any attempt at independent mobilization. Even if Mayan peasants in Campeche deeply opposed neoliberal agricultural reforms and had no access to democratic mechanisms of protest, the absence of autonomous leaders and mobilizing structures prevented them from taking up arms.

Figure 5.2 finally shows that the impact of indigenous protest on the probability of rebellion is not constant at high levels of autocracy. Yet as we had already identified in the simulations based on Model 5, our ability to discern the effect of governance on protest at high levels of autocracy is limited. This is an important limitation that will guide case selection for the controlled qualitative comparison I present in the following section: we will assess how even small differences between autocratic regimes may significantly distinguish between small and large-scale rebellions.

In summary, in spite of limitations owing to small sample size and the skewed nature of the distribution of levels of rebel activity, the regression results help us establish a reasonable association between subnational governance practices and the likelihood of rebellion. In the context of the most radical transformation of agricultural policy in Mexico's postrevolutionary history, we have reasonable evidence to suggest that states where the spread of electoral competition prevented governors from adopting repressive practices to manage indigenous protest and provided grassroots movements with an institutional mechanism to seek alternative forms of policy negotiation had a low chance of experiencing the outbreak of rebellion. Although we have some grounds to believe that the repressive handling of indigenous protest significantly increased the chances of rebellion, regression outcomes involve too much uncertainty to substantiate a strong claim. To improve our confidence that this association exists, that it is not spurious and is likely to be causal, I turn to a controlled paired comparison of two states with histories of autocratic governance.

SOUTHERN POLITICS IN MEXICAN STATES

Up to this point, the combination of descriptive statistics and multivariate analysis has enabled us to suggest that the various strategies of governance that Mexican governors followed in implementing a nearly universally opposed neoliberal agricultural reform may be associated with the escalation of protest into rebellion. To more effectively isolate the likely effect of the authoritarian governance of the reform on the escalation of peaceful protest into armed rebellion, and to understand the causal link between changes in governance and the radicalization of rural indigenous movements, in this section I develop a comparative study of the governance of rural indigenous protest in two states that share many similarities: the neighboring southern states of Chiapas and Oaxaca.

Even though there are many important differences between these two states, if we look at the most basic indicators of economic development used in quantitative studies of political violence, Chiapas and Oaxaca are strikingly similar. As illustrated in Table 5.3, in 1990 Chiapas and Oaxaca were the two Mexican states with the lowest GDP per capita, the highest level of poverty, the highest Gini index of income inequality, the highest proportion of rural households, and the largest number of ethnic groups. Both states had similar mountainous terrains and the largest percentage of socially shared land.

The two states also shared similar histories of rural indigenous mobilization and comparable trajectories of repression. As Figure 5.3a shows, the trajectories of rural indigenous protest in both states were roughly similar up to 1991 but diverged dramatically thereafter. Figure 5.3b also shows that both states shared similar histories of government repression up to 1991 and then diverged markedly when Chiapas experienced a dramatic threefold increase in unlawful arrests and assassinations of rural indigenous population while Oaxaca underwent a threefold decline.

To add stricter controls to the paired comparison, I focus on the governance strategies that Chiapas and Oaxaca elites followed to politically implement the unpopular neoliberal agricultural reform in two particular regions: the Diocese

TABLE 5.3. *Controlled Comparison of Two Mexican States, 1990*

	Oaxaca	Chiapas	National Mean
Controls			
GDP per capita, U.S. $	2,162	2,011	4,111
Poverty[a]	3.74	4.04	1.74
Income inequality[b]	0.62	0.63	0.49
Altitude	2,610 m	2,730 m	1,465 m
Indigenous (%)	39.12	26.14	8.57
Ethnic groups[c]	2.5	1.78	1.22
Rural population (%)	52.87	58.34	27.14
Socially shared land (%)[d]	71.10	51.87	41.16
Social Bases			
Catholic progressive practice and networks	Yes[e]	Yes[f]	
Cycle of rural protest	Yes	Yes	
Governance			
Compensatory measures	Yes	No	
Tolerated protest	Yes	No	
Electoral liberalization	Yes	No	
Outcomes			
Rebel activity	Small rebellion[g]	Large-scale rebellion[h]	

Note: All data are as of 1990; *a*: Marginality index; *b*: Gini index; *c*: Effective number of ethnic groups; *d*: Sum of communal and ejido land; *e*: Diocese of Tehuantepec; *f*: Diocese of San Cristóbal de Las Casas; *g*: Although the EPR was active in some parts of Oaxaca, it had no meaningful activity in the Diocese of Tehuantepec; *h*: The Zapatista rebellion took place primarily in the Diocese of San Cristóbal de Las Casas.

of San Cristóbal de Las Casas (Chiapas) and the Diocese of Tehuantepec (Oaxaca). As we extensively discussed in Chapter 3, these dioceses were led by progressive Catholic bishops who spearheaded the rise of powerful and extensive social networks and movements for rural indigenous mobilization. Although a wide range of organizations actively participated in each of the regions' intense cycles of protest, as we discussed in Chapter 4, two nearly identical organizations – COCEI and CIOAC – played a dominant role. Finally, the geography of both dioceses is fairly similar: it is divided between extensive highlands and a deep rainforest.

Given that the end of land reform and the liberalization of land tenure meant that partial material concessions associated with land tenure and agricultural subsidies were no longer available for PRI governors to offer to independent rural communities and movements, the critical question is what PRI subnational elites of Chiapas and Oaxaca did to transform rural governance without stimulating widespread mobilization. Both governors knew the end of land reform and the liberalization of land tenure were two fundamental policy

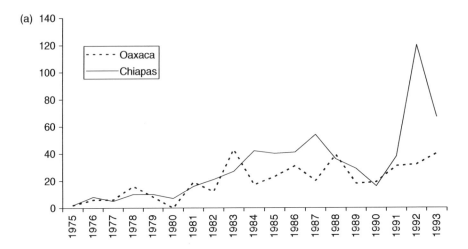

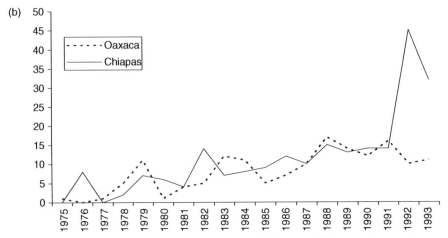

FIGURE 5.3. (a) Indigenous protest in Oaxaca and Chiapas. (b) Repression against indigenous populations in Oaxaca and Chiapas.

requirements for the negotiation of NAFTA – the cornerstone of the presidency of Carlos Salinas (1988–1994). Both governors knew that the reforms evoked deep opposition, grievances, and moral indignation. Their challenge was to politically implement the reforms while averting any possibility of social insurrection.

As summarized in Table 5.3, our goal is to show that despite similarities in economic and demographic structures and in spite of similar trajectories of contention, a punitive governance strategy adopted by the governor of Chiapas fueled the escalation of protest into rebellion in the municipalities that conform the Diocese of San Cristóbal de Las Casas, whereas in neighboring Oaxaca, a more compensatory set of policies created conditions for the deepening of institutional and nonviolent forms of policy negotiation in the Diocese of Tehuantepec. Let us assess these different governance strategies through the point of view of the governors.

Chiapas

A lawyer educated in Mexico City and London, son of a former governor of Chiapas, and grandson of a radical anticlerical PRI governor of the neighboring state of Tabasco, Patrocinio González was elected governor of Chiapas in 1988, following a major episode of electoral fraud in the 1988 presidential elections. González took office in the midst of a major cycle of social mobilization in Mexico and in Chiapas. From the outset, the new governor announced that his administration would follow strict "law and order" policies.

Knowing that a major agricultural reform was underway, from the early days of his administration, Governor González focused most of his energies on credibly convincing Chiapas's rural indigenous villagers that the land reform program was coming to an end and that his administration would no longer negotiate with social movements in the streets. He was emphatic from the outset that his government would no longer tolerate land invasions and that he would end all land programs operated by his predecessor, General Absalón Castellanos, by which government authorities purchased invaded plots from landowners and transferred them to campesinos (see Chapters 2 and 4).

In his second annual address to the Chiapas legislature, González (1990) was clear about the new strategy of rural governance in the state. He forcefully stated:

> The agrarian reform is over in Chiapas; there is no more land for redistribution. Land invasions are a thing of the past.... This government categorically rejects any policy by which the state government will purchase invaded private land plots to give them to the campesinos; we can not and should not buy private land for redistribution. Enhancing agricultural productivity and tightening birth control represent the solution to Chiapas's acute agrarian problems.

A year later, Governor González (1991) framed his third address to the state legislature in terms of the "rule of law." He devoted a large segment of his speech to defending the legislative bill that President Salinas was about to send to Congress to reform Article 27 of the Constitution, establishing the legal base for the liberalization of land tenure. He concluded with an unusual warning to Bishop Samuel Ruiz and his pastoral team at the Diocese of San Cristóbal de Las Casas – "the greatest promoters of land invasions in the state," according to González – that no one would be above the law.

Shortly after the governor's third annual address, in the fall of 1991, the Chiapas state legislature approved a reform of the state's criminal law that increased the punitive powers of the state government and *criminalized* social protest. Even though peaceful social protest had become an acceptable and widespread form of policy bargaining in Mexico since the 1977 liberalization

TABLE 5.4. *Penalties Associated with Different Forms of Collective Action in Chiapas's Criminal Law, 1991*

Type of Action as Defined in the Law	Article	Penalty
Mutiny (marches, demonstrations, sit-ins)	225	2–5 years
Road blockades	234	3–5 years
Invasion of property (land occupation)	202	2–6 years
Conspiracy, sedition, and contribution to public disorder (e.g., resisting eviction from occupied land)	222	2–4 years
Possession of arms while engaging in conspiracy, sedition, etc.	222	10–40 years
Possession of arms while disturbing public peace or pressuring government for policy concessions	237	10–40 years
Holding or kidnapping public officials to pressure government for policy concessions	148	10–30 years

Source: Gobierno del Estado de Chiapas, *Código Penal*, 1991.

of authoritarian rule, the 1991 reform of Chiapas's criminal law removed the streets and the public plazas from the repertoire of legitimate sites for independent movements to negotiate policy concessions with state authorities. For all practical purposes, in preparation for the liberalization of land tenure, González's new law abolished the basic civic rights and liberties de facto gained in Mexico since 1977.

Table 5.4 summarizes the penalties associated with the most common forms of social protest in Chiapas in the 1980s. Under this new law, a leader of a peasant movement who invaded a private land plot and then resisted eviction by the state judicial police could spend up to ten years in prison. If the leader carried weapons – or the state judicial police alleged he did, even if they showed no proof – the sentence could increase to up to forty-six years in prison. If members of the movement took to the streets to peacefully protest the imprisonment of their leader and took part in a demonstration in the state's capital, followed by a sit-in in the capital's main plaza, and blocked a road in the downtown area, they could face up to ten years in prison.

In summary, under the 1991 law, a leader or an activist of a rural indigenous movement participating in what had been the most common acts of social protest and policy bargaining in Chiapas in the 1980s could spend up to half a century in prison! Note that a key element of this law was the wide range of time in prison prescribed for violations, particularly those in which dissidents allegedly possessed weapons. This gave great discretionary powers to state authorities to apply the law arbitrarily.

Because law enforcement had been a subject of negotiation in Chiapas for decades, Governor González decided to show his resolve to enforce the 1991 penal law and the criminalization of protest by backing the law with the sword. Between 1989 and 1993, Chiapas experienced an unprecedented rise in government repression against rural indigenous movements and their secular leftist and Catholic religious allies. This combination of de jure and de facto repression would prove to be critical in shaping peasants' perception of a security dilemma and their preference for war.

During the first three years of the González administration, villagers in the rural indigenous regions of Chiapas – particularly those in the Diocese of San Cristóbal de Las Casas – suffered a dramatic increase in unlawful arrests. Whereas in the first three years of the administration of General Absalón Castellanos (1983–1985), there were, on average, 73 illegal arrests per year, during the first three years of Governor González's administration, there were, on average, 451 arrests per year. In 1991, the year when the new criminal law was adopted, nearly 700 leaders and activists were arrested.[4]

Extensive interviews with social movement leaders and activists and former members of the EZLN confirm that people on the ground did observe and extensively discuss this unprecedented rise in repression. Antonio Hernández, a former CIOAC Tojolabal leader from Las Margaritas in eastern Chiapas, and a general coordinator of CIOAC in the state, recalls the dynamics of government repression under Governor González:

Repression under Patrocinio [González] was more severe than with any of his predecessors. He invented the "rule of law." But it was the "rule of Patrocinio." He said: "There will be no more land invasions," and he welcomed the World Bank into Chiapas and forbade peasant and teacher mobilization.

Hernández continues:

When Patrocinio and Congress issued the new penal law, social movement leaders talked a lot about it. It was a time of repression but also of co-optation.[5]

Andrés Díaz, a Tzotzil Catholic catechist and a local CIOAC leader from Simojovel in northern Chiapas, elaborates on Hernández's latter point:

When [the governor] announced the end of land reform and tried to sign agreements with CIOAC leaders to demobilize the rank and file in exchange for personal kickbacks, CIOAC splintered. Some leaders betrayed the movement. But those who continued to demand land redistribution and carried on with land invasions were met with severe repression. It was within this context that Father Joel Padrón was arrested and sentenced to three decades in prison.[6]

If the unlawful arrests of hundreds of indigenous leaders were powerful signals that Governor González and the local PRI would seek to check rural indigenous mobilization with an iron fist, the arrest of Father Joel Padrón moved Chiapas into a new era of repression. One of Bishop Ruiz's closest

[4] These figures are based on information from the local press in Chiapas, particularly from the daily *Tiempo*.
[5] Interview with Antonio Hernández.
[6] Interview with Andrés Díaz.

collaborators and confidants in the Diocese of SCLC, in the early 1980s Padrón was transferred from Comitán in eastern Chiapas to Simojovel in the northern part of the state. A CIOAC stronghold, during the 1980s Simojovel became one of the three most important focal points of peasant mobilization and land invasion in Mexico. Facing rising levels of Protestant competition in his parish, from the outset, Padrón and his pastoral team sided from the outset with poor rural Toztzil communities in their struggle for land, started hundreds of Bible study groups and cooperatives, and established close collaboration with the CIOAC. As catechist Andrés Díaz recalls, Padrón was very active in developing a religious justification for land struggle:

He was not the organizer of land invasions; he only accompanied us. He would say to us: "Who created this land? God did. And he created it for the natives. You are the ones who have the right to live and work for the land because it belonged to your ancestors, not to Chiapas's German landowners."

In the midst of a new wave of land invasions in October 1991, the state judicial police arrested Padrón without a warrant and the state filed nine charges against him, including robbery, invasion of property, sedition and conspiracy against the state, and possession of weapons. Padrón was sentenced under the new criminal law to more than two decades in prison. In a country that had experienced a civil war in the 1920s, in which Catholic militias from central and northern Mexico took up arms to dispute the implementation of Mexico's anticlerical laws, the incarceration of Padrón reopened old wounds.

The timing of Father Padrón's incarceration was not random in the least. A few months before Congress in Mexico City would vote in the unpopular constitutional reform to liberalize land tenure, Padrón's arrest was meant to be a clear signal of Governor González's resolve to end land invasions and to bring to "justice" anyone who participated in struggles for land redistribution, as he had warned in his third address to the state legislature. For Father Padrón, the message behind his arrest was clear: "Whereas his predecessors – including General Absalón Castellanos – had followed policies of carrots and sticks, [González] wanted to show everyone in Chiapas that he was prepared to rule with a big stick in his hand."[7]

Even though Governor González's shift in governance strategy was aimed at preventing a major social insurrection, in the context of a hugely unpopular radical transformation of traditional agrarian policies in which the state's rural indigenous populations had no meaningful access to electoral channels for policy contestation, the criminalization of protest had the unintended effect of radicalizing communities and social movements. This had an important impact on rebel recruitment. Whereas between 1983 and 1988, the mestizo founders of the EZLN had succeeded in recruiting barely a dozen influential rural indigenous leaders from eastern Chiapas and the highlands, between 1989 and 1992 Zapatism became a mass movement.

A series of invaluable interviews conducted by journalists who traveled with the Zapatistas across the Lacandón jungle in eastern Chiapas a few months

---

[7] Interview with Father Joel Padrón.

after the outbreak of rebellion in 1994 provide rich information about the expectations that led Zapatista combatants and militants to join the EZLN in the late 1980s and early 1990s.[8] There is compelling evidence to suggest that for several Zapatista combatants and *milicianos*, the end of six decades of land reform and the liberalization of land tenure meant a major threat of reversion back to the zero-sum agricultural world dominated by *fincas*, which had enslaved their parents and grandparents for many decades.

Although we have ample historical evidence showing that by the 1990s the *finca* system had almost disappeared from the rural landscape of Chiapas (Villafuerte et al., 1999), the fact is that the memories of the plantation economy that had dominated agrarian life across northern and eastern Chiapas for most of the twentieth century remained alive in the minds and hearts of the most politicized rural indigenous households.[9] Not only were these memories still vivid because their parents and grandparents, who had been born in the *fincas* and had escaped from them, were still alive, but also because these experiences represented the backbone of the Theologies of Land developed by members of the pastoral team of the Diocese of San Cristóbal de Las Casas and Bible study groups. The Biblical reinterpretation of these indigenous experiences in the light of the Jewish exodus from slavery and their search for the Promised Land had been part of weekly Bible study meetings and discussions since the mid-1970s. This narrative served as a framework for reinterpreting the liberalization of land tenure and González's punitive implementation of the reform as a likely return to slavery.

Juan, a Zapatista combatant from San Quintín, Ocosingo, in the heart of the Lacandón jungle, succinctly expressed the fears associated with a likely economic reversion:

Things became worse with the reforms of Article 27 because our problems with land tenure law became more severe. Even women became frightened when remembering their own stories [at the *fincas*] and feared that their children would go through the same things. Now land can be sold. Who's going to sell it? It'll be the campesinos out of need or ignorance. Who's going to buy? The landowners will. Our analysis revealed to us that this year [1994] things were going to get worse for us, that's why we took up arms, because most campesinos are selling their land and they will never buy it back. They will not have any place to go other than the *finca* again (Rovira, 1994).

Eduardo López, a Tojolabal deacon from Las Margaritas, and a former militant of the EZLN, recalls the expectations his family and community held in 1991 and 1992:

We talked a lot about [the reform of Article 27] in the Bible study groups and in the ejido union. We were furious and felt disenfranchised. But we knew that the land was ours, even if the laws changed. Though there was no way to negotiate land redistribution

---

[8] In Chapter 6, I supplement these journalistic sources with additional information I gathered from extensive interviews with former Zapatista militants between 2009 and 2010.

[9] In fact, these memories have led revisionist scholars to reassess the history of the *finca* system in several regions in Chiapas. See Saavedra (2008) for Las Margaritas, Legorreta (2008) for Ocosingo, Bobrow-Strain (2007) for Chilón, and Toledo (2002) for Simojovel.

with the government, the land was ours. We thought the reform would send us back to the time when the land was in the hands of a few people, but we would avoid it by every means. Landowners would have to recover their land by means of force because we were not going to willingly sell our land; the land is our mother, our flesh, our body.[10]

There is extensive qualitative evidence that the fear of economic reversion was coupled with fears of a likely political regression to an authoritarian status quo ante, particularly after González's reform of the criminal law in 1991 and the unprecedented wave of repression in 1989–1992. Whereas the country as a whole was slowly moving toward greater electoral competition, Chiapas remained the PRI's foremost subnational authoritarian bastion. Worse yet, the unprecedented wave of human rights violations in the early 1990s signaled that the few civil and political liberties won by independent social movements over the course of the 1980s could be permanently reversed. The dense network of human rights NGOs that emerged in these years, including the influential Fray Bartolomé de Las Casas Human Rights Center, helped members of Catholic social networks and their associated social movements keep detailed records of the state's punitive actions, and served as an invaluable input to update their beliefs and expectations.

In one of the first Zapatista communiqués after the outbreak of war, the rebels referred to González's 1991 criminal law as "the most absurd and repressive [law] that ever existed" (EZLN, 1994). Maribel, a young Zapatista combatant from Las Margaritas, summarized how the changing strategies of repression reshaped the strategies of mobilization for herself and her peers:

As a response [to popular independent protests, the government] would send the army and illegally arrest the leaders. There was no way to continue fighting like that. Soon we didn't have any more leaders or some comrade would disappear. Thus the people realized that the rich had the soldiers on their side but the poor had to become soldiers in order to defend themselves" (Rovira, 1994).

Another Zapatista commander from the Chiapas highlands effectively conveyed the sense of generalized repression in the state: "There have been repression and [illegal] detentions all over … so much injustice that we said: enough!" (Rovira, 1994). Subcommander Marcos, the mestizo spokesman and military leader of the EZLN, eloquently captured the sense of a security dilemma: "It was [ultimately] a question of survival and self-defense" (Le Bot, 1997).

Oaxaca

An Indian Mixteco lawyer trained in Mexico City, Heladio Ramírez was elected governor of Oaxaca in 1986. Initially recruited into the PRI by populist President Luis Echeverría in the 1970s, Ramírez's political career has been associated with the PRI's peasant branch, the National Peasant Confederation (CNC). As a leader of the CNC, Governor Ramírez was perfectly aware that

---

[10] Interview with Deacon Eduardo López.

the end of land reform and the liberalization of land tenure entailed – to use the language of Yashar (2005) – the disenfranchisement of Indian peasants as rural citizens. To compensate for these losses and avoid a major insurrection, Ramírez and his cabinet focused most of their attention in the second half of his administration to implementing rights-based compensatory measures to avoid a major insurrection as a response to the end of land reform and the liberalization of land tenure. Ramírez focused on two areas: elections and ethnicity.

During Ramírez's term, major opposition electoral victories in municipal elections were accepted for the first time in the state and the governor did not reverse outcomes ex post. Whereas leftist parties had made only modest inroads in the indigenous regions of Chiapas in the 1980s and PRI authorities had thwarted the electoral progress of the left through coercion or sheer fraud in such places as Las Margaritas or Simojovel, in 1989 in Oaxaca, the left emblematically came to power in Juchitán, the largest city of the Isthmus of Tehuantepec and the undisputed Zapotec cultural and political epicenter.

Led by the COCEI, the influential coalition of peasants, students and workers discussed in Chapter 4, the left had been making significant inroads in the Isthmus region since the late 1970s. Even though an earlier victory in 1983 had been reversed and the COCEI leaders removed from power, persecuted, and nearly assassinated by the military and state security forces,[11] by 1989, the national PRI elite in coordination with Governor Ramírez and the local PRI accepted the COCEI victory in Juchitán and allowed the leftist coalition to take office. Héctor Sánchez, a Zapotec founding leader of COCEI, took office in 1989. It was during these years that Ramírez began a close collaboration with COCEI and even co-opted some of the movement's most influential young activists into his cabinet.[12] They would become a privileged source of local information for the governor and successive PRI administrations in Oaxaca City.

The COCEI electoral victory in 1989 sent shockwaves throughout Oaxaca and signaled the availability of elections as a potentially effective channel for social and policy contestation. The fact that the most emblematic and influential social movement in Oaxaca had finally gained municipal power meant that the revolutionary option was fading in the state. Since the mid-1970s, insurgent groups such as *La Liga 23 de Septiembre* had unsuccessfully approached COCEI leaders to recruit their leaders and members into revolutionary politics.[13] COCEI's early commitment to electoral politics and the 1977 liberalization of authoritarian rule prevented the group from taking up arms.

Against the background of the repressive policies of the early 1980s that had illegally removed COCEI leaders from office, and in the context of the liberalization of land tenure, another fraud against COCEI in 1989 would have provided a strong signal that elections were not an option for independent

[11] Interviews with Leopoldo de Gyves, Héctor Sánchez, and Bishop Emeritus Arturo Lona. For a detailed study of the politics of indigenous mobilization in Juchitán, see Rubin (1997).

[12] Interview with Bishop Emeritus Arturo Lona.

[13] Interview with Héctor Sánchez.

rural indigenous movements. However, the COCEI victory in Juchitán signaled to rural indigenous communities that a new era of multiparty competition was a viable institutional option for recovering as voters what they had lost as peasants.

Governor Ramírez and his team of anthropologist advisers also shifted their attention from class-based agrarian politics to multicultural rights. As Recondo (2007) explains, Ramírez and his advisers played a key role in persuading President Salinas to recognize Convention 169 of the International Labor Organization, which recognized extensive indigenous rights to autonomy and self-determination. A few months before the Mexican Congress approved the liberalization of land tenure in 1992, Ramírez introduced a pioneering, albeit limited, constitutional reform that recognized the existence of indigenous peoples as culturally distinct groups in Oaxaca and mandated state authorities to devise the institutional mechanisms to protect and promote indigenous cultures. Whereas the national agrarian reform closed the door of class politics to rural indigenous communities, local reforms in Oaxaca opened a small window of opportunity for them to begin channeling their needs and grievances through ethnic politics. Some of the most politicized indigenous communities across the state were quick to notice and embrace this ethnic turn (Elizarrarás, 2003; Recondo, 2007; Eisenstadt, 2011). While Tojolabal and Tzeltal Indians in Chiapas were preparing for war, the Mixe and the Zapotec in Oaxaca were discussing how to push for further multicultural institutional reforms.

The Ramírez administration's attempt to establish a legal basis for partial and limited (ethnic) policy concessions to independent rural indigenous communities was a clear signal that the state would continue with traditional carrot-and-stick policies. Newspaper records from the MII data set show that state repression against rural indigenous communities continued to be an important governance mechanism during the Ramírez administration. The relevant point, however, is that unlike Chiapas, where Governor González had given up on any meaningful material concessions to independents and had adopted repression as a dominant strategy of governance, in Oaxaca, Governor Ramirez tried to compensate for agrarian losses with limited ethnic rewards, did not introduce new repressive laws, and did not seek to incarcerate or eliminate all of the state's major social and religious leaders.[14]

A year before the liberalization of land tenure was approved by the Mexican Congress, the contrast in rural governance between Chiapas and Oaxaca could not have been starker: While Governor González had approved a law that criminalized protest, provided no meaningful compensation for the upcoming agrarian losses, and "ruled with a big stick in his hand," Governor Ramírez had conceded to meaningful leftist opposition victories in municipal elections, had introduced limited multicultural reforms, and continued to use carrots as well as sticks. To put it succinctly, whereas the end of land reform and the

---

[14] For specific compensatory policies Governor Ramírez adopted in the state's most important agricultural sectors, particularly in the coffee sector, see Snyder (2001a).

liberalization of land tenure disenfranchised Indians as peasants, the policies adopted by Governor González also disenfranchised them as citizens. In contrast, in Oaxaca, the governor's actions empowered indigenous communities to start thinking about two new forms of representation: multicultural and liberal citizenship.

Over the course of the next decade, indigenous communities and movements from the Diocese of San Cristóbal de Las Casas in Chiapas and the Diocese of Tehuantepc in Oaxaca followed very different trajectories: Whereas in Chiapas communities followed a path of revolutionary action, fruitless peace negotiations with government authorities, and irregular warfare with paramilitary forces, in Oaxaca they continued to contest policy change primarily through peaceful protest and began to actively explore electoral politics and multicultural institutions. When the EPR declared war on the government in the southern state of Guerrero and moved some of its operations to Oaxaca, the response of the state's rural indigenous communities was not overwhelming. Unlike the Zapatistas, who were able to create a mass base after the 1992 reform in the rural indigenous regions of the Diocese of San Cristóbal de Las Casas, the EPR was unable to grow into a mass-based rebel movement in Oaxaca and built no significant bases in the Diocese of Tehuantepec. The crucial differentiating factor, as we have argued, was the different governance strategies adopted by the Chiapas and Oaxaca governors.

Accounting for Different Governance Strategies

If the difference in governance strategies the Chiapas and Oaxaca elites adopted to politically implement a universally opposed agricultural reform explains the different trajectories of collective action that rural indigenous villages from these states followed, we must account for the factors that led governors to adopt repressive or compensatory policies in the first place. Three factors can explain these differences: (1) the governors' beliefs and expectations of the revolutionary capacity of Indians; (2) the state's history of strategic interaction between government officials and social movements; and (3) political constraints.

Beliefs. Like all rulers in autocracies, Governors González and Ramírez operated under conditions of severe information asymmetries. Survey evidence coming from the Office of the President told them that the liberalization of land tenure evoked deep emotional opposition. They knew that although villagers privately opposed the reform, the greatest opposition came from the streets: from the state's powerful rural indigenous movements. Hence, their challenge was to prepare the ground for an implementation of the reform without a major social uprising; their main limitation, however, was that they were unsure about the resilience of rural dissident groups to repression and their true revolutionary potential. Here is where the local information available to González and Ramírez became crucial in shaping beliefs and expectations.

There is extensive evidence for the claim that Governor González in Chiapas strongly believed that the state's powerful rural indigenous movements were dominated by Bishop Ruiz and his pastoral team and by outside leftist mestizo social activists. The governor was convinced that these centralized movements had not developed deep and widespread support in the state's rural indigenous communities. In his third state of the union address, he made explicit and repeated references to the "… the clerical and socialist agitators…" that "… manipulated the Indians for their own religious and political causes" (González, 1991).

In the language of network analysis, Governor González believed these movements were part of centralized networks dominated by a few powerful clerical and secular leaders. By removing these leaders, he assumed, the collective action capacity of these groups would be compromised and their revolutionary potential arrested. The ultimate goal of González's new penal law and the major wave of unlawful arrests of leaders that accompanied it was to decapitate what he believed was a centralized movement with no meaningful village-level association networks.

There is reasonable evidence to suggest that Governor Ramírez in Oaxaca believed that the state's major rural indigenous movements, particularly those in the Isthmus of Tehuantepec, had extensive local leadership structures and local associational networks to resist a repressive implementation of the neoliberal agricultural reform. The state authorities had seen the collective action capacity of the COCEI and the state's social movements when the *coceistas* launched a major civil resistance campaign to defend their electoral victory in Juchitán in 1983. Moreover, through the COCEI local leaders that joined his team in the late 1980s, Ramírez had firsthand information about the density of the Catholic network structure developed by Bishop Lona and his pastoral team.

Governor Ramírez adopted compensatory measures and actively opened alternative sources of compensation for peasants because he had information that reasonably led him to assume that a purely repressive response would backfire. Unlike Governor González, Ramírez did not assume that removing the leadership would lead to the collapse of opposition networks; rather, he considered that opposition movements from below had to be neutralized or channeled into institutional paths of contestation through reformist and compensatory policies. Unlike Chiapas, where de facto racial segregation had prevented the white and mestizo elite from having any intimate information about the Indian world, in Oaxaca the indigenous and nonindigenous worlds were intimately connected – indigenous local elites, like Governor Ramírez himself and the COCEI local leaders Ramírez had recruited onto his team, had privileged access to local information that informed governance decisions.

The History of State-Peasant Strategic Interaction. The different histories of land reform in Chiapas and Oaxaca and the different patterns of strategic interaction between governments and peasant movements prior to the 1992 reform led to different governance strategies to implement the liberalization of land tenure. Although Chiapas and Oaxaca in the early 1990s were the two Mexican states with the largest share of socialized land (ejido and communal land), historically land redistribution had taken longer in Chiapas than in Oaxaca. The last phase of redistribution in Chiapas in the 1980s was achieved through ad-hoc policies, such as the Agrarian Rehabilitation Program described in Chapter 2, by which state authorities bought land plots from landowners and gave them to PRI and non-PRI affiliates.

Given that land redistribution for independents in Chiapas had been achieved through land invasion and street protest during the 1980s, by the time Governor González announced that this time land redistribution was truly over, that his government would no longer accept land invasions as a legitimate mechanism to negotiate land redistribution, and that the streets were not longer a legitimate site for policy negotiation, he faced a major credibility problem. To overcome the government's reputation deficit, Governor González *overcommitted* himself to a punitive path; a course of action in which material concessions were no longer on the table and repression was the dominant strategy of rural governance.

The history of land reform in Oaxaca provided Ramírez with a major strategic advantage: Oaxaca was the single Mexican state with the largest proportion of communal land tenure. According to Mexico's agrarian laws, the state could grant land to groups of families that constituted themselves into ejidos or to already constituted (indigenous) communities.[15] Governor Ramírez took advantage of this communal structure to offer mechanisms for government transfers to communities based on ethnic criteria. For the most politicized leaders of municipalities with communal land tenure in Oaxaca, the politicization of ethnicity from above became a plausible way to compensate "as Indians" what they had lost "as peasants."

Political Constraints. Even though Chiapas and Oaxaca were two of the least democratic states by the early 1990s, there were small, albeit important, differences in terms of gubernatorial power. By 1992, the left in Oaxaca had become a major player in gubernatorial (ENP = 1.74) and state legislative (ENP = 1.67) elections and had a meaningful presence in the state legislature (ENLS[16] = 1.47), whereas in Chiapas, multiparty competition was severely constrained and the state legislature remained under the hegemonic control of the PRI (ENLS = 1.16).

Differences in state-level multiparty competition provided different structures of checks and balances for governors in the two states. Whereas in Chiapas, Governor González could single-handedly pass a draconian law like the 1991 reform of the state's criminal law, Governor Ramírez in Oaxaca

---

[15] For an insightful analysis of the impact of land tenure structures on indigenous individual political and cultural attitudes in Oaxaca and Chiapas, see Eisenstadt (2011)

[16] ENLS stands for the effective number of legislative seats.

faced greater constraints on passing punitive laws. Although these checks and balances did not effectively deter Ramírez from entirely resorting to repressive policies, they did stop him from opting for purely repressive actions as González had in Chiapas.

The importance of checks and balances can also be seen retrospectively in Oaxaca's history. Whereas a PRI-dominated legislature had allowed Ramírez's predecessor to "legally" remove the COCEI-Communist municipal president in 1983, in 1989 Ramírez was compelled to accept the COCEI victory; removing the new leftist-Zapotec major was untenable within the context of a more pluralistic legislature.

CONCLUSION

In their seminal article on the outbreak of insurgencies and civil wars, Fearon and Laitin (2003) suggest that the outbreak of insurgencies is more likely in societies where financially poor states are incapable of policing criminal movements that arise in the rural and mountainous countryside of developing countries and prevent them from plundering natural resources and taking up power. Although the article correctly points to governance and conditions for rebel recruitment as the two central explanatory factors, its use of such indicators as GDP per capita and rurality and mountainous terrain conceals the actors, processes and dynamics of strategic interaction that typically determine whether groups take up arms or not.

Focusing on the literature of governance of dissent (Lichbach, 1987) and on the literature on cycles of protest (Della Porta and Tarrow, 1986; Brockett, 2005), in this chapter we put to test an alternative explanation of the outbreak of insurgencies that emphasizes the governance strategies that incumbents in hybrid regimes adopt to "manage" protest in times of major economic crises or major unpopular policy shifts. Our focus was on the outbreak of indigenous insurgencies in Mexico that followed the introduction of radical neoliberal agricultural reforms that put an end to six decades of land reform and liberalized land tenure.

Survey evidence on peasants' views showed that neoliberal agricultural reforms indeed evoked deep grievances, a profound sense of relative deprivation, and moral indignation in the Mexican countryside. Yet data on the geography of rebellion across states and municipalities revealed that these shared emotions led to many different responses, ranging from acquiescence, to peaceful protest, to armed rebellion. This contrasting evidence suggests that grievances, relative deprivation, or moral indignation are limited explanations of the outbreak of indigenous rebellion: They may explain the timing of rebel activity but fail to explain spatial variation. This does not mean that emotions are irrelevant. It does mean that their effect is conditional – on the governance strategies elites choose to implement unpopular reforms.

Based on quantitative and qualitative evidence, and controlling for economic, demographic and geographic factors typically associated with the outbreak of armed insurgencies, the analyses in this chapter showed that the governance strategy that Mexican governors followed to politically implement neoliberal reforms distinguished states where rural indigenous communities and movements took up arms from those where they did not.

In states where electoral constraints and checks and balances prevented governors from harshly repressing peaceful rural protest and where the spread of local competition provided Indian peasants with opportunities for redistribution through democratic means, rural indigenous movements challenged reforms in the streets and at the ballot box but not in the mountains. As the evidence of the governance strategies followed by subnational elites in Oaxaca revealed, when governors in traditionally authoritarian settings adopted new policy measures to compensate for their losses, consented to opposition electoral victories in meaningful jurisdictions, and continued to rule by means of carrots and sticks, peasants continued to take their demands to the streets; neoliberal reforms stimulated protest but not the escalation of protest into rebellion.

Where unconstrained governors in autocratic states adopted repressive strategies to prevent widespread peasant mobilization, protest was most likely to lead to rebellion. The strategy followed by the Chiapas governor of abandoning any meaningful economic concession in favor of independent grassroots movements and his attempt to dissuade peasant mobilization through punitive measures signaled a likely reversion to the former world of landowners and *fincas*. The fear of a dual economic and political regression to an authoritarian status quo ante raised a serious security dilemma and activated the path of revolutionary action to prevent the return to a punitive plantation economy.

Evidence from this chapter suggests that major changes in governance strategies in the ascending phase of a cycle of peaceful mobilization can provide new incentives for radicalization in electoral autocracies. The dynamics of indigenous insurgency across Mexican states showed that the withdrawal of major economic and political rights won in the political liberalization phase can provide powerful incentives for the escalation of protest into rebellion. The important theoretical lesson is that when elites implement unpopular reforms that take away fundamental economic rights by withdrawing limited political rights, they create conditions for the radicalization of peaceful social movements.

Yet as the next chapter explores, in a statewide context of repression, not all affected communities and villagers join rebel groups. Facing similar threats of a dual reversion in Chiapas, not all rural indigenous communities and villagers in the state joined the EZLN. Regime reversion threats may create revolutionary contexts but they do not on their own explain revolutionary action. To understand the conditions under which revolutionary contexts actually become revolutionary action, we shall turn in the next chapter to analyze the microdynamics of recruitment from social movements into armed rebel groups.

6

From Social Movement to Armed Rebellion

Religious Networks and the Microdynamics of Rebel Recruitment

Major threats of regime reversion in liberalizing autocracies provide members of independent grassroots and social movements with meaningful incentives for radical collective action. In the face of these threats, however, not all leaders and social activists may become combatants and not all villages become social bases for insurgent action. As Fearon and Laitin (2003) remind us, it all depends on the conditions for rebel recruitment.

Classic theories of rebel recruitment have typically emphasized economic, ethnic, and demographic structures. Students of revolutions since Marx have sought to identify a proto-revolutionary class. In his classic study of insurgencies and revolutions in Latin America, Wickham-Crowley (1992) identified landless peasants and rural migrants as members of a proto-revolutionary group. Gurr (1993) has suggested that marginalized and discriminated ethnic minority groups can become a potentially revolutionary actor. And Fearon and Laitin's (2002) influential study suggests that rebel recruitment takes place in rural and mountainous regions.[1]

Following the pioneer work of Gould (1995), a group of scholars have recently pointed out the importance of social networks for rebel recruitment (Petersen, 2001; Wood 2003; Berman, 2009). In line with this literature, and building on recent developments of network theory, in Chapter 1 we argued that recruitment from social movements into armed insurgencies will be more likely when social movements are structured as decentralized organizations with multiple interconnected local leaders who are supported by dense communal associational networks.

For rebel groups for which social capital is one of the main sources of power, establishing direct intimate relationships with rural community leaders, grassroots organizations, and social movements is absolutely crucial (Guevara, 1967/2006; Weinstein, 2006). If these rural communities and movements represent the civilian bases for war and resistance, building a long-term relationship

---

[1] For a thorough treatment of the effect of rurality on insurgency and civil war, see Kocher (2005).

with them becomes one of the most important politico-military strategies for rebel success.

The focus of this chapter is on the municipal and village-level dynamics of rebel recruitment in a context of statewide repression such as that which prevailed in Chiapas between 1989 and 1992. Whereas in Chapter 5 we analyzed the effect of state-level governance on the escalation of protest into rebellion, in this chapter we look at the microdynamics of recruitment from communities, grassroots organizations, and social movements into armed rebel groups.

Within a context of statewide repression, we want to know whether EZLN commanders recruited their social base on the basis of class, ethnicity, or geographic location, or whether Catholic associational networks served as the main conduit for recruitment. Our question is whether recruitment took place in (1) the most cohesive corporate and traditional indigenous communities in isolated and mountainous terrains, (2) communities experiencing major internal transformations as a result of the dynamics of religious competition between Catholic and Protestant churches, or (3) communities that were fully integrated into the state's powerful rural indigenous movements via leftist secular movements. In the language of social movement scholarship, our inquiry is about the mobilizing structures for rebel recruitment.

Testing in this chapter relies on quantitative and qualitative evidence, and I combine information from multiple levels of analysis: municipalities, villages, and local leaders.

Based on a new index of levels of community involvement in the EZLN by municipality and controlling for economic, geographic, and demographic factors typically associated with rebel recruitment, statistical results from order probit models show that municipalities with intense histories of religious competition between Catholic and Protestant churches – where members of the pastoral team of the Diocese of San Cristóbal de Las Casas had become major promoters of Catholic social networks and peasant movements for land redistribution – more commonly joined the EZLN than those where the Catholic Church monopoly remained intact. Statistical results also show a strong association between those municipalities experiencing the most intense histories of rural indigenous protest and rebel recruitment into Zapatism.

Contrary to the dominant narrative that suggests that Zapatista recruits were the villagers who experienced the most brutal levels of state repression, statistical results show that villagers from the municipalities experiencing the harshest levels of repression *did not* join the EZLN, but their neighbors *did* – that is, those who knew from their participation in Catholic trans-regional networks of the extent of repression elsewhere in the state but who did not themselves face the harshest repressive actions.

Because the statistical analyses do not help us disentangle the effect of religious and secular networks on rebel recruitment, we resort to case studies to gain a better understanding of the mechanics of recruitment. I first assess dynamics of rebel recruitment in the municipality of Las Margaritas – a municipality with a history of intense religious competition and rural mobilization, where the Zapatistas established their headquarters.

Based on the life histories of five Tojolabal CIOAC leaders with nearly identical personal stories except for the fact that two of them were part of secular networks while the others were part of Catholic networks, I present a tightly controlled comparison of rebel recruitment. Through the life stories of these leaders I provide unambiguous micro evidence showing that participation in Catholic social networks was the single factor that distinguished poor Mayan peasants who joined the EZLN from those who did not.

These comparative life stories show that rebel recruitment took place through religious rather than secular connections because the main structural features of Catholic social networks facilitated rebel recruitment while the secular networks did not. The analysis shows that the decentralized, horizontal structure of Catholic social networks with multiple local leaders (catechists) who enjoyed unique access to dense local associational networks was more conducive to rebel recruitment than the centralized and hierarchical organization of leftist secular networks (see H.6).

A brief analysis of the Tzeltal municipality of Amatenango del Valle, near Margaritas, shows that in the absence of religious competition, communities in these municipalities did not have the associational networks that attracted rebels, despite their high levels of poverty, inequality, and economic exploitation.

Finally, the in-depth analysis of an outlier discloses crucial information about the effect of state repression on rebel recruitment. With a long history of religious competition, Catholic social activism, and intense peasant mobilization, the Tzotzil municipality of Simojovel in the northern highlands would have seemed to be the ideal context for rebel recruitment into the EZLN. Even though miles away, Simojovel was like a twin municipality of Margaritas; yet villagers from Simojovel did not play a prominent role in Zapatism because the municipality was under heavy military and police surveillance and control at the time when Zapatism was growing into a mass movement. Recruitment was too dangerous for Zapatista commanders, Catholic catechists, and local grassroots leaders. Yet the dissemination of information about repression practices in Simojovel through Catholic regional networks was crucial for communities elsewhere in their decision to go to war.

In the following two sections, I provide a historical overview of the different stages of recruitment and expansion of Zapatism and present an original index of the geography of levels of community support for the EZLN prior to the outbreak of war. The third section discusses the statistical results, and in the fourth part I present the inter-municipal and intra-municipal case studies. In the conclusion, I discuss the contribution of this chapter to our understanding of rebel recruitment based on religious networks.

THE GEOGRAPHY OF COMMUNITY-LEVEL SUPPORT FOR THE EZLN

Whereas in Chapter 5 I tested for rural indigenous rebel *activity* by state, in this chapter I test for the municipal level of community *participation* in the EZLN prior to the outbreak of war. The latter is a crucial indicator for rebel groups for which community support is the main source of power. Access to these networks enables guerrilla groups to hide after carrying out surprise attacks on their enemies. In protracted conflicts, it is these community networks that provide rebel groups with a social base for establishing territorial control.

Scholars have classified levels of support for rebel groups based on the logistical and material aid communities render to rebels and on community members' degree of involvement in rebel military operations. Following Wickham-Crowley (1992) and based on interviews with former Zapatistas, I divide positive involvement in Zapatism into four levels: 0 – none; 1 – passive support (sympathizers); 2 – logistical and material assistance (*milicianos*); and 3 – full-time combatants (combatants). Classifying these elements requires more than a count of rebel actions or battle deaths; it requires information about the prewar social and political activity of rebels, communities, and social movements.

Founded in 1983 by a group of young northern middle-class urban mestizo rebels who survived the Dirty War of the 1970s and did not join electoral politics after the 1977 legalization of the Mexican Communist Party and the 1978 Amnesty Law, the EZLN spread from the Lacandón forest in eastern Chiapas to the state's northern region and the highlands in less than a decade (Tello, 1995; Legorreta, 1997). Scholars of Zapatism and Zapatistas themselves identify two major periods of recruitment before the outbreak of war: an initial stage of unsuccessful mass recruitment attempts between 1983 and 1988, in which the EZLN founders were able to recruit no more than twenty community leaders and activists, followed by a second stage of mass recruitment between 1989 and 1993, in which the EZLN amassed an extensive network of community support.

Elite Recruitment, 1983–1988

In practically every publicly available interview, Subcommander Marcos and indigenous Zapatista commanders acknowledge that between 1983 and 1988 the mestizo founders of the EZLN were only able to recruit a small elite of community and grassroots leaders and failed to appeal to the rural masses. It was during these years that they recruited some of the most energetic and socially respected catechists and deacons from the extensive Catholic social networks in the heartland of the Lacandón jungle. These lay leaders had positioned themselves at the center of many religious and secular networks and played a prominent role in the networks of rural cooperatives that sprang up throughout the Lacandón jungle after the 1974 Indigenous Congress and in the multiple cycles of rural mobilization throughout the state.[2] Subcommander

---

[2] Legorreta (1997) provides extensive accounts of the recruitment of catechists and Catholic communities into the EZLN. For personal accounts by Zapatista commanders, see interviews with Commander Tacho by Le Bot (1997) and by Reza (1995). For the recruitment of Lázaro Hernández, the most prominent deacon in the Lacandón forest, see De Vos (2002).

Marcos, one of the founding leaders of the EZLN, has always referred to these
first recruits as a "highly politicized elite" of indigenous leaders with "great
organizational skills" (Castillo and Brisac, 1995) and "great political experience in mass movements" (Le Bot, 1997).

A growing frustration with the political inefficacy of peaceful protest to
advance the struggle for land redistribution drove some of the early recruits
into the EZLN. Ana María, a Tzotzil commander from the Chiapas highlands
and one of the first recruits into Zapatism, confirmed this sense of frustration:

As a small girl I participated in la *lucha pacífica* (non-violent struggle). My family were
the type of people who would always get organized and fight for a more dignified life,
but we never achieved it. [...] Since I was eight years old, I would go to demonstrations and that is how I became conscious that with *la lucha pacífica* one gets nothing.
[...] There was only one alternative: to organize for armed struggle. (Rovira, 1994,
214–215)

The experience of Central American revolutionary movements in the 1980s –
widely discussed in the catechist training courses and the secular rural movements – served these early recruits as a historical point of reference to justify
their view on the futility of social protest and the need for revolutionary
action.[3]

Status differentiation was a second important motivation for these early
recruits.[4] After the 1974 Indigenous Congress, when Bishop Ruiz reached
out to professional activists to aid his diocese in building a "popular power,"
a wide range of organizations approached the region in search of the precious social capital the Catholic Church had built in the indigenous regions of
Chiapas. From leftist parties (such as the PCM) and rising agrarian movements
(CIOAC, the Emiliano Zapata Peasant Organization – OCEZ, the Plan de Ayala
National Confederation-CNPA, among others) to rebel groups (EZLN), activists (Popular Power – PP), and NGOs (the Center for the Social and Economic
Development of Indigenous Mexicans – DESMI), deacons and catechists sud-
denly found themselves in a position to choose political partnerships.

Some of the rising stars of the catechist movement and the ejido unions
entered into fierce competition for local power, recognition, and status. In this
context, joining the EZLN meant moving into a different status layer. The first
recruits attended special training camps in EZLN safe houses in Mexico City,
had access to weapons similar to those used by the Mexican army, and became

[3] At the annual meetings of the Diocese of San Cristóbal de Las Casas pastoral team, priests,
missionaries, and catechists extensively discussed the revolutionary experiences of Guatemala,
El Salvador, and Nicaragua. Bishop Ruiz and his diocese provided financial and moral support
to Guatemalan refugees fleeing the country's bloody civil war in the late 1980s. Throughout the
1980s, several SCLC priests and members of the religious orders spent short periods of time
in parishes in Nicaragua and El Salvador. (Interviews with Fathers Ramón Castillo and Joel
Padrón.)

[4] For a detailed discussion of social status as a mechanism for rebel recruitment, see Petersen
(2001).

the communities' military branch (Tello, 1995) – the ones who would defend the community from the state judicial police.

But even with the assistance of some of the most powerful community and grassroots leaders from the highlands and the Lacandón jungle, the EZLN was unable to reach the status of a mass movement in the mid-1980s. Mass recruitment for a popular war was unsuccessful because for most members of Catholic social networks and secular rural movements, *la lucha pacífica* remained a viable mechanism for policy negotiation with the state government. Despite the repressive and sometimes brutal actions of Governor Absalón Castellanos (1982–1988), the streets and public plazas remained effective sites for the negotiation of government concessions. Although partial and limited, as we showed in Chapter 4, these concessions motivated the most networked leaders and activists to carry out protests and to discount repression as a *sunk cost* they had to pay to receive any concessions at all.

Subcommander Marcos vividly recalls the frustration and fears that dogged their failed attempts at mass recruitment in the early years of Zapatism: "And always accompanying us [in these years] was the ghost of Che [Guevara] in Bolivia and the lack of campesino support for an artificially implanted guerrilla movement" (Castillo and Brisac, 1995: 135).

Mass Recruitment, 1989–1992

As we discussed in Chapter 5, the dramatic transformation of rural governance in Chiapas in the years leading to the liberalization of land tenure in 1992 changed the incentives for rebellion and opened a unique window of opportunity for mass recruitment into the EZLN. The star catechists the Zapatistas had been able to recruit in the mid-1980s became the leading EZLN recruiters. Prior to 1988, their attempt to convince other catechists and communities of the futility of social protest had been entirely unsuccessful. But as various sources reported in Chapter 5 suggest, in the context of a new law that criminalized protest, an unprecedented rise in government repression and the imminent marketization of land tenure, the message of the Zapatista recruiters began to attract the attention of other catechists and community members. As Subcommander Marcos recalls:

We thought that we were persuading people [to join the EZLN]. But, in truth, it was something else that was convincing them to join: the Salinas reform of Article 27 ... the cancellation of Mexico's agrarian reform and the liberalization of land tenure. With these reforms, even the ejidos could be bought and sold. Then there was no more hope; it was all over. Armed struggle was the only alternative option. (Le Bot, 1997: 179)

To more actively penetrate the rich Catholic community networks and the rural social movements that had sprung up in the previous decades, in the early 1990s the EZLN created a civilian arm – the Emiliano Zapata National Independent Alliance (ANCIEZ). Under the leadership of Commander Tacho, a former star catechist and CIOAC member from Las Margaritas, ANCIEZ

became an umbrella organization that drew members of Catholic social networks and defectors from some of the state's largest peasant organizations into
a new phase of EZLN-linked social activism. The ANCIEZ was an active participant in most acts of peaceful protest that took place during 1991 and 1992
(Tello, 1995; De Vos, 2002).

Yet after the Zapatista commanders decided in a meeting in the fall of
1992 to take military action against the Mexican government and the army,
ANCIEZ virtually disappeared from the public scene. The organization would
no longer seek to recruit new members but to consolidate their base in preparation for war. ANCIEZ members were last seen on October 12, 1992 in San
Cristóbal de Las Casas – the picture on the cover page of this book – during
the unprecedented indigenous demonstration condemning the Quincentenary
of the Conquest of the Americas.[5] They would reappear fifteen months later as
EZLN members hidden behind ski masks and carrying AK-47 assault rifles.

An Index of Community Support for Zapatism

I use reports from the local Chiapan press on ANCIEZ activities to identify
the geography of Zapatism during the mass recruitment phase between 1991
and 1993.[6] I create an index of Zapatism based on two indicators related to
ANCIEZ collective action. The first is a simple count of all acts of social protest
in which ANCIEZ members were involved and all acts of government repression against ANCIEZ members between 1991 and 1992. The second indicator
identifies municipalities that experienced a marked decline in ANCIEZ protest
during 1993. I use this indicator of abrupt demobilization as evidence that
ANCIEZ members went underground to prepare for war. A combination of
these two indicators gives a four-point scale of municipal levels of support for
Zapatism: 0 – no Zapatista presence; 1 – sympathizers; 2 – *milicianos* (bases of
logistic and material support); and 3 – full-time combatants.

Map 6.1 shows municipalities where the EZLN operated between 1992 and
1993 – the time period when the 1994 attack was planned. The map shows fifteen Zapatista military strongholds in Tzeltal/Tojolabal municipalities in eastern Chiapas, the northern Chol region, and the Tzotzil highlands. The eastern
front operated mainly in the Lacandón jungle, where the EZLN built up its
military bases drawing full-time combatants from Tzeltal and Tojolabal villages in the municipalities of Altamirano, Chilón, Palenque, Ocosingo, and Las
Margaritas. Some military recruits also came from northern Chol municipalities, including Sabanilla, Salto de Agua, Tila, Tumbalá, and Yajalón. A few
additional military units came from the highland municipality of San Andrés

---

[5] Interview with Antonio Hernández, then statewide CIOAC leader and general coordinator of the
October 12, 1992 mass demonstration in San Cristóbal de Las Casas, Chiapas.
[6] I use information from the daily newspaper *Tiempo* and supplement the information with the
CIACH report – a monthly summary of news reports on contentious events based on the Chiapas
press. See Appendix A.

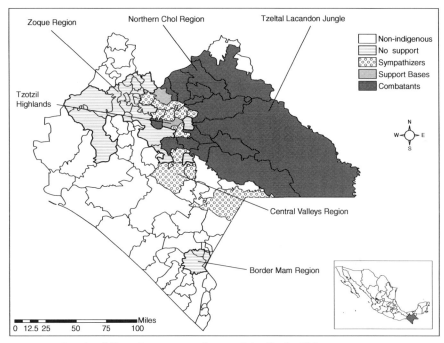

MAP 6.1. Levels of Zapatista support by municipality in Chiapas, 1992–1993.

Larráinzar and Tzotzil urban neighborhoods of San Cristóbal de Las Casas. Northern and eastern Chiapas and the highlands were strategically connected by the Tzeltal/Tzotzil municipalities of Chanal, Huixtán, and Oxchuc, which served as a military bridge between these three regions.

Although most of the EZLN military bases were concentrated in the eastern and northern parts of the state, the highland municipalities provided important bases of logistic support and sympathizers. During the preparations for war in 1992 and 1993, the EZLN developed logistic support bases in the Tzotzil municipalities of Chenalhó (highlands) and Huituipán (northern highlands). Zapatista sympathizers were concentrated around the Larráinzar/Chenalhó stronghold and within the San Cristóbal de Las Casas, Huituipán, and Simojovel area. In the southeastern part of the state, sympathizers were mostly located around Las Margaritas, mainly in the municipality of La Trinitaria.

Map 6.1 also shows twenty-eight indigenous municipalities that initially stayed aloof from Zapatism. The Zoque region in the western part of the state stands out as the single indigenous region in Chiapas that never participated in the EZLN. Recall that in previous chapters we had already highlighted these municipalities as the only region in Chiapas that did not partake in any of the state's major cycles of indigenous mobilization – the Zoque did not participate in the influential Indigenous Congress of 1974 or in any major wave of land invasion, let alone the Zapatista uprising.

In the next two sections, we will assess whether class, ethnicity or participation in religious or secular networks served as the basis for recruitment of local leaders and community members into Zapatism.

ACCOUNTING FOR THE GEOGRAPHY OF REBELLION: QUANTITATIVE EVIDENCE

The Dependent Variable

The dependent variable for statistical analysis in this section is the *level of community involvement* in the EZLN for the period immediately before the outbreak of war, 1992–1993. I focus on this period because our goal is to explain the recruitment of community, grassroots, and social movements into the EZLN prior to the 1994 outbreak of war. Rather than test these dynamics on all Chiapan municipalities, consistent with the prior analysis of indigenous protest discussed in Chapter 2, here I take as the statistical universe all of the state's municipalities that at any time between 1970 and 1990 had at least 10 percent indigenous population (N = 59).

Explanatory Factors

To test whether the EZLN recruited from communities with dense social networks and from rural indigenous movements, I focus on prior histories of Catholic social activism and of peasant collective action in the 1980s. From the early days of the rebellion, students of Zapatism have argued that Catholic communities and deacons and catechists associated with the progressive theological and pastoral practices adopted by Bishop Samuel Ruiz and his diocese in Chiapas since the 1970s became the social base and leadership of the EZLN (Leyva, 1995; Legorreta, 1997; Womack, 1999). In several interviews, Zapatista leaders and commanders themselves have explained at length that many of their recruits came from the most politicized peasant movements operating in the state throughout the 1980s.

Religious Competition and Catholic Social Networks. Building on results from Chapters 2 and 3, we know that Catholic bishops and priests built a vast network of Bible study groups and economic and social cooperatives in rural indigenous regions facing growing levels of Protestant competition. Quantitative and qualitative evidence showed that religious competition gave rise to these social networks and that these networks, in turn, served as the social base for the rise of peaceful indigenous mobilization.

In this section, I test whether the dynamics of *Religious competition* produced the social networks that served as community bases of support for the EZLN. Following the same strategy as in Chapter 2, I use the effective number of religions (ENR) in 1990 as an indicator of the presence of pastoral practices geared to the development of dense Catholic social networks. Note that most municipalities in the sample belonged to the Diocese of San Cristóbal de Las Casas, under the jurisdiction of Bishop Ruiz.

Although Ruiz's diocese had the highest level of religious competition in the country, there were significant intra-diocesan differences among municipalities and parishes. Competition was higher in Tzeltal and Tojolabal municipalities in eastern Chiapas and the northern Chol region, followed by the Tzotzil highlands. The central valleys registered low levels of competition. It is noteworthy in this geography of religion that the Zoque in the western region of the state were the only major indigenous ethnolinguistic group that remained outside of the ecclesiastic jurisdiction of the Diocese of San Cristóbal de Las Casas. As members of the Diocese of Tuxtla Gutiérrez, a predominantly mestizo jurisdiction that adopted charismatic practices to respond to the predominantly neo-evangelical and Pentecostal competition, traditionalist and charismatic clergy did not encourage the formation of community networks for peasant mobilization.

History of Social Protest. To assess whether the EZLN also recruited part of its leadership and social base from the state's powerful rural indigenous movements, I test for a *History of protest* by dividing the raw number of rural indigenous protest events in the period between 1980 and 1992 by the municipal population. I classified these into four categories: low, medium, high, and severe protest. The two CIOAC strongholds, Simojovel in the northern part of the state and Las Margaritas in the eastern region, were two focal points of intense mobilization. Venustiano Carranza in the central valleys was also a major site of mobilization. In addition, several Chol/Tzeltal municipalities in northeastern Chiapas and the Tzeltal/Tojolabal corridor in the eastern part of the state experienced high levels of mobilization. The local press in Chiapas consistently reported no protest in the western Zoque region.

History of Repression. We know from the state-level statistical analysis in Chapter 5 that the governance strategies adopted by the Chiapas ruling elite to manage protest in the state in the years prior to the liberalization of land tenure was a critical factor motivating the radicalization of Chiapas's peasantry. We recall that two key elements of the new governance strategy were the introduction of a law that criminalized protest and an unprecedented rise in acts of physical aggression and unlawful arrests of social movement leaders and activists.

I generate two indicators of repression to capture the effect of Governor González's punitive strategies to implement the 1992 neoliberal agricultural reforms: one that captures the municipality's own experience of repression victimization, *History of repression*, and a second that captures the information that villagers in the municipality had about the prevailing ecology of repression in the state, *Repression information networks*.

I use the product of the municipal count of acts of repression and the numbers of repression victims per capita, 1980–1992, to assess the direct impact of government repression on the creation of the social bases for the EZLN. I would like to know whether it was villagers from the most repressed municipalities who were most likely to become involved in Zapatism. Unlawful arrests of social movement activists represented the most common type of repression, followed by physical aggression and assassinations. Geographically, the most severe levels of repression clustered in the highlands, the central valleys, and northeastern Chiapas, followed by the municipalities in the Lacandón jungle in the eastern part of the state. Zoque municipalities had the lowest levels of repression.

To capture the likely effect of the dramatic rise of government repression in the state on the decision-making processes of villagers, I created an index of repression information networks. My goal is to assess how news of government repression traveled from one region to another through the two most frequent channels of interregional communication: Catholic diocesan networks and interregional family migration networks.

In 1989, Bishop Ruiz created a human rights center to publicize information about human rights violations in the indigenous regions of Chiapas and to provide legal counseling to victims. Information about government repression traveled across the most closely connected regions in the diocese, including the Tzotzil region in the highlands, the Chol region in the northeast, and the Tzeltal and Tojolabal regions in eastern Chiapas. The central valleys were loosely connected to these information networks, while the Zoque region remained out of the loop. Kinship ties between families of internal migrants also served as channels communicating news of repression, particularly along the migratory routes connecting the highlands and central valleys with the Lacandón jungle in eastern Chiapas. The index of repression information networks is calculated by arithmetically adding levels of repression across the most closely connected regions.

History of Electoral Competition. We know from the state-level results that the absence of meaningful electoral channels for social contestation was associated with rebel activity in the 1990s. Compared to other states, Chiapas showed the lowest levels of electoral competition and alternation of power in the early 1990s. As we showed in Chapter 4, however, indigenous municipalities experienced different histories of electoral competition in the 1980s. I test for the mean effective number of parties per municipality in the 1980s to assess the likely impact of local *Democracy* on levels of community support for Zapatism.

Controls

I include as statistical controls a battery of economic factors typically associated with rebellions: a *Poverty* index, a Gini index of *Land inequality*, and the municipal proportion of land devoted to *Coffee* (a commodity typically associated with revolutionary action). Note that poverty and inequality at this level are significantly correlated, but the association is negative – that is, the poorest and most indigenous municipalities are the most egalitarian ones. As revisionist economic historians and anthropologists have shown, between 1970 and 1990 several regions in Chiapas underwent an economic transition from a plantation economy dominated by *fincas* and *haciendas* to agrarian contexts characterized by the proliferation of miniscule land plots for subsistence agriculture (Villafuerte et al., 1999). As a result of this process of economic transformation, white and mestizo middle-class landowners migrated to Chiapas's main urban centers and these predominantly rural municipalities became more Indianized (Viqueira, 1994).

I also test for demographic factors typically associated with rebellions, including the *Proportion of indigenous population*, the *Proportion of young males*, and levels of *Out-migration* (INI, 1993). Finally, to incorporate a measure of the nature of the terrain, I include the natural log of municipal altitude (*Mountains*).

Statistical Model

Because of the ordinal nature of the dependent variable, I employ ordered probit models. Because most of the economic variables are correlated and because the proportion of indigenous population is highly correlated with poverty, I test these variables in separate models. Both the McKelvey and Zavoina's R^2 and the BIC statistic suggest that Models 2 and 3 are preferable to Model 1.

Results

Table 6.1 summarizes statistical results. Results across models confirm that recruitment into Zapatism was more likely in municipalities with stronger Catholic social networks and with more intense histories of rural indigenous protest.

Results in Models 2 and 3 show that rebel recruitment was more likely in areas with more intense histories of religious competition. Building on the quantitative and qualitative evidence from previous chapters, we can safely conclude that the EZLN recruited from within the hundreds of Bible study groups and economic and social cooperatives that Catholic authorities had built as a response to U.S. Protestant missionary work in Chiapas. Results from simulations using Clarify (Tomz, et al., 2003) show that a municipality under undisputed Catholic monopoly was 80 percent likely to reject Zapatism and had only a 3.7 percent chance of having local villagers join the EZLN as combatants. In contrast, a municipality with 2.5 effective religions was only 34 percent likely to reject Zapatism and had a 25 percent chance of contributing full-time combatants. That is, a municipality with 2.5 effective religions was eight times more likely to have Zapatista combatants than one in which the monopoly of the Catholic Church remained undisputed.

Models 2 and 3 show that Zapatista leaders also recruited from within the peasant indigenous movements that had mushroomed throughout Chiapas

TABLE 6.1. *Ordered Probit Models of Levels of Community Involvement in the EZLN across Indigenous Municipalities in Chiapas, 1992–1993*

	Model 1	Model 2	Model 3
Economic structures			
Poverty	0.788**		
	(0.367)		
Land inequality		1.202	1.251
		(1.853)	(1.924)
Coffee	0.116	0.070	0.137
	(0.236)	(0.225)	(0.210)
Sociopolitical processes			
Religious competition	0.510	0.820**	0.867**
	(0.345)	(0.410)	(0.403)
History of protest, 1975–1992	0.633***	0.879***	0.879***
	(0.232)	(0.251)	(0.220)
History of repression, 1975–1992	−0.010**	−0.015**	−0.016**
	(0.004)	(0.006)	(0.006)
Repression information networks			0.029**
			(0.014)
Democracy, 1985–1991	−0.027	−0.045	−0.026
	(0.058)	(0.066)	(0.071)
Controls			
Proportion indigenous population		0.031***	0.024***
		(0.006)	(0.006)
Proportion of young population (15–25)	14.007	20.01*	19.67*
	(8.725)	(10.82)	(10.61)
Out-migration	0.021	0.062	0.131
	(0.145)	(0.158)	(0.158)
Mountains (ln altitude)	0.466	0.311	0.187
	(0.636)	(0.762)	(0.812)
N	59	59	59
Cut 1	8.370	10.765	10.382
Cut 2	9.086	11.669	11.376
Cut 3	9.199	11.806	11.515
Log-Like.	−58.48	−49.97	−47.96
Chi-squared	20.99	51.16	62.82
Significance	0.012	0.000	0.000
Pseudo R^2	0.125	0.252	0.282
McKelvey and Zavoina's R^2	0.339	0.594	0.623
BIC	−69.803	−82.778	−82.737

***Significant at the 0.01 level; ** Significant at the 0.05 level; * Significant at the 0.1 level. Robust standard errors in parentheses.
Note: Data on poverty comes from SNIM (2003) and data on land from INEGI (1991 b).

during the 1980s. Although the Catholic networks played a major role in the creation of these movements, communist and socialist parties and unions were also actively engaged in protest activities. It was these independent peasant movements that negotiated land redistribution and policy concessions in the streets. Results from a simulation tell us that a municipality with the highest level of protest had a 3 percent chance of rejecting Zapatism and an 80 percent chance of having contributed full-time combatants to the EZLN.

Given the importance, discussed in Chapter 5, that government repression played in dividing states with rebel activity from those without, one of the most surprising results in Table 6.1 is the negative association between state repression and levels of community support for the EZLN. Contrary to the common wisdom about repression and rebellion in Chiapas, results across models show that within a statewide context of growing repression, indigenous municipalities facing the most severe levels of repression *did not* become a breeding ground for rebel recruitment.

However the statewide ecology of repression was not irrelevant at all. The results from Model 3 suggest that people from municipalities that were part of cross-regional information networks about human rights violations in the state were more likely to join the higher ranks of Zapatism. A simple simulation shows that the most regionally networked municipalities, in which communities learned firsthand about human rights violations committed against their coethnics, coreligionists, and family members living elsewhere in the state, were twice as likely to provide combatants to the EZLN as municipalities that were outside these informational loops.

While these networks were closely connected through migrant kinship ties, the most important channels of communication were the Catholic social networks and human rights NGOs linked to the Diocese of San Cristóbal de Las Casas. In the biannual meetings of the Diocese's pastoral team, catechists from all over Chiapas received fresh information about the state of human rights in all of the diocesan regions and brought this information back to their communities.

I take these results to be a reasonable indication that the statewide dynamics of repression in Chiapas created an ecological context of coercion in which communities developed a preventive rationale for the escalation of peaceful mobilization into violent action. Between 1989 and 1992, the most politicized rural indigenous communities and peasant movements that learned from firsthand sources about the increasingly punitive behavior of Governor González and the state judicial police against their peers and family members elsewhere were those who preventively took up arms before the government could crush them.

Results from control variables provide important information. One of the most significant findings is that whereas poverty is strongly associated with support for Zapatism, land inequality is not. Given that our poverty index measures characteristics of indigenous households and the provision of public goods and services, it is reasonable to conclude – following Fearon and

Laitin (2002) – that poverty in this case can be an indicator of weak state capacity. Based on results from Model 1, we can suggest that recruitment into Zapatism was more likely in municipalities that had historically received fewer public goods and services (public education, health, and roads) and where the state government's most active presence had been confined to a clientelistic and piecemeal redistribution of land. In the qualitative section, I present additional evidence to support this conclusion.

The fact that the Gini index of inequality is not statistically significant at the municipal level should not be surprising. As the influential work of revisionist anthropologists and historians has shown in recent years, the Zapatista rebellion was not fundamentally a class conflict between poor peasants and rich landowners but one between poor anti-PRI and pro-PRI Mayan peasants fighting over land (Favre, 2001). Even though in the 1990s Chiapas was the most unequal Mexican state in terms of income distribution, and although the state had historically been dominated by a landed oligarchy, the fact is that throughout the 1980s, the federal and state governments bought large quantities of land from Chiapan landowners to distribute among PRI loyalists and independents (Villafuerte et al., 1999). During this transition, landowners gradually transferred their wealth from fixed assets (land) in the rural periphery to mobile wealth in the growing service sector (tourism) of the state's major urban centers.

Although municipal land inequality in the 1990s does not correlate with support for the EZLN, in the qualitative section I show that the prevalence of state-level income inequalities and the *memories* of land inequality associated with the infamous *finca* system that prevailed in the state until the 1970s informed decisions by individuals and communities to join Zapatism; as the interviews reported in Chapter 5 show, memories of historical inequalities influenced their fears that after the liberalization of land tenure, oligarchs would return to the countryside to rebuild the former *finca* system.

THE SOCIAL BASES OF REBELLION: QUALITATIVE EVIDENCE

Even though the statistical analyses suggest that participation in Catholic social networks and in prior histories of rural mobilization are strong predictors of levels of involvement in the EZLN, the results do not allow us to conclude whether religious or secular networks served as the main conduits for rebel recruitment. Moreover, because poverty and the proportion of indigenous population are positively and significantly associated with community levels of support for Zapatism, we cannot rule out the possibility that rebel recruitment was made on the bases of class and ethnicity.

To gain greater understanding of the social base for rebel recruitment and to explore in greater historical detail the motivations and mechanisms of mass recruitment into Zapatism, in this section I compare the mobilization experience in three municipalities: Las Margaritas, Amatenango del Valle and Simojovel. Roughly similar along important economic and demographic dimensions typically associated with rural insurgencies, these municipalities have different histories of Catholic activism, peasant mobilization, and EZLN participation. A bastion of Zapatism and home of the EZLN's military head-quarters, Margaritas has a long history of religious competition and peasant protest. The nearby municipality of Amatenango del Valle, in contrast, had a limited history of religious competition and peasant mobilization and a low level of involvement in Zapatism. Finally, Simojovel is an outlier: Having experienced one of the most intense histories of religious competition, Catholic social activism, and rural mobilization in Chiapas, Simojovel nonetheless did not play an important role in Zapatism prior to 1994.

Las Margaritas

The life histories of five Tojolabal leaders from Las Margaritas provide us with unique ethnographic evidence to directly test in a highly controlled environment whether Catholic religious networks or secular leftist networks served as conduits for rebel recruitment into Zapatism. This is a group five men from the same age cohort, the same ethnic group, and the same municipality: Antonio Hernández, Roberto Alfaro, Eduardo López, Límbano Vázquez and Humberto Trejo (or Commander Tacho).

This group of Tojolabal leaders share similar family histories in the *fincas* in the region and they all actively participated in peaceful mobilizations for land in the 1980s, particularly with the CIOAC, the most important rural organization in the region. Yet there are two important differences between them: network connections and place of residence. Hernández and Alfaro lived near Margaritas's municipal seat and were part of the secular networks of bilingual teachers linked to the CIOAC, while López, Vázquez and Trejo lived either in the periphery or in the Lacandón jungle and they were active participants in the Catholic networks that were part of the CIOAC.

Map 6.2 shows where these five leaders lived in Las Margaritas. The map is divided into three major zones. Zone I includes the municipal seat, the city of Margaritas, which is surrounded by the rural Margarita Valleys. Although in the late 1980s the city was a semi-urban municipal seat, there were unpaved roads that connected it with Comitán, the third-largest city in Chiapas, and with the rest of the state. The federal and state governments had a small presence in the municipal seat as providers of basic education and health services. Antonio Hernández lived in Ejido Veracruz and Roberto Alfaro, although born in Ejido Artículo 27, lived in Margaritas.[7]

Zone II is a predominantly rural area and in the 1980s access to the villages in the central part of Margaritas was already problematic because the roads were barely, if at all, passable. To travel to the municipal seat from Ejido Tabasco took approximately half a day. The state presence in terms of public

---

[7] Each ejido represents a village. Map 6.2 identifies only the relevant ejidos and villages under study.

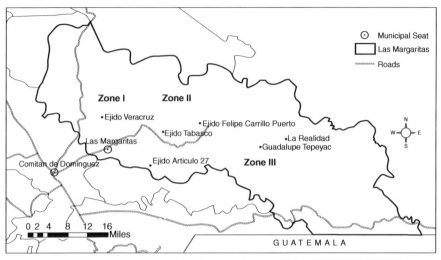

	Zone I	Zone II	Zone III
Terrain	Semi-urban	Rural	Jungle
State Presence	High	Low	None
Networks	Loose/secular	Dense/Catholic	Dense/Catholic
Rebel Support	Sympathizers	Support Base	Combatants
Leaders	Antonio Hemandez Roberto Alfaro	Eduardo Lopez Limbano Vazquez	Humberto Trejo

MAP 6.2. Geography of rebel support by village in Las Margaritas, Chiapas, 1992–1993.

goods provision was very low, but the state judicial police had some presence in these villages suppressing land conflict. Eduardo López lived in Ejido Tabasco and Límbano Vázquez lived in Ejido Carrillo Puerto.

Zone III belongs to the Lacandón jungle and lies along the border with Guatemala. Access to the ejidos and villages in the heart of the jungle in Zone III was problematic – they were at least twenty-four hours from the municipal seat. During the rainy season in the summer, many communities in the Lacandón jungle were completely inaccessible. The state had practically no presence in this region except for the crucial delimitation of property rights. Humberto Trejo, Tacho, lived in La Realidad.

Extensive in-depth interviews with these leaders and with secular and religious actors revealed why religious networks, rather than secular class-based organizations or ethnic ties, served as the privileged channel for recruitment into Zapatism. In what follows I use these narratives to show the microdynamics of rebel recruitment in Margaritas.

Religious Networks. Father Ramón Castillo, the charismatic Catholic diocesan priest who headed *La Castalia*, the diocesan training center for catechists in Comitán/Margaritas discussed in Chapter 3, is explicit about the social origins of the indigenous leaders of the region's peasant movements and Zapatism: "They are all my children!" – he proudly claims.[8]

Humberto Trejo, or Tacho, the indigenous leader with the highest rank in the EZLN, was a student at *La Castalia* in the 1970s. Father Castillo remembers that as a precocious thirteen-year-old, Trejo tried to sneak into the three-month workshops for catechists. When Castillo learned Trejo was under fifteen – the required age for joining the workshops – he asked him to leave. An old Marist brother, Don Tacho, took Trejo under his protection and insisted he stay. The young Trejo became a leading participant in the training sessions, and returned to his village in the heart of the Lacandón jungle in eastern Margaritas.

Over the course of the next decade, Trejo became an influential catechist in the region, one of the founders of Lucha Campesina and a member of CIOAC. As he consolidated his position as an influential religious and social leader in the Lacandón jungle, Trejo was recruited into the EZLN in the mid-1980s. As the leader of ANCIEZ, the civilian branch of the EZLN, between 1989 and 1992 Trejo led the recruitment of thousands of indigenous villagers connected through the Catholic social networks, becoming the rebel group's most effective recruiter of dissident communities. In homage to Don Tacho and other Marist brothers with whom he had actively worked throughout prior to joining the EZLN, Trejo adopted "Tacho" as his *nom de guerre*.

Deacon Eduardo López, a charismatic, influential catechist in the 1970s and a former *miliciano* in the EZLN, recalls how the extensive regional networks of catechists and Catholic Bible study groups and cooperatives in Margaritas served as the preeminent vehicles for rebel recruitment into Zapatism. Personal access to these networks was absolutely crucial for rebel recruitment. López provides an important description of Tacho's own extensive network connections:

Tacho was a great catechist; he was very good at evangelizing, and fearless. He was my guide when I proselytized in the jungle and I was his guide when he came to this region [the long rural stretch between Margarita's municipal seat and the jungle]. Tacho was a very well-known catechist and over the years he was able to build solid trans-community networks in the Tojolabal region. He knows how to build trust among villagers. He was very active in the ejido unions.

López is explicit about the Zapatista methods of recruitment and the motives for targeting such places as the Ejido Tabasco to develop a social base for rebellion:

EZLN commanders first came to Tabasco to recruit in 1989. They were my friends. I knew them all. They would first contact the community authorities; the catechists. Then they would organize a meeting with the community. Tabasco eventually became Zapatista – communities provided logistic and material support and local leaders became *milicianos*. [...] For purposes of recruitment, Zapatista commanders went

---

[8] Interview with Father Ramón Castillo.

where they had access to trustworthy people – they approached Catholic communities, not Presbyterians. It was a security issue.

Límbano Vázquez, a former catechist, former CIOAC regional coordinator in the Lacandón jungle, and himself a former Zapatista commander in 1995, recalls the dynamics of recruitment into Zapatism: "Tacho was a member of a regional network of catechists under my supervision. Once he gave up his lay religious duties and joined the EZLN … he played a key role in recruiting and organizing the social base of Zapatism. When the EZLN began a phase of active recruitment between 1988 and 1992, everything was done underground."

Reflecting about his dual identity as catequist and CIOAC leader, Vázquez is assertive about the preeminence of Catholic religious networks as a privileged channel for underground recruitment. Vázquez recalls that his extensive contacts within the dense Catholic social networks provided him both with key information and with unique access for recruitment. He is emphatic about this point: "Everything I knew about recruitment into the EZLN was because I was a catechist, not because I was a member of the CIOAC. In fact, few of the high-level CIOAC leaders actually knew who joined Zapatism and who stayed out."

The testimony of Pedro Méndez, a Presbyterian villager from La Realidad, one of the villages in Margaritas that became the headquarters of the EZLN, adds important evidence about the secrecy of these networks. A small village of approximately 1,000 inhabitants, La Realidad, like most ejidos in Margaritas, does not seem to be the type of place where enrollment into a rebel group would go unnoticed. And yet, Méndez – then a small child – reports that he was completely taken by surprise when he saw his village neighbors wearing *pasamontañas* (ski masks) and carrying rifles on the morning of January 1, 1994. He recalls the awe of his parents and grandparents, who were among the first converts into the Presbyterian Church in the 1950s: "We knew nothing about Zapatism because all the combatants and *milicianos* were Catholics and we did not participate in Catholic social networks. We found out about the EZLN on January 1, 1994!"[9]

Other municipalities in eastern and northern Chiapas and in the highlands, including Altamirano, Ocosingo, Palenque, Chilón, and San Andrés Larráinzar went through similar processes of recruiting from within the extensive Catholic social networks and social movements, like the process described for Margaritas. A few leading catechists and deacons, including Tacho and David – the highest indigenous commander in the highlands – played a crucial role in recruiting communities within their home regions and beyond.

Members of the diocesan pastoral team and members of religious orders responded differently to the recruitment of their star catechists and social base into Zapatism: some tried to block the Zapatista commanders' access to their region (such as the Jesuits of the Mission of Bachajón) while remaining sympathetic to the movement, but others (such as diocesan priests) simply let

---

[9] Interview with Pedro Méndez.

communities decide. Still others remained intimately close to those communities that joined the EZLN (such as the Dominicans).[10] As the single religious order that had been most clearly identified with the *finca* system (the Dominican Order had been the largest landowner in the region in the nineteenth century), facilitating recruitment to Zapatism was a clear opportunity for Dominican friars to reverse this historical reputation deficit.

Despite the different strategic responses adopted by members of the pastoral team of the Diocese of San Cristóbal de Las Casas, they were all united by one goal: to protect the precious Catholic social capital they had built up in previous decades and to avoid a major defection from Catholicism in the event of a major uprising. To serve this end the clerics and nuns, like their parishioners, kept the secret of their communities' underground rebel recruitment to Zapatism. Moreover, after the outbreak of war in 1994 Bishop Ruiz became a crucial mediator in the first round of peace negotiations between the EZLN and the federal government.

Secular Networks. Professor Roberto Alfaro, a rural bilingual teacher and CIOAC leader with no access to the Catholic social networks, did not join the EZLN in any capacity. When I openly asked why he did not join, he gave three reasons: "By then I was persuaded that it was easier to achieve economic and social goals through electoral competition than through military action. Furthermore, I was not prepared militarily and I lived near the municipal seat of Margaritas where the army had easy access."

Antonio Hernández, one of the most prominent CIOAC leaders, was not a catechist but, as we extensively discussed in Chapter 4, had significant contacts with Catholic social networks, and also lived in the Valleys of Margarita. He did not participate in the EZLN until after the outbreak of war, when he served for a very brief period of time as political liason for the rebels. When asked why he did not join the EZLN in the late 1980s, he offers two reasons: "At that time I was actively involved in civilian and political life and because I was not a member of the Catholic social networks."

Even though CIOAC secular leaders like Luiz Hernández, Antonio's brother, and Antonio Vázquez became strategic supporters of the EZLN in 1994, the fact remains that the mestizo leadership of the EZLN never seriously tried to recruit these leftist socialist leaders and their networks. After 1995, they moved into electoral politics and, following Margarito Ruiz, led the development of a powerful national pan-Indian organization that rivaled with the Zapatistas for the vanguard in the struggle for the rights to autonomy and self-determination for indigenous peoples – the National Indigenous Assembly for Autonomy, or ANIPA.

Why Rebel Recruitment Relied on Religious Networks. These testimonials clearly suggest that it was Catholic social networks, rather than secular

---

[10] For an important discussion of the strategic differences between the Jesuits of Bachajón and the Dominican Order on the question of support for the EZLN see De Vos (2002).

Catholic   Socialist

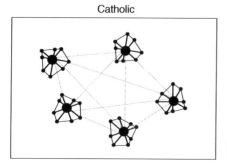
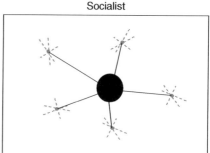

FIGURE 6.1. Social networks and rebel recruitment.

networks and movements, that served as the virtually exclusive vehicle for mass recruitment into the EZLN. It is puzzling that the mestizo and predominantly secular leadership of the EZLN decided from the outset to primarily target lay religious leaders and communities to create their social base for guerrilla warfare. Although Tojolabal leaders initially recruited by the Communist Party and trained in Cuba, like Antonio Hernández, were ideologically closer to them, the EZLN founders went after the catechists and their networks to build a popular base for war.

Figure 6.1 presents two illustrations that help us resolve this puzzle: religious networks were more conducive to successful rebel recruitment and guerrilla warfare than secular socialist networks. Whereas the decentralized and horizontal network connections Catholic clergy had built in response to the spread of U.S. Protestantism had the structural features that facilitated rebel recruitment, the leftist parties' centralized and hierarchical networks constructed to fight fraud and develop a core electoral constituency did not.

Leftist secular networks had two structural weaknesses that made them unattractive for rebel recruitment: centralized leadership structures and weak local associational networks. Organized under principles of "democratic centralism," as we extensively discussed in Chapter 4, secular networks of dissident rural bilingual teachers were dominated by a few charismatic leaders – including Margarito Ruiz, the Hernández brothers, Antonio Vázquez, and Roberto Alfaro, among others – but with weak associational networks in the ejidos and the villages. Any meaningful connection in this network passed through the centralized leadership.

In a context in which subnational authorities had adopted repressive policies targeting social movement leaders, a centralized network structure entirely dependent on a few leaders was highly vulnerable. Given the structure of interactions in this network, an attack on the leadership would bring the group to a near collapse.[11] In fact, the arrest or assassination of a few important individuals would end the revolutionary potential of the group. Moreover and

---

[11] I follow Siegel (2011) here.

equally important, the structure of these secular networks did not provide the communal associational density, trust, and secrecy that facilitates underground rebel recruitment and that provides the social capital that rebels use to hide during guerrilla warfare.

In contrast, religious networks had structural features that facilitated rebel recruitment: decentralized and horizontal regional structures that connected multiple local lay leaders (catechists) who had access to dense local associational networks (Bible reflection groups and economic and social cooperatives). Unlike the small centralized secular leadership of teachers, which was vulnerable to targeted repression, this structure of multiple local lay leaders was highly resilient to leadership removal. Moreover and most importantly, the structural position of each catechist gave him access both to dense local associational networks and to other leaders with equally powerful local associational structures. As the in-depth interviews with Eduardo López and Límbano Vázque suggest, unlike the weak secular village-level connections, the dense Catholic associational networks provided the trust, friendship and secrecy for underground recruitment. And the linkages that connected catechists across villages and regions proved to be privileged connections for recruiters to reach communities beyond their own home regions – to spread information and to give access to Commanders David and Tacho and other Zapatista recruiters.

The mestizo founders of the EZLN worked tirelessly to penetrate these Catholic associational networks. Once they had succeeded in recruiting a few important catechists in the mid-1980s, through them, the EZLN gained access to these powerful religious networks. As Tacho's personal trajectory makes clear, the first indigenous recruits into Zapatism made extensive use of their personal relationships with other catechists and their privileged access to the dense Catholic social networks to build the leadership and social base of the rebel group. These were networks of friendship and trust that had developed during nearly two decades of community religious organization (to prevent the further expansion of Protestant churches) and of secular mobilization (for land redistribution).

These experiences of social interaction and clearly demarcated group boundaries along religious lines provided Zapatista commanders such as Tacho with the trust, secrecy, and exclusivity to recruit the social base and leadership of Zapatism from within Catholic social networks. Mayan peasants who were not part of these Catholic social networks were not subjects of recruitment even if they were poor, exploited peasants from marginalized and discriminated ethnic groups like the Catholics who were recruited into the EZLN.

Amatenango del Valle

Geographically situated halfway between the city of San Cristóbal de Las Casas in the highlands and Las Margaritas in eastern Chiapas, the poor, predominantly indigenous agrarian municipality of Amatenango del Valle did not become a major locus of Zapatista recruitment. Up to the early 1990s, the municipality had been served by a traditionalist priest who had barely left the parish house in the municipal seat for more than a decade.[12] Facing no significant competition for indigenous souls in the municipality and despite the high levels of poverty among Tzeltal villagers, Father Juan organized no Bible study groups, economic and social cooperatives, or any rural or indigenous movement.

With no meaningful religious challenge, Bishop Ruiz did not direct any clerical capital – by then fully engaged in major battles for indigenous souls elsewhere in the state – to Amatenango. By the time Tacho and some of the most influential former catechists were recruiting the social base for Zapatism in the late 1980s, there were no reliable contacts in Amatenango who might have brokered the entry of Zapatista recruiters into the communities, nor any dense associational networks to hide Zapatista combatants. Hence, they did not recruit Amatenango communities into the EZLN. In fact, Amatenango shared a feature with the twenty-eight municipalities identified in Map 6.1 as places with no Zapatista presence: in the late 1980s, they were not part of the extensive Catholic associational networks.

The sudden and rapid spread of Christian-based sects and Pentecostal missions in Amatenango in the late 1980s and early 1990s led Bishop Ruiz to appoint Father Ramón Castillo – the former director of *La Castalia* in Comitán/ Margaritas – as parish priest. Assisted by an energetic team of nuns, Castillo soon developed a small network of Bible study groups and economic and social cooperatives and recruited some of the most promising community leaders to build social networks and social services that would serve to prevent large-scale defections from Catholicism.

As the Zapatistas were preparing for war in 1993, some members of these new associational networks were enlisted at the last minute into the EZLN as sympathizers. On January 1, 1994, as the Zapatistas traveled from the jungle to the highlands – Father Castillo recalls – Tzeltal villagers from Amatenango were cheering the commanders.

The Puzzle of Simojovel

The absence of a strong combatant base in the Tzotzil municipality of Simojovel in the northern part of the Chiapas highlands is particularly puzzling. Even though Father Joel Padrón had worked tirelessly throughout the 1980s to develop a dense network of Bible study groups and unions, and even though the CIOAC had led hundreds of land occupations in Simojovel, neither catechists nor grassroots leaders from Simojovel became Zapatista combatants. Although some communities eventually became more involved in the rebel group after 1994, it is strange that one of the most activist and combative municipalities in Chiapas did not become a military bastion for the EZLN.

The testimony of Father Joel Padrón, the Catholic diocesan priest who was unlawfully arrested in 1990, provides key clues for understanding the

---

[12] Interview with Father Ramón Castillo.

absence of a Zapatista military post in Simojovel. When asked to reflect on the difference in the Zapatista experience between Las Margaritas and Simojovel, Padrón is explicit about the cause: the unprecedented presence of military, police and secret service personnel in the municipality in the late 1980s and early 1990s.

Following the 1988 presidential campaign, in which the CIOAC and Catholic social networks overwhelmingly supported the leftist opposition candidate and provided the mass following for his campaign in Simojovel, the federal government sent federal military troops stationed in the neighboring state of Tabasco to the municipality. Between 1990 and 1991, Simojovel was under siege; approximately 300 state judicial police and federal troops were permanently stationed in the municipality. Padrón recalls the scene: "State police presence was permanent in Simojovel. This did not allow for any underground activities." He reports that a stranger shadowed him continuously for much of 1990 and 1991, until his arrest.[13]

The municipality having suffered through one of the most punitive waves of government repression in Chiapas in the 1980s, the constant military and police presence made it too risky for Zapatista recruiters from the highlands to approach Catholic social networks in Simojovel the way Tacho was doing in the Lacandón jungle. Recruiters such as David, the highest-ranking indigenous commander in the highlands region, were able to contact some of the leading catechists in Simojovel, but the few local leaders who joined the rebels as combatants moved away from Simojovel and those communities that joined the EZLN did so only as sympathizers.

The case of Simojovel shows that during the stage of mass recruitment into Zapatism between 1989 and 1992, the moral indignation sparked by state repression among its victims did not suffice to drive Simojovel villagers into the arms of Zapatism. It also shows that a powerful sense of religious duty and a high regard for rebellion as a productive process in the search for the Promised Land was not sufficient motivation to join the rebels either. Instrumental calculations associated with security concerns did play a major role in the decision-making processes of communities and their leaders, even the most religious ones.

Religious and secular leaders from San Juan Chamula (in the highlands) and Venustiano Carranza (in the Central Valleys), the two other municipalities that experienced the harshest levels of repression in Chiapas in the 1970s and 1980s, adopted a similar strategy to that of villagers in Simojovel and kept their distance from Zapatism. If anyone from these communities joined the rebels and participated as a combatant or *miliciano*, it was outside the municipality, for it was impossible to conduct any meaningful recruitment within it.[14] Even though the statewide context of repression and the dual threat of economic and political reversion created a revolutionary context, the strong

[13] Interview with Father Joel Padrón.
[14] Interviews with Fathers Ramón Castillo and Joel Padrón.

state presence and the history of repression in Simojovel, San Juan Chamula and Venustiano Carranza did not allow for rebel recruitment, even when dense Catholic networks existed.

But the repressive experiences of these municipalities – particularly under the new criminal law approved in 1991 – served as important input to create a sociotropic perception of repression among villagers closely connected to them. Members of the pastoral team of the Diocese of San Cristóbal de Las Casas used the extensive Catholic social networks to disseminate news of government repression from such places as Simojovel, San Juan Chamula and Venustiano Carranza all the way to tiny Catholic communities in the Lacandón jungle.

CONCLUSIONS

Karl Marx famously claimed in the nineteenth century that peasants and clerical authorities were quintessential reactionary actors. Clerics represented the interests of the ruling class and their religious message was nothing less than "the opium of the masses" (Marx, 1844/1994). And peasants were no more than "sacks of potatos" waiting to be manipulated against progressive change (Marx, 1854/1994). Yet students of revolutions in the twentieth century discovered that peasant support was a sine qua non for successful guerrilla warfare and in the past few decades social scientists have discovered the power of religion for insurgent collective action (Wickham-Crowley, 1992). Most explanations rest on peasant's class position or on the ability of religion to foster radical attitudes.

In seeking to explain the revolutionary actions of Mayan indigenous peasants from Chiapas, Mexico, in this chapter we have put to test the social base of recruitment into the Zapatista National Liberation Army (EZLN). Using a wide variety of original sources of quantitative and qualitative evidence, one of the main findings in this chapter is that class, occupation, place of residence, or ethnicity did not guide rebel recruitment, but participation in religious networks did.

Within a subnational context in which authoritarian elites were adopting punitive measures to end a six-decade-old program of land reform and liberalize land tenure in Chiapas, Catholic social networks built in response to the spread of U.S. Protestant missions were the primary vehicle for the recruitment of communities and social movements into the EZLN. As we refined our analytical lens and moved from the study of municipalities to villages, hamlets, and individuals, the evidence consistently showed that participation in Catholic social networks was the crucial factor that distinguished those poor indigenous peasants who joined the rebel group from those who did not.

Gould's (1995) pioneer research showed that residential networks, rather than class positions, served as the associational glue for the revolutionary actions of the Paris Commune of 1871, and here we have provided new evidence to suggest that Catholic religious networks served as the main mobilizing vehicle for rebel recruitment into the EZLN in late twentieth-century Chiapas. This finding is consistent with Wood's influential (2003) work, in which she provides extensive micro level data showing the crucial role that Catholic communities and networks played in forging the connections, social norms and emotions that sustained peasant revolutionary action in El Salvador.

Although Catholic progressive Theologies of Land and Resistance provided powerful narratives to justify rebellion, the main factor that made progressive Catholicism a crucial source for rebel recruitment was the structural characteristics of Catholic social networks. The systematic comparison of religious and secular networks makes this point evident.

Responding to the decentralized evangelizing strategy of U.S. Protestant missionaries, Catholic clergy in Chiapas's indigenous regions developed decentralized, horizontal social networks that connected hundreds of local community leaders (catechists) with unique access to dense community associational networks. Unlike centralized secular leftist organizations with weak local leaders, these Catholic social networks provided the ideal social infrastructure for rebel recruitment and for the development of a communal base of support for rebellion. In the context of a major regime reversion threat, those villages and communities that were part of Catholic social networks were more likely to join rebel groups to thwart the likely regression to an authoritarian status quo ante.

The chapter further showed that within a statewide context of repression, catechists and members of Catholic social networks did not, however, behave like martyrs but instead followed a preventive strategy in response to the punitive implementation of market reforms. Those facing the harshest levels of repression did not rebel, but those closely connected to them preventively joined the Zapatistas and took up arms to contest what they believed was an imminent return to a plantation economy sustained by an oligarchic subnational political regime. Community leaders and activists who joined the EZLN were employing a preventive strategy: attacking the government before they could be crushed by the subnational elites. Note, however, that the information they received about rising levels of repression was to a great extent the result of their participation in cross-regional Catholic networks.

State-level results from Chapter 5 and the municipal and village-level results reported in this chapter show the need for a multilevel approach to understanding the microdynamics of the escalation of protest into rebellion and recruitment from grassroots movements into insurgent groups. Even though this chapter has shown that religion played a crucial role in the development of the social bases for Zapatism, we must bear in mind that this dynamic was activated the decision of Chiapas's secular elites to adopt a punitive strategy to implement an unpopular market liberalization reform. In the absence of these punitive policies, as we showed in Chapter 5, radical Catholic practices did not serve as a vehicle for recruitment into a rebel group in the Diocese of Tehuantepec in Oaxaca.

Up to this point, we have analyzed how religion and politics combine to provide the social networks, ideological resources, and political opportunities and threats for peaceful protest and for the escalation of protest into rebellion. But the competition for indigenous souls and votes also played a crucial role in another important transformation within Mexico's cycle of rural indigenous protest: the politicization of ethnicity. We now turn to explain the sudden and unprecedented rise of ethnic identities in late-twentieth-century Mexico.

PART IV

THE POLITICIZATION OF ETHNICITY

7

Politicizing Ethnicity

The Breakdown of Religious and Political Hegemonies and the Rise of Indigenous Identities

Ethnic minorities do not always make ethnic claims. Millions of people throughout the world speak minority languages at home and their daily personal interactions in their communities are structured by traditional ethnocultural norms, but many of them nonetheless do not publicly articulate their claims in ethnic terms. The quintessential intellectual victory of the constructivist paradigm – the dominant school in the study of social identities – is to have forced us to ask about the conditions that allow people to politicize their shared identities.[1]

One of the most common explanations of the politicization of social identities in recent years points to globalization (Nash, 2001; Olzak, 2006). Scholars suggest that the threats and opportunities associated with globalization have facilitated the mobilization of ethnic minorities in ethnic terms. While economic and trade liberalization may threaten the livelihood of ethnic minorities and their traditional ways of life, the globalization of rights – religious, ethno-territorial, democratic, for example – enable them to contest these threats on multicultural grounds. What is unclear in this literature, however, is how minorities manage to act collectively and respond to the threats and capitalize on the opportunities afforded by globalization.

The literature on the unprecedented wave of indigenous mobilization in Latin America has contributed important insights to explanations of the rise of ethnic identities. Based on the idea of cultural survival, some scholars propose that indigenous communities that were able to preserve their most fundamental cultural traditions and communal norms through centuries of colonial rule and mestizo cultural hegemony took to the streets and mobilized under an ethnic banner when the penetration of capitalist global markets endangered their traditions and ancient ways of life (Nash, 2001).

A prominent alternative explanation suggests that while the neoliberal turn in agricultural policies ended Indians' opportunities to mobilize as peasants

---

[1] The crucial claim is that social identities do not give rise to collective mobilization but the other way around – identities are the contingent outcome of social mobilization. See Laitin (1986), Przeworski and Sprague (1988), Kalyvas (1996), and Hechter (2000).

(Le Bot, 1994; Van Cott, 1995; Yashar, 2005), the rise of a new system of international law favoring indigenous peoples' rights opened the door to demands for ethnic autonomy and self-determination (Brysk, 2000). In this explanation, cultural survivors from the lowlands and indigenous communities that had persisted under the façade of rural corporatist organizations in the highlands took advantage of these new international legal instruments to publicly articulate their ethnic claims (Yashar, 2005).

In Chapter 1 we developed a new explanation in which indigenous ethnic minorities experiencing the most intense processes of political and cultural differentiation, rather than homogenous communities of cultural survivors, responded to global threats and took advantage of global opportunities by mobilizing in the name of ethnicity.

Focusing on the breakdown of Catholic hegemonic controls, we suggested that the spread of U.S. Protestant competition, the translation of Bibles to local languages and the training of native pastors would motivate Catholic clergy to become major promoters of indigenous languages, cultures and rights. Focusing on the breakdown of authoritarian secular controls, we suggested that the introduction of government-controlled elections and the spread of electoral competition would motivate opposition parties to initially embrace and promote minority demands. If elections became free and fair and opposition parties became major contenders for power, parties would drop ethnic minority demands. But fraud and coercion and the threat of political reversion might radicalize minorities in embracing radical agendas for territorial autonomy and self-determination.

The first goal of this chapter is to test whether the introduction of a new international regime of indigenous rights and the introduction of neoliberal agricultural reforms are associated with the rise of indigenous ethnic identities (see H.7). Based on information from the MII Dataset, I show that rural indigenous movements did not begin to make ethnic claims until eighteen years into the cycle of indigenous protest and that the rise of ethnic claims took place only *after* the introduction of neoliberal agricultural reforms and the globalization of indigenous rights.

The second goal of the chapter is to assess whether homogenous communities of cultural survivors or communities experiencing the most intense levels of religious and electoral competition responded to these macro international and domestic changes by raising the ethnic banner (see H.2b and H.3b).

I provide extensive statistical evidence showing that religious competition was a strong predictor of ethnic claim-making: ethnicity was not politicized in closed corporate communities dominated by the Catholic Church but in communities where Protestant churches succeeded in challenging the Catholic hegemony. Based on extensive fieldwork in northeastern Chiapas – Mexico's most dynamic religious market place – I show how one of the most successful U.S. Protestant missionary experiences in Latin America led the Society of Jesus – the fiercest defenders of the Catholic Church – to become major promoters of the Tzeltal language, culture, and governance practices. By analyzing the competitive process of Bible translations to the Tzeltal language by SIL and Jesuit missionaries, the Jesuits' defense of the patron saint system against Protestant challenges, and the Jesuits' promotion of organic export agriculture based on indigenous ancient practices, I show why the spread of U.S. Protestantism led the Catholic Church to become a long-term promoter of ethnic identities and to the rise of a new indigenous ethnic pride.

I also provide new statistical evidence showing that the rise to power of leftist political parties in rural indigenous municipalities shaped the politicization of ethnicity in important ways. I show that their initial spread was associated with a rise of ethnic claims but the consolidation of leftist parties as major power contenders led them to incrementally drop ethnic claims. Based on extensive fieldwork in northeastern and southeastern Chiapas, I show how some of the most influential Tzeltal and Tojolabal social leaders and long-time promoters of ethnic rights and identities strategically diluted radical ethnic claims when it became evident that electoral victories were dependent on their ability to build cross-class and pluralistic electoral coalitions and to appeal to the median voter, who was not always indigenous or who did not endorse ethnic claims despite being indigenous.

The final goal of this chapter is to extend theory testing to the surprising transformation of the Zapatista National Liberation Army (EZLN) from a peasant insurgency into a self-determination movement. This is a puzzling case because Latin America's most emblematic indigenous insurgency of the twentieth century only articulated a programmatic agenda of ethno-territorial demands twelve years after its foundation and twelve months after it declared war on the Mexican government. It is also puzzling because neither Mexico's neoliberal agricultural reforms nor a new international regime of indigenous rights initially motivated the EZLN to go ethnic.

I provide original evidence showing that the transformation of the EZLN into a self-determination movement was a strategic response to electoral fraud and coercion: although Mexico's authoritarian elites consented to relatively free *federal* elections, they deterred the move of the Zapatistas into *subnational* politics in Chiapas via fraud. Together with the evidence on peaceful ethnic protest, this finding allows us to show that whereas the deepening of political liberalization into democratization dilutes ethnic minority demands, political reversal via fraud and coercion against minorities moves them into become radical self-determination movements (see H.8).

The chapter begins with definitions of ethnicity and the politicization of ethnicity, it moves on to discuss empirical evidence on the rise of ethnic mobilization in Mexico, and then it proceeds to theory testing. In the final section, I discuss theoretical implications of this chapter's findings for a more general understanding of the renegotiation of social identities in times of major cultural and political transformation.

POLITICIZING ETHNICITY

This chapter makes a crucial distinction between ethnicity and the politicization of ethnicity. This is the distinction drawn between an individual's social identity and the collective articulation of this identity in the public arena. I refer to the process of public articulation of ethnic identities as the politicization of ethnicity. To understand the politicization of ethnicity, we need to have a basic definition of ethnicity.

Ethnicity

I understand ethnicity as a social category that serves to identify group members on the basis of individual characteristics associated both with descent (Horowitz, 1985; Chandra, 2007) and shared histories of domination (Weber, 1956/1978). Indigenous communities are groups larger than families but smaller than nation-states that (1) speak a shared pre-Hispanic language; (2) never became racially mixed with the Spanish conquistadores or with their mestizo descendants; (3) survived three centuries of colonial rule and two centuries of independent mestizo governments; and (4) developed communal governance practices and social and cultural norms distinct from all other members of the colonial and postcolonial societies.

Using narrow linguistic criteria, the 1990 Mexican census reported that nearly 10 percent of Mexico's population was indigenous. With approximately sixty-two different ethnolinguistic groups dispersed mainly across central and southern states and the Gulf of Mexico, in absolute terms Mexico's indigenous population is the largest of any Latin American country. Historically dispersed across subnational political and administrative jurisdictions, language has not been a source of aggregation of indigenous communities. As historians and anthropologists have noted, the indigenous social norms and institutions that historically evolved within municipal boundaries became the main source of ethnic identification (Bonfil 1987/1996; Dehouve, 2001).

Since colonial times, the municipality has been the level within which common cultural norms and governance practices are shared. Some of these norms and practices have persisted; others have been dramatically transformed. Over time, however, the municipality remained the essential domain for the persistence and reinvention of ethnicity. Scholars of religion have shown that the Catholic municipal "patron saint" and the festivities and cultural norms associated with it have played a crucial role in the development of indigenous identities. In fact, the indigenous symbols and institutions associated with the municipality and the municipal patron saint became a major source of indigenous identities. Hence, Mayan-Tzotzil-speakers from the highlands of Chiapas did not identify as Mayans (pan-ethnic) or Tzotzils (ethnolinguistic), but adopted local identities associated with the patron saint of their municipality – for example, "pedranos," those from San Pedro Chenalhó.

The Politicization of Ethnicity

The prevalence of ethnic practices at the community and municipal level does not imply that ethnicity serves as an important cleavage for politics.

In this definition, the politicization of ethnicity entails a process of public aggregation and expression of demands based on ethnic criteria. Hence, I understand the politicization of ethnicity as the process by which social and political actors frame their public collective claims in ethnic (indigenous) terms. Ethnicity is politicized when communities, social movements, or insurgent groups take to the streets or take up arms demanding rights and benefits for ethnically defined groups; when political parties draft their ideological platforms and run campaigns using explicit ethnic categories and appeal to ethnolinguistic populations; and when states establish political institutions or follow public policies with the explicit purpose of favoring ethnically defined populations.

In this chapter, I focus on the politicization of indigeneity via social mobilization – social protest and armed insurgency. I define indigenous *ethnic* mobilization as a process of social contestation against state authorities undertaken by indigenous populations, in which ethnic claims become the critical demand. Note that in this definition I impose the requirement that only indigenous populations can make public claims related to indigeneity. Yet the crucial underlying assumption in this definition is that when indigenous populations mobilize, the claims they make are not necessarily ethnic. Here I assume that ethnicity is politicized only when indigenous populations mobilize for ethnically defined purposes. Hence indigenous mobilization is not the same as ethnic mobilization.

Note that consistent with this definition, I do not use language as an indicator of ethnic mobilization. Rather, in the analysis I use linguistically defined indigenous populations to delimit the sample population and then assess the dynamics of ethnic claim-making in municipalities that at any time between 1970 and 2000 had at least 10 percent indigenous population (the national mean for this period). Indigenous ethnic claims in Latin America have traditionally focused on rights (Van Cott, 2000; Yashar, 2005) rather than policy outcomes and have included a broad spectrum of rights ranging from demands for cultural recognition and bilingual and intercultural education to demands for autonomy and self-determination.

EMPIRICAL EVIDENCE OF THE POLITICIZATION OF ETHNICITY IN MEXICO

Ethnic Claim-Making in Mexico's Cycle of Indigenous Protest

Drawing on information from the MII Dataset, Figure 7.1 illustrates the evolution of indigenous demands during the cycle of rural indigenous protest. The MII identifies 5,120 protest claims made in 3,553 protest events. This means that there were, on average, 1.2 collective claims per event. To facilitate the empirical analysis, I collapse the forty-two most common demands into three main social categories that form the indigenous identity repertoire: economic (class), political (liberal citizenship), and ethnic (multicultural citizenship).

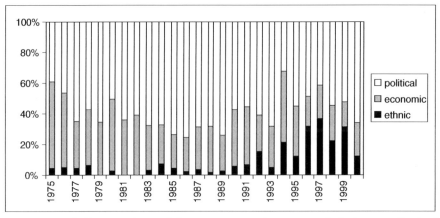

FIGURE 7.1. Indigenous demands in protest events by category (relative contribution).

Economic demands include mainly demands for the provision of social services, claims for land redistribution, and objections to neoliberal reforms (free trade and market liberalization). Political demands encompass the democratization of municipal power structures, respect for human rights, the end of government repression, and religious freedoms. Ethnic demands involve the provision of social services earmarked for indigenous populations, constitutional recognition of indigenous peoples, and constitutional rights to autonomy and self-determination for indigenous peoples. These are not individual claims, but collective group demands as expressed in collective acts of contention.[2]

I take group protest claims as reported by Mexican journalists in daily newspapers as an indicator of the politicization of social identities. Note that I do not use the journalists' description of the protesters' identity as an important piece of information. My main source of information is the journalists' report of the demands the group make in the public arena. Although there were significant differences in how journalists from different newspapers described the same group of protesters,[3] there were rarely any significant differences in the report of the group's demands.

One of the most significant features of Mexico's cycles of indigenous protest is that indigenous claims evolved during the course of the cycle of protest, undergoing a series of transitions from material demands for land redistribution, to claims for civil and political liberties, to demands for ethnic autonomy and self-determination. Economic demands dominated the cycle at the start but declined sharply from a historical high of 60 percent in 1975 to 20 percent

[2] Individual preferences do not always coincide with the claims and demands made by collective actors. Based on a pioneering survey of indigenous and nonindigenous citizens conducted in three Mexican states in 2002, Eisenstadt (2006) reports that ethnicity is not a good predictor of community attitudes associated with ethnic claims.
[3] Descriptions included "*campesinos*," "*labriegos*," "*comuneros*," "*ejidatarios*," "*indígenas*," and in other instances journalists described protesters as members of specific ethnolinguistic groups.

in 2000. Political demands were dominant throughout the cycle, particularly in the 1980s when they represented two-thirds of all claims. Ethnic demands rose from near nonexistent to almost 40 percent in 1996–1997.

Disaggregating indigenous collective claims reveals critical aspects of the cycle. Land redistribution was indisputably the dominant indigenous economic claim. Sixty-four percent of all economic demands involved some claim to land and 30 percent concerned the provision of social services. Demands for land reform exploded in the 1970s and represented almost half of all peasant indigenous claims between 1975 and 1982, but declined to 25 percent in the remainder of the decade. In the years leading up to the liberalization of land tenure, land demands returned to the forefront, and in 1994 – the year of the Zapatista rebellion – land redistribution became the dominant indigenous claim in the country. After 1994, land demands subsided to a historical low of 13 percent.

Respect for human rights was the leading political claim. Sixty-two percent of all political demands involved claims against police and military repression and petitions for the release of political prisoners, and 30 percent involved requests for municipal democratization. In the 1980s Mexican indigenous protesters made demands for liberal citizenship, including respect for human rights and municipal democratization. After a dramatic slowdown of political demands in 1994, protest against human rights violations rapidly increased as the Mexican military expanded its operations across Mexican indigenous regions in the southern and central states, and paramilitary groups emerged in the Zapatista conflict zone in Chiapas.

The right to autonomy for indigenous peoples was the leading ethnic indigenous claim in Mexico. Fifty percent of all ethnic demands involved calls for autonomy and self-determination, 40 percent for cultural recognition, and 10 percent for ethnically earmarked anti-poverty funding. Nineteen-ninety-two marked a turning point in the contemporary history of Mexico's indigenous movement, as many rural indigenous organizations made a strategic shift from class to ethnic identities. In the early years (1992–1995) of the initial politicization of ethnicity, demands involved the expansion of bilingual education programs, interpreters in the courts, and constitutional recognition of indigenous peoples as part of the Mexican nation. The right to autonomy and self-determination became the leading demand of Mexico's indigenous movements only after the EZLN embraced a programmatic agenda for ethnic autonomy and self-determination in 1995.

Even though substantive claims and identities evolved throughout the cycle of rural indigenous mobilization, from class to liberal citizenship to multicultural claims, what remained constant was the "rights-based" nature of indigenous demands. In each of the three major categories, indigenous claims involved demands for rights: rights to land (economic); human rights and rights to free and fair elections (political); and ethno-territorial and cultural rights (ethnic). There is, indeed, a legalistic and rights-based nature to indigenous struggles in Mexico and throughout Latin America. This has been evident in our discussions of rights to land redistribution from previous chapters and

TABLE 7.1. *Leading Zapatista Demands in Two Rounds of Peace Negotiations*

1994[a]	1995–96[b]
1. Work	1. Indigenous Rights and Cultures
2. Land	2. Democracy and Justice
3. Housing	3. Development and Welfare
4. Food	4. Indigenous Women in Chiapas
5. Health care	
6. Education	
7. Independence	
8. Freedom	
9. Democracy	
10. Justice	
11. Peace	

[a] All items were part of a general negotiation.
[b] Items were discussed sequentially in different negotiation rounds. Peace negotiations did not progress beyond item #2.

will become crucial in the discussions that follow about rights to autonomy and self-determination.

Rebel Demands for Ethnic Autonomy and Self-Determination

When the EZLN declared war on the Mexican government in 1994, the rebel claims were those typically associated with a rural insurgency (Collier, 1994). Their claims were for land and democracy (Harvey, 1998). A year later, however, the Zapatistas underwent a dramatic metamorphosis and became a self-determination movement. Table 7.1 provides evidence of this major transformation. It summarizes the main items of negotiation during the first and second rounds of peace talks between the Zapatistas and the federal government.

During the first round of peace negotiations in 1994, the main items for negotiation included land redistribution, public goods and services for indigenous communities, social transfers, access to a fair judicial system, and free and fair elections. As Moreno Toscano (1996), a member of the government delegation, recalls, the agenda for negotiation was laid out by the Zapatistas themselves and was a replica of the list of claims the rebels had raised in their first public communiqué – the *First Declaration of the Lacandón Jungle*. As shown in Table 7.1, this collection of claims resembled a leftist program of material and pro-democracy demands rather than the ethno-territorial agenda of a self-determination movement. Even though the language of indigeneity and racial discrimination against indigenous peoples was widely used in the first weeks after the outbreak of war, the EZLN never outlined a program of ethnic demands during the first round of peace negotiations – that is, Mexico's most emblematic indigenous insurgency of the twentieth century did not initially politicize ethnicity.

During the second round of peace negotiations in 1995–1996, however, the EZLN explicitly included an ambitious programmatic agenda of ethno-territorial demands. Although the Zapatistas wanted to negotiate a major agenda of national electoral and judicial reforms first and then move on to discuss indigenous cultures and rights, the federal government pressed for giving priority to the indigenous agenda, as shown in Table 7.1.[4]

After a few months of intense negotiations, an agreement was reached by both parties on item one, by which the federal government and the Zapatistas agreed to a list of ambitious constitutional changes granting autonomy and self-determination rights to indigenous peoples. However, President Ernesto Zedillo (1994–2000) did not honor the agreement and the PRI froze a limited bill on indigenous rights in Congress until the end of Zedillo's administration.[5] During these years, the Zapatistas consolidated a network of municipal and regional de facto autonomous governments claiming legitimacy under ILO Convention 169.

Both the evidence on the rise of ethnic claims after two decades of indigenous protest and the transformation of the EZLN into a self-determination movement suggest that the public expression of ethnic claims was the result of a complex process of strategic interaction between incumbent authorities and indigenous movements and their social and political allies. Before we try to account for this surprising process of politicization of indigeneity, however, we need to explain why ethnic claims and identities were originally so conspicuously absent from Mexico's political landscape.

ACCOUNTING FOR THE HISTORICAL ABSENCE OF ETHNIC CLAIMS IN MEXICO

Colonial empires and autocracies in independent countries have historically been brutally successful in shaping, reinventing, or suppressing ethnic identities (Laitin, 1986; Posner, 2005). Colonial and authoritarian elites strive to homogenize multiethnic societies; they construct authoritarian controls on the basis of one or a few cleavages while suppressing most other sources of collective identification. In the Mexican experience, while Spanish colonial institutions created the institutional base for the rise of communal indigenous identities, the PRI's policies of state-building nationalism in the twentieth century actively sought to suppress indigenous ethnic identification and replace it with class (peasant) identities.

Colonial Rule

Ruled under the Spanish empire for three centuries, between 1521 and 1821, the Mesoamerican region underwent one of most remarkably complete

---

[4] In Chapter 8, I explain the federal government's motivations to prioritize indigenous rights in the peace negotiation with the Zapatistas.
[5] Chapter 8 provides an extensive explanation of Zedillo's decision.

experiences of diversity destruction and homogenization in modern world history. Through coercive colonial institutions, the Spanish empire reengineered the cleavage structure of Mesoamerican societies and dramatically reduced to a few categories a myriad of racial, religious, linguistic, tribal, territorial, and class cleavages that had previously existed in the civilizations and societies that inhabited the region in pre-Columbian times (Bonfil, 1987/1996).

The invention of the "Indian" as one of the principal colonial categories was one of the most important legacies of three centuries of Spanish rule in the Americas. Throughout this long period, entire native societies and hundreds of different ethnolinguistic groups were lumped together and recategorized as "Indians." In New Spain, the Spanish Crown established "Indian Republics" ruled by councils of elders and communal assemblies under a set of internally defined rules that would later be known as indigenous customary laws and traditions. In exchange for this sphere of political and judicial autonomy, native members of these "Indian Republics" would pay taxes and tribute and provide labor to the conquistadores, their descendants, and the Catholic Church. Native Mesoamerican populations were able to survive under these colonial rules and categories, and the "Indian" or "indigenous" identity became a synonym of cultural resistance and survival.

Single-Party Hegemony

A century after independence, the second most brutal and successful attempt at reengineering the cleavage structure of Mexican society took place under the PRI hegemony, from 1929 to 2000. Unlike the Spanish colonial empire, which had created and sustained the "Indian" identity as a dominant racial and political category for autocratic governance, the postrevolutionary PRI regime consistently and systematically pursued a policy of nation building that suppressed indigenous identities (Gutiérrez, 1999; Jung, 2003). Like most populist authoritarian regimes in Latin America and elsewhere in the developing world, the PRI sought the assimilation of a still rather diverse ethnocultural indigenous mosaic into a mestizo hegemonic project. Rural indigenous populations would be encouraged to increasingly abandon their languages and cultures and embrace the Spanish language instead; to express their grievances as peasants (class) but not as Indians (ethnicity); and to channel their claims within the corporatist rural organizations of the PRI.

Revolutionary nationalism – the PRI's homogenizing strategy – rested on three policy areas: agriculture, education, and language. Agricultural policies served as the preferred government tool to turn Indians into peasants (Bartra, 1993). Beginning in the 1930s, based on new postrevolutionary agrarian laws, PRI officials encouraged rural indigenous populations to join the rank and file of the party's National Peasant Confederation (CNC) and frame their demands in material rather than cultural terms. As members of the CNC, rural indigenous populations could apply for land reform, credit, price subsidies, and special aid for marketing agricultural products. As Indians, however, their land

and economic resources were severely limited. Although land was distributed to groups of individual households (ejidos) and to communities (communal ejidos, mainly indigenous), the preferred and most rewarded channels for redistribution were the PRI's corporatist, class-based organizations.

Education policy was a major tool for building a national consciousness around the mestizo hegemonic mainstream. Modeled on the Napoleonic system of centralized, secular public education, Mexico's national education curricula for elementary education exposed students to an exhaustive coverage of the history of Aztec, Mayan, Olmec, Zapotec, and other major pre-Hispanic civilizations, but conspicuously ignored their living descendants (Gutiérrez, 1999). Instead, *mestizaje* was celebrated in national history textbooks (Aguilar Rivera, 2001) as the racial synthesis that defined the country – "the cosmic race," in Vasconcelos's infelicitous language. Racial discrimination was disguised under the illusion that people of mixed race would not discriminate against their own indigenous roots. However, as experimental studies show (Aguilar-Pariente, 2008), the opposite was true: indigenous phenotypical features came to be stigmatized as backward and undesirable.

Spanish was never defined as the official language of the Mexican education system because the Mexican state pursued an active policy of bilingual education. However, the main goal of the government's bilingual education programs was not to promote indigenous languages but to Hispanicize indigenous populations (Gutiérrez, 1999). Following the advice of William Townsend and the SIL discussed in Chapter 3, Mexican education policy makers were persuaded that the most effective way to assimilate indigenous populations to the mestizo mainstream was to first make them literate in their mother tongues and then introduce them to Spanish and assimilate them into the mestizo Spanish-speaking world (Gutiérrez, 1999; Hartch, 2006).

State-building nationalism under the PRI was a powerful and effective authoritarian ethnic assimilation experiment. State policies and institutions defined a structure of payoffs that dissuaded Mexican indigenous populations from adopting ethnic identities and encouraged them instead to adopt class (peasant) identities in virtually every public aspect of their lives. Faced with few prospects of social, economic, or political mobility as Indians, rural indigenous persons were compelled to relinquish most forms of public ethnic identification in order to participate in Mexico's twentieth-century authoritarian institutions. Indigenous languages and customary practices remained alive across hundreds of indigenous municipalities and thousands of communities, but the political institutions of single-party autocracy provided no meaningful incentives for indigenous communities to articulate ethnicity in the public arena.

MACRO INCENTIVES TOWARD ETHNIC MOBILIZATION

How did the robust authoritarian equilibrium the PRI had built around class and *mestizaje* unravel? A series of major international and domestic transformations that developed around 1992 contributed to undermining the positive

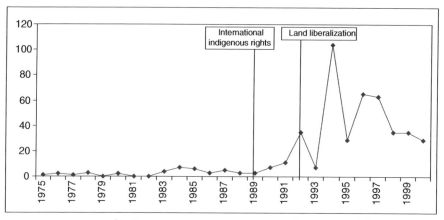

FIGURE 7.2. Count of indigenous protest events with explicit ethnic claims.

payoffs historically associated with peasant identities while at the same time revaluing ethnic forms of identification for Mexico's rural indigenous populations. The literature on Latin American indigenous mobilization has persuasively argued that the neoliberal turn in agricultural policy across the region (Van Cott, 1995; Yashar, 2005) and the creation of a new international indigenous rights regime (Brysk, 2000) provided powerful incentives for the politicization of ethnicity.

Figure 7.2 provides visual quantitative evidence of the likely causal association between the major macrostructural reforms of the early 1990s and the rise of ethnic demands within Mexico's cycle of indigenous protest. Although some minor ethnic claims were made in the 1970s and in the 1980s, Figure 7.2 clearly shows that ethnic claims became an important demand in the identity menu of rural indigenous movements only *after* 1992.

As we discussed in previous chapters, the end of Mexico's ambitious program of land reform and the liberalization of land tenure in 1992 represented the final blow for rural mestizo and indigenous rural households to a six-decade-long agrarian pact between the Mexican postrevolutionary regime and the country's peasantry. The dissolution of the Mexican state's commitment to redistribute land to the peasantry and to subsidize the production, marketing, and consumption of agricultural commodities contributed to undermining incentives for Indian peasants to continue expressing their grievances under peasant identities. Even though the reform would turn mestizo and Indian rural villagers into private owners of land who would no longer have to work and live on lands that actually belonged to the state (ejidos), survey evidence cited in previous chapters suggested that up to three-quarters of Mexico's rural households strongly opposed the reform.

At the international level, in the context of the Quincentennary of the Conquest of the Americas in 1992, international organizations introduced a new international law regime for indigenous peoples. The centerpiece of the new system was *The Indigenous and Tribal Peoples Convention, No. 169*, approved by the ILO, an independent agency affiliated with the United Nations, in 1989. Convention 169 called for the recognition of indigenous peoples as subjects of group rights and defined a long list of collective rights in such diverse areas as language, education, customary law, governance, and property rights over land and natural resources (ILO, 1989/2004). The Mexican Senate approved the adoption of Convention 169 in 1989, and one year later the Mexican Congress introduced an important amendment to the federal constitution recognizing indigenous peoples as the founding ethnic groups of the Mexican nation.

As several scholars have argued and indigenous activists have recognized, when the agrarian policies that supported the adoption of peasant identities went into crisis, the adherence of the Mexican state to ILO Convention 169 and the important, albeit limited, multicultural constitutional reforms raised hopes for ethnocultural rights and identities among rural indigenous organizations (Sánchez, 1999; López Bárcenas 2002; Jung, 2003; Mattiace, 2003).

MICRO INCENTIVES FOR ETHNIC PROTEST

Even though incentives to switch from class to ethnicity involved all Mexican rural indigenous population and movements, only a few actually did so. To account for spatial variation in the intensity of ethnic mobilization, we need to understand the process that gave rise to the formation of a proethnic coalition and the subnational contextual conditions that motivated the politicization of ethnicity. We test whether homogenous communities of cultural survivors capitalized on opportunities for ethnic mobilizaton or whether it was those experiencing the most intense processes of religious and electoral competition who did so.

Quantitative Evidence

The Dependent Variable. I take indigenous ethnic mobilization as an indicator of the politicization of ethnicity. I measure ethnic mobilization as the number of ethnic claims made in indigenous protest events. Following the same criteria used to measure the number of protest events in Chapter 2, I do not take the raw number of ethnic demands (N = 462) reported in the MII data set as a measure of the dependent variable, but rather the number of municipalities making ethnic claims per protest event (N = 1,143). To be sure, this is a different set of events from the ones tested in Chapter 2. For one thing, it is not a measure of protest events but of *claims*. The MII reports on average 1.26 claims per protest event. For another, this indicator only counts ethnic claims (13 percent of total protest event claims) and excludes economic (29 percent) and political (58 percent) demands. I cover the 1975–2000 period.

Explanatory Factors. I first test for macro incentives for the politicization of ethnicity. To test for the effect of major macro international and domestic changes,

I include a dummy variable for the 1992–2000 period, *Post-1992 dummy*, to distinguish between the years before and after the liberalization of land tenure and the emergence of a new international regime of indigenous rights. I also introduce a dummy variable to identify the years of major *Economic policy shifts*, as in Chapter 2.

Although most students of Latin American indigenous mobilization agree on the macro shocks that stimulated ethnic mobilization, the mobilizing agents that promoted the politicization of ethnicity remain under dispute. The central argument of this book is that the breakdown of religious and political monopolies led to the renegotiation of traditional hegemonies in Mexico's rural indigenous regions. In Part II of this book, I showed that this renegotiation empowered rural indigenous communities to mobilize for land redistribution. Here I want to test whether this renegotiation facilitated the rise of ethnic identities in the 1990s.

I test for the effect of *Religious competition* on ethnic mobilization using the effective number of religions (ENR). I test for the level and *Growth rate of religious competition* (1970–2000) on ethnic claim-making. Recall that my theoretical argument was that the translation of Bibles to indigenous languages by U.S. Protestant missionaries and the creation of local churches led by native pastors would encourage Catholic authorities in competitive districts to become major promoters of indigenous languages, cultures, ethnic identities and rights. Hence, I hypothesized that the spread of religious competition would be associated with the rise of a new ethnic pride (see H.2b).

I also test for the effect of the spread of *Electoral competition* and the presence of leftist opposition parties using the effective number of municipal parties (ENP). Given that leftist parties were the main opposition to the PRI in rural indigenous regions up to the late 1990s, ENP captures dynamics of both electoral competition and leftist presence. My theoretical argument was that in their dual attempt to fight fraud and establish a core electoral constituency, opposition parties would initially establish socio-electoral coalitions with independent indigenous movements – such as those nurtured by Catholic communities – and embrace their ethnic claims but once the opposition became competitive and elections relatively free and fair party leaders and candidates would drop radical ethnic claims. Hence I test for ENP and ENP^2 (see H.3b).

I test for government attempts to oppose ethnic claims via state *Repression* using a count measure of government repression from the MII Dataset. I assume that PRI governments would prefer to channel rural indigenous demands via class-based material claims, as they did for most of the twentieth century.

I test the religious and electoral competition hypotheses against two alternative mobilization vehicles for ethnic claim-making: corporatism and community survival. In some accounts, peasant indigenous leaders of underfunded rural corporatist unions and cohesive indigenous communities that received collective land and succeeded in safeguarding indigenous cultural autonomy served as mobilizing agents for the politicization of ethnicity (Yashar, 2005). I use the same indicator of *Corporatism* as in Chapter 2 and continue to use *Indigenous pop. (%)* as an indicator of cultural survival.

I include seven controls: economic (*Poverty* and *Economic crises*), demographic (*Indigenous pop., ln*), and geographic (*South*), as well as a one-year lag of *Economic, Ethnic* and *Political protest* to assess whether ethnic claims grew out of prior ethnic or nonethnic claims.

Statistical Models. Table 7.2 presents the results of fitting negative binomial regression models to the total frequency of ethnic claim-making by indigenous municipality for the period between 1975 and 2000. Models 1 and 2 show results from random (RE) and fixed effects (FE) models covering the 1975–2000 period. In Model 3 I aggregate all ethnic claims for the 1990s and run cross-sectional regressions. I concentrate on the 1990s for two reasons: (1) the large substantive effect of the *Post-1992 dummy* on ethnic claim-making in Model 2 confirms that this is indeed a critical time period for analysis; and (2) as Figure 7.2 shows, hardly any ethnic claims were made prior to the 1990s. By focusing on this segment of the cycle, Model 3 partially reduces the potential for bias because of the large number of zero counts. In this model I introduce two additional variables: *Communal Land* (the municipal proportion of nonprivate land plots, 1990) to further assess the mobilizing role of autonomous communities, and guerrilla presence, *Rebellion*, to assess the effect of the EZLN and other rebel groups on ethnic claim-making. Note that I average all explanatory variables for the 1990–2000 period, the only exception being the protest lags which result from the aggregation of all protest events in the 1980s and the rate of growth of religious competition (1970–2000). For interpretation I rely on RE models.

Statistical Results. The statistical results confirm that the major international and domestic macro-institutional changes Mexico experienced in 1992, including a new international regime of indigenous rights, the liberalization of land tenure, and the constitutional recognition of indigenous peoples, were crucial reasons why peasant indigenous movements raised the ethnic banner in the 1990s. The results specifically show that major economic policy shifts in agricultural policies were associated with sudden and large – threefold – increases in ethnic claims.

When we look at the dynamics of micro-mobilization, the results show that ethnicity was politicized not in the more culturally and politically homogenous indigenous municipalities, but in the more heterogeneous ones – in larger and more racially mixed municipalities, where religious and partisan competition, as well as political protest and the presence of the EZLN, had been more intense.

Models 1–3 show that the level and growth rate of religious competition are strong predictors of indigenous ethnic claim-making. Model 1 shows that for every additional religion in an indigenous municipality's religious marketplace,

TABLE 7.2. *Negative Binomial Models of Intensity of Ethnic Claim-Making by Mexican Indigenous Municipality, 1975–2000*

Indep. Var.	Model 1 (TSCS, 1975–2000)			Model 2 (TSCS, 1975–2000)		Model 3 (CS, 1990s)
	RE	IRR	FE	RE	IRR	Coeff.
Shocks						
Economic	1.288***	3.628	1.366***	0.844***	2.327	
policy shifts	(0.088)		(0.090)	(0.102)		
Post-1992				1.309***	3.705	
dummy				(0.151)		
Micro-mech.						
Religious	0.983***	2.672	1.075***	0.831***	2.297	0.993***
competition	(0.162)		(0.229)	(0.160)		(0.379)
Electoral	1.466***	4.334	1.384***	0.933***	2.543	0.469
competition	(0.330)		(0.359)	(0.320)		(0.334)
Electoral	−0.227***	0.796	−0.231**	−0.153***	0.857	
competition²	(0.073)		(0.081)	(0.070)		
Repression	0.053***	1.055	0.045***	0.047***	1.048	0.001
	(0.015)		(0.016)	(0.014)		(0.011)
Rebellion						0.690***
						(0.189)
Controls						
Corporatism	−1.159***	0.313	−1.297***	−1.321***	0.266	0.274
	(0.303)		(0.330)	(0.309)		(0.649)
Indigenous	−0.988***	0.372	0.158	−1.587***	0.204	−2.434***
pop. (%)	(0.296)		(0.563)	(0.301)		(0.433)
Poverty	−3.018***	0.048	−5.262***	0.247	1.281	2.800***
	(0.581)		(0.643)	(0.686)		(1.021)
Economic crises	−0.376***	0.686	−2.482**	−0.133	0.874	
	(0.118)		(0.116)	(0.120)		
Indigenous	1.099***	3.003	0.518***	1.105***	3.021	1.047***
pop. (ln)	(0.084)		(0.170)	(0.080)		(0.098)
Ethnic prot $_{t-1}$	0.012	1.012		0.000	1.000	
	(0.022)			(0.022)		
Constant	−12.859***		−6.850***	−13.464***		−11.060***
	(0.785)		(1.414)	(0.779)		(1.193)
T × N	21,543		5,412	21,543		871
Log Like.	−2,463.10		−1,598.53	−2,423.45		−795.47
Wald chi²	852.21		645.01	864.46		321.58

***Significant at the 0.01 level; ** Significant at the 0.05 level; * Significant at the 0.1 level. Standard errors in parentheses (Model 3, robust standard errors).

RE = random effects; FE = fixed effects; IRR = incidence rate ratios; TSCS = time-series-cross-section models; CS = cross-section models.

Note: Religious competition in Model 3 measures the rate of growth, 1970–2000; *South, Communal Land* and the lags for economic and political *Protest* not shown.

ethnic claims are likely to increase by 167.2 percent (IIR = 2.672). Model 3 shows, moreover, that not only high levels but a history of religious competition can become an important predictor of ethnic mobilization. This finding provides a strong basis for suspecting that where the competition for indigenous souls was more intense, communities experienced a linguistic and cultural renaissance and a sizeable boost in ethnic pride. Results from previous chapters lead us to believe that Catholic clergy in competitive regions were a major institutional player in the rise of a proethnic coalition.

Models 1–2 show that the spread of electoral competition had considerable, albeit distinct, effects on ethnic mobilization. Model 1 shows that during the initial phase of electoral competition opposition parties embraced and actively mobilized ethnic demands and identities, but as competition became more widespread they discouraged ethnic forms of identification. This finding suggests that leftist opposition parties were only an opportunistic member of a proethnic coalition during the stage in which opposition parties fought to establish a minimal electoral coalition and combat electoral fraud, but became a deterrent of ethnic mobilization thereafter.

Comparing the results of different models shows that ethnic claims were endogenous to the cycle of indigenous protest. Models 1 and 2 show that municipalities where rural indigenous movements had embraced an agenda of universal respect for human rights and free and fair elections by the 1980s were more likely to engage in ethnic claim-making in the 1990s. Results also show that a history of government repression did not discourage but stimulated ethnic mobilization. These findings hint at a potential metamorphosis from liberal rights to multiculturalism in municipalities where civil rights and liberties were effectively denied via electoral fraud and movements repressed.

The models show that the emergence and spread of Zapatism in Chiapas was a powerful stimulus for the politicization of ethnicity. The rise and transformation of the EZLN into a self-determination movement did, therefore, have a powerful effect in provoking a switch to ethnicity among rural indigenous movements. As I discuss later in the chapter, as soon as the EZLN embraced a program of ethnic autonomy and self-determination, Zapatism became the lead actor in Mexico's proethnic coalition.

Finally, the results suggest that corporatism depressed, rather than encouraged, ethnic mobilization. This should not be surprising. After Mexico's CNC survived the neoliberal turn in agricultural policy and continued to be a key institutional member of the ruling coalition (Gibson, 1997), PRI-affiliated rural indigenous villagers became major detractors of ethno-territorial claims. The statistical output also shows that neither cultural autonomy nor communal land tenure structures provided the structural context for the politicization of ethnicity. Because the smallest and most culturally homogenous communities were under the monopoly of the PRI, neither the PRI nor the CNC were part of the proethnic independent coalition, as these results show.

Qualitative Evidence

Progressive Catholic clergy, leftist parties, rural indigenous movements, and Zapatism were the four constitutive actors of a proethnic coalition. This section discusses the motivations that led clerics, partisan leaders, and social activists to embrace ethnicity. In the following section, I assess the motivations that caused Zapatism to become a self-determination movement.

Why the Catholic Church Became an Unconditional Promoter of Ethnic Identities. Under the pressure of U.S. Presbyterian and Pentecostal competition, Catholic clergy in competitive districts became one of the most important institutional promoters of ethnic identities and rights in Mexico. As part of a member-retention strategy, Catholic bishops and their pastoral teams actively promoted (1) indigenous languages and cultures and local autochthonous churches; (2) indigenous customary law; and (3) ancient indigenous agricultural practices and the development of organic agricultural cooperatives, particularly coffee for export. These actions established the Catholic Church in competitive regions as a long-term sponsor of ethnic identities and contributed to the rise of a new ethnic pride (see H.2a).

Ethno-linguistic revival. As in sixteenth-century Europe (Anderson, 1991), the Protestant translation of Bibles to "vernacular" languages led to a major linguistic revival and to the rise of a new ethnic pride. The fact that U.S. Protestant missionaries not only translated Bibles to indigenous languages but also promoted the formation of new native clergy who used indigenous languages for evangelizing shifted the arena of religious competition to the ethnic camp.

Unable to decentralize ecclesiastic hierarchies to the extent that their competitors did, Catholic clergy in competitive districts sought to avoid a major defection to Protestantism by introducing a radical reinterpretation of the Gospel, based on indigenous cultures, histories and ways of life. Known as "inculturation" theology, the Catholic member-retention strategy entailed a major interpretative shift in Christian theology and the rise of indigenous theologies.

The experience of the Tzeltal region in northeastern Chiapas – Mexico's most competitive religious marketplace – illustrates how these competitive dynamics contributed to the revival of ethnic identities. Led by U.S. SIL missionary and linguist Marianna Slocum, a team of professional linguists worked in the translation of the Bible to the Tzeltal language throughout the 1950s and 1960s and well into the last quarter of the twentieth century. The availability of the Gospel in the Tzeltal language was an instant success; it triggered an unprecedented wave of conversions to the Presbyterian Church and turned the northeastern Tzeltal region into one of Mexico's most religiously contested areas.

The Jesuit Mission of Bachajón, Chilón, initially established in 1959 to arrest the growth of U.S. Protestantism in the region, led one of the most ambitious attempts of reinterpretation of the Christian Gospel based on Tzeltal history. Although the Jesuits had adopted Tzeltal as their pastoral language in the 1970s, it was not until the 1990s that they undertook a major Bible translation, involving expert linguists, Tzeltal deacons and catechists, and Bible study groups.[6] Unlike SIL linguists who had made *literal* translations of the Bible, the Jesuits adopted a *contextual* translation in which major passages of the scriptures and crucial religious symbols were retold in terms of Tzeltal history, culture, and ancient indigenous religious beliefs. This process involved more than a decade of intense community discussions in which the Bible was practically reinterpreted based on major elements of Mayan religious and cultural traditions. Published in 2010, the Catholic Tzeltal Bible marked a major event in contemporary Tzeltal history.

As a result of six decades of competition between Protestant and Catholic missionaries for indigenous souls, the Tzeltal language and culture became fundamentally ingrained into Christianity. But there were fundamental differences that reflect how far churches were willing to go to enlist or retain indigenous souls into their fold: Whereas the Protestant God learned to *speak* Tzeltal, the Catholic God *became* Tzeltal. These historical transfigurations of Christian deities that resulted from intense processes of competition contributed to a linguistic revival and the rise of a new ethnic consciousness.

Defending customary practices. Hegemonic institutions often strategically adopt policies that contradict their own traditional practices to safeguard their dominant position. After centuries of actively seeking to suppress pre-Hispanic religious practices, Catholic clergy in competitive districts became fierce defenders of what had been considered for centuries one of the most "pagan" institutions in rural indigenous regions: the system of municipal patron saints.

Since colonial times, the annual festival of the patron saint has been a fundamental institution of traditional indigenous governance. The annual festival honoring a white European Catholic saint is both an opportunity to legitimate those community members who have reached positions of power through the cargo system and a chance to reaffirm community cohesion. As discussed in Chapter 1, the cargo system is the ladder to positions of power in the community and an institutional mechanism of group survival established during colonial times. Male heads of households climb the communal power ladder through service, through their contribution of free labor for the provision of communal public goods and services and through unpaid administrative work.

Refusing to participate in the annual festival of the municipal patron saint is the first indicator that a rural indigenous household has converted to a non-Catholic Christian faith. Catholic clergy in competitive districts have become fierce defenders of the patron saint system and by default of the cargo system;

---

[6] This section is based on in-depth interviews with key participants in the process of translating the Bible to the Tzeltal language, including Father Felipe J. Ali Modad, SJ, who coordinated the translation project, Verónica Martínez, the Bible's artistic designer, and Gilberto Moreno, a native catechist and linguistic adviser.

in fact, Catholic authorities have conveniently turned the defense of the patron saint system against Protestant and Pentecostal attacks into a defense of indigenous customary law and practices and of cultural survival – a matter of community ethnic rights.

Here, too, the experience of the Tzeltal region in northeastern Chiapas is relevant. In the 1980s the Jesuit Mission of Bachajón had encouraged the formation of human rights NGOs to support peasant struggles for land and democracy, and in the mid 1990s the Jesuits transformed these NGOs into advocacy groups for indigenous rights to autonomy and self-determination. The defense of the patron saint system has become an essential part of this struggle. Based on ILO Convention 169, Catholic clergy in competitive districts have come to question the religious liberties of Protestants and Pentecostals on multicultural grounds; they claim that by boycotting the annual festival, non-Catholic Christian churches are undermining the cultural rights of indigenous communities.[7]

The Jesuit struggle in favor of the patron saint system and of indigenous customary practices has become a crucial member-retention strategy. A Jesuit missionary put it to me plainly during the annual festival of Santo Domingo in Chilón, Chiapas: "Our survival in the indigenous world is tied to the survival of the patron saint system."[8]

A new "indigenous" economy. As avid readers of Italian Marxist Antonio Gramsci, Catholic clergy in competitive districts know that social identities do not survive in the absence of a strong material base.

After 1992 and particularly after the transformation of Zapatism into a self-determination movement, Catholic clergy became major sponsors of cooperatives for organic agriculture, particularly organic coffee for export to the United States and Western Europe. As part of the fair trade movement, these cooperatives have become successful cases of a new brand of social capitalism in which the justification of organic agriculture is based on indigenous ethnic and Christian religious narratives. The financial success of these cooperatives and the justification of their existence based on ancient indigenous agricultural practices have contributed to creating the material bases to sustain indigenous ethnic identities.

The experience of the Jesuit Mission of Bachajón is instructive here again. During a fieldtrip to the Jesuit mission, my visit to the headquarters of the mission's human rights center in Chilón was telling of Chiapas's identity shifts. As I went into the center, I saw offices at the entrance of the house full of boxes and files of human rights violations and posters of Christian human rights martyrs. As I moved into the patio, there were rooms where people discussed indigenous rights. But in the backyard, at the end of the house, I found a remarkable coffee production site, where the son of one of the region's founding catechists was processing organic coffee beans and packing them for export

---

[7] This is one of Marroquín's (2007) central arguments in the context of Oaxaca.
[8] Interview with Father Oscar González, SJ.

to the United States and Europe. Father Oscar González, SJ, the center's director and the chief financial officer of the coffee cooperative, was clear about the center's new activities: In the absence of economic options, young Tzeltal men will leave for the United States; the production of coffee keeps them close to their community and their traditions. In Gramsci's terms, we may add, it provides the material bases for the prevalence of indigenous cultures and Catholic hegemony.

Why Leftist Parties Became Opportunistic Promoters of Ethnic Claims. Unlike the Catholic Church, which became a long-term promoter of indigenous rights and identities, leftist opposition parties strategically embraced ethnic claims on their path to local power but then became institutional detractors of the politicization of ethnicity. Not only did the rise of the Left to local power entail the demobilization of a major cycle of rural indigenous protest; it also involved the depoliticization of ethnic claims. After the 1996 national electoral reform, which guaranteed free and fair elections, and as the PRD was becoming the largest opposition force in Congress and a major power contender in Mexico's countryside, Leftist leaders rapidly began to distance themselves from the EZLN and its radical demands for autonomy and self-determination.

The experience of the CIOAC in the eastern municipality of Las Margaritas in Chiapas helps explain the mechanics behind this process. Influenced by their participation in international indigenous conferences, in the late 1980s CIOAC leaders developed a coherent program calling for indigenous rights to autonomy and self-determination for the Tojolabal region of Las Margaritas (Mattiace, 2001). Although Catholic social networks had worked for more than a decade to develop a linguistic renaissance and foster Tojolabal pride, it was the secular CIOAC leaders who first developed an ethno-territorial rights agenda for indigenous peoples.

As Antonio Hernández – the CIOAC leader whose story was told in Chapter 4 – recalls, communist and socialist parties initially viewed their emerging agenda of ethnic demands with suspicion but were supportive of their claims as long as the CIOAC contributed with anti-PRI votes and helped combat electoral fraud.[9] In fact, the national leadership of the PRD was a major promoter of ethnicity in the years leading up to the major mobilizations against the Quincentennary of the Conquest of the Americas in 1992. And in the aftermath of the Zapatista uprising, the PRD even introduced an internal statutory reform to create a council for indigenous peoples as an institutional forum for the hundreds of rural indigenous leaders who had joined the party in the preceding years. Between 1995 and 1996, the PRD provided financial support enabling leaders and activists of the leading indigenous movements from southern and central Mexico to organize national social forums in Mexico City to discuss the legal implications of a likely reform of the constitution to introduce rights to autonomy and self-determination for indigenous peoples.

[9] This section draws from three rounds of interviews with Antonio Hernández.

After the 1996 electoral reform and more specifically after the PRD became
a major power contender in national and local politics, however, party leaders
gradually withdrew their financial and institutional support for ethnic agendas.
Hernández bitterly recalls that a prominent PRD leader warned him of this
new reality in 1997: "The doors have closed," he was told. As we discussed in
Chapter 4, in Margaritas, Chiapas, the CIOAC splintered into a pro-Zapatista
group, CIOAC-Independiente led by Antonio Hernández and committed to
an agenda of ethno-territorial rights, and another group, CIOAC-Histórico,
constructed a multi-class coalition in which ethnic claims were diluted. Even
though Antonio Vázquez, a Tojolabal leader from CIOAC-Histórico, had been
sworn in as rebel president of the de facto Zapatista Municipality of San Pedro
Michoacán in 1995, in 2001 he ran for office on a PRD ticket supported by
a cross-class constituency that included the town's mestizo economic elite.
Ethnicity played *no* role in his campaign or in his administration. In fact, during the years in which CIOAC-Histórico ruled in Margaritas in the 2000s,
ethnicity faded as the CIOAC became a clientelistic machine and clientelistic
rewards were distributed by class and residence criteria.

Former indigenous leaders who were committed to the politicization of ethnicity in the 1980s tell similar stories of the erosion of ethnic identities as
they rose to power with the Left. Manuel Gómez, one of the most respected
Tzeltal social leaders of the Catholic social networks associated with the Jesuit
Mission of Bachajón, did not embrace any ethnic agenda when he became the
first Tzeltal president of the municipality of Chilón in 1996. Héctor Sánchez,
the historic Zapotec leader of the COCEI, and the first indigenous mayor of
Juchitán in the Oaxaca Isthmus, similarly dropped all major ethnic claims after
he won the municipal presidency in 1989. As a PRD candidate for the governorship of Oaxaca in 1998, Sánchez never articulated a programmatic ethnic
agenda during his campaign. Other important leaders in Guerrero and Tabasco
also dropped ethnic agendas as soon as they came to power as PRD senators,
deputies, or mayors.

Indigenous leaders and activists who joined the PRD and came to power
abandoned ethnic claims for purely electoral and governance reasons. As the
PRD became a national party in an increasingly level playing field, their ambi-
tion to persuade the median (mestizo) voter led PRD leaders to drop ethnic
minority claims, by then associated with an increasingly essentialist ethnic
agenda espoused by the Zapatistas. Given that indigenous populations do not
represent a majority in any of Mexico's thirty-one states, this strategy was
extended to the subnational level.[10] And in the municipalities, as Gómez and
Sánchez reported, the politicization of ethnicity would have politically and
financially alienated them from the state and federal governments, where ethnic criteria were not prevalent. On their way to power, indigenous leaders and
activists campaigned in both Spanish and indigenous languages, dressed in
both Western and indigenous clothes, but never embraced an ethnic program.

[10] For the importance of the population size of ethnic minorities on electoral politics, see Posner
(2005).

In summary, indigenous regions and municipalities with histories of intense religious competition experienced a renaissance of indigenous languages and ethnic pride after 1992. Yet, in those regions and municipalities that also experienced intense electoral competition processes, the rise of leftist parties to power eventually entailed the depoliticization of ethnic demands and identities; ethnicity faded as the left transformed itself from an opposition movement-party to a ruling party. In contrast, in subnational jurisdictions where the spread of multiparty competition was thwarted by coercion and fraud, dissident movements embraced radical ethno-territorial claims. This was the emblematic case of the Zapatistas.

FROM PEASANT INSURGENCY TO SELF-DETERMINATION MOVEMENT

Unlike a large number of rural indigenous independent organizations, which were eventually absorbed by leftist parties and dropped ethnic claims, the EZLN remained a staunch defender of indigenous peoples' rights to autonomy and self-determination. Why did a rebel group that had declared war on the Mexican government demanding land and democracy so rapidly transform itself into a movement for autonomy and self-determination for indigenous peoples? To understand this metamorphosis, we need to account for the timing of the transformation and then explain spatial variation in rebel ethnic claims across Zapatista-controlled areas.

Going Ethnic

As Figure 7.3 shows, the dramatic metamorphosis of the EZLN from a classic peasant armed insurgency into a self-determination movement took place *after* 1994. It illustrates the proportion of ethnic demands made by the Zapatista civilian bases of support in 118 contentious actions between 1994 and 1999. It shows that after 1994, the EZLN radically funneled an important proportion of the movement's demands into a program of ethno-territorial rights. Given the de facto power that the Zapatistas had up to the end of the Zedillo administration, this strategic choice turned them into the most radical promoters of indigenous ethnic identities and the de facto leading organization in the struggle for indigenous autonomy and self-determination in Mexico.

Three major events account for this shift. The first was a fraud-ridden gubernatorial election in Chiapas. While the Zapatista uprising motivated a major national electoral reform that guaranteed a relatively free, albeit unfair, presidential election in 1994, the election for the governorship of Chiapas in 1994 was marred by fraud. An influential local journalist, Amado Avendaño, received support from an unusual coalition that brought together the state's leading rural indigenous movements, the PRD, and the EZLN. After a rough campaign in which Avendaño lost by a fifteen-point margin, the Zapatistas and the coalition denounced the election as a massive fraud. Independent electoral

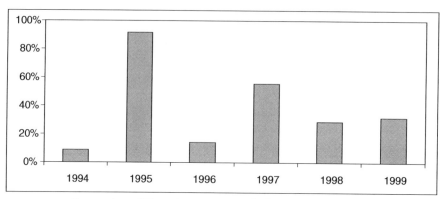

FIGURE 7.3. Proportion of Zapatista actions with claims of ethnic autonomy and self-determination.
Note: The Zapatista occupation of 34 municipalities starting 12/19/1994 is included in 1995.

watchdog organizations provided compelling evidence of coercion, vote buying, and vote rigging (Alianza Cívica, 1994).

Postelection public opinion surveys conducted by the Office of the President showed that 60 percent of the Chiapas electorate demanded a new election (Oficina de la Presidencia, 1994c). Given the government's refusal, the Zapatistas called for a period of civil disobedience and had Avendaño sworn in as "rebel governor" and head of a de facto parallel government. In a dramatic transformation that took place during the fall of 1994, the Zapatista language of civil disobedience and rebel authorities rapidly shifted from liberal democracy to multiculturalism and from universal rights to rights to autonomy and self-determination for indigenous peoples.

The second major event was an unprecedented wave of occupation of municipal presidencies. Throughout 1994, at least one-half of the state's 119 municipalities were occupied by members of Chiapas's leading rural indigenous movements, many of which were Zapatista sympathizers (Burguete, 1998). This wave of de facto occupations of government buildings empowered Zapatistas and their sympathizers to envision their own civilian forces as rulers of de facto governments protected by Zapatista military forces. The electoral fraud in the gubernatorial election reinforced this view of de facto rebel autonomous municipalities. By the end of 1994, in fact, the EZLN invaded more than thirty municipalities in Chiapas and established parallel de facto local governments in a number of them claiming legitimacy under OIT Convention 169.

The third major event was a dramatic wave of land invasions throughout 1994, in which Zapatistas and non-Zapatistas alike took advantage of the political crisis triggered by the rebellion and invaded the largest number of hectares of private and national lands in the history of Chiapas. Even though the 1992 constitution had ended Mexico's six-decade-long program of land reform, the federal and state governments' response to this wave of land invasions was to buy an unprecedented amount of occupied land from private owners and distribute it among PRI-affiliated and independent peasants – as local authorities had done in the 1980s. As a counterinsurgency strategy, this new wave of land reform was aimed at draining the social base of Zapatism.[11] Embracing an agenda of ethno-territorial rights and gaining de facto territorial controls would be the rebel's counterstrategy to secure land for their own cadres and avoid major defections.

The program for ethnic autonomy and self-determination for indigenous peoples that Tojolabal Indians from the CIOAC had devised in the late 1980s and early 1990s served the EZLN as the initial grammar for translating their de facto actions into juridical language, as they gained control over territory covering at least 38 of the state's 119 municipalities by the end of 1994 (Mattiace, 2003). With the advice of PRD legislators and intellectuals who had served as advisers to the Sandinista government in Nicaragua when the Sandinista National Liberation Front (FSLN) established regional autonomous regimes for the Miskito Indians, the Zapatistas were able to rapidly develop a detailed programmatic agenda demanding the rights to autonomy and self-determination for indigenous peoples during the second round of peace negotiations in 1995 and 1996 (Sánchez, 1999).

Building De Facto Indigenous Autonomy: Cross-Regional Variation

Between 1995 and 2000 the EZLN developed a network of Zapatista Rebel Autonomous Municipalities (MAREZ) and Zapatista Autonomous Regions (RAZ) across 30 of Chiapas's 119 municipalities.[12] Claiming legitimate jurisdiction on the basis of ILO Convention 169, the Zapatistas established a system of "dual sovereignties" and de facto parallel governments. These were municipalities where constitutionally elected governments ruled by the PRI coexisted with de facto Zapatista governments. EZLN forces protected these territories, federal and state authorities were banned, and Zapatista civilian authorities were responsible for providing basic public goods, including security, education and health services and criminal and civil justice.

The unprecedented agreement on indigenous rights signed by the federal government and the EZLN reached in the second round of peace negotiations was supposed to establish the legal bases to institutionalize some of these de facto autonomous governments. Yet the peace negotiations stalemate and President Zedillo's decision not to honor the agreement led to a period of violent territorial disputes between MAREZ and RAZ members and PRI-sponsored paramilitary forces. These were conflicts between poor coethnic peasants who belonged to different networks: Catholics and Zapatistas on the one hand and the PRI on the other. This conflict led to one of the most violent

---

[11] For a pioneering discussion on the role of land reform as a counterinsurgency policy, see Albertus and Kaplan (2010).
[12] See Burguete (1998, 1999).

periods in Chiapas's contemporary history, exemplified by the ignominious Acteal massacre of forty-five Tzotzil women and children in 1997.[13]

I construct an index of Zapatista autonomy governments as a proxy for the politicization of ethnicity. The index is based on two indicators. One is the per capita number of acts of protest, inter-community conflicts, and acts of government repression in which Zapatistas were involved while making claims for ethno-territorial control in the 1996–2000 period. The second indicator is a weighted average of the number of MAREZ and RAZ that operated across Chiapan municipalities.[14] I create a three-point scale of levels of autonomy by summing the two indicators.

If we compare the levels of community support for Zapatism when the rebel group was a peasant movement in 1994 with levels of support when Zapatism had become a self-determination movement, we can observe a sizeable decline: Up to 25 percent of the state's municipalities expressed their support for Zapatism in 1994, but only one-quarter of these Zapatista municipal supporters became involved in the creation of MAREZ and RAZ. In fact, many of the communities and villagers that had joined Zapatism between 1989 and 1992 and later on in 1994 slowly faded from the support base as the movement entered a long phase of construction of radical de facto autonomous governments.

Table 7.3 summarizes the results of an ordered probit regression model of the likelihood of Zapatista militants establishing de facto ethno-territorial control within constitutionally defined municipal boundaries in Chiapas during the 1996–2000 period.

Consistent with previous findings, regression results show that a history of *Religious competition* is a strong predictor of the creation of Zapatista-controlled ethno-territorial governments in indigenous regions in Chiapas. A simple simulation based on Model 1 shows that a municipality with no prior history of religious competition was 87 percent likely to reject the Zapatista ethnic option in 1996. On the other hand, a municipality experiencing the highest rate of growth of religious competition had a 46 percent chance of supporting a de facto autonomy arrangement. This result suggests that former catechists and Catholic associational networks within Zapatism played a prominent role in the construction of autonomous rebel governance.

Results also show that autonomy arrangements emerged in municipalities that had experienced some level of *Ethnic protest* prior to the emergence of Zapatism. Chapter 6 established that Zapatism was initially an outgrowth of

---

[13] On the Acteal massacre, see CDHFBC (1998).

[14] Although the EZLN claimed officially that rebel authorities were present in at least thirty-eight municipalities, when these numbers are compared with national and local press reports, one finds that Zapatista rebel governments operated in a more limited number of municipalities and that MAREZ were more real than RAZ. Hence the index of ethno-territorial control weights MAREZ more heavily than RAZ. For detailed narratives on Zapatista de facto autonomy arrangements during this period, see Burguete (1998, 1999), Eber (2001), Leyva (2001), and Mattiace (2001).

TABLE 7.3. *Ordered Probit Regression Estimates of the Establishment of a Zapatista Rebel Autonomous Municipality (MAREZ) in Chiapas, 1996–2000*

Independent Variables	Model 1 Coefficient	Model 2 Coefficient
Religious competition	0.7044*	0.796**
	(0.373)	(0.367)
Electoral competition	−0.982**	−1.086**
	(0.476)	(0.467)
Economic protest (1983–2000)	−0.012	−0.016
	(0.036)	(0.035)
Political protest (1983–2000)	−0.001	−0.001
	(0.021)	(0.020)
Ethnic protest (1983–2000)	0.537**	0.616***
	(0.172)	(0.167)
Repression (1995–2000)	−0.031	−0.038*
	(0.023)	(0.022)
EZLN (1994)	0.409*	
	(0.2370)	
Paramilitary activity	0.706	1.124**
	(0.594)	(0.533)
Controls		
Corporatism	−6.725**	−6.093**
	(3.211)	(3.113)
Proportion indigenous population	1.014	0.966
	(0.888)	(0.883)
ln Indigenous population	0.112	0.319
	(0.372)	(0.347)
Cut 1	0.1322	1.840
Cut 2	1.776	3.362
Cut 3	3.389	4.900
N	58	58
Log Likelihood	−34.873	−36.379
Chi^2	66.03	63.01
Pseudo-R^2	0.4863	0.4641
McKelvey and Zavoina's R^2	0.805	0.798

***Significant at the 0.01 level; ** Significant at the 0.05 level; * Significant at the 0.1 level. Standard errors in parentheses

the state's cycle of contention, but the statistical results in Table 7.3 further show that the EZLN drew from indigenous movements' prior programmatic development of ethno-territorial demands. This was particularly true of the CIOAC, the most influential peasant indigenous organization in Chiapas to have embraced a program of ethnic demands prior to the Zapatista uprising (Burguete, 1998, 1999; Sánchez, 1999; Jung, 2003; Mattiace, 2003).

Government *Repression* and *Paramilitary activity* are both strong predictors of the development of de facto autonomy arrangements. The lethal spread of paramilitary activity persuaded many villagers of the high cost of neutrality, driving them to join Zapatista-controlled autonomous regions.[15] Autonomismo and paramilitarismo thus became endogenously related. As the EZLN established territorial controls, PRI-sponsored paramilitary forces employed violent means to try to prevent the Zapatistas from taking over any of the state's territory. In search of protection from paramilitary violence, villages in the northern and eastern parts of the state and in the highlands joined autonomous regions.

Finally, the statistical results show that local *Electoral competition* was an important deterrent to the formation of Zapatista autonomous territories. Holding all else constant, a municipality under tight PRI control had only a 20 percent chance of rejecting the de facto ethno-territorial option, but one with a 3.5-party system was 80 percent likely not to enter any type of Zapatista autonomous arrangements. Consistent with the findings on peaceful ethnic protest, results here suggest that the spread of electoral competition was a deterrent for the politicization of ethnicity by both social movements and armed insurgent groups.

Overall, the results suggest that members of Catholic social networks and some of the most radical members of the state's rural indigenous movements served as the social base for the development of Zapatista de facto territorial controls and autonomous governments. These constituencies established parallel governments in Chiapan regions where opposition presence was weak in or before 1996 and where PRI-sponsored paramilitary groups engaged in violent disputes with Zapatistas for land and territorial control.

Various sources suggest that former deacons and catechists and members of Catholic social networks became the core constituency that sustained the transformation of MAREZ and RAZ into *Juntas de Buen Gobierno* (councils of good government) after 2003. Within these local de facto governments, Zapatista authorities issued birth certificates and other civil documents, administered local justice, provided education and health services, and continued to build economic and social cooperatives. With financial aid from international donors and some local European governments, these communities worked to show all political parties and governments that the Zapatistas could survive and build a better world without any government interference. Their territorial sphere of influence, however, dramatically shrank after the PRI lost power in Mexico and in Chiapas in 2000.

Eduardo López, a Tojolabal deacon from Margaritas and a former EZLN *miliciano*, respectfully refers to his former comrades in the Autonomous Municipality of San Pedro Michoacán as *la resistencia*. He says some of them are people who are still in search of the Promised Land. Others, he says, have come to see their journey of defiance as a religious duty.

---

[15] This result is consistent with Kalyvas's (2006) influential claim that indiscriminate violence against civilians is less likely in areas controlled either by rebel or government forces.

In the language of Wood (2003), these are rural indigenous villagers moved by process-regarding motivations, who are building alternative forms of governance as a moral duty. They are, at the same time, people driven by moral indignation – a deep sense of moral outrage against a history of electoral fraud and anti-insurgent repression and against the government betrayal in the second round of peace talks. In building their alternative forms of governance, many of them have transformed indignation into a process by which the construction of autonomy has become a process of reaffirming their own dignity. Driven by process-regarding and moral-religious motivations, these are the radical and long-term communal guarantors of the rights to autonomy and self-determination for indigenous peoples.[16]

CONCLUSIONS

In this chapter we have presented new evidence showing that the simultaneous globalization of indigenous rights and introduction of neoliberal agricultural reforms opened new opportunities for indigenous peoples in Latin America to mobilize on ethnic grounds. We have also shown that not all indigenous villagers have seized these opportunities to take up the ethnic banner.

Challenging dominant explanations of indigenous ethnic mobilization in Latin America, which claim that homogenous indigenous communities of cultural survivors raised the ethnic banner against the penetration of capitalist markets in their communities, this chapter provided extensive quantitative and qualitative evidence showing that the politicization of ethnicity in Mexico was led by communities experiencing the most intense processes of modernization resulting from novel experiences of religious and political differentiation. Ethnicity was politicized – we show – where the twin processes of erosion of local religious and political hegemonies resulted in the rise of associational networks and the creation of an ethnic coalition that encouraged the mobilization of indigenous ethnic identities.

The chapter showed that the successful spread of U.S. Protestant missions and widespread religious conversions in rural indigenous regions motivated the Catholic Church to become a major promoter of indigenous cultures, languages, and communal institutions. In trying to keep indigenous souls in the Catholic fold, Catholic clergy in competitive regions became long-term promoters of ethnic identities and rights, and the major theological changes they adopted to integrate indigenous cultures and traditions into the Christian gospel and in their daily pastoral strategies contributed in significant ways to the renaissance of a new indigenous ethnic pride.

But this finding is not entirely novel. In his classic study, Anderson (1991) showed how the breakdown of the Catholic Medieval Order and the Protestant Reformation led to the rise of nationalism in Western Europe. In his account, the

---

[16] See interviews by Saavedra (2008) in Chapter 7. For a critical view of how these Zapatista autonomous territories have operated in recent years, see essays in Saavedra and Viqueira (2010).

Protestant translation of the Bible to "vernacular" languages led to a linguistic renaissance, and the invention of the printing press allowed these new linguistic networks to "imagine" themselves as national communities. Looking at an entirely different world region and many centuries later, the contribution of this chapter is to underscore religious competition as the mechanism that motivates the rise of new ethnic identities.

The chapter also showed that despite the endorsement of major social actors such as the Catholic Church, the politicization of ethnicity was crucially shaped by electoral incentives. We showed that the introduction of government-controlled multiparty elections in Mexico motivated leftist opposition parties to establish socio-electoral coalitions with rural indigenous movements and to support ethnic demands. As elections became relatively free and fair and opposition parties became more competitive in subnational elections, opposition party leaders and indigenous leaders themselves diluted their ethnic claims; as they built cross-class and pluralistic coalitions to conquer the median voter, class-based cleavages replaced ethnic identities.

While democratization and leftist local victories institutionalized rural indigenous movements and marginalized radical ethnic demands, the chapter showed that when elites deterred the electoral mobilization of indigenous movements through fraud and repression, they created the conditions for the rise of radical movements for territorial autonomy and self-determination. This chapter presented original evidence showing that the radical transformation of the EZLN from a peasant insurgency into a self-determination movement was the result of fraud, deceit and repression.

We know since the seminal study of Przeworski and Sprague (1988) that the introduction of mass democracy in authoritarian contexts affects group mobilization and social identities. Working class movements in nineteenth-century Europe had to give up working class identities and dilute radical worker demands to become electorally viable. This chapter presented evidence of a similar electoral logic of identity dilution in Mexico's indigenous regions as indigenous movements and leaders had a chance to win local power. We introduced a new element, however: authoritarian regression as a motivation for the radicalization of ethnic minorities and for the rise of self-determination movements.

Even though the Zapatistas became one of the most powerful political actors in late twentieth century Mexico, the movement eventually failed to translate their de facto power into de jure power. The Zapatistas and their allies did not see their claims for the ethno-territorial reconstruction of Mexico on ethnic grounds materialize. A few years after the end of the transition to democracy, ethnicity rapidly faded from public discourse and it never became a major cleavage for politics. It is to the twilight of indigenous mobilization and to the defeat of claims for indigenous autonomy and self-determination in Mexico that we now turn our attention.

8

The Twilight of Ethnicity

Democratization as an Elite Strategy to Avert
Mexico's Indigenous Insurgency

One of the most influential discoveries in the study of democratization in recent years is that the threat of major insurrections and civil war can motivate authoritarian elites to democratize.[1] Based on the Western European experience, scholars suggest that elites in nineteenth-century Europe consented to the universal male franchise and introduced mass democracy to prevent a working class revolution (Acemoglu and Robinson, 2006; Przeworski, 2009). Democracy was a credible institutional arrangement to negotiate wealth and income redistribution through peaceful means (Boix, 2003). Based on the experience of developing countries in Africa and Latin America, Wood (2000) shows that radical mobilizations from below in highly unequal societies motivated economic elites to democratize to avoid a revolutionary breakdown.

Despite these recent findings, students of Latin America's unprecedented wave of indigenous mobilization have not actively explored a potential link between indigenous collective action and democratization. To be sure, the literature has persuasively shown how indigenous mobilizations have sought to transform democratic regimes by demanding the recognition of multicultural rights (Van Cott, 2000, 2001; Postero, 2006). Yet dominant explanations have analyzed indigenous mobilizations as post-authoritarian phenomena; scholars suggest that the rise of liberal democracy facilitated indigenous collective action and provided the political space for the renegotiation of citizenship rights on ethnic grounds (Yashar, 2005). But they have not explored the potential impact of indigenous mobilizations on transitions from authoritarian rule to liberal democracy.

[1] For the pioneering analyses on the literature of "democratization from below," see Bermeo (1997), Collier and Mahoney (1997), and more recently McAdam, Tarrow and Tilly (2001) and Tilly (2006). Most of the initial scholarship stressed the importance of working class mobilization on democratization but did not extensively articulate the idea that the threat of civil war could motivate elites to democratize. Wood (2000), Boix (2003), Acemoglu and Robinson (2006), and Przeworski (2009) have established this connection in a more detailed way. For a less explicit, albeit important, connection of the threat of civil war and democratization in Costa Rica, see Lehoucq and Molina (2002).

Following scholars of "democratization from below," my goal in this chapter is to explore the potential impact of indigenous insurgent collective action on Mexico's democratic transition. Students of Mexico's democratization have persuasively shown (1) that a series of major electoral reforms provided Mexican voters with the means to end seven decades of uninterrupted PRI rule and (2) that a series of major macroeconomic crises undermined the PRI's ability to buy off voters and granted voters substantive reasons to throw the rascals out. Yet, a systematic explanation of the motivations that led authoritarian elites to relinquish their ability to manipulate fraud remains a major omission in this account.

This chapter seeks to specifically test whether the outbreak of the Zapatista rebellion in 1994 and the transformation of the Zapatista National Liberation Army (EZLN) into a self-determination movement in 1995 motivated Mexico's authoritarian elites to relinquish the government's ability to manipulate electoral outcomes through two major electoral reforms in 1994 and 1996. In Chapter 1 we conjectured that authoritarian elites would democratize only if they (1) feared a major social insurrection leading to a potential systemic breakdown, (2) expected to win or remain a major player in a new democratic system and (3) believed a new democratic configuration of power would not lead to a major redistribution of income and wealth (see H.9).

I test the "democracy from below" hypothesis against three rival explanations. Scholars of Mexico's democratization have suggested that market-oriented reforms and the dynamics of economic and trade liberalization led to political liberalization. Others have suggested that the spread of subnational electoral competition and the incremental victories of the opposition in Congress and the Senate created the minimum winning coalitions for reform. Still others suggest that reforms were the result of major waves of peaceful mobilization initially triggered by the 1968 student massacre.

The chapter draws on a unique combination of qualitative and quantitative sources to establish a causal connection between the Zapatista uprising and the Mexican elite's decision to reform the country's electoral institutions and guarantee free and fair elections. Information from memoirs and public speeches from some of the key decision makers in these stories of electoral reform, including presidents, secretaries of the interior, and chief negotiators with the Zapatistas presents important evidence of the elite's expectations and fears.

The most important piece of information, however, comes from a systematic analysis of the biweekly public opinion surveys that the Office of the President in Mexico conducted throughout the administrations of Presidents Carlos Salinas (1988–1994) and Ernesto Zedillo (1994–2000). After the outbreak of the Zapatista rebellion and until the end of the Zedillo administration, the Office of the President conducted more than one hundred surveys that included relevant information about the EZLN. I specifically focus on surveys that assessed the approval rates of the rebels and their actions among residents of Mexico's major metropolitan centers.

The great advantage of analyzing these surveys is that they provided the information that Presidents Salinas and Zedillo used to create their expectations about the likely spread of Zapatismo into the country's major urban centers and about the likely creation of a revolutionary alliance between the EZLN and leftist urban dissidents. I also assess the survey information that served presidents to forge their expectations about likely electoral outcomes at the time when they accepted to relinquish authoritarian electoral controls.

The analysis of the *sequential* evolution of historical events allows me to show that the outbreak of war in Chiapas in January 1994 and the territorial expansion and dramatic transformation of the Zapatistas into a self-determination movement seeking to reinvent Mexico's federal structure along ethno-territorial lines at the end of 1994 were the antecedents of the major electoral reforms of 1994 and 1996 by which the PRI and the government relinquished their ability to manipulate electoral outcomes.[2] My argument rests on the temporal ordering and proximity of events but also on evidence about elite beliefs and expectations. In fact, the information from the government surveys and memoirs provides crucial micro evidence of the information, beliefs and expectations that led authoritarian elites to consent to reform national electoral institutions and avoid a generalized social insurrection.

Through the sequential analysis of events, I am also able to rule out alternative explanations: Major market-oriented reforms such as NAFTA gave rise to limited electoral reforms but not to the crucial 1994 and 1996 reforms; the electoral expansion of opposition parties in subnational positions of power and in legislative chambers was the result, not the cause of the 1994 and 1996 reforms; and major waves of social protest in the 1980s only gave rise to minor reforms – in fact, social movements became an effective force for electoral change only after the Zapatista uprising.

The chapter is divided into four sections. The first part analyzes how the Zapatista uprising led to the 1994 electoral reform. In the second section I assess how the transformation of Zapatism into a self-determination movement in 1995 led to the 1996 electoral reform. In the third part I discuss how the 1996 reform and the major electoral victories of the Left led to the rise of a powerful coalition of social movements and leftist parties from which Zapatism was marginalized. I show how this major transformation in the alliance structure of the Left provided Mexico's elite with the political capital to block the Zapatista struggle for ethno-territorial reforms. In the final section I assess why the advent of democracy meant the twilight of ethnicity.

1994: CONFRONTING A PEASANT UPRISING AND THE THREAT
OF NATIONAL INSURRECTION

A Military Response

After ten days of combat between the EZLN and the Mexican army, with approximately 150 casualties, on January 12, 1994, the federal government

---

[2] For insightful discussions about strategies of sequential historical analysis, see Büthe (2002), Mahoney, Kimball and Koivu (2009) and Grzymala-Busse (2010).

called for a ceasefire and for peace negotiations with the Zapatistas. The government abandoned a purely military response after government officials and military strategists became convinced that despite the army's undisputed military superiority, the rebels' advantage in having access to a dense network of communal support in the highlands and the Lacandón jungle made a swift, clean, unambiguous government military victory highly unlikely.

In a presidential election year, a protracted anti-insurgency war with the potential to produce thousands of civilian casualties would have been a risky political action. As the biweekly public opinion surveys conducted by the Office of the President made evident to policy makers, the initial negative reaction evoked by the uprising among Mexico's urban population was rapidly transformed into sympathy for the Indian cause (see discussion later in the chapter). Moreover, because Mexico was under the international spotlight with NAFTA going into effect the very day of the Chiapas rebellion, a protracted war against the country's indigenous peoples would have exposed the Mexican regime internationally as a repressive autocracy.

A Political Response

As the Zapatistas were preparing for peace negotiations in Chiapas, the federal government made a surprising call to all national opposition parties to immediately begin negotiations in Mexico City to reform Mexico's electoral institutions and guarantee a free and fair presidential electoral process in the summer of 1994. Six weeks after the start of the Zapatista uprising, all major opposition political parties were negotiating a serious of major constitutional and legal changes with the federal government to transform the government-controlled Federal Electoral Institute (IFE) into an independent institution.

Even though the 1977 reform had legalized all political parties and allowed multiparty elections, the federal government had retained tight control of the organization of national elections. As President Miguel de la Madrid candidly revealed in his own memoirs (2004), these legal prerogatives had allowed the federal government to manipulate election results in the contested 1988 presidential election.

Twelve weeks after the Zapatista uprising, the Mexican Congress and the Senate unanimously approved a major constitutional reform that laid the institutional foundation for free national elections in Mexico. Even though the federal government retained a seat on the governing council of IFE, under the new rules the council would be governed by a group of independent citizens appointed by a two-thirds congressional majority. Additional changes in the federal electoral law expanded citizen control over district-level electoral councils, which were the IFE local authorities charged with organizing the logistical aspects of the elections, and provided legal status to watchdog citizen groups and international observers. Changes in the federal criminal code expanded the number of electoral felonies and the penalties associated with coercing voters, vote buying, and a long list of specific forms of fraud that had been widely used in the 1980s. Although the federal government retained a major advantage in terms of access to sponsorship and policy resources, as well as media air time during election campaigns, the constitutional and legal changes approved in the spring of 1994 made an electoral fraud like that of 1988 virtually impossible.

Why did President Salinas and the PRI introduce a democratizing reform that every single administration – his own included – had fiercely opposed since the federal government and the PRI consented to multiparty elections in 1977?

Free Elections to Keep the PRI in Power and Avoid a Systemic Collapse. In this section I present primary evidence from government-sponsored surveys and from the personal memoirs of top decision makers showing that the Mexican government and the PRI consented to free elections to avoid a major social insurrection after the outbreak of the Zapatista rebellion in Chiapas. The chief goal of electoral democratization was to avert the formation of a revolutionary coalition that would join the partisan and social lefts together under the banner of Zapatism and unite revolutionary forces from the countryside with Mexico's major urban centers. As the evidence shows, the federal government crucially consented to free elections at a time when public opinion surveys undisputedly confirmed a likely PRI victory, even after the major legitimacy crisis triggered by the Zapatista rebellion.

Personal recollections by the chief government decision makers confirm the fear evoked by the Zapatista uprising among government elites and their goal of preventing a major social insurrection by reforming the country's electoral institutions. In his own memoirs, written in political exile in Cuba and Ireland in the late 1990s, President Salinas confirms that the main goal of the reform was "to avoid armed rebellion becoming the only effective channel of political negotiation" and to prevent that "politics [be] moved to the jungle" (2000: 1046–1047). Jorge Carpizo, the Secretary of Interior who presided over the reform, confirms that the reform was aimed at "preserving peace." But elections could only become a credible path toward peace, Carpizo recalls, if the leftist PRD, the main victim of the 1988 electoral fraud, would also consent to the reform. The challenge thus was to turn the Left into a parliamentary force committed to the electoral path as the "…the only means to negotiate political differences" (Carpizo, 1995: 47–50).

In the political context of 1994, the elite's fear of the rise of a revolutionary coalition in which the partisan Left (the PRD) and the country's major social movements would rally behind the Zapatistas in trying to end PRI hegemony was not without foundation. As illustrated analytically in Figure 8.1a, in 1994 the PRD was divided into a reformist and a radical wing. The leaders of the moderate wing were PRI defectors who had abandoned the ruling party when a "neoliberal" candidate was handpicked as the PRI presidential candidate in 1987. The radical wing was made up of a wide range of actors linked to the "social" and "revolutionary" lefts of the 1970s, including (1) former members

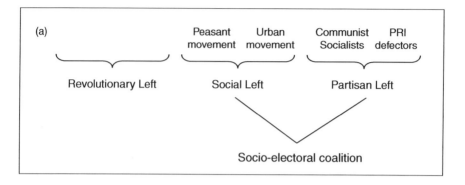

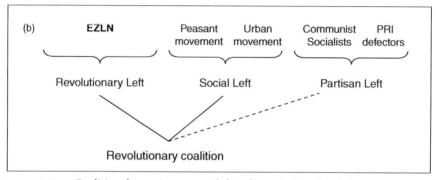

FIGURE 8.1. Coalition formation among leftist forces in Mexico: (a) 1977–1993 and (b) 1994–1996.

of guerrilla groups who had fought in the 1970s and joined electoral politics under the 1978 Amnesty Law; (2) communist and socialist party militants whose parties had been outlawed until 1977; and (3) leaders and activists of the urban and rural social movements that mushroomed throughout the 1980s.

As Chapters 2 and 4 demonstrated, during the 1980s and early 1990s, the radical wing of the PRD developed important socio-electoral coalitions with rural indigenous movements and became major institutional supporters of peasant struggles for land in exchange for their support in mobilizing against fraud. Studies of Mexican urban politics show that the PRD established similar political coalitions with the country's major urban popular movements in the 1980s (López-Leyva, 2007). At the time of the Zapatista uprising, the PRD was a movement-party rather than a traditional party. And the party's most radical militants had few incentives to pursue an electoral path exclusively.

As illustrated in Figure 8.1b, the Zapatista uprising opened up the possibility that the radical wing of the PRD and the country's urban and rural social movements would shift even further to the left and join Zapatism in their armed struggle "against neoliberalism and the PRI dictatorship." This conclusion could be drawn from Mexico's recent history: Not only had President

Salinas's victory in the 1988 election involved a major election fraud operation against Cuauhtémoc Cárdenas, the founder of the PRD, but approximately 360 PRD militants had been assassinated during the Salinas administration.[3] With virtually no chance of their party becoming a serious electoral contender in the 1994 presidential election, a number of PRD leaders and activists were almost immediately attracted to Zapatism and the insurgent path. Moreover, the country's major social movements, including university students, dissident teachers, peasants, and Indians, were also attracted to the rebel cause.

Evidence from biweekly public opinion surveys conducted by the Office of the President reveals the enthusiastic support that Zapatism evoked among Mexicans in general and among PRD voters in the country's major urban centers in particular. Figure 8.2a shows that public support for Zapatism and its main demands nearly doubled from a 25.3 percent approval rate in the second week of the conflict to 44.1 percent by the sixth week. Like most Mexicans, during the first days of the conflict, PRD voters viewed Zapatism with surprise and skepticism.[4] As Figure 8.2b shows, however, six weeks after the outbreak of war, two-thirds of likely PRD voters already supported Zapatism and its demands. This high approval rate in favor of the rebels would persist throughout 1994 and 1995. As the information in Figure 8.2b illustrates, likely PRD voters were between two and three times more likely to support the EZLN than sympathizers of other parties.

In the midst of the great uncertainty the Zapatista rebellion introduced to Mexican politics, this survey evidence and other sources of information persuaded President Salinas and his administration that a sizeable segment of PRD-Zapatista sympathizers might respond positively to the Zapatista's call to establish a revolutionary coalition that would link the rural countryside with Mexico's major urban centers. In their first communiqué, the Zapatistas had called for the removal of President Salinas and for the selection of a civilian commission that would organize free and fair elections. During the first days of combat in Chiapas, a number of bombs had been set off in the mall of a middle-class neighborhood in Mexico City nurturing the fear that the rebels had the capacity and revolutionary alliances to expand their struggle into Mexico's main urban centers (Salinas, 2000).

By opening a credible channel for negotiation of a major electoral reform, the government's chief goal was to establish elections as a credible institutional mechanism for conflict resolution. The goal was to dissuade the most radical PRD affiliates and the country's grassroots organizations and social movement leaders and activists from joining a Zapatista-led revolutionary coalition to oust the PRI from power by violent means.

---

[3] A brief description of every case can be found in the monthly publication on human rights violations by the Fray Francisco de Vitoria Human Rights Center.

[4] *La Jornada*, Mexico's leading leftist newspaper, initially condemned the rebellion in a fiery editorial published on January 2, 1994. The paper became an enthusiastic Zapatista sympathizer shortly thereafter.

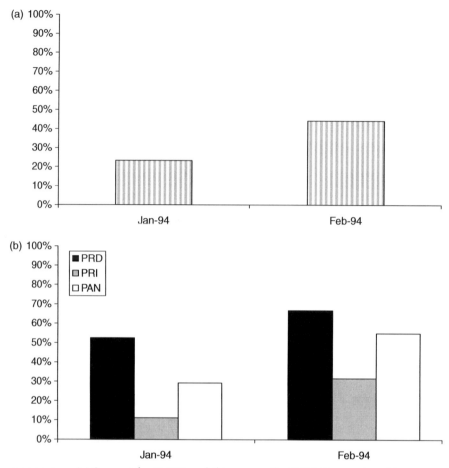

FIGURE 8.2. (a) Support for EZLN and (b) support for EZLN by partisanship.
Source: See Appendix D.

Survey evidence gathered by the Office of the President during the first two quarters of 1994 consistently showed that despite the Zapatista uprising, the PRI candidate was the undisputed frontrunner for the 1994 presidential election. A survey conducted on February 27 reported that the PRI candidate had a 57 percent of the national vote intention; the second closest competitor, the candidate of the PAN, received only 18 percent (Oficina de la Presidencia, 1994a).

This information persuaded the incumbent elite that the ruling party could remain in power even if impartial authorities organized a free electoral contest; that is, if the government relinquished its ability to manipulate electoral outcomes – as they had done in 1988 – the PRI nevertheless would have a high probability of remaining in power and Mexico's economic structures would most likely remain unchanged. Hence consenting to free elections after the Zapatista uprising was not viewed as a major threat either to the PRI or to the country's political and economic elites. Free elections would not result in a major transfer of power or in a major economic redistribution. Facing a real threat of major social insurrection and a potential systemic collapse, liberalizing electoral controls entailed lower costs than no reform and became the most effective way for the PRI to remain in power.

Alternative Explanations of the 1994 Electoral Reform. Although some of the most influential explanations of the democratization of Mexico's electoral institutions do acknowledge the effect of Zapatism in triggering the 1994 reform (Becerra, Salazar and Woldenberg, 2000; Magaloni, 2006, 2010), explanations of the mechanics of institutional change during Mexico's transition to democracy rarely put the emphasis on insurgent collective action. Instead, scholars have emphasized the democratizing effect of market-oriented reforms, electoral competition, and peaceful protest. Yet as I show here, none of these explanations persuasively accounts for the *timing* of the reforms.

Economic liberalization. Scholars of economic reforms have suggested that market liberalization led to political liberalization in Mexico (Rubio, 1998). The historical record shows, however, that the most radical market-oriented reforms introduced during the 1980s and early 1990s did not produce major electoral reforms. NAFTA is a prominent example. Joining NAFTA – the most radical market liberalization in Mexico's contemporary economic history – only motivated the creation of a government-controlled Human Rights Commission in 1990 and a series of incremental electoral reforms that improved the quality of the national electoral roll and introduced a voter identification card. The importance of these reforms should not be minimized, but the fact remains that up to the early days of 1994, the federal government and the PRI remained firmly in control of the IFE. Unlike the European Union, which required new member countries to comply with a series of stringent democratic requirements, NAFTA membership entailed no political requisites. Market-oriented reforms did not motivate political elites to democratize Mexico's electoral institutions.

Electoral competition. Students of Mexican electoral institutions suggest that the spread of electoral competition and the increased presence of opposition forces in Congress empowered opposition parties to pressure the PRI into giving up its control over the country's electoral institutions (Lujambio, 2000; Merino, 2003). A simple inspection of the evolution of federal election results shows, however, that the most substantive opposition gains in federal elections were a consequence, not a cause, of major electoral reforms.[5] For example, the 1988 election – which saw the greatest increase in opposition votes since the introduction of government-controlled multiparty competition in 1977 – motivated only limited electoral reforms.

Mexico's major 1994 electoral reform took place at a time when the PRI had already recovered from the 1988 "electoral earthquake" and was positioned to

---

[5] This is not the case for reforms of state-level electoral commissions. Ley (2006) shows that the spread of electoral competition in gubernatorial elections is the single most important explanatory factor of the wave of subnational electoral reforms in the late 1990s.

enjoy major presidential and legislative victories in that year's federal elections. It took place at a point in time when the electoral opposition was weak and divided and the PRI strong. Hence, although the growth of opposition presence facilitated the logistics of a congressional negotiation of the 1994 reform, the growth of electoral competition was not the factor that motivated Mexico's ruling elite to relinquish electoral control.

Social protest. Students of social movements suggest that the protracted wave of social mobilization that began with the 1968 student movement motivated PRI elites to democratize (Cadena-Roa, 2003). However, evidence on social protest in Mexico shows that the most intense waves of social mobilization during the 1980s had no effect in motivating PRI elites to relinquish governmental control over the organization of elections. Multiple waves of protests by workers, teachers, students, peasants, and urban dwellers in the 1980s contributed to the growth of opposition parties but did not generate incentives for the democratization of electoral controls. And the major waves of post-election protest in the late 1980s and early 1990s motivated incremental changes but did not prompt the definitive democratizing reforms.

In the absence of credible insurgent threats – we must say – peaceful mobilization alone did not trigger major episodes of meaningful electoral reform in Mexico. After 1994, however, when rural indigenous and urban movements had a chance to join Zapatism, their bargaining power dramatically increased and it was then that the potential, even likely creation, of a revolutionary coalition led to Mexico's most fundamental democratizing reforms.

In summary, after two decades of government-controlled multiparty elections, the Zapatista rebellion and the threat of a major social insurrection prompted Mexican authoritarian elites to finally consent to creating the institutional infrastructure for free elections. The Zapatista uprising stimulated a major change in authoritarian governance. Whereas in the past, incumbent authorities had tried to derail a potential coalition of social movement and leftist parties (see Chapter 4), after the Zapatista uprising their goal was to empower the reformist wing of the PRD and to foment the institutionalization of social and grassroots movements into electoral politics. After 1994, the PRD was no longer the chief enemy of Mexico's electoral autocracy; Zapatism and the specter of a grand revolutionary coalition had become the regime's worst nightmare. Consenting to free elections was the regime's attempt to eliminate this shadow.

Subnational Autocracy Despite National Democratization. Even though the federal authorities and the PRI had agreed to establish the institutional basis for free elections at the national level, the government did not create conditions for free and fair elections for the 1994 gubernatorial contest in Chiapas. Although the Chiapas legislature did introduce an important electoral reform that legally removed the governor from the state electoral commission and empowered the legislature to elect the commission's governing council (Ley, 2006), the PRI's hegemonic control of the state legislature[6] meant that the PRI governor de facto maintained all control over organization of the election. Whereas at the national level, President Salinas and the PRI had made every effort to signal that the 1994 presidential election would be free and fair, their message in Chiapas had consistently been that the PRI would defend their hold on power by means of fraud and coercion.

The federal government and the PRI did not pursue a path of subnational electoral democratization in Chiapas because they had firsthand evidence that a PRI victory in Chiapas's gubernatorial election was far from sure. Moreover, and most importantly, they had reasonable suspicion that a victory of the PRI's main challenger – a Zapatista-supported leftist candidate – would likely lead to a major transformation of the state's political and economic structures and to a period of major wealth redistribution. Uncertain about electoral outcomes and fearful of major redistributive losses, federal and subnational PRI elites opted for fraud and coercion rather than democratization.

After the unsuccessful conclusion of the first round of peace negotiations with the federal government and in the midst of a year of unprecedented social mobilization, the EZLN decided to participate in Chiapas's gubernatorial election under a coalition that united the social, partisan, and revolutionary lefts. Headed by Amado Avendaño, one of Chiapas's most influential journalists and a close ally of Bishop Ruiz, the coalition brought together the PRD, the state's most influential rural indigenous movements and the EZLN.

Evidence from pre-election surveys conducted by the Office of the President shows that two months before the gubernatorial election, the PRI enjoyed only a 42.5 percent of vote intention – a colossal drop from the PRI's traditional 90 percent support in gubernatorial races in Chiapas. Even though the leftist coalition only held approximately 13 percent of the intended vote, there was a great degree of uncertainty because 30 percent of likely voters did not reveal their preferences. More importantly, however, official surveys two months before the election showed that the Zapatistas held a high approval rate of up to 42 percent of Chiapan voters (Oficina de la Presidencia, 1994b).

Even though the EZLN had rejected the federal government's offer to lay down arms in exchange for extensive economic and social transfers for Chiapas's poor rural indigenous regions, the Chiapas electorate attributed most of the blame for the ongoing conflict and the high levels of personal and societal insecurity they experienced to federal and state authorities. In a context in which the Zapatista uprising had eliminated many historical fears and had exposed the federal and local governments as weak and illegitimate authorities, a virtual tie between the PRI and the Zapatistas at a 42 percent approval rate, was an unusually uncertain scenario for a hegemonic party.

After a rough election campaign, in which the leftist candidate nearly lost his life in a suspicious car accident, the PRI won by a margin of 15 percent.

---

[6] The effective number of legislative seats (ENLS) for 1994 in Chiapas was 1.2.

Influential international and local NGOs provided compelling evidence of vote buying, coercion, and blatant fraud (Alianza Cívica, 1994). Whether these were sufficient to push the election into a PRI victory remained unclear, but, as we discussed in Chapter 7, the EZLN and the state's leading peasant indigenous movements responded with a massive campaign of civil disobedience that eventually led to the transformation of Zapatism into a self-determination movement.

1995–2000: CONFRONTING A SELF-DETERMINATION MOVEMENT

By December 1, 1994, when PRI president-elect Ernesto Zedillo took office, Zapatism and Chiapas's most influential peasant indigenous movement were undergoing a radical metamorphosis into a self-determination movement. While nonindigenous rural and urban leftist movements continued to conduct land invasions, post-electoral mobilization, and acts of civil disobedience, some of the state's most influential rural indigenous movements were already articulating a new discourse for ethnic autonomy rights.

Antonio Hernández, the CIOAC leader whose life history served as the guide for Chapter 4, was the keynote speaker at a major demonstration in San Cristóbal de Las Casas on October 12, 1994. A newly elected federal deputy for the PRD, Hernández outlined the most detailed program for autonomy and self-determination for indigenous peoples that anyone had articulated in the post-Zapatista era. A few weeks after Hernández's influential speech, Zapatista commanders and civilian forces established de facto regional and municipal parallel governments in approximately one-third of Chiapas's municipalities, claiming legitimacy under ILO Convention 169.

A Military Response

Even though a personal envoy from President Zedillo traveled to the Lacandón jungle to establish a basis for renewed dialogue with the Zapatistas, two months after assuming office the president ordered military troops to recover control over territory won by the Zapatistas in December 1994 and to arrest Subcommander Marcos and the main rebel indigenous commanders. The Mexican military recovered some of the territory under Zapatista control, but they were unable to successfully penetrate into the core areas of Zapatism in the Lacandón jungle, where communities hid their leaders effectively.[7] This failed raid on the Zapatistas reminded the Mexican military that the dense networks of community support rendered a militarily poor group strategically powerful.

A Political Response

Massive demonstrations in Mexico's major urban centers and around the world as well as the inability of the armed forces to penetrate the Zapatista core

---

[7] Interview with Deacon Eduardo López.

areas forced a military retreat. In the midst of a major macroeconomic crisis and facing renewed mobilization in Chiapas and across the country, President Zedillo called for a political solution to the conflict. To show his commitment to peace, the president forced the newly elected PRI governor of Chiapas to resign, issued an amnesty law for Zapatista rebels, and called for a new round of peace negotiations between the Zapatistas and the federal government.

Unlike in 1994, when the Zapatistas had accepted that peace negotiations would take place in Chiapas and center on local social and economic demands from the state's rural indigenous communities, in 1995 the rebels demanded national talks in Mexico City centered on two major topics: (1) a profound reform of the country's political institutions and (2) a constitutional reform that recognized indigenous peoples' rights to autonomy and self-determination.

As Marco A. Bernal, Zedillo's chief negotiator, recalls in his coauthored memoirs of the peace negotiations, President Zedillo consented to the Zapatistas' two substantive concerns but shrewdly demanded that the negotiations be held in Chiapas and that the thematic order of negotiations be reversed: rights to autonomy and self-determination for indigenous peoples first and the national agenda for electoral reform later (Bernal and Romero, 1999). Zedillo made this request because his administration wanted to curtail the Zapatistas' ability to influence the national agenda and also because it sought to limit the Zapatista sphere of influence to indigenous affairs.

Even though the president's team consented on paper to discuss reforms to the country's electoral institutions with the Zapatistas, the fact was that while the EZLN and the federal government were engaged in major discussions on indigenous rights, the federal government launched a parallel negotiation of the country's electoral reforms with Mexico's major political parties. Over the course of 1995 and 1996, the Secretary of the Interior and the country's main opposition parties negotiated what came to be known as the "definitive electoral reform" – the set of institutional changes that guaranteed free and fair elections in Mexico.

After a long series of negotiations, in 1996 the Mexican Congress approved a series of constitutional and legal reforms that (1) entirely removed the federal government from the IFE, (2) empowered Congress to appoint all IFE councilors by a two-thirds majority, (3) granted institutional independence to a federal electoral tribunal, (4) changed electoral laws to guarantee a more equitable provision of public funding for political campaigns, and (5) provided opposition parties with unprecedented access to public television and radio and subsidies for private broadcasts. Within the next four years, most Mexican states reformed their own subnational electoral institutions to make their laws compatible with the federal constitution and laws (Ley, 2006).

Against the background of a major macroeconomic debacle in 1995, and with a new set of electoral rules that guaranteed free and relatively fair elections at the national and subnational levels, between 1996 and 2000 opposition parties experienced a dramatic electoral expansion. The leftist PRD went on to become the largest opposition party in Congress in the midterm 1997 election;

Cuauhtémoc Cárdenas, PRD founder and the main target of a major fraud in the 1988 presidential election, emblematically became the first democratically elected mayor of Mexico City; and local PRD candidates became mayors in urban, rural, and indigenous regions. The center-right National Action Party (PAN), in turn, won several governorships, became the country's second-largest opposition party in Congress in 1997, and, most critically, won the presidency in 2000, ending seven decades of uninterrupted PRI rule.

In contrast to the successful electoral reform and the meteoric electoral gains of opposition parties, the negotiation over indigenous rights between the federal government and the Zapatistas sank into a stalemate. Although the federal government and the Zapatistas had reached an unprecedented agreement that unambiguously recognized indigenous rights to autonomy and self-determination, President Zedillo did not honor the agreement, which required that the president, together with the congressional commission that oversaw the peace negotiation – the Commission for Peace and Reconciliation (COCOPA) – send a bill to the legislature that would transform the agreement into law.

Unlike the 1996 electoral reform, in which President Zedillo had acted expediently to reach an agreement through Congress and put a new law in place for the 1997 midterm election, in the case of the "indigenous bill," Zedillo called for an extended pause for legal consultation and finally sent a watered-down initiative that languished in congressional committees during the remainder of his term in office. The president's bill differed radically from the one prepared by the COCOPA and endorsed by the Zapatistas. Between 1996 and 1998, the federal government waged a major public opinion battle to attribute the responsibility for the stalemate in peace negotiations to the Zapatistas. At the same time, paramilitary forces of Mayan peasants affiliated with the local PRI and enjoying de facto military protection led an anti-insurgency campaign to delimit the expansion of Zapatista Autonomous Municipalities and Regions.

Democratizing Elections to Avoid a National Insurrection. In this section I present evidence from government-sponsored surveys and memoirs by key decision makers showing that President Zedillo, like his predecessor, consented to the democratization of Mexico's electoral institutions to avert the formation of a revolutionary coalition that would launch a major social insurrection. The president's chief goal was to undo a potential national coalition between the PRD, the EZLN, and the country's urban, rural, and indigenous movements, which by the end of 1994 seemed to be coming together in Chiapas under the banner of de facto authorities and parallel governments. The Zapatista radical demand for indigenous autonomy and self-determination and the constitution of de facto rebel governments in places where constitutionally elected governments were seen as fraudulent was a galvanizing ideological framing for PRD nonindigenous militants engaged in post-election mobilizations to denounce fraud across the country.

Eleven months after the outbreak of the 1994 Chiapas rebellion and half a year after the assassination of the PRI presidential candidate, in the midst of major post-election mobilizations and widespread civil disobedience the newly elected President Zedillo openly addressed the need for significant electoral reform to halt the escalation of conflict. In his inaugural speech, President Zedillo unambiguously identified electoral reforms as the only means of preventing a major social insurrection: "The nation demands a definitive political reform. In the absence of a profound and consensual reform of the state, in the months ahead the country will enter into a path of violence and confrontation of unpredictable dimensions." (Andrade, 1997: 12)

In his coauthored day-by-day recollection of the events of the second round of peace negotiations, Zedillo's chief negotiator in Chiapas reveals that the expansion of Zapatista territorial controls and the establishment of local rebel governments in December 1994 represented a major revolutionary threat (Bernal and Romero, 1999). This concern may be interpreted as an ex post facto justification of the government's renewed military attacks in January 1995, but it can also be considered as prima face evidence that the multiple sovereignties the Zapatistas had created in Chiapas by the end of 1994 evoked revolutionary fears among the presidential elite. Bernal's account also reveals that the presidential elite saw the creation of rebel territories in municipalities that shared international borders with Guatemala as a serious national security problem.

Results from a series of important surveys conducted by the Office of the President in Mexico's major urban centers between December 1994 and January 1995, inquiring directly about approval for the Zapatista de facto occupation of municipal territories in Chiapas, provided crucial information that nurtured elite fears of the rise of a revolutionary coalition. The results provided the president with important evidence about the profound sympathy of PRD voters for the Zapatistas and their new revolutionary actions. As Figure 8.3 shows, by December 19, 1994, when the Zapatistas had established control over nearly one-third of Chiapas' municipalities, 43.5 percent of PRD voters in Mexico's major urban centers approved the rebel actions. Nearly a month later, on January 11, this level of support remained unchanged.

In the context of major post-election mobilizations and civil disobedience in Chiapas and the neighboring state of Tabasco, the evident enthusiasm of PRD voters for de facto Zapatista governments was a powerful signal to President Zedillo that if elections were to have any real effect in undoing what then appeared to be the imminent rise of a leftist revolutionary coalition, the 1994 electoral reform had to be both deepened at the federal level and extended to the states. To prevent this coalition from materializing, it became clear to Mexico's ruling elite that the "definitive electoral reform" had to tie the government's hands once and for all and credibly prevent it from intervening in the country's increasingly competitive national and subnational electoral contests. By conceding to free and fair elections, Zedillo's goal was to stimulate PRD moderates and social movement and grassroots leaders across the country to choose the path of electoral participation and unambiguously reject the revolutionary path.

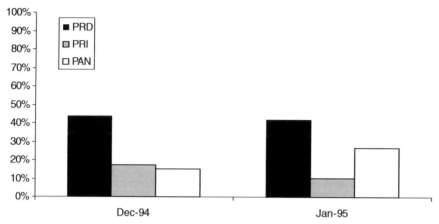

FIGURE 8.3. Approval of Zapatista armed invasion of municipal territories by partisanship.
Source: See Appendix D.

The ambitious 1996 electoral reforms and major PRD victories in federal and subnational elections both strengthened the appeal of the electoral route and the power of the moderate wing of the PRD. As Chapters 2 and 4 showed, as the PRD became a major power contender in local municipal races and as PRD candidates became office holders, the newly elected deputies and mayors absorbed a significant number of social movement leaders and grassroots activists into government positions and made important contributions to the demobilization of subnational cycles of rural indigenous protest. From Chiapas to Guerrero, from Oaxaca to Tabasco, as rural and indigenous leaders and activists either became political candidates or were absorbed into local governments, the PRD and their social movement allies increasingly moderated their actions and demands. This meant, as we showed in Chapter 7, that rural indigenous movements moderated their ethnic claims and increasingly distanced themselves from Zapatism and its struggle for the political reconfiguration of the country along ethno-territorial lines.

Why Democratization Facilitated the Capitulation on Ethnic Autonomy Rights. Whereas the 1994 electoral reform did no eliminate the threat of a major social insurrection and that a national revolutionary coalition would seek to oust the PRI from power through violent means, the 1996 reform and the leftist electoral victories in 1997 established the partisan Left as a stakeholder of Mexico's political regime, marginalized Zapatism from the country's major social movements, and provided the federal government with the political capital to bury the Zapatista's quest for the reconstruction of Mexican federalism on ethno-territorial grounds. Surrendering their ability to manipulate election outcomes was the price authoritarian elites paid to successfully suppress indigenous revolutionary threats and their ambitious program of ethno-territorial transformations.

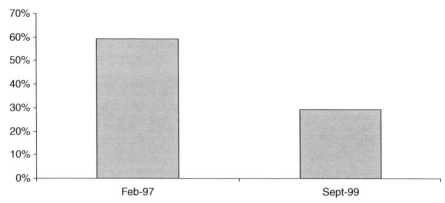

FIGURE 8.4. Sympathies for EZLN among leftist voters before and after the 1997 midterm elections.
Source: See Appendix D.

Evidence from the biweekly surveys conducted by the Office of the President reveal that President Zedillo had privileged access to information showing a dramatic decline in approval rates and support for the Zapatistas in Mexico's major urban centers after 1997. Figure 8.4 shows that before the 1997 midterm elections, PRD voters had greater sympathy for the EZLN (60 percent) than for the government. Yet, after the 1997 Leftist victories in the midterm election and in Mexico City, as the PRD became a major stakeholder and a key player of Mexico's nascent competitive electoral democracy, sympathies for the EZLN among PRD voters declined sharply (30 percent).[8] This information shows that after 1997, the PRD was no longer a movement-party and PRD leaders and voters increasingly behaved like a political party engaged in electoral battles to please the median voter rather than a niche party seeking to please the interests of groups with preferences located at the extremes of the ideological spectrum (Greene, 2007).

Evidence that the 1996 reforms and the 1997 PRD election victories had undermined the potential for a revolutionary coalition and committed the social and partisan Left to a path of electoral participation provided President Zedillo with the political force to renege on his promises to the Zapatistas and to marginalize the rebel group and its ethno-territorial agenda.

Together with PRI governors and the country's main business and trade associations, during 1997 and 1998 President Zedillo launched a massive public opinion campaign framing the rights to autonomy and self-determination for indigenous peoples as a major threat to the country's political stability. Mexico's political and economic elites strongly opposed any meaningful constitutional

---

[8] Unfortunately these questions are not comparable with the questions the Office of the President asked in the 1994 and 1995 surveys. However the February 1997 and September 1999 questions are identical and allow for an assessment of likely PRD voters' sympathies before and after the 1997 midterm election, when the 1996 reform was tested and proved successful. See Appendix D.

reform granting autonomy and self-determination rights to indigenous peoples because these reforms would entail a major redistribution of political power, public resources, and economic wealth. In President Zedillo's own words, a reform that opened the possibility of redefining Mexico's internal boundaries along ethno-territorial lines could lead to "the Balkanization" of the country.

As we discussed in Chapter 7, this national campaign against the Zapatistas' struggle for autonomy and self-determination for indigenous peoples was matched on the ground with anti-insurgency actions conducted by Mayan peasants affiliated with the local PRI in Chiapas. Although direct links between the federal government and the army and these local paramilitary forces have not been firmly established, what is clear is that neither the federal government nor the military played an active role in deterring these paramilitary groups from acting against the Zapatistas and their allies. There is reliable evidence from the Acteal massacre victims' families that despite their presence in the area the day of the massacre, and in spite of their knowledge of the actions taking place that day, neither the army nor the state police tried to stop the brutal murder of 45 Tzotzil villagers by paramilitary forces in 1997 (CDHFBC, 1998).

After their electoral victories in the 1997 midterm elections, PRD candidates, newly elected senators, federal and local legislators, and mayors were too busy learning the ABC's of governance and courting the Mexican median voter to pay much attention to the whereabouts of the Zapatistas. Once the anti-indigenous autonomy coalition succeeded in derailing the multicultural constitutional reform process, PRD leaders and public officials along with social movement leaders and grassroots activists publicly criticized the government but did not take to the streets in defense of the Zapatistas or engage in acts of civil disobedience to force the government into honoring the peace agreements. Although PRD leaders and social activists rhetorically condemned the anti-insurgency actions against the Zapatistas, neither the country's major social movements nor the PRD actively took to the streets in defense of the Zapatistas' human rights.

THE TWILIGHT OF AUTONOMY AND SELF-DETERMINATION AT THE NATIONAL LEVEL

The end of seven decades of uninterrupted PRI rule in 2000 and Mexico's long-awaited democratization brought the country's prolonged cycle of rural indigenous protest to an end and prepared the terrain for the final defeat of the Zapatista struggle for the rights to autonomy and self-determination for indigenous peoples. After President Zedillo's success in marginalizing the Zapatista rebels from a leftist parliamentary coalition of parties and social movements, the EZLN lost their final battle in Mexico's legislative assemblies and in the Supreme Court.

In his first public act as Mexico's first post-authoritarian president, President Vicente Fox sent the COCOPA legislative bill to Congress to transform the agreements the federal government and the PRI had reached with the Zapatistas in 1996 into law. Drafted by a multipartisan legislative commission in 1997, and approved by the EZLN, the COCOPA initiative was never embraced by President Zedillo and the PRI, and the bill remained frozen in Congress. The fact that Mexico's first post-authoritarian president sent a legislative bill to improve the lives of the country's most marginalized and excluded groups in society signaled the beginning of a new era.

Yet President Fox never defended "his" legislative bill in Congress, delegated the constitutional reform process to a group of experienced PAN and PRI senators, and moved on to negotiate the core of his government program – "second-generation" neoliberal reforms. After an unprecedented visit to Congress, in which a Zapatista commander, Esther, addressed Mexico's legislatures in a nationally televised event to defend the COCOPA bill, the EZLN returned to the highlands and the Lacandón jungle to await the legislative outcome. Like President Fox, they delegated the reform process to professional politicians.

A group of senators from the PRI and the PAN prepared a watered-down version of the reform, which was unanimously approved by the Senate, passed by simple majority in Congress, and approved by the minimum number of state legislatures required to become law. From the heart of the Lacandón jungle, the Zapatistas immediately condemned the new "indigenous law" as a democratic sham. Within the next few months, several municipal authorities and rural indigenous movements submitted constitutional challenges to the Mexican Supreme Court. But these never prospered and the reform prevailed.

As various scholars soon pointed out, the constitutional reform contained vague language acknowledging shallow multicultural rights for Mexican indigenous communities. The reform introduced new mechanisms for earmarked federal transfers to states with significant indigenous populations, but transferred most of the responsibility for articulating any meaningful rights to autonomy and self-determination to subnational legislatures. In a country in which ethnolinguistic groups are spread across state borders, this meant that the possibility of creating autonomous regions to reconstitute indigenous peoples' identities had been erased. It also eliminated the possibility of creating special electoral districts for ethnolinguistic groups to provide indigenous peoples with permanent seats in Congress or the Senate (López Barcena, 2002).

With the limited legal "ceiling" defined in the federal constitution, the states were, in turn, limited in the scope of their reforms. Given that natural resources remained the property of the nation, the constitutional reform eliminated any possibility that state lawmakers could redefine property rights over natural resources. Most subnational reforms would take place at the municipal level, reifying the colonial status of Indians as communities rather than as peoples.

It is puzzling that the most emblematic indigenous movement of the post-Cold War world, and one of the most powerful social actors in contemporary Mexico, failed to translate its de facto power into de jure changes. Following Van Cott's (2000 and 2001) insightful analysis of multicultural constitutionalism in Latin America, we can identify two factors that explain Mexico's lackluster multicultural reform. First, having no direct presence and no meaningful parliamentary allies in the Senate or in Congress, the Zapatistas did not participate in the legislative process. And, second, the reform did not take place at a time of major regime crisis, but at a point in time in which the president and Mexico's democratic institution enjoyed their highest approval rates.

Despite three decades of rural indigenous mobilization and the Zapatista uprising, Mexico's indigenous movements did not have a direct representative actor in the 2000 constitutional reform process. The PRD, the ideologically most proximate actor to the Zapatista-led movement for ethnic autonomy and self-determination, had by the late 1990s ended any allegiance with the Zapatistas. A radical reform granting extensive rights to autonomy and self-determination to indigenous peoples would have undermined the power of the PRD in the southern and central states. Outside the congressional halls, the collective action power that rural indigenous movements had once won was waning as the cycle of protest came to an end. Most leaders and activists of the country's major rural indigenous movements were already part of PRD partisan bureaucracies or were busy serving in new subnational government offices.

Unlike most cases of major multicultural reforms elsewhere in Latin America in which countries were reforming their institutions and introducing multicultural rights in the midst of major political crises, Mexico's multicultural reform was sent to Congress at a time when the first democratically elected president enjoyed an unprecedented approval rate of 80 percent and Mexicans appeared to be highly confident about their nascent political regime and institutions. The Mexican regime was not facing a legitimacy crisis that would motivate parliamentary actors to seek new sources of legitimacy in multicultural institutions; after the PRI's defeat in 2000, Mexico's nascent democracy enjoyed the highest level of support that it would ever achieve. Furthermore, any attempt by the Zapatistas to contest the legislative outcome in the mountains or in the streets would receive little social approval in a country in which citizens showed high levels of support for the new political regime.

It remains a historic irony that the same democratic institutions and actors that the Zapatista rebellion and its transformation into a self-determination movement had helped consolidate became the forces that facilitated the demise of Mexico's indigenous insurgency. By the end of seven decades of uninterrupted PRI rule, the country had completed an *uneven transition*: Mexico's indigenous insurgency had facilitated the spread of electoral competition and the consolidation of electoral democracy but the country's democratization had in turn facilitated the twilight of the Zapatistas' ethno-territorial demands.

THE BIRTH OF LIMITED SUBNATIONAL MULTICULTURALISM

Although the Zapatista agenda for a radical reconstruction of Mexico along ethno-territorial lines did not materialize, the rebellion triggered the rise of a series of limited, albeit important, multicultural reforms in the states. This wave of limited subnational reforms was the most important legacy of Zapatism in terms of multicultural rights.

At the outset of his administration, particularly after the peace negotiations with the Zapatistas fell into a stalemate, President Zedillo decided to allow limited multicultural rights at the subnational level. Between 1995 and 2000, PRI governors introduced a range of limited and symbolic rights in the central and southern states. Reforms ranged from constitutional recognition of ethnolinguistic groups in state constitutions and the promotion of bilingual education to the introduction of multicultural considerations in criminal and electoral procedures.

The introduction of indigenous customary laws for the selection of municipal presidents in the southern state of Oaxaca became the most ambitious reform and an example of how far the administration of President Zedillo would be willing to go in terms of multicultural reforms. No new administrative boundaries were established and there were no discussions about ethno-territorial rights or rights over natural resources.

A simple statistical analysis shown in Appendix B, Table A.B.2, shows that subnational multicultural reforms in the late 1990s more commonly took place in states experiencing the most intense histories of ethnic protest where rebel contagion across borders was most likely to occur. Some authors suggest that electoral incentives drove PRI governors to introduce multicultural rights in competitive states, but these results show that the risk of rebel diffusion across borders, particularly in states experiencing the most intense waves of ethnic protest, was the main impetus for reform. To prevent the spread of Zapatism into their territories, PRI governors adopted limited reforms to open alternative institutional channels for rural indigenous movements. As the results in Model 6 show, the limited, albeit most ambitious, reforms in such places as Oaxaca were introduced to purposefully reduce the risk of rebel contagion across borders.

As students of indigenous politics in Oaxaca have suggested, the introduction of customary law for the selection of three quarters of Oaxaca's municipal presidents was mainly the result of the Zapatista uprising and its transformation into a self-determination movement (Elizarrarás, 2003; Recondo, 2007). Before the Zapatista uprising, a similar reform had been partially curtailed in the state congress in 1991, when the governor was able to introduce indigenous communities as subjects of rights but did not recognize customary law. After the Chiapas uprising, however, indigenous customary law was constitutionally recognized, becoming the flagship reform for the federal government and was unanimously approved by all PRI legislators in Oaxaca's state congress. It introduced an institutional mechanism that discouraged the state's grassroots and indigenous movements from following the Zapatista example of radical ethno-territorial claims.

CONCLUSION

The study of Mexico's democratization – like the study of democratization in the social sciences – has been dominated by political economy and institutionalist explanations. As the Mexican economy went into a series of crises and the ruling elite was compelled to introduce an ambitious program of market-oriented reforms – political economists suggest – the PRI lost its privileged access to public resources and patronage that had in the past enabled it to win electoral majorities at all levels of government.[9] Subnational and legislative opposition victories – institutionalists have suggested – led to incremental electoral reforms.[10] Electoral reforms, in turn, allowed opposition voters to punish the PRI for multiple economic crises and economic mismanagement.[11] This generated greater opposition presence, additional reforms, and eventually the possibility for the Mexican median voter to end seven decades of uninterrupted PRI rule.

Students of political economy and institutions have succeeded in showing how Mexican citizens voted the PRI out of office; however, we still lack a systematic explanation of the motivations that led authoritarian incumbents to relinquish control over the electoral process. Following students of democratization from below (Wood, 2000; Acemoglu and Robinson, 2006), in this chapter I have presented new evidence showing that the 1994 and 1996 democratizing electoral reforms in Mexico were a direct response to the Zapatista uprising and its dramatic transformation into a self-determination movement.

Based on public opinion surveys conducted by the Office of the Mexican President in the 1990s and the sequential analysis of historical events and policy decisions, I show that the objective of these two historical reforms was to prevent the rise of a revolutionary coalition that would seek to remove the PRI from power by violent means. Both reforms sought to empower the partisan Left while marginalizing Zapatism. The government's goal was to provide leftist parties with the political power and resources to absorb the country's grassroots and social movements in rural and urban regions and to both deter Zapatista growth outside Chiapas and leave the rebels without a social base. I showed that the government's success in institutionalizing the partisan and social Lefts provided Mexico's authoritarian elites with the political space to apply an anti-insurgency policy against Zapatism without the risk of a major leftist mobilization.

Whereas Acemoglu and Robinson (2006) and Przeworski (2009) have argued that the threat of a revolutionary uprising of the working class led authoritarian elites in nineteenth-century Western Europe to democratize, this chapter has shown that it was an uprising of Indian peasants, rather than of workers, that motivated Mexican elites to consent to free and fair elections. This is a surprising finding, because the literature in the social sciences has traditionally associated peasant and ethnic collective action with antidemocratic politics and outcomes. There are important exceptions. Wood (2000) for example, suggests that campesino revolutionary action motivated economic

[9] See Magaloni (2006) and Greene (2007).
[10] See Lujambio (2000).
[11] See Magaloni (2006).

elites to demand democratization to avoid a revolution in El Salvador. Here we have suggested that the revolutionary actions of Mayan peasants and their transformation into a self-determination movement motivated authoritarian elites to establish the institutional basis for free and competitive multiparty elections in Mexico.

Although the Zapatistas failed to translate their de facto collective action power into meaningful de jure multicultural institutions, the fact remains that the insurgent actions of a group of Mayan peasants motivated Mexican authoritarian elites to finally consent to develop democratic electoral institutions. Faced with the unprecedented possibility of empowering Mexico's indigenous peoples, Mexico's political elites opted instead to empower the country's major political parties. Three decades of rural indigenous peaceful protest and a few years of insurgent collective action had major political consequences for indigenous and nonindigenous Mexicans: Indigenous collective action played a crucial and hitherto unrecognized role in the creation of the institutional base for Mexico's democratization. Without this institutional base, the mestizo median voter would have not been able to vote the PRI out of office in 2000.

Conclusion

The scene of thousands of ordinary people taking to the streets to defy authoritarian regimes across the Arab world has become an iconic image of the twenty-first century. Social networks have connected people and empowered them to struggle for political change in the streets. They have enabled citizens around the world to follow these extraordinary journeys almost by the hour; we have all been witnesses of courageous struggles for freedom and democracy in the streets and the public plazas of Northern Africa and the Middle East.

This book has analyzed a similar journey of defiance that took place several decades earlier and thousands of miles away from the Arab world, in which the poorest and most marginalized members of Mexican society led one of the most protracted and publicly unrecognized cycles of mobilization of the last quarter of the twentieth century. This journey of peaceful protest – which began with demands for land redistribution from rulers who had used land tenure as a tool of authoritarian control – would lead hundreds of rural indigenous communities into a path of armed rebellion and see their initial claims for land transformed into demands for autonomy and self-determination for indigenous peoples.

This mobilization by the poorest and most marginalized members of Mexico's society and the revolutionary potential unleashed by their actions eventually pushed Mexican authoritarian elites to establish the legal basis for free and fair national elections. Seeking to avoid a major social insurrection, the elites democratized to avert an indigenous insurgency. In their quest for land redistribution and ethno-territorial controls, Mexican indigenous movements contributed in a crucial and yet unrecognized way to Mexico's democratization.

Making sense of this extraordinary journey of indigenous collective mobilization has led us on a long journey of research. It led us first to develop a series of general theoretical propositions about the rise, development, and demise of cycles of popular mobilization in autocracies.

In developing a theory of popular mobilization in autocracies, our emphasis was on the transformational role of one specific social mechanism: competition.

Focusing on poor, unequal societies ruled by a single party and served by a single religious supplier, we suggested that the entry of a new religious supplier and the spread of local *competition for poor peoples' souls* would lead the former monopoly clergy to become major promoters of autonomous social networks and popular movements for material redistribution as a member-retention strategy.

We also suggested that the introduction of government-controlled multi-party elections and the spread of local *competition for poor peoples' votes* would lead challengers to initially establish socio-electoral coalitions with autonomous social networks and independent movements and become major promoters of social mobilization as a member-expansion strategy.

We argued that the continuous spread of electoral competition and local electoral victories by opposition parties would eventually lead the opposition to discourage radical mobilization and contribute to the demise of cycles of social protest. But the *elimination of competition* as a mechanism of political change in the midst of a major cycle of mobilization would lead popular movements into radical action. We proposed that when elites responded to major economic crises by rescinding the limited economic, civic and political rights granted during the liberalization phase, signaling a likely reversion to an authoritarian status quo ante, popular movements would move to a new phase of radical politics: to the transformation of peaceful collective action into armed insurgency and to the adoption of previously suppressed social identities such as ethnicity. We suggested that radicalization would be more likely where poor rural villagers were part of decentralized horizontal regional networks that connected powerful local leaders with access to dense communal associational networks.

We finally explored the conditions under which insurgent collective action would lead authoritarian elites to democratize. We argued that elites democratize when they believe democratization would avoid the escalation from insurgency to civil war and when they have reliable information showing that under democracy (1) they would remain important political players and (2) the new configuration of power would not lead to an era of major wealth redistribution.

In testing our basic theoretical propositions we gathered microlevel data of three decades of indigenous mobilization across Mexico's 883 indigenous municipalities. To rule out alternative explanations and establish causal associations connecting religious and electoral competition with indigenous mobilization, we relied on quantitative and qualitative data to conduct different types of tests. We went from analyzing 22,958 observations (883 municipalities × 26 years), to conducting matched comparisons of a few states and municipalities, to studying the life histories of clerics and of a few village leaders from a single municipality over time. Our goal was to gather different types of evidence (quantitative and qualitative) and use very different techniques (from maximum likelihood estimation models to natural experiments and life histories and paired comparisons) to improve confidence in our causal claims.

Although the use of multiple sources of *micro* evidence may be a good strategy for hypotheses testing, one of the main challenges that any microlevel study faces is the external validity of its causal claims: The reader may have wondered throughout the book whether our findings were specific to Mexican indigenous municipalities or if they could travel beyond this statistical universe.

My goal in this chapter is to explore whether the findings and mechanisms presented in this book are generalizable beyond Mexico and to assess the theoretical contributions of this study to four areas of research on collective action and social movements: (1) social movements and cycles of protest in autocracies; (2) the transformation of social movements into rebel groups and the outbreak of armed insurgencies in liberalizing autocracies; (3) the impact of protest and rebellion on democratization; and (4) the study of indigenous politics in Latin America.

POPULAR MOVEMENTS AND CYCLES OF PROTEST IN AUTOCRACIES

A comprehensive understanding of collective action and social protest in autocracies compels us to answer four specific questions: How do autonomous associational networks that enable collective action ever arise in autocracies? How do these networks become politicized and when do members of these networks engage in cycles of peaceful protest? When do government attempts to co-opt or repress movements actually deter protest and when do they stimulate further mobilization? How do cycles of protest come to an end? In this book we have carefully identified and isolated a number of causal mechanisms that help answer these questions and hence improve our understanding of social protest in autocracies.

Religious Competition and the Creation of Autonomous Associational Networks for Popular Collective Action

Three decades of research on collective action and social movements have succeeded in establishing the importance of social networks and a movement's organizational structure for social protest (McAdam, McCarthy, and Zald, 1996; Tarrow, 1998; Diani and McAdam, 2003). Scholars have argued that in the absence of mobilizing vehicles, major crises and grievances may not translate into collective action.

Although the literature has firmly established the importance of social networks and organizations, we know little about the social processes by which these networks come into existence.[1] Answering this question is crucial for our understanding of collective action in autocracies because rulers in closed autocracies discourage the existence of autonomous networks in the first place.

Extending some of the basic propositions of the political economy of religion (Iannaccone, 1996; Gill, 1994, 1998) to the study of social movements,

---

[1] This is the case in the social movement literature as well as in network theory.

I have explored how the spread of U.S. Protestant missionary activity and the breakdown of Catholic monopolistic controls in rural indigenous regions led Catholic clergy to become major promoters of autonomous associational networks and independent movements for land redistribution and indigenous rights in Mexico. Unable to decentralize ecclesiastic hierarchies to the extent that Protestant missionaries did and to avoid a defection en masse to the competition, Catholic clergy stepped into the secular realm and promoted the construction of decentralized horizontal regional networks of powerful local lay leaders (catechists) and dense communal associational networks of Bible study groups and economic and social cooperatives. These religious networks served as the organizational infrastructure for the rise of powerful secular peasant and indigenous movements.

Our finding on the effect of religious competition on rural indigenous mobilization in Mexico has major implications for our understanding of why traditional clergy become major promoters of progressive movements for social transformation and why religious social networks can be such powerful vehicles for sustained collective action, particularly under conditions of high risk. After centuries of believing that religion was "the opium of the people" and one of the major sources of backwardness and social control, in recent decades we have come to understand that religion is Janus-faced: it can be a source of obedience but also an important source for dissent and progressive transformation. The problem is, however, that we are just beginning to understand what makes religion such a potentially powerful source for dissident collective action.

This book has provided extensive evidence showing that the spread of religious competition and the breakdown in local religious monopolies can be a causal mechanism that may stimulate former monopoly clergy to transform themselves from guarantors of the status quo to major promoters of secular movements for social transformation. Whereas scholars of religion and politics have successfully shown that church-state conflicts can be a mechanism that explains the transformation of religious authorities into major promoters of secular collective action (Kalyvas, 1996), building on Gill (1994, 1998), we have shown here how religious competition can be another mechanism for explaining why clerical authorities become promoters of the social basis for independent popular mobilization. This finding is particularly important for the study of autocracies, where religion is one of the few sources for the rise of autonomous movements.

This book has also provided important evidence showing that it was not radical religious ideas that gave Catholic social networks their powerful potential for dissident collective action; rather, it was the *structural characteristics* of the Catholic social networks that facilitated the transformation of peaceful religious groups into powerful secular social movements. We have shown that in response to the decentralized Protestant evangelizing strategy and as a member-retention strategy, Catholic clergy in competitive districts developed decentralized horizontal regional network structures composed of multiple local leaders with access to dense communal associational networks.

We presented primary evidence showing that the leaders and communities that belonged to these networks had the social power to defy government co-optation and repression. It was the structural characteristics of the social connections resulting from religious competition that turned religious networks into such powerful vehicles for secular protest in autocracy.

A rich literature based on experiences of rural indigenous and nonindigenous mobilization in specific Latin American countries provides reliable micro evidence suggesting that religious competition transformed traditional Catholic clergy into major promoters of grassroots organizations and secular movements for economic redistribution and social transformation beyond Mexico. Here are some examples.

We have ethnographic evidence that in response to the spread of U.S. Protestantism and the entrenched prevalence of *la costumbre* (folk Catholicism), U.S. Maryknoll and Guatemalan and European Jesuit missionaries played a prominent role in building the social base for the rise of powerful peasant indigenous movements in Guatemala in the 1960s and 1970s, particularly in the Dioceses of Quiché, San Marcos, and Huehuetenango.[2] We also have good micro evidence about the important effect of the spread of U.S. Protestantism and the missionary work of the Summer Institute of Linguistics on the transformation of Bishop Leónidas Proaño in Chimborazo, Ecuador, from a conservative cleric into one of the founding fathers of Andean Theology and one of the most important institutional sponsors of the social basis for the rise of a powerful peasant indigenous movements in Ecuador.[3] Le Bot (1994) provides secondary evidence of the impact of religious competition on the rise of indigenous movements in Bolivia and Brazil.[4]

As in Mexican indigenous regions, it is religious competition, rather than radical religious ideas, that explains why traditional clerics in these countries became champions of the poor. And the nature of Protestant evangelizing strategy – emphasizing material rewards, decentralization of ecclesiastic hierarchies, and the creation of a native local clergy – explains why these Catholic clergy built the decentralized network structures that would enable rural indigenous communities to engage in powerful movements for land redistribution and indigenous rights.

Evidence from Guatemala, Ecuador, Bolivia, and Brazil shows that the social networks Catholic clergy built in response to the proselytizing activity of U.S.

[2] See the influential work by Le Bot (1995) and Brockett (1991, 2005). For detailed accounts of four decades of rural indigenous organizing, see Bastos and Camus (1995) and Quino (2006).
[3] See the pioneering anthropological work by Santana (1992) and the most recent sociological work by Andrade (2004).
[4] The work by Potter, Amaral, and Woodberry on the impact of Protestant missionary activity on household income in Brazil provides additional clues. The maps of religious plurality they present show a remarkable visual correlation between areas of high religious competition and areas where we know Catholic clergy played a leading role in the development of indigenous movements and of the Landless Rural Workers Movement (MST), Brazil's powerful landless peasants' movement. For a general overview of the MST, see Wright and Wolford (2003).

Protestant missionaries served many different secular purposes. In some cases, these networks became the mobilizing structure for the rise of powerful cycles of peaceful social protest, in others for the spread of opposition political parties, and in others for the rise of armed insurgencies. Why some of these religious networks took nonviolent or violent paths, however, is beyond the affairs of God; the explanation lies in the secular world of Caesar.

Electoral Competition and the Rise of Cycles of Popular Protest

Students of social movements generally consider the rise of cycles of social protest as a result of the expansion of political opportunities (Eisinger, 1973). When levels of repression decline, elites splinter, or countries undergo party realignments, social movements can more effectively politicize their claims in the streets (McAdam, McCarthy, and Zald, 1996). Building on this argument, scholars of social movements in autocracies have suggested that periods of autocratic liberalization give rise to waves of independent protest (Almeida, 2003).

One of the most common criticisms of the political opportunity argument is that it is tautological: the opening of opportunities allows movements to search for opportunities. Although this criticism carries important intellectual weight, it is not a lethal attack. A way to eliminate the tautological elements of the political process argument is to identify social actors and political incentives and to link political processes with societal actions. This is what some of the most influential students of social movements have been urging us to do: to explore the connections of *electoral* processes and political parties with social movements and the dynamics of protest; to connect the logic of ballots with the logic of the streets (McAdam and Tarrow, 2010).

Extending some of the basic intuitions drawn from the study of elections in autocracies (Schedler, 2002; Greene, 2007) to the study of political processes and social movements, in this book I have explored how the introduction of government-controlled multiparty elections in Mexico's authoritarian regime led leftist opposition parties to develop *socio-electoral coalitions* with autonomous rural indigenous networks and independent movements and to become major sponsors of peasant indigenous protest. Because elections in autocracies are "nested games," in which opposition parties compete for office while at the same time contesting the rules of competition, we found extensive evidence showing that in their attempt to establish a core electoral constituency and develop a social base to fight fraud, leftist opposition parties recruited social leaders and activists and became major sponsors of social movements for land redistribution and indigenous rights. In exchange for the movement members' votes and support in post-election rallies to contest fraud, opposition parties provided resources, support and protection for street mobilization in non-electoral times.

Our finding establishing a causal association between the spread of electoral competition and peaceful protest has important implications for our understanding of the widespread existence of cycles of peaceful protest in hybrid regimes or electoral autocracies and for the intimate relationship between social movements and opposition parties in these regimes – social movements rapidly become politicized and opposition parties look and act more like social movements than political parties. Whereas most explanations in the literature emphasize the inconsistent capacity of hybrid regimes to repress, here we have outlined an electoral rationale that accounts for socio-electoral coalitions and protest.

This book has produced extensive evidence showing that social protest is endogenous to electoral competition in electoral autocracies. The Mexican experience shows that in these political regimes opposition parties become major promoters and sponsors of social protest for purely electoral purposes. Ideology did not drive leftist parties to embrace rural indigenous movements, particularly those linked to Catholic social networks; rather, opposition parties opportunistically partnered with rural indigenous movements because they were a crucial actor for their electoral goals. Hence the introduction of government-controlled elections in autocracies gives rise to incentives toward the creation of socio-electoral coalitions and for the development of cycles of peaceful protest.

This book has also presented important evidence showing that rural indigenous movements rapidly became politicized under electoral autocracy – demands for land redistribution soon became demands for human rights respect and free and fair elections. Even if the struggle for free and fair elections is not initially part of their ideological repertoire, lay movements and religious networks become politicized as a result of their socio-electoral partnership. And even if democracy is not part of their initial set of demands, peasant movements become politicized to achieve their demands for land redistribution. It is not that they will achieve their material goals through electoral means; it is that the electoral connection empowers them to take their claims to the streets.

We have reliable evidence of the development of socio-electoral coalitions and the rise of independent protest in authoritarian regimes that have introduced government-controlled elections throughout Latin America. This includes a wide variety of authoritarian regimes, from civilian to military.

Guatemala provides an important example, where the military regime consented to government-controlled multiparty elections in the 1970s and opposition parties, particularly the Christian Democratic Party of Guatemala, built strong socio-electoral coalitions with Catholic social networks and peasant indigenous movements as they tried to establish themselves as credible electoral alternatives for municipal and then national elections.[5] We have similar evidence that the Christian Democratic Party of El Salvador and various leftist opposition parties established socio-electoral coalitions with Catholic social networks and peasant movements after the military regime consented to government-controlled multiparty elections. As opposition forces tried to create local electoral core constituencies and fight fraud in the 1970s, party

---

[5] For extensive discussions of these linkages, see Brockett (1991, 2005) and Le Bot (1995).

leaders became major promoters of street mobilization.[6] Similar socio-electoral coalitions emerged in Ecuador and Bolivia between leftist parties and peasant indigenous movements, where leftist opposition parties became strategic promoters of social mobilization for purely electoral purposes.[7]

The introduction of government-controlled multiparty elections in Brazil also provided powerful incentives for opposition parties to establish socio-electoral coalitions with progressive Catholic movements, workers' unions, and peasant movements. In a nonindigenous context, Chile under Augusto Pinochet provides a surprising example, in which the 1978 constitutional reform and the call for a plebiscite in 1988 opened the way for the rise of powerful socio-electoral partnerships between a wide variety of social movements and the Christian Democrats and Socialist parties; these opposition socio-electoral coalitions impelled multiple waves of peaceful protest in Chile throughout the 1980s.

Persistent Protest Despite Co-optation and Repression

Students of collective action and social movements have traditionally assumed that government repression is a cost that dissuades dissident social protest and that through repressive actions governments can either deter or bring cycles of protest to an end (McAdam, McCarthy, and Zald, 1996). Yet numerous studies of repression and social mobilization have found contradictory results: Repression sometimes quells independent protest, but in other cases it stimulates additional mobilization.[8] In trying to make sense of these contradictory effects, scholars of contentious politics have refined their arguments by distinguishing between different strategies of repression (e.g., random versus targeted and preventive versus reactive), but the results remain contradictory.

Building on the study of governance in autocracies, in this book I have suggested that although incumbents in electoral autocracies may consent to government-controlled multiparty elections, they adopt governance strategies that seek to minimize opposition party growth and hence try to prevent the formation of socio-electoral opposition coalitions. The Mexican experience showed that authoritarian incumbents actively sought to co-opt leaders and activists of independent movements through selective incentives and limited material concessions (e.g., land) to their movements. If co-optation did not work, rulers sought to keep protest under control through moderate forms of targeted repression, particularly unlawful arrests of leaders and activists.

In this book we have presented important micro evidence showing that the success of government attempts to "manage" independent protest through co-optation or repression was conditional on the nature of social networks.

---

[6] See Almeida (2003, 2008).
[7] See Van Cott (1995, 2008).
[8] The two volumes edited by Davenport (2000, 2005) provide a good overview of fascinating, albeit contradictory, results in the literature.

Co-optation and repression worked most effectively in closed corporate indigenous communities where no independent associational networks existed and communities remained internally united by traditional customary practices but externally isolated from other independent villages. Co-optation and repression had more modest, albeit important, demobilizing effects when peasant indigenous movements were structured as centralized hierarchical organizations with a few leaders at the top. But they were least effective in dampening protest when movements were organized as decentralized and horizontal regional networks of multiple local leaders with access to dense associational local community organizations.

We showed that the decentralized horizontal social base the Catholic Church contributed to building in response to the spread of U.S. Protestant missionary activity was a resilient structure for independent mobilization because this network structure worked as a social safety and security net for leaders, activists, and community members. The collective provision of social services and public goods by economic and social cooperatives allowed group members to resist the short-term benefits of authoritarian co-optation and wait for greater gains. In the event of government repression, when a leader was incarcerated, other local leaders stepped up and kept the movement going. Moreover, the strong local bonds that leaders and activists had with the dense local associational networks would assure them that their comrades would not give up until they achieved their release from jail.

The most important implication of these findings is that the impact of government attempts to deter independent protest via co-optation or repression is conditional on social networks. As Siegel's (2011) influential article suggests, the same act of government repression can have different and seemingly contradictory effects, depending on the social connections of victims. In this book, we have provided extensive evidence showing that decentralized regional networks with multiple local leaders supported by dense local associational networks were highly resilient structures to co-optation and repression. The removal of one or a few leaders did not lead to a network collapse. And the different components of the network rapidly mobilized to rescue or restore the missing leader.

Our findings support pioneering studies by Osa (2003), Schock (2005), and Siegel (2011) in suggesting that the impact of authoritarian governance and repression on independent social protest should not be studied as a direct relationship but as a conditional phenomenon. In the language of social movement theory, our suggestion is to systematically integrate the study of political opportunities and threats with the study of mobilizing vehicles; to bring back social network structures in the study of political processes.

A second important finding is that lay religious leaders were more resilient than secular leftist leaders in the face of repression or co-optation. As the experiences of indigenous mobilization in Mexico have shown, radical progressive theologies did not make rural indigenous movements more resilient than socialist activists; rather, it was the decentralized horizontal network connections of Catholic social networks that enabled their leaders and members to become the main drivers of a powerful cycle of independent mobilization. Leftist secular rural indigenous movements, in contrast, were less resilient to co-optation and repression because these movements would collapse once the centralized leadership was successfully removed.

We have reliable evidence that peasant and/or indigenous movements that emerged from within the decentralized horizontal Catholic social networks were particularly resilient in the face of co-optation attempts and government repression throughout Latin America.

The experience of the United Peasants Committee (CUC) in Guatemala – the powerful peasant movement that developed on the basis of the dense Catholic associational networks built by Maryknoll and Jesuit missionaries in the 1960s and 1970s – is instructive here. Students of social mobilization in Guatemala have called attention to the resilience of these movements in the face of harsh military repression (Brockett, 1991). Although explanations have emphasized the role of emotions (Brockett, 2005), my findings in this book would suggest that the decentralized horizontal structure of the social networks on which the CUC was built contributed to the development of the social incentives and social power that sustained peasant indigenous collective action in Guatemala.

In a nonindigenous context, the experience of the Christian Federation of Salvadoran Peasants (FECCAS) – the powerful federation of peasants that Jesuit priests were instrumental in building in El Salvador – is also instructive. In the face of government co-optation attempts via land redistribution and lethal selective repression in the 1970s, the peasants linked through these Catholic social networks were the least likely to abandon independent protest. Influential studies (Wood, 2003) have underscored the role of Catholic progressive ideology and emotions in making Salvadorean campesinos overcome fear and brutal repression, but here I offer an alternative explanation: the structure of social connections that progressive Catholic priests built in response to Protestant competition empowered campesions to remain defiant.

How Cycles of Protest Come to an End

An enduring question in the study of social movements is about the conditions that bring cycles of social protest to a close. In the case of electoral autocracies, the question is whether democratization brings about demobilization or whether expanding political opportunities under democracy stimulate greater mobilization.

Building on electoral theories in autocracies, in this book I have suggested that the expansion of electoral competition and opposition electoral victories in subnational contests would provide incentives for opposition party leaders and candidates to eventually discourage radical mobilization and de-emphasize

radical demands. We showed that in their attempt to satisfy the policy preferences of the median voter, even former leaders of indigenous movements
embraced moderate forms of mobilization and adopted moderate platforms
when they ran for office or when they became mayors. In exchange for patronage and government resources, leaders and activists of social movements and
their rank and file left the streets and moved their politics into parliaments and
city halls.

Although this institutionalizing effect was more pronounced among members
of centralized, hierarchically organized social movements, it was also important among those organized in decentralized horizontal networks. Members of
Catholic networks abandoned protest as they embraced democratic politics,
and their political choice contributed to bringing protracted cycles of protest
to an end.

The main theoretical implication of our exploration of socio-electoral cycles
is that electoral incentives can explain both the rise and demise of cycles of
independent protest in electoral autocracies. At the initial stages of competition, parties build socio-electoral coalitions and sponsor social movements
to politicize their demands in the streets. But once opposition parties become
truly competitive and elections are increasingly free and fair, party leaders and
candidates face significant incentives to discourage radical mobilization, contributing to the institutionalization of social movements and to the demobilization of cycles of independent protest.

We do not have much evidence in Latin America to support this finding
because autocratic liberalization processes were dramatically interrupted
by civil war in Guatemala and El Salvador, and because after democratization, traditional party systems collapsed in several Southern Cone countries
and indigenous movements went on to create their own political parties. The
experiences of Guatemala and El Salvador show that on their way to power,
Christian Democratic parties strongly discouraged independent mobilization
and radical demands from peasants and workers. The electoral connection was
relevant here, but the main factor that drove moderation was the repressive
practices military regimes had already adopted as these countries plunged into
civil war.

In a different context, Chile provides an instructive case outside the indigenous sphere of how democratization and opposition electoral victories may
result in the institutionalization of social movements. After the opposition victory in 1988, the powerful cycle of social protest of the 1980s came to an end
and many of its key social leaders and activists were absorbed into party or
government positions. The institutionalization of social movements into parliaments and city halls was so rapid and effective that in the aftermath of Chile's
democratization, one of the leading students of the country's social movements
published an article emblematically entitled "Where did all the protesters go?"
(Oxhorn, 1994).[9]

---

[9] See also Hipsher (1996).

FROM POPULAR PROTEST TO ARMED REBELLION

Even though students of social movements since Tilly (1978) and Della Porta and Tarrow (1986) have immersed themselves in the study of political violence and revolution, the social movement literature has not been able to establish an enduring theoretical connection between social protest and the rise of political violence.[10]

Economic and demographic explanations emphasizing structural factors dominate the study of the outbreak of insurgencies and civil war. Although levels of economic development, inequality, rurality, and mountainous terrain are macro variables that do help us identify countries that are more likely to experience insurgency and civil war, the explanatory power of these macro variables declines as we move away from using nation-states as units of analysis and ask about subnational variation in levels of insurgent activity between provinces, municipalities, villages, hamlets, and individuals. The micro evidence on the ground often shows that the same rural, mountainous context of poverty gives rise to different strategies: from villagers who rebel, to those who do not, and to those who take up arms as paramilitaries to fight their rebel neighbors.[11]

Building on theories of conflict escalation (Della Porta and Tarrow, 1986; Lichbach, 1987), in this book we have focused our understanding of the outbreak of armed insurgencies on the governance strategies followed by incumbents in electoral autocracies to deal politically with major economic crises or implement unpopular shifts in economic policy. Our goal was to understand how different governance strategies elites adopt to manage the crisis in the midst of major cycles of peaceful mobilization can provide incentives either for further peaceful mobilization or for the transformation of social movements into armed insurgency and the escalation of protest into rebellion.

Through the systematic analysis of the governance strategies subnational elites in Mexico adopted to implement a widely unpopular reform that ended six decades of land reform and set the legal basis for the liberalization of land tenure, we showed that where governors adopted compensatory policies and deepened electoral democratization, rural indigenous protest increased but did not become rebellion. In contrast, where governors rescinded basic political rights and liberties and adopted purely punitive strategies to implement the marketization of agricultural life, signaling a likely reversion to a status quo ante, their new governance strategies gave rise to incentives for revolutionary action.

One key finding of the book, however, was that revolutionary incentives became revolutionary action only where rebel recruitment was possible. We found that closed corporate traditional indigenous communities or centralized socialist networks and unions were not the main vehicle for rebel recruitment.

---

[10] See Tarrow (2007) for an extensive discussion of ways to connect the social movement literature with studies of insurgency and civil war.
[11] See Viterna (2006) and Humphreys and Weinstein (2008).

Instead, recruitment took place primarily through Catholic social networks, where social movements and communities were organized on the basis of decentralized horizontal regional networks with multiple local leaders (catechists) and strong community associational networks (Bible study groups and economic and social cooperatives).

These findings have important implications for the study of the outbreak of armed insurgencies. Punitive governance of a major negative economic shock in the midst of a major cycle of protest can provide incentives for radicalization; however, in such a punitive context, revolutionary feelings translate into revolutionary action only where rebel recruitment is possible.

The first important theoretical implication is that once autocracies engage in political liberalization processes and grant limited economic, political, and civic rights and liberties, the removal of any of these fundamental rights in the midst of a major cycle of social and political mobilization will radicalize people in the streets. Large-scale electoral fraud, changes in criminal codes that criminalize protest, and the assassination of previously immune individuals (e.g., party leaders or members of the clergy) may serve as powerful signals of a likely regime reversion. Facing the possibility of a regression to a punitive status quo ante, people in the streets might have incentives for revolutionary action.

The quantitative cross-national literature has observed that the outbreak of insurgencies and civil wars is more likely in hybrid regimes and electoral autocracies (Hegre, et al., 2001; Goldstone, et al., 2010). We do not, however, know why. Our findings suggest that regime reversion threats in hybrid regimes are an invitation to insurgent collective action. We showed that inconsistent political management of major economic crises or major and unpopular economic policy shifts can render these regimes vulnerable to revolutionary action. Once autocrats enter onto a path of partial political liberalization and grant limited rights and liberties, they create expectations for dissidents to negotiate limited policy concessions in the streets and through the ballot box; when elites adopt reforms that rescind fundamental economic rights and seek to deter a major social insurrection by rescinding recently granted civil rights and political liberties, they will nurture revolutionary motives.

The second implication is the important observation that revolutionary incentives translate into revolutionary action only where professionals in violence can recruit from within social movements; in other words, the effect of authoritarian governance on revolutionary action is conditional on the nature of social networks. In the absence of the social networks for rebel recruitment, regime reversion threats may lead to demobilization. And where social networks exist, not all structural configurations of networks will lend themselves to rebel recruitment. When rebel leaders want to build a social base for guerrilla warfare – the military technique of militarily inferior groups – they approach social movements and communities that are part of decentralized horizontal structures where powerful local leaders are supported by communities densely organized in multiple associational networks. This structure minimizes the risks of underground recruitment and maximizes the extent of popular support.

Since 9/11, a number of studies have explored the revolutionary capacity of religious groups. In his influential explanation of the significant role religious communities have played in terrorist acts around the world, Berman (2009) has suggested that strict religions that develop "club"-like organizational structures and create social norms that increase the costs of defection are more likely to generate radical actors and radical actions. Focusing on the organizational structure of Catholic indigenous communities in Mexico and Latin America, we have developed a different explanation based on network connections. In a punitive context marked by threats of regime reversion, in our story catechists and Catholic social networks in rural indigenous regions became a major conduit for rebel recruitment because they had the structural characteristics and connections that facilitated recruitment.

The experience of peasant indigenous collective action in Latin America provides additional evidence that regime reversion threats in liberalizing autocracies may motivate strongly networked religious communities to engage in revolutionary action. Conflict escalation in these cases was the result of dramatic changes in governance that gave rise to regime reversion threats; these threats were capitalized mainly by professionals in violence who were able to recruit combatants from decentralized Catholic associational networks.

After a decade of limited political liberalization in Guatemala, fearful that a revolutionary contagion effect from Nicaragua would embolden Guatemalan social movements and opposition parties to join rebel groups, a newly elected military government abandoned liberalization and embraced repression as a dominant governance strategy. The generals tried to decapitate the opposition, and the state's security forces went on to assassinate previously untouched leaders, including foreign-born Catholic clergy, opposition mayors, leading political figures, and peasant and indigenous leaders (Le Bot, 1995; Brockett, 2005). These radical actions did not dismantle the Catholic decentralized regional networks with multiple local leaders, but served as a powerful signal to Guatemala's peasant movements and Catholic communities that the era of liberalization was over. The imminent return to a punitive closed authoritarian regime stimulated a period of mass recruitment from Guatemala's leading peasant movements into the Army of Guatemala's People (EPG).

As in Chiapas, rebel recruitment in Guatemala took place predominantly among Mayan peasants who were connected through the decentralized horizontal networks built by the Catholic Church in response to Protestant competition (Stoll, 1993; Le Bot, 1995). These were regional networks of communities with dense local associational networks in which catechists played a major leadership role; professionals in violence coming from northeastern Guatemala into the western highlands had access to these rich network structures only after communities became convinced they were facing a security dilemma: they either attacked the state or the military would crush them.

A similar experience of regime reversion threats and the escalation of protest into rebellion took place in El Salvador, where, after fifteen years of political liberalization, a newly elected military government reformed the country's criminal code to criminalize protest and began a period of unprecedented repression between 1977 and 1982 (Brockett, 2005). Seeking to avoid a revolution as in neighboring Nicaragua, the government's security forces assassinated key political figures, social movement leaders, and members of the Catholic clergy (Almeida, 2003; Brockett, 2005). These were years of mass recruitment into fragmented rebel groups that eventually united into a powerful revolutionary coalition. In the countryside, rebel recruitment took place mainly through decentralized horizontal Catholic social networks and rural movements that Jesuit priests and other missionaries had contributed to building in the rural countryside in the 1970s and early 1980s (Wood, 2003; Brockett, 2005).

It is noteworthy that similar Catholic progressive practices throughout Latin America's rural and indigenous regions gave rise to a wide range of experiences of collective mobilization, from revolutionary action to cycles of peaceful protest to electoral participation. Progressive practices linked to Liberation and Indigenous Theologies led catechists and movements from Chiapas (Mexico), Guatemala, and El Salvador into becoming the mass base for revolutionary collective action. However, similar progressive practices did not lead to rebellion in Oaxaca (Mexico), Bolivia, Ecuador, or Brazil.

We know from the comparison of Oaxaca and Chiapas that the punitive policies that signaled a regime reversion threat in Chiapas created a revolutionary context that motivated members of Catholic social networks to join the EZLN. A path of reform and democratization, rather than regime regression, led rural indigenous movements in Oaxaca to take their claims to the streets and the ballot boxes rather than to the mountains. Comparisons of Guatemala and El Salvador to Bolivia, Ecuador and Brazil suggest that, in the absence of regime reversion threats, decentralized social networks will not serve as vehicles for rebel recruitment but for the continuous spread of peaceful social protest or the consolidation of electoral politics.

INSURGENT COLLECTIVE ACTION AND DEMOCRATIZATION

Cycles of protest and the outbreak of armed insurgencies can lead to civil war or to democratization. Although scholars of social movements have been conspicuously silent about the institutional consequences of social protest, in recent years, based on the Western European experience of democratization, students of regime change have suggested that major waves of working class mobilization and the rise of revolutionary threats can motivate elites in authoritarian regimes to democratize (Acemoglu and Robinson, 2006; Przeworski, 2009).

Extending theories of democratization from below in developing countries (Wood, 2000) to the study of rural indigenous mobilization, in this book I have shown that the potential rise of an indigenous-led revolutionary coalition and the threat of a major national uprising led Mexican authoritarian elites to establish the institutional basis for free and fair national elections. We provided original data showing that elites consented to democratization to avoid a rebel indigenous army leading the country's major rural and urban independent movements into a grand Leftist revolutionary coalition to topple the PRI from power and to reconstruct the country's political institutions along ethno-territorial lines.

Establishing a legal base for free and fair elections was a mechanism to empower the partisan left and enable it to lead the country's social movements into a path of electoral participation. We showed that authoritarian elites consented to free and fair elections because they knew they could win or remain as key players under competitive elections, and because economic elites were persuaded that Mexico's three-party system did not entail major risks of economic redistribution or claims for retroactive justice.

Whereas research in political science has traditionally argued that the mobilization of peasants and ethnic minorities gives rise either to insurgencies and civil war or to the development of authoritarian regimes, my research provides extensive evidence showing that the contentious and revolutionary actions of Indian peasants was the single factor that motivated authoritarian Mexican elites to democratize. Contrary to most narratives of Western European democratization that emphasize the proto-democratic role of the working class (Acemoglu and Robinson, 2006), the middle class (Lipset, 1960/1981), or the bourgeoisie (Moore, 1966/1993), and the pro-authoritarian nature of peasant collective action in predominantly rural societies (Boix, 2003), in my account, the collective action of rural and ethnic minorities played a crucial role in stimulating the democratization of Mexico's electoral institutions.

Whereas the literature on Latin America's unprecedented wave of indigenous mobilization has suggested that national democratization facilitated local indigenous collective action (Yashar, 1998, 2005), here I have made the case that the reverse was true: Local indigenous collective action contributed to national democratization. More specifically, I argued that when indigenous movements shifted from peaceful protest to armed rebellion and from demanding land redistribution to claiming rights to autonomy and self-determination for indigenous peoples, authoritarian elites consented to free and fair elections to avert Mexico's indigenous insurgency.

This finding suggests a new mechanism of democratization: authoritarian elites may embrace a path of *liberal* democratization to undermine self-determination movements fighting for major ethno-territorial reforms. It is a strategy by which authoritarian elites choose a second best political outcome: liberal-democratic institutions to empower political parties rather than self-determination movements seeking to rebuild a country's internal political boundaries along ethno-territorial lines.

Even though the impact of peasant and indigenous mobilization on democratization is a relatively underexplored area in Latin America, we have important evidence of the impact of rural insurgent collective action in the democratization of El Salvador. As Wood's (2000) work has persuasively shown, El Salvador represents a prominent case in which campesino insurgent collective action and the extension of civil war into the country's major cities motivated economic and political elites to democratize. Oligarchic economic elites demanded democratization and military elites consented to give up power only when the country's elites were persuaded that a right-wing party could effectively represent their interests in a democratic system and could work as an effective check on the redistributive ambitions of popular movements and leftist parties.

RETHINKING INDIGENOUS COLLECTIVE ACTION

Competition and the Social Basis for Indigenous Collective Action

The dominant academic and popular interpretation of indigenous collective action in contemporary Latin America suggests that the most cohesive, homogenous, isolated indigenous communities of cultural survivors – those who successfully resisted three centuries of colonial rule and two centuries of assimilation attempts by postcolonial mestizo societies – led major cycles of mobilization against neoliberal agricultural policies and capitalist penetration into indigenous habitats.

Using a wide variety of quantitative and qualitative data, in this book I have shown that the most culturally cohesive and racially homogenous and isolated indigenous communities did not participate in Mexico's major cycles of independent mobilization and remained under the clientelistic domination of traditional authoritarian controls. It was, instead, indigenous communities undergoing the most intense processes of social, cultural, and political differentiation that spearheaded major independent movements for land redistribution and indigenous rights.

Emphasizing the unprecedented rise of the competition for indigenous *souls* and *votes*, the book showed that the spread of sociopolitical plurality in Mexico's rural indigenous regions transformed the internal structures of communal power and the external articulation of these communities with their coethnic villages and with nonindigenous society. The most important transformation was the rise of new local leadership structures and new associational networks that were not necessarily built on traditional kinship ties.

Indigenous collective action – from social protest, to armed insurgency, to the politicization of ethnic identities – took place on the base of these new associational networks instead of on the base of traditional customary leadership structures and cultural norms. And external agents – churches and parties – did not impose these new associational connections. As this book has shown using micro ethnographic evidence, the competition for souls and votes empowered members of indigenous communities to demand new sources of power, status, and differentiation from their churches and parties. The renegotiation of traditional allegiances empowered rural indigenous villagers to demand new religious and political relationships with those who wanted to win or retain their loyalties.

Even though primordialism has been questioned on theoretical and empirical grounds and a constructivist consensus currently dominates the social sciences, studies of indigenous politics in Latin America and comparative quantitative studies of ethnic politics continue to assume that shared linguistic, religious, or racial traits can serve as the basis of collective action. The findings of this book show that it was not these inherited traits that represented the most powerful base for the rise of rural indigenous movements, cycles of protest, and armed insurgencies. Instead, the associational networks – the mobilizing vehicles – external agents and communities created through processes of competition and conflict became the organizational infrastructure for indigenous struggles for economic, political and cultural rights.

The Political Consequences of Indigenous Collective Action

Students of indigenous politics have argued that the unprecedented wave of indigenous mobilization that took place in Latin America in the last quarter of the twentieth century was a *post-authoritarian* phenomenon. In this narrative, indigenous movements benefited but did not participate in Latin America's near universal shift from authoritarian rule to democracy.

Although students of democratization in Mexico do recognize the important effect of the 1994 Zapatista rebellion in motivating authoritarian elites to introduce one of the most important democratizing electoral reforms to pave the way for the demise of seven decades of uninterrupted PRI rule (Becerra, Salazar and Woldenberg, 2000; Magaloni, 2006 and 2010), in the grand narrative of Mexico's prolonged democratization, macrostructural factors such as economic crises and electoral competition are identified as the causal factors of political change. In the dominant narrative, external economic shocks, opposition parties, and most importantly Mexican voters were the key actors of the country's transition to democracy.

Even though indigenous communities and movements are absent from dominant narratives of democratization in Mexico, this book is an attempt to show that the end of seven decades of uninterrupted PRI rule and the country's democratization would have not taken place without the three decades of indigenous collective action that preceded it. If this book only succeeds in persuading the academic and nonacademic community of this finding, the long journey of research that enabled us to make sense of an unprecedented wave of indigenous mobilization in Mexico will have been worth every second.

Appendix A

Collecting Protest Event Data in Autocracies
Indigenous Protest in Mexico

The main objective of the Mexican Indigenous Insurgency Database (MII) is to provide systematic, representative, reliable quantitative data on indigenous protest, group claims, rebel activities, and government repression in Mexico during the period between 1975 and 2000. The MII includes information on 21 Mexican states and 883 indigenous municipalities. The data cover only those municipalities that at any time between 1970 and 2000 had at least 10 percent indigenous population (the national mean). The MII contains detailed information about 3,553 protest events, 5,120 claims, and 1,765 actions of government repression.

My guiding principle for data gathering was to minimize any sources of spatial and temporal bias. Because my ultimate goal was to gather data to enable inferential statistical analyses, I did not try to build a record of the exact number of protest and repression events that took place in Mexico in the last quarter of the twentieth century; rather, I strove to gather the best data available while minimizing any sources of bias.

In this appendix, I describe the information sources I used to build the MII database and the criteria I followed to select my news sources. I discuss how the use of multiple sources contributes to minimizing sources of bias in the reporting of contentious events, particularly in autocracies, where freedom of the press is not always guaranteed. I conclude by highlighting limitations of the data.

SOURCES

Unlike most single-country studies, which rely on a single newspaper for data collection (e.g., *The New York Times* in the study of social protest in the United States), in constructing the MII, I followed the example of Beissinger (2001) and used multiple national sources for data collection – eight Mexican *daily* newspapers. The use of multiple news sources helps minimize sources of spatial and temporal bias. I personally collected data from *El Día* (1975–1976), *Unomásuno* (1977–1983), and *La Jornada* (1984–2000), and then complemented the data from Prodato's collection of more than 3 million news clips.

The latter is based on a systematic review of Mexican daily newspapers from 1968 to the present.

CRITERIA FOR NEWSPAPER SELECTION

I initially collected data from *El Día*, *Unomásuno*, and *La Jornada* because these newspapers had the best team of editors and reporters on social protest in Mexico. *La Jornada* is the Mexican daily newspaper with the best coverage of rural indigenous affairs. The editorial team and reporters of *La Jornada*, founded in 1984, came mainly from *Unomásuno*. In turn, the editorial team and reporters of *Unomásuno*, founded in 1977, came mainly from *Excelsior*.

In the mid-1960s, *Excelsior* became Mexico's pioneer newspaper in investigative journalism and one of the news sources most critical of authoritarian rule under the PRI. Julio Scherer, then *Excelsior*'s chief editor, trained many generations of reporters who specialized in dissident social movements and opposition politics in urban and rural areas. In 1976, *Excelsior* suffered a "coup," in which the government removed Scherer from his post as director and replaced him with a pro-regime chief editor who led the newspaper for nearly three decades.

Trained at *Excelsior* in the 1960s and 1970s, reporters from *Unomásuno* (1977–1983) and *La Jornada* (1994–2000) provided the best coverage of Mexico's rural and indigenous affairs. I did not use *Excelsior* for the 1975–1976 period because the editorial team of the paper was busy surviving the "coup" rather than accurately reporting contentious events in Mexico's rural periphery. In the absence of *Excelsior*, *El Día* offered the best alternative coverage.

After comparing protest and repression counts from these three news sources against secondary sources, I realized that *Unomásuno* and *La Jornada* had a good coverage of southern and central Mexican states but their coverage was uneven in other parts of the country, particularly in northern and southeastern states. To minimize this important source of bias, I decided to use other daily newspapers with better coverage in these particular regions.

The Prodato collection was my main source of information to overcome regional biases from my initial news sources. Since its foundation in the late 1960s by Jesuit priests, the Prodato (then under the name of SIPRO) team has been conducting a systematic analysis of the Mexican press on a *daily* basis. The Prodato team – now an independent family business – collects newspaper reports on social movements, protest, insurgencies, and human rights violations for the whole country. For the 1968–1981 period, data on protest and repression are summarized in monthly bulletins. For the period covering 1982 to the present, Prodato collects newspaper clips by social sector or topic (e.g., "peasants," "workers," "urban popular movements," "government repression"). These news clips are filed by sector and by month in binders stored at the Prodato office. A single person, Mauro Monreal, has been in charge of data collection since the late 1960s. The data collection criterion of Prodato and the criterion I followed for gathering information from *El Día, Unomásuno*, and *La Jornada* are fairly similar.

Together with a research assistant, I collected data from the monthly SIPRO bulletins and selected the relevant news from the Prodato newspaper clips from the sections classified under "peasant/indigenous," "government repression," and "Chiapas."

Only four newspapers from the Prodato collection cover the entire 1976–2000 period: *Excelsior, El Universal, El Día*, and *El Sol de México. Unomásuno* covers 1977–2000; *La Jornada*, 1984–2000; *El Nacional*, 1976–1990s; and El Financiero, 1989–2000.

El Universal, El Sol de México, and the post-1976 *Excelsior* have good coverage of the regions in which *La Jornada* and *Unomásuno* were weak. Some newspapers are left-wing (*La Jornada*), others right-wing (*El Sol de México*), others pro-PRI (*Excelsior* and *El Nacional*), and others relatively neutral (*El Universal* and *El Financiero*).

Overall, this set of eight newspapers helped me (1) minimize uneven coverage across regions from a single source and (2) cross-verify events. This latter point was particularly important in the 1970s and early 1980s (see more later). When the newspaper information was not sufficient, I used secondary literature (such as ethnographic accounts from scholarly research) to learn more about specific contentious events.

OVERCOMING SOURCES OF GEOGRAPHIC BIAS

As a whole, the eight national daily newspapers I used for data gathering cover all Mexican states and all major urban and rural regions. For purposes of inferential data analysis, I can safely say that even though this group of newspapers does not report the universe of protest and repression events, underreporting of events is not systematically biased in favor of or against any state or region. To be sure, let me reiterate that my main methodological concern for data collection was to minimize biased underreporting. Ultimately, MII gets as close as possible to the universe of events while minimizing sources of bias.

OVERCOMING SOURCES OF TEMPORAL BIAS

Recent experiences of data collection of protest and repression events based on newspaper sources shows that through the use of *multiple national daily sources* one can maximize coverage of events while minimizing temporal and spatial biases. Potential for temporal biases is an important concern in data collection in countries undergoing transitions from authoritarian rule to democracy.

Gathering contentious event data in closed autocracies requires a combination of national and international news sources, but this is not necessarily the case in *electoral* autocracies – as Mexico was between 1977 and 2000 – where the domestic press operates in a context of greater, albeit limited, freedoms.

Indeed, after the Mexican government removed *Excelsior*'s chief editor in 1976, between 1977 and 2000 no other national newspaper was closed down or manipulated to the same extent. To be sure, coercion and corruption were major issues throughout the transition, and editors and reporters were under close scrutiny from national government officials and PRI governors.[1] But national elites had incentives to let information flow – not only to learn about governors' and municipal presidents' performance, but also to learn about protesters' preferences and revolutionary potential.[2]

In the early years of the transition, 1977–1988, the main source of conflict between government officials and the press was not necessarily reporting but the interpretation of events. Newspapers would report the facts, but reporters would add their own interpretation of events depending on the political affiliations of their employers. Cross-verification of information about contentious events during these years is essential to separate the wheat from the chaff. When there was divergence in the reporting of facts, we resorted to multiple news sources and to the rich regional historical, anthropological, and sociological accounts of peasant indigenous mobilization from Mexican and international scholars. This strategy helped us overcome temporal biases associated with the transition. Moreover, as the transition to democracy progressed, newspaper reports became increasingly more factual and less interpretative.

LIMITATIONS

One of the main problems in building a database of protest events is that newspaper reporters do not always report the main characteristics of the protest event. For example, in 40 percent of the news reports I gathered, reporters did not report the number of participants. There was simply no way for me to reliably estimate this number, and as a result, the statistical analysis does not weight for the numbers of participants. As I explain in Chapter 2, I use the municipal place of residence of protesters as a proxy for the number of participants. Another limitation in the data is that in 10 percent of protest events (around 350 cases), reporters failed to report the place of residence of protestors. In most cases, I was able to impute the municipal origins of protestors by analyzing secondary sources and prior histories of local protest.

SUBNATIONAL SOURCES

The MII database contains a special collection on contentious events in Chiapas based on subnational news sources. For purposes of data collection, I followed a similar strategy as in the national data collection, gathering information from a single source and then complementing the data set with multiple sources.

---

[1] For the role played by the press in Mexico's democratization, see Lawson (2002).
[2] Huang (2007) makes this argument about governance in China.

My main source of information was the newspaper *Tiempo*, 1970–1993. I reviewed this source at the home and office of *Tiempo*'s chief editor, Amado Avendaño, in San Cristóbal de Las Casas, Chiapas.

Tiempo was the oldest newspaper in the highlands of Chiapas, and from its inauguration in the late 1960s until it disappeared in the late 1990s, it had the best coverage of indigenous affairs in the southern state. After analyzing the data for the 1970–1993 period, I realized that *Tiempo* had very good coverage of the Chiapas highlands but that its coverage of other regions, particularly the northern, eastern, and southern portions of the state, was not as complete. For that reason I decided to complement the data set with information from other sources.

For the 1976–1985 period, I relied partially on information contained in the report *Chiapas: Cronología de un Etnocidio* (1975–1987), drafted by anthropologist Araceli Burguete (1987), which is a report on indigenous dissidence based on local newspapers and CIOAC archives.

For the 1986–1993 period, I relied on information from the monthly press reports *Resúmen Informativo* (1986–1993) and *La Palabra* (1997–1999), edited by the Center of Information and Analysis of Chiapas (CIACH). *Resúmen Informativo* reports were based on three local newspapers: *El Orbe*, *La Voz del Sureste*, and *Tiempo*. *La Palabra* reports were based on the local newspapers *Cuarto Poder*, *Expresso*, and *La Foja Coleta*.

Appendix B

Additional Statistical Results

TABLE A.B.1. *Negative Binomial Models of Intensity of Indigenous Protest by Indigenous Municipality in Chiapas, 1987*

Independent Variable	Model 1 Coefficient	IRR
Religious competition	0.957***	2.606
	(0.430)	
Electoral competition	1.619**	5.048
	(0.802)	
Repression $_{t-1}$	0.850***	1.089
	(0.254)	
Land plots to independents $_{t-2}$ (%)	1.262**	3.534
	(0.586)	
Controls		
Indigenous population (%)	−0.496	0.608
	(0.763)	
Indigenous population (ln)	−0.016	0.983
	(0.232)	
Corporatism	0.777	2.175
	(1.125)	
Constant	−2.91	
N	57	
Log Likelihood	−81.27	
Wald chi^2	43.57	

***Significant at the 0.01 level; ** Significant at the 0.05 level; * Significant at the 0.1 level.
Robust standard errors in parentheses.
Source: Data on distribution of land plots by political affiliation from Reyes (1992).

RESULTS FOR CHAPTER 8

TABLE A.B.2. *OLS Regression Estimates of Extent of Indigenous Rights by State in Mexico, 2000*

	Indigenous Rights Index			Self-Government Rights Index		
	Model 1	Model 2	Model 3	Model 4	Model 5	Model 6
Electoral Threats						
Electoral competition in gubernatorial elections (1997–2000)	−0.482 (0.769)	−0.838 (0.703)	−0.325 (0.715)	0.160 (0.349)	−0.181 (0.410)	0.499 (0.391)
Electoral competition in municipal elections (Rate of growth, 1990–2000)	1.539*** (0.518)	1.522*** (0.509)	1.254*** (0.480)	0.503 (0.412)	0.481 (0.432)	0.046 (0.425)
Systemic Threats						
Rebel activity index, 1997	0.464* (0.247)			0.449* (0.234)		
Rebel diffusion index, 1997			−0.476 (0.508)			0.025 (0.225)
Ethno-Territorial Threats						
Ethnic protest, 1990s		0.416** (0.208)	−0.453* (0.245)		0.414* (0.28)	−0.474* (0.233)
Rebel diffusion × ethnic protest			0.729*** (0.179)			0.725*** (0.199)
Controls						
Economic development (ln GDP/k), 1995	0.684 (0.818)	0.435 (0.737)	0.977 (0.896)	0.116 (0.452)	−0.114 (0.470)	0.821* (0.410)
Indigenous population (ln), 1990	0.314*** (0.116)	0.287*** (0.114)	0.344*** (0.125)	0.137 (0.086)	0.106 (0.067)	0.120* (0.058)
N	31	31	31	31	31	31
R^2	0.493	0.505	0.706	0.369	0.397	0.799

***Significant at the 0.01 level; ** Significant at the 0.05 level; * Significant at the 0.1 level. Robust standard errors in parentheses.
Notes: (1) I use principal component analysis to calculate the index of indigenous rights. The index is based on rights introduced in Mexico's thirty-one state constitutions and in each of the states' electoral, education, and criminal laws in the 1990s. It includes a wide range of rights from recognition of an ethnolinguistic group in a state constitution to the introduction of ethnic criteria for criminal and electoral procedures. Whereas the indigenous rights index includes all rights, the self-government rights index focuses only on the latter.
(2) Electoral competition is measured as the effective number of parties. I use the rebel index discussed in Chapter 5. The rebel diffusion index is the arithmetic sum of the rebel activity index of a state's neighbors. Ethnic protest is a count of ethnic claims.

Appendix C

Criteria for Targeted Fieldwork and Ethnographic Interviews

In the summers of 2009 and 2010, I conducted two rounds of fieldwork in southern Mexico. Building on the statistical results and with the purpose of overcoming some of the limitations of the statistical analyses, I conducted twenty-eight targeted in-depth interviews with Catholic clerical authorities, catechists and deacons, members of non-Catholic Christian churches, social movement leaders, former members of the EZLN, former mayors affiliated with the leftist PRD, and advisers to clerical authorities and social movement leaders.

These were targeted interviews because I approached individuals from places and organizations I could identify through my regression results; that is, I used as research sites places of which I knew beforehand whether they were typical (located along the regression line) or atypical (outliers). Because I had deliberately chosen these places and organizations, I had substantial fine-grained information about the social and political context in which my interviewees operated and about the likely causes of protest, rebellion, and ethnic identification (or their absence) in the particular places of my choice. Moreover, in many cases I had important information about the individuals I wished to interview and the organizations to which they belonged.

Unlike most fieldwork in which scholars rely on the advice of local academics and local brokers for the selection of interviewees, I decided not to make use of my own connections built over a decade of research on indigenous politics in Mexico and opted, instead, to make direct contact with the interviewees I had selected based on the statistical results. Although most scholars do not address this issue when reporting their fieldwork, mediation by local *academic brokers* is a major source of bias. Local academics are not always unbiased observers and, as a result, qualitative studies often end up reproducing the same information as the networks of these local brokers would yield. After establishing direct contact with the interviewees from the places of my choice, I used the principles of snowball sampling and followed their respective network connections. The important difference, however, is that I was following the *subject*'s network and not that of an academic broker.

Most of my interviews involved long in-depth conversations ranging between two and five hours. These were not primarily exploratory or open-ended interviews, in which the interviewees freely set the agenda or in which most of the information provided is of a descriptive nature. I conducted the interviews by asking specific questions and then left time for open-ended reflections.

Because my goal was to bring agency into my research and explore different causal mechanisms, I decided to frame the questions in the singular and always followed a biographical approach. By focusing the interview in terms of the choices individuals made throughout their clerical, social, and political personal histories, I was able to extract invaluable information about individual preferences, motivations, expectations, and perceptions of context and incentives for action. I was not a passive interviewer and often either questioned their narratives or asked about alternative interpretations of their causal stories.

The open-ended reflections at the end of the interview provided valuable information that is also reported throughout the book. After several hours of retrospectively reflecting on their personal life stories, many of my interviewees went deeply into exploring the motivations that had guided their choices at different moments in their religious and/or political life.

The information from the structured and unstructured parts of the interviews provided the input for the life histories in Chapters 3, 4, 5, and 6. It allowed me to present these life histories as analytic narratives, in which emphasis was placed on the choices actors made and opportunities foregone (Bates et al., 1998).

All the interviews were conducted in Spanish and in all cases interviewees were asked to reflect on issues that pertained mostly to the past. Unlike scholars doing fieldwork in southern Mexico in the 1990s, when mobilization and conflict was unfolding, I conducted fieldwork in a post-conflict context. This had advantages and disadvantages. Speaking in a less contentious context allowed interviewees to express their views more freely than they would have done earlier. Although memories seemed to be very fresh in the minds of interviewees, there was always a danger of ex post facto reinterpretation of events. To avoid this, I often confronted interviewees with questions about specific details of their motivations and context and inquired about alternative explanations. After the interviews, I constantly conducted cross-verification of the information I had received that might have called the individual's conclusions into question.

Although I did not live for extended periods of time in many of the villages and towns where I conducted my interviews – as anthropologists *used* to do – two prior experiences prepared me to gain the trust, sensitivity, and immersion that are quintessential features of ethnographic work (Schatz, 2009).

First, as a secular social activist in the late 1980s, I worked with Jesuit missionaries in grassroots organization of urban popular, rural, and indigenous movements in Mexico City, Coahuila, and Veracruz. Through contacts with the Diocese of San Cristóbal de Las Casas in Chiapas, I spent a brief period of time with Guatemalan refugees living in the Comitán/Margaritas region. As a scholar living in Mexico between 1997 and 2005, I actively participated in multiple fora of discussion of the peace process in Chiapas and of indigenous rights in a wide range of places, including Mexico City, Acapulco (Guerrero), and Oaxaca City (Oaxaca). These discussions took place in the Senate, in Congress, at the Federal Electoral Institute, and in various academic settings, and involved direct conversations with government officials, political representatives, social movement leaders, and members of the EZLN. Finally, between 2000 and 2005, I was a regular participant (by invitation) in the quarterly meetings of SERAPAZ – Service for Peace, the Mexico City-based NGO founded by Bishop Samuel Ruiz and some of the former lay members of his diocese – where leaders of human rights NGOs and of indigenous movements discussed challenges and strategies for social and political action.

None of the information I gathered through these experiences serves as evidence to test any of the theoretical arguments I make in this book. I did not use any of the contacts established through my participation in these events to conduct fieldwork. These experiences did prepare me, however, to quickly establish the trust and persuade a wide variety of local actors to share their life histories with me.

Second, the long periods of time I spent in Mexico City and in San Cristóbal de Las Casas, Chiapas, collecting data from local newspaper sources – see Appendix A – and the unique access I gained to detailed local histories proved to be absolutely crucial in establishing a frank conversation with my interviewees. Sharing this information with them – sometimes reminding them of local facts and events – was an important signal that I was not seeking general background information and helped me quickly move the conversation into motivations and mechanisms for action. Sharing this information with them also helped establish trust, particularly with members of non-Catholic Christian churches.

Even though I claim that these in-depth interviews have an ethnographic character, the reader must be reminded that in this book I use several sources of information for hypothesis testing and to explore the causal mechanisms that lead to indigenous collective action (and inaction). Within a research that uses multiple sources of evidence, quantitative and qualitative, my "ethnographically" informed research is a window onto the agency, motivations, expectations, and context that even the most disaggregate quantitative data fail to capture.[1]

Table A.C.1 provides a detailed list of the interviewees. I have identified the name of the interview subject, their past affiliations, and their affiliation at the time of the interview. Information on past affiliations helps the reader understand why I interviewed this group of individuals, and information on their affiliation at the time of the interview provides relevant clues to assess whether the data and motivations they reported was informed by a process of ex post facto reinterpretation to improve their current political situation.

---

[1] See Allina-Pisano (2009) for an insightful discussion of the advantages that ethnographically informed qualitative research provides to identifying causal mechanisms and improving causal inference.

TABLE A.C.I. *List of Interviewees*

Name	Past affiliations	Affiliation at the time of interview	Place of interview
Catholic clerical authorities			
Bishop Arturo Lona	Bishop of Diocese of Tehuantepec, Oaxaca, and Rector of Seminary in Huejutla, Hidalgo	Bishop Emeritus	Santa María Petapa, Oaxaca
Father Marcelino Rivera	Seminarian under Lona's mentorship, SERESURE graduate	Parish priest	Santa María Petapa, Oaxaca
Pedro Sosa	Legal adviser to Archdiocese of Oaxaca	Assistant to Father Wilfrido Mayrén	Oaxaca City, Oaxaca
Father Felipe J. Ali Modad, S.J.	Jesuit priest, coordinated Bible translation to Tzeltal	Jesuit priest	Chilón, Chiapas
Father Oscar González, S.J.	Jesuit priest, director of Human Rights NGO	Coordinator of Coffee Export Cooperative	Chilón, Chiapas
Father Carlos Camarena, S.J.	Jesuit parish priest of Chilón	Parish priest	Chilón, Chiapas
Father Ramón Castillo	Director of catechist training center for the Tojolabal region and former parish priest in Venustiano Carranza and Amatenango del Valle	Director of catechist training center *La Castalia*	Comitán, Chiapas
Father Joel Padrón	Parish priest of Simojovel and El Bosque	Retired priest in San Andrés Larrainzar	San Andrés Larrainzar, Chiapas
Father Miguel Saldaña	Assistant priest to Father Joel Padrón in El Bosque	Parish priest of Simojovel	Simojovel, Chiapas
Catholic lay leaders			
Gilberto Moreno	Catechist, linguist, and social activist	Catechist	Chilón, Chiapas
Don Manuel	Catechist and social activist	Catechist	Chilón, Chiapas
Deacon Gómez	Catechist	Deacon	Chilón, Chiapas
Verónica Martínez	Designer for Bible translation into Tzeltal	Adviser to Jesuit Mission	Chilón, Chiapas
Andrés Díaz	Catechist and member of CIOAC	Catechist	Simojovel, Chiapas
Eduardo López	Catechist, member of Tierra y Libertad and CIOAC and former miliciano of the EZLN	Deacon	Ejido Tabasco, Las Margaritas, Chiapas

(*continued*)

TABLE A.C.I. *(continued)*

Name	Past affiliations	Affiliation at the time of interview	Place of interview
Members of non-Catholic Christian churches			
Sr. Gutiérrez	Member of Presbyterian Church	Member of Presbyterian Church	Ocosingo, Chiapas
Mariano Jiménez	Member of Pentecostal Church	Member of Pentecostal Church	San Cristóbal de Las Casas, Chiapas
Pedro Méndez	Grandson of founding members of Presbyterian Church in the Lacandón jungle	Law student and Member of Presbyterian Church	Las Margaritas, Chiapas
Don Elías	Member of Presbyterian Church of Chenalhó, Chiapas	Migrant worker and member of Presbyterian Church	Las Margaritas, Chiapas
Anonymous	Member of Seventh-Day Adventist Church	Member of Seventh-Day Adventist Church and CIOAC militant	Las Margaritas, Chiapas
Social/political leaders			
Amado Avendaño+	Editor of *Tiempo* and former gubernatorial candidate under a leftist coalition	Editor of *La Foja Coleta*	San Cristóbal de Las Casas, Chiapas
Manuel Gómez	Yomlej leader and former mayor of Chilón	Social leader	Chilón, Chiapas
Leopoldo De Gyves	COCEI leader, former mayor of Juchitán (removed)	COCEI leader	Oaxaca City, Oaxaca
Hector Sánchez	COCEI leader and former mayor of Juchitán	Government official	Oaxaca City, Oaxaca
Antonio Hernández	Leader of CIOAC and CIOAC-Independiente and former federal legislator	Green Party social and political activist	Las Margaritas, Chiapas
Límbano Vázquez	Catechist, CIOAC leader in Lacandón jungle, former EZLN commander	Green Party social and political activists	Las Margaritas, Chiapas
Roberto Alfaro	Teacher, leader of CIOAC and CIOAC-Histórico	Retired teacher and PRD candidate for municipal presidency of Las Margaritas	Las Margaritas, Chiapas
Araceli Burguete	Former political adviser of CIOAC and human rights activist	Anthropology professor at CIESAS	San Cristóbal de Las Casas, Chiapas

+ This interview was conducted in 2000.

Appendix D

Questions from Public Opinion Surveys

All surveys used in this book were conducted by the Office of the President (Mexico) between 1991 and 1999. All the surveys are housed in the library of the Centro de Investigación y Docencia Económicas (CIDE) in Mexico City.

CHAPTER 5

Table 5.1

Source: Presidencia de la República, "Ejido: Reforma al artículo 27 constitucional," November 1991.

Q.19. Do you think it would be a good or a bad thing that ejidatarios can buy and sell their land plots?

Good
Bad
Indifferent

Q.32. Do you believe land redistribution should continue or come to an end?

Continue
End

Q.45. Do you believe the liberalization of land tenure contradicts the principles of the Mexican Revolution?

Yes
Partially yes
No

Q.37.   Do you think there will be land hoarding (*acaparamiento*) if
        ejidatarios can sell their land plots?

        Yes
        No

CHAPTER 8

Figures 8.2a and 8.2b

Source: Presidencia de la República, "Conflicto EZLN," January 15, 1994.

**Do you personally support the Zapatista movement or the
government and the army?**

EZLN
Government and army

Figures 8.2a and 8.2b

Source: Presidencia de la República, "Conflicto EZLN," February 27, 1994.

Do you personally sympathize with the motivations of the EZLN?

Yes
No

Figure 8.3

Source: Presidencia de la República, "Conflicto EZLN," December 19, 1994.

**Last week the EZLN carried out the military invasion of the
municipality of Simojovel in Chiapas. Do you personally agree
with the rebels' actions?**

Agree
Do not agree

Figure 8.3

Source: Presidencia de la República, "Conflicto EZLN," January 11, 1995.

**Last week the EZLN carried out the military invasion of the
municipality of Chicomuselo in Chiapas. Do you personally
agree with the rebels' actions?**

Agree
Do not agree

Figure 8.4

Source: Presidencia de la República, "Negociación de paz," February 1997 and September 1999.

Do you believe the government is trying to trick (*engañar*) the EZLN in the peace negotiations?

Yes
Partly yes
No

References

Acemoglu, Daren and J. A. Robinson. 2006. *Economic Origins of Dictatorship and Democracy*, Cambridge: Cambridge University Press.

Aguayo, Sergio. 2001. *La charola: Una historia de los servicios de inteligencia en México*, Mexico City: Grijalbo.

Aguilar-Pariente, Rosario. 2008. "Effect of Phenotypic Prejudice on Voters' Evaluation of Electoral Candidates in Mexico," paper delivered at the Midwest Political Science Association.

Aguilar Rivera, José Antonio. 2001. *El fin de la raza cósmica*, Mexico City: Océano.

Albertus, Michael and O. Kaplan. 2010. "Land Reform as a Counterinsurgency Policy: Evidence from Colombia," Typescript, Stanford University.

Alianza Cívica. 1994. "Observación 1994: Informe de la muestra estratificada." Mimeo, August 23.

Allina-Pisano, Jessica. 2009. "How to Tell an Axe Murderer: An Essay on Ethnography, Truth, and Lies" in E. Schatz (ed.) *Political Ethnography: What Immersion Contributes to the Study of Power*, Chicago: The University of Chicago Press.

Almeida, Paul D. 2003. "Opportunity Organizations and Threat Induced Contention: Protest Waves in Authoritarian Settings," *American Journal of Sociology*, vol. 109, no. 2.

2008. *Waves of Protest: Popular Struggle in El Salvador, 1925–2005*, Minneapolis: University of Minnesota Press.

Anderson, Benedict. 1991. *Imagined Communities. Reflections on the Origins and Spread of Nationalism*, London: Verso.

Andrade, Eduardo. 1997. *La Reforma Política de 1996 en México*, Mexico City: UNAM.

Andrade, Susana. 2004. *Protestantismo indígena. Procesos de conversion en la provincia de Chimborazo*, Quito: FLACSO.

Arce, Moisés and P. Bellinger. 2007. "Low-Intensity Democracy Revisited: The Effects of Economic Liberalization on Political Activity in Latin America," *World Politics*, vol. 60, no. 1.

Arce, Moisés and R. Rice. 2009. "Societal Protest in Post-stabilization Bolivia," *Latin American Research Review*, vol. 44, no. 1.

Azzi, Corry and R. Ehrenberg. 1975. "Household Allocation of Time and Church Attendance," *Journal of Political Economy*, vol. 84, no. 3.

Bakke, Kristin and E. Wibbels. 2006. "Diversity, Disparity and Civil Conflict in Federal States," *World Politics*, vol. 59, no. 1.

(Banamex) Banco Nacional de México. 2001. *México Electoral*, Mexico City: Banamex.

Bartra, Roger. 1993. *Agrarian Structure and Political Power in Mexico*, Baltimore: The Johns Hopkins University Press.

Bastos, Santiago and M. Camus. 1995. *Quebrando el Silencio: Organizaciones del Pueblo Maya y sus Demandas, 1986–1992*, Guatemala: FLACSO.

Bates, Robert. H., A. Greif, M. Levi, J. L. Rosenthal, and B. Weingast. 1998. *Analytic Narratives*, Princeton, NJ: Princeton University Press.

Becerra, Ricardo, P. Salazar, and J. Woldenberg. 2000. *La mecánica del cambio político en México*, Mexico City: Cal y Arena.

Benítez, Fernando. 1967. *Los indios de México*, Mexico City: Era.

Beissinger, Mark. 2001. *Nationalist Mobilization and the Collapse of the Soviet State*, Cambridge: Cambridge University Press.

Berman, Eli. 2009. *Radical, Religious, and Violent*, Cambridge, MA: MIT Press.

Bermeo, Nancy. 1997. "Myths of Moderation: Confrontation and Conflict during Democratic Transitions," *Comparative Politics*, vol. 29, no. 3.

Bernal, Marco Antonio and M. A. Romero. 1999. *Chiapas: Crónica de una negociación*, vol. 1 and 2, Mexico City: Rayuela.

Bobrow-Strain, Aaron. 2007. *Intimate Enemies: Landowners, Power, and Violence in Chiapas*, Durham, NC: Duke University Press.

Bonfil, Guillermo. 1987/1996. *Mexico Profundo: Reclaiming a Civilization*, Austin, TX: University of Texas Press.

Boix, Carles. 2003. *Democracy and Redistribution*, Cambridge: Cambridge University Press.

Brockett, Charles D. 1991. "The Structure of Political Opportunities and Peasant Mobilization in Central America," *Comparative Politics*, vol. 23, no. 3.

2005. *Political Movements and Violence in Central America*, Cambridge: Cambridge University Press.

Bruhn, Kathleen. 2008. *Urban Protest in Mexico and Brazil*, Cambridge: Cambridge University Press.

Brysk, Alison. 2000. *From Tribal Village to Global Village: Indian Rights and International Relations in Latin America*, Palo Alto, CA: Stanford University Press.

Buendía, Jorge. 1997. "Incertidumbre y comportamiento electoral en la transición democrática: la elección mexicana de 1988," *Política y Gobierno*, vol. 4, no. 2.

Burguete, Araceli. 1987. "Chiapas: Cronología de un etnocidio (1975–1987)," Typescript.

1998. "Poder local y autonomía indígena en Chiapas: Rebeliones comunitarias y luchas municipalistas," in M. E. Reyes Ramos et al. (coords.) *Espacios Disputados: Transformaciones Rurales en Chiapas*, Mexico City: UAM and ECOSUR.

1999. "Empoderamiento indígena. Tendencias autonómicas en la región Altos de Chiapas," in A. Burguete Cal y Mayor (coord.) *México: Experiencias de Autonomía Indígena*, Copenhague: IWGIA.

Büthe, Tim. 2002. "Taking Temporality Seriously: Modeling History and the Use of Narrative as Evidence," *American Political Science Review*, vol. 96, no. 3.

Cadena-Roa, Jorge. 2003. "State Pacts, Elites, and Social Movements in Mexico's Transition to Democracy," in J. A. Goldstone (ed.), *States, Parties and Social Movements*, Cambridge: Cambridge University Press.

Cameron, Colin A. and Pravin K. Trivedi. 1998. *Regression Analysis of Count Data*, Cambridge: Cambridge University Press.

Camp, Roderic A. 1997. *Crossing Swords. Politics and Religion in Mexico*, Oxford: Oxford University Press.

Carpizo, Jorge. 1995. "Algunos aspectos de la reforma federal electoral de 1994," in Miguel López Ruiz (ed.) *Un homenaje a Don César Sepúlveda*, Mexico City: UNAM.

Castellanos, Laura. 2007. *México Armado*, Mexico City: ERA.

Castillo, Carmen and T. Brisac. 1995. "Historia de Marcos y los Hombres de la Noche. Entrevista con el Subcomandante Marcos," in A. Gilly et al. (eds.) *Discusión sobre la historia*, Mexico City: Taurus.

CDHFBC (Centro de Derechos Humanos Fray Bartolomé de Las Casas) . 1998. *Acteal: entre el Duelo y la Lucha*, San Cristóbal de Las Casas: CDHFBC.

CIDAC (Centro de Investigación para el Desarrollo, A.C.). 2009. *Base de Datos Electorales*, CIDAC: http://www.cidac.org/esp/Acerca_de_CIDAC.php

Chandra, Kanchan. 2007. "What Is Ethnic Identity and Does It Matter?" *Annual Review of Political Science*, vol. 9.

Chávez, Emilio. 2005. *La expansión de la educación media-superior en las comunidades tseltales del norte de la Selva Lacandona, Chiapas, 1994–2004*, Tesis de Licenciatura en Ciencia Política y Relaciones Internacionales, CIDE, Mexico City.

Chesnut, Andrew. R. 2003. *Competitive Spirits: Latin America's New Religious Economy*, New York: Oxford University Press.

Chong, Dennis. 1991. *Collective Action and the Civil Rights Movement*, Chicago: The University of Chicago Press.

Cleary, Edward and T. J. Steigenga. 2004. "Resurgent Voices: Indians, Politics, and Religion in Latin America," in C. Cleary and T. J. Steigenga (eds.) *Resurgent Voices in Latin America: Indigenous Peoples, Political Mobilization, and Religious Change*, New Brunswick, NJ: Rutgers University Press.

Collier, George with E. L. Quaratiello. 1994. *Basta! Land and the Zapatista Rebellion in Chiapas*, Oakland, CA: Food First Books.

Collier, Paul. 2000. "Rebellion as a Quasi-Criminal Activity," *Journal of Conflict Resolution*, vol. 44, no. 6.

Collier, Paul et al. 2005. *Breaking the Conflict Trap. Civil War and Development Policy*, Washington, DC: The World Bank.

Collier, Ruth and J. Mahoney. 1997. "Adding Collective Actors to Collective Outcomes: Labor and Recent Democratization in South America and Southern Europe," *Comparative Politics*, vol. 29, no. 3.

Davenport, Christian (ed.). 2000. *Paths to State Repression. Human Rights Violations and Contentious Politics*, Lanham, MD: Rowman and Littlefield.

2005. "Introduction. Repression and Mobilization: Insights from Political Science and Sociology," in C. Davenport, H. Johnston, and C. Mueller (eds.) *Repression and Mobilization*, Minneapolis: University of Minnesota Press.

De la Madrid, Miguel. 2004. *Cambio de rumbo: testimonio de una presidencia, 1982–1988*, Mexico City: FCE.

De Nardo, James. 1985. *Power in Numbers. The Political Strategy of Protest and Rebellion*, Princeton, NJ: Princenton University Press.

De Vos, Jan. 2002. *Una tierra para sembrar sueños. Historia reciente de la Selva Lacandona, 1950–2000*, Mexico City: Fondo de Cultura Económica.

Dehouve, Danièle. 2001. *Ensayo de geopolítica indígena. Los municipios Tlapanecos,* Mexico City: Miguel Angel Porrúa.

Della Porta, Donatella and S. Tarrow. 1986. "Unwanted Children: Political Violence and the Cycle of Protest in Italy," *European Journal of Political Research,* vol. 14, no. 5–6.

Diani, Mario and D. McAdam. 2003. *Social Movements and Networks: Relational Approaches to Collective Action,* Oxford: Oxford University Press.

DGE (Dirección General de Estadística). 1972. *IX Censo General de Población 1970,* Mexico City: DGE.

Dunning, Thad. 2008. "Improving Causal Inference: Strengths and Limitations of Natural Experiments," *Political Research Quarterly,* vol. 61, no. 2.

Eber, Christine. 2001. "Liberation through Autonomy in San Pedro Chenalhó, 1970–1998," *Latin American Perspectives,* issue 117, vol. 28, no. 2.

Eisenstadt, Todd. 2004. *Courting Democracy in Mexico. Party Strategy and Electoral Institutions,* Cambridge: Cambridge University Press.

2006. "Indigenous Attitudes and Ethnic Identity Construction in Mexico," *Mexican Studies,* vol. 22, no. 1.

2011. *Politics, Identity and Mexico's Indigenous Rights Movement,* Cambridge: Cambridge University Press.

Eisinger, Peter, K. 1973. "The Conditions of Protest Behavior in American Cities," *American Political Science Review,* vol. 67, no. 1.

EZLN (Ejército Zapatista de Liberación Nacional). 1994. "De qué nos van a perdonar?" Centro de Documentación sobre Zapatismo.

Elizarrarás, Rodrigo. 2003. *Gobernabilidad y Autonomía Indígena: Motivos y Efectos en el Reconocimiento de los Usos y Costumbres en Oaxaca,* Tesis de Licenciatura en Ciencia Política, Mexico City: ITAM.

Esparza, Manuel. 2004. "La Iglesia Católica al Fin del Siglo," in Victor R. Martínez Vásquez (coord.), *Oaxaca: Escenarios del Nuevo Siglo,* Oaxaca: UABJO

Esponda, Hugo. 1986. *El Presbiterianismo en Chiapas,* Mexico City: Publicaciones El Faro.

Favre, Henri. 2001. "Chiapas: Intento de análisis de una situación de insurreción," CIDE, División de Historia, Documento de Trabajo, no. 14.

Fazio, Carlos. 1994. *Samuel Ruiz. El Caminante,* Mexico City: Espasa Calpe.

Fearon, James and David Laitin. 2003. "Insurgency, Ethnicity and Civil War," *American Political Science Review,* vol. 97, no. 1.

Florescano, Enrique. 1996. *Etnia, estado y nación: Ensayo sobre las identidades colectivas en México,* Mexico City: Aguilar.

Freire, Paulo. 1970. *Pedagogy of the Oppressed,* New York: Continuum.

Gandhi, Jennifer and A. Przeworski. 2007. "Authoritarian Institutions and the Survival of Autocrats," *Comparative Political Studies,* vol. 40, no. 11.

Garma, Carlos. 1994. "Afiliación religiosa en el México indígena de 1990," INI, typescript.

1998. "Afiliación religiosa en municipios indígenas de Chiapas según el censo de 1990," in E. Masferrer (coord.) *Chiapas: El factor religioso,* Revista Académica para el Estudio de las Religiones, Mexico City.

Geddes, Barbara Geddes. 2003. *Paradigms and Sand Castles: Theory Building and Research Design in Comparative Politics,* Ann Arbor: The Michigan University Press.

Gibson, Edward. 1997. "The Populist Road to Market Reform: Policy and Electoral Coalitions in Mexico and Argentina," *World Politics,* vol. 49, no. 3.

Gill, Anthony. 1994. "Rendering unto Caesar? Religious Competition and Catholic Political Strategy in Latin America, 1962–1979," *American Journal of Political Science*, vol. 38, no. 2.

　　1998. *Rendering unto Caesar: The Catholic Church and the State in Latin America*, Chicago: The University of Chicago Press.

　　2007. *The Political Origins of Religious Liberty*, Cambridge: Cambridge University Press.

Gilly, Adolfo. 1998. *Chiapas: La razón ardiente. Ensayo sobre la rebelión del mundo encantado*, Mexico City: Era.

Goldstone, Jack A., R. Bates, D. Epstein, T. Gurr, M. Lustik, M. Marshall, J. Ulfelder, and M. Woodward. 2010. "A Global Model for Forecasting Political Instability," *American Journal of Political Science*, vol. 54, no. 1.

González, Patrocinio. 1990. *Segundo Informe de Gobierno*, Tuxtla Gutiérrez: Gobierno del Estado de Chiapas.

　　1991. *Tercer Informe de Gobierno*, Tuxtla Gutiérrez: Gobierno del Estado de Chiapas.

Gould, Roger. V. 1995. *Insurgent Identities: Class, Community, and Protest in Paris from 1848 to the Commune*, Chicago: The Chicago University Press.

Granovetter, Mark. 1973. "The Strength of Weak Ties," *American Journal of Sociology*, vol. 78, no. 6.

Greene, Kenneth. F. 2007. *Why Dominant Parties Lose: Mexico's Democratization in Comparative Perspective*, Cambridge: Cambridge University Press.

Gross, Toomas. 2003. "Protestantism and Modernity: The Implications of Religious Change in Rural Oaxaca," *Sociology of Religion*, vol. 64, no. 4.

Grzymala-Busse, Anna. 2010. "Time Will Tell? Temporality and the Analysis of Causal Mechanisms and Processes," *Comparative Political Studies*, vol. 44, no. 9.

Guevara, Ernesto. 1967/2006. *The Bolivian Diary*, New York: Ocean Press.

Gurr, Ted R. 1993. *Minorities at Risk. A Global View of Ethnopolitical Conflicts*, Washington, DC: United States Institute of Peace Press.

Gurr, Ted R. and W. H. Moore. 1997. "Ethnopolitical Rebellion: A Cross-Sectional Analysis of the 1980s with Risk Assessments for the 1990s," *American Journal of Political Science*, vol. 41, no. 4.

Gutiérrez, Natividad. 1999. *Nationalist Myths and Ethnic Identities. Indigenous Intellectuals and the Mexican State*, Lincoln: Nebraska University Press.

Guzmán, Luis. 1989. "Entrevista al arzobispo de Yucatán," *Cuadernos de la Casa Chata*, vol. 167, no. 7.

Hafez, Mohammed M. 2004. *Why Muslims Rebel. Repression and Resistance in the Islamic World*, Bolder, CO: Lynne Rienner.

Hardin, Russell. 1995. *One for All: The Logic of Group Conflict*, Princeton, NJ: Princeton University Press.

Hardy, Clarissa. 1984. *El Estado y los campesinos: la Confederación Nacional Campesina*, Mexico City: Nueva Imagen.

Hartch, Todd. 2006. *Missionaries of the State: The Summer Institute of Linguistics, State Formation, and Indigenous Mexico, 1935–1985*, Tuscaloosa: The University of Alabama Press.

Harvey, Neil. 1998. *The Chiapas Rebellion. The Struggle for Land and Democracy*, Durham, NC: Duke University Press.

Hechter, Michael. 2000. *Containing Nationalism*, Oxford: Oxford University Press.

Hedstrom, Peter and Richard Swedberg (eds.). 1998. *Social Mechanisms. An Analytic Approach to Social Theory*, Cambridge: Cambridge University Press.

Hegre, Havard, T. Ellignsen, S. Gates, and N. Gleditsch. 2001. "Toward a Democratic Civil Peace? Democracy, Political Change, and Civil War, 1816–1992," *American Political Science Review*, vol. 95, no. 1.

Hernández Díaz, Jorge. 2001. *Reclamos de la Identidad: La Formación de las Organizaciones Indígenas en Oaxaca*, Mexico City: Miguel Angel Porrúa.

Hernández Valdéz, Alfonso. 2000. "Las causas estructurales de la democracia local en México, 1989–1998," *Política y gobierno*, vol. 7, no. 1.

Hipsher, Patricia. L. 1996. "Democratization and the Decline of Urban Social Movements in Chile and Spain," *Comparative Politics*, vol. 28, no. 3.

Hirschman, Albert. O. 1970. *Exit, Voice, and Loyalty: Responses to Decline in Firms, Organizations, and States*, Cambridge MA: Harvard University Press.

Horowitz, Donald. L. 1985. *Ethnic Groups in Conflict*, Berkeley, CA: University of California Press.

Huang, Haifeng. 2007. "Media Freedom, Governance, and Regime Stability in Autocracies," Paper presented at the annual meeting of the Midwest Political Science Association, Chicago, IL.

Humphreys, Macartan and J. Weinstein. 2008. "Who Fights? The Determinants of Participation in Civil War" *American Journal of Political Science*, vol. 52, no. 2.

Iannaccone, Laurence R. 1996. "Rational Choice: Framework for the Scientific Study of Religion," in Lawerence A. Young (ed.) *Rational Choice Theory and Religion*, New York: Routledge.

Inclán, María. 2008. "From ¡Ya Basta! to the *Caracoles*: Zapatista Protest Mobilization under Transitional Conditions," *American Journal of Sociology*, vol. 113, no. 5.

INEGI (Instituto Nacional de Estadística, Geografía e Informática). 1985. *X Censo General de Población y Vivienda 1980*, Mexico City: INEGI.

  1991a. *XI Censo General de Población y Vivienda 1990*. Mexico City: INEGI.

  1991b. *VII Censo Agrícola-Ganadero*. Mexico City: INEGI.

  2001. *XII Censo General de Población y Vivienda 2000*. Mexico City: INEGI.

INI (Instituto Nacional Indigenista). 1993. *Indicadores socioeconómicos de los pueblos indígenas de México*, Mexico City: INI.

ILO (International Labor Organization). 2004. *The Indigenous and Tribal Peoples Convention, No. 169*, http://www.ilo.org/public/english/index.htm

Iribarren, Pablo. 1985. "Experiencia: Proceso de la Diócesis de San Cristóbal de Las Casas, Chiapas, México. Comunidades de San Cristóbal y Ocosingo," Typescript.

Jung, Courtney. 2003. "The Politics of Indigenous Identity," *Social Research*, vol. 7, no. 2.

Kalyvas, Stathis. 1996. *The Rise of Christian Democracy in Europe*, Ithaca, NY: Cornell University Press.

  2006. *The Logic of Violence in Civil War*, Cambridge: Cambridge University Press.

King, Gary and E. Powell. 2008. "How Not to Lie Without Statistics," Working Paper, Institute for Quantitative Social Science, Harvard University.

Kitschelt, Herbert P. 1986. "Political Opportunity Structures and Political Protest: Anti-Nuclear Movements in Four Democracies," *British Journal of Political Science*, vol. 16, no. 1.

  2003. "Landscape of Political Interest Intermediation: Social Movements, Interest Groups and Political Parties in the Twenty-First Century," in Pedro Ibarra (ed.) *Social Movements and Democracy*, New York: Palgrave-MacMillan.

Knight, Jack. 1992. *Institutions and Social Conflict*, Cambridge: Cambridge University Press.

Kocher, Matthew. 2005. *Human Ecology and Civil War*, PhD Dissertation, University of Chicago.

Kuran, Timur. 1991. "Now Out of Never: The Element of Surprise in the Eastern European Revolution of 1989," *World Politics*, vol. 44, no. 1.

    1997. *Private Truths, Public Lies: The Social Consequences of Preference Falsification*, Cambridge, MA: Harvard University Press.

Laitin, David D. 1986. *Hegemony and Culture: Politics and Religious Change among the Yoruba*, Chicago: The University of Chicago Press.

    2002. "Comparative Politics: The State of the Discipline," in I. Katznelson and H. V. Milner (eds.) *Political Science: State of the Discipline*, New York: W.W. Norton & Company.

Lawson, Chappell. 2002. *Building the Fourth State. Democratization and the Rise of a Free Press in Mexico*, Berkeley, CA: University of California Press.

Le Bot, Yvon. 1994. *Violence de la modernité en Amérique latine. Indianité, société et pouvoir*, Paris: Karthala.

    1995. *La guerra en tierras mayas. Comunidad, violencia y modernidad en Guatemala (1970–1992)*, Mexico City: FCE.

    1997. *Subcomandante Marcos. El sueño zapatista*, Barcelona: Plaza & Janés.

Legorreta Díaz, María del Carmen. 1997. *Religión, política y guerrilla en Las Cañadas de la Selva Lacandona (1973–1995)*, Mexico City: Cal y Arena.

    2008. *Desafíos de la emancipación indígena. Organización señorial y modernización en Ocosingo, Chiapas (1930–1994)*, Mexico City: UNAM.

Lehoucq, Fabrice. 2003. "Electoral Fraud: Causes, Types and Consequences," *Annual Review of Political Science*, vol. 6.

Lehoucq, Fabrice and I. Molina. 2002. *Stuffing the Ballot Box: Fraud, Electoral Reform, and Democratization in Costa Rica*, Cambridge: Cambridge University Press.

Ley, Sandra. 2006. *Descentralización e independencia electoral*, Tesis de Licenciatura en Ciencia Política y Relaciones Internacionales, CIDE, Mexico City.

Leyva, Xochitl. 1995. "Catequistas, misioneros y tradiciones en las Cañadas," in J. P. Viqueira and M. H. Ruz (eds.) *Chiapas: los rumbos de otra historia*, Mexico City: UNAM, CIESAS, CEMCA, UdeG.

    2001. "Regional, Communal, and Organizational Transformation in Las Cañadas," *Latin American Perspectives*, issue 117, vol 28, no. 2.

Lichbach, Mark I. 1987. "Deterrence or Escalation? The Puzzle of Aggregate Studies of Repression and Dissent," *Journal of Conflict Resolution*, vol. 31, no. 2.

    1996. *The Rebel's Dilemma*, Ann Arbor: Michigan University Press.

Lieberman, Evan. 2005. "Nested Analysis as a Mixed-Method Strategy for Comparative Research," *American Political Science Review*, vol. 99, no. 3.

Lipset, Seymour. M. 1960/1981. *Political Man: The Social Bases of Politics*, Baltimore: The Johns Hopkins University Press.

Lisbona, Miguel. 2006. "Olvidados del neozapatismo: Los zoques chiapanecos," *Estudios Sociológicos*, vol. 24, no. 71.

Long, Scott J. 1997. *Regression Models for Categorical and Limited Dependent Variables*, Thousand Oaks, CA: Sage Publications.

Long, Scott J. and J. Freese. 2001. *Regression Models for Categorical Dependent Variables Using Stata*, College Station, TX: Stata Press.

López Bárcenas, Francisco. 2002. *Legislación y Derechos Indígenas en México*, Mexico City: Casa Vieja/La Guillotina.

López-Leyva, Miguel. 2007. *La encrucijada. Entre la protesta social y la participación electoral (1988)*, Mexico City: Plaza y Valdés Editores.

Lujambio, Alonso. 2000. *El poder compartido. Un ensayo sobre la democratización en México*, Mexico City: Océano.

Magaloni, Beatriz. 2006. *Voting for Autocracy: Hegemonic Party Survival and Its Demise in Mexico*, Cambridge: Cambridge University Press.

2008. "Credible Power-Sharing and the Longevity of Authoritarian Rule," *Comparative Political Studies*, vol. 41, no. 4/5.

2010. "The Game of Electoral Fraud and the Ousting of Authoritarian Rule," *American Journal of Political Science*, vol. 54, no. 3.

Mahoney, James, E. Kimball, and K. Koivu. 2009. "The Logic of Historical Explanation in the Social Sciences," *Comparative Political Studies*, vol. 42, no. 1.

Mainwaring, Scott. 2003. "Party Objectives in Authoritarian Regimes with Elections or Fragile Democracies: A Dual Game," in S. Mainwaring and T. Scully (eds.), *Christian Democracy in Latin America: Electoral Competition and Regime Conflicts*, Stanford, CA: Stanford University Press.

Mainwaring, Scott and A . Wilde. 1989. "The Progressive Church in Latin America: An Interpretation," in S. Mainwaring and A. Wilde (eds.) *The Progressive Church in Latin America*, Notre Dame, IN: University of Notre Dame Press.

Marroquín, Enrique. 2007. *El conflicto religioso. Oaxaca, 1976–1992*, Mexico City: UNAM & UABJO.

Marx, Karl. 1844/1994. "Critique to Hegel's Philosophy of Rights," in J. O'Malley (ed.), *Marx: Early Political Writings*, Cambridge: Cambridge University Press.

1852/1994. "The Eighteenth Brumaire of Louis Bonaparte," in Robert C. Tucker (ed.), *The Marx-Engels Reader*, New York: W. W. Norton & Company.

Mattiace, Shannan. 2001. "Regional Renegotiation of Space. Tojolabal Ethnic Identity in Las Margaritas, Chiapas," *Latin American Perspectives*, issue 117, vol. 28 no. 2.

2003. *To See with Two Eyes: Peasant Activism and Indian Autonomy in Chiapas, Mexico*, Albuquerque: University of New Mexico Press.

2009. "Ethnic Mobilization among the Maya of Yucatán Today," *Latin American and Caribbean Ethnic Studies*, vol. 4, no. 2.

McAdam, Doug. 1996. "Political Opportunities: Conceptual Origins, Current Problems, Future Directions," in D. McAdam, J. McCarthy, and M. Zald (eds.) *Comparative Perspectives on Social Movements: Political Opportunities, Mobilizing Structures, and Cultural Framings*, Cambridge: Cambridge University Press.

1982/1999. *Political Process and the Development of Black Insurgency, 1930–1970*, Chicago: The University of Chicago Press.

McAdam, Doug, J. McCarthy, and M. N. Zald. 1996. "Introduction: Opportunities, Mobilizing Structures, and Framing Processes – Toward a Synthetic, Comparative Perspective on Social Movements," in D. McAdam, J. McCarthy, and M. Zald (eds.) *Comparative Perspectives on Social Movements: Political Opportunities, Mobilizing Structures, and Cultural Framings*, Cambridge: Cambridge University Press.

McAdam, Doug and S. Tarrow. 2010. "Ballots and Barricades: On the Reciprocal Relationship between Elections and Social Movements," *Perspectives on Politics*, vol. 8, no. 2.

McAdam, Doug, S. Tarrow, and C. Tilly. 2001. *Dynamics of Contention*, Cambridge: Cambridge University Press.

Mejía, María Consuelo and S. Sarmiento. 1987. *La lucha indígena: un reto a la ortodoxia*, Mexico City: Siglo XXI.

Merino, Mauricio. 2003. *La transición votada*, Mexico City: FCE.

Meyer, David, S. 2004. "Protest and Political Opportunities," *Annual Review of Sociology*, vol. 30.

Misión Jesuita de Bachajón. 2010. *Huellas de un caminar*, Mexico City: Universidad Iberoamericana.

Montemayor, Carlos. 1999. *La guerrilla recurrente*, Ciudad Juarez: UACJ.

Moore, Barrington Jr. 1966/1993. *Social Origins of Dictatorship and Democracy*, Boston, MA: Beacon Press.

Morales Bermúdez, Jesús. 1995. "El Congreso Indígena de Chiapas: Un Testimonio," *América Indígena*, vol. 40, no. 1/2.

Moreno Toscano, Alejandra. 1996. *Turbulencia política: Causas y razones del 1994*, Mexico City: Editorial Océano.

Nash, June. 2001. *Mayan Visions: The Quest for Autonomy in an Age of Globalization*, New York: Routledge.

Norget, Kristin. 1999. "Progressive Theology and Popular Religiosity in Oaxaca, Mexico," in C. Smith and J. Prokopy (eds.) *Latin American Religion in Motion*, New York, Routledge.

    2004. "'Knowing Where We Enter': Indigenous Theology and the Popular Church in Oaxaca," in C. Cleary and T. J. Steigenga (eds.) *Resurgent Voices in Latin America: Indigenous Peoples, Political Mobilization, and Religious Change*, New Brunswick, NJ: Rutgers University Press.

Oficina de la Presidencia. 1991. "Ejido: Reforma del artículo 27 constitucional," November.

    1994a. "Conflicto EZLN," February 27, 1994.

    1994b. "Conflicto en Chiapas," June 20, 1994.

    1994c. "Conflicto en Chiapas," December 15, 1994.

Olson, Mancur. 1966. *The Logic of Collective Action. Public Goods and the Theory of Groups* Cambridge, MA: Harvard University Press.

Olzak, Susan, 2006. *The Global Dynamics of Racial and Ethnic Mobilization*, Stanford, CA: Stanford University Press.

Osa, Maryjane. 2003. *Solidarity and Contention: Networks of Polish Opposition*, Minneapolis: University of Minnesota Press.

Oxhorn, Philip. 1994. "Where Did All the Protesters Go? Popular Mobilization and Transition to Democracy in Chile," *Latin American Perspectives*, vol. 21, no. 3.

Petersen, Roger D. 2001. *Resistance and Rebellion: Lessons from Eastern Europe*, Cambridge: Cambridge University Press.

Philpott, Daniel. 2007. "Explaining the Political Ambivalence of Religion," *American Political Science Review*, vol. 101, no. 3.

Pierskalla, Jan. 2010. "Protest, Deterrennce and Escalation: The Strategic Calculus of Government Repression," *Journal of Conflict Resolution*, vol. 54, no. 1.

Presidencia de la República Mexicana. 1974. *Nueva Ley Federal de Reforma Agraria y Leyes Complementarias*, Mexico City: Anaya Editores.

Posner, Daniel N. 2005. *Institutions and Ethnic Politics in Africa*, Cambridge: Cambridge University Press.

Postero, Nancy. 2006. *Now We Are Citizens: Indigenous Politics in Postmulticultural Bolivia*, Stanford: Stanford University Press.

Potter, Joseph, E. Amaral, and R. Woodberry. n.d. "The Growth of Protestantism in Brazil and Its Impact on Income, 1970–2000," unpublished paper.

Przeworski, Adam. 2009. "Conquered or Granted? A History of Suffrage Extensions," *British Journal of Political Science*, vol. 39, no. 2.

Przeworski, Adam and J. Sprague, 1988. *Paper Stones: A History of Electoral Socialism*, Chicago: The University of Chicago Press.

Quino, José Vicente. 2006. "El Movimiento Indígena en Guatemala: Entre el sujeto y la razón instrumental," Master's Thesis, FLACSO-Guatemala.

Recondo, David. 2007. *La política del gatopardo: Multiculturalismo y democracia en Oaxaca*, Mexico City: CIESAS.

Remes, Alain de. 2000. "Las Elecciones Municipales en México," CD-Rom, Mexico City: CIDE.

Remmer, Karen.2010. "Political Scale and Electoral Turnout: Evidence from the Less Industrialized World," *Comparative Political Studies*, vol. 43, no. 2.

Reyes, María Eugenia. 1992. *El reparto de tierras y la política agraria en Chiapas, 1914–1988*, Mexico City: UNAM.

    1998. "Los Acuerdos Agrarios en Chiapas: ¿una política de contención social?" in M. E. Reyes Ramos et al. (coords.) *Espacios Disputados: Transformaciones Rurales en Chiapas*, Mexico DF: UAM and ECOSUR.

Reza, Rocío. 1995. "Paz con justicia y dignidad para los pueblos indios." Testimonios: Comandante Tacho y Mayor Moises. *Documentos de la Selva Lacandona*, III, vol. I, Mexico City: Medios del Sur, Videotapes.

Ríos, Julio. 2005. *Siglo XX: muerte y resurrección de la Iglesia Católica en Chiapas*, Mexico City: UNAM.

Rivera, Silvia. 1986. *"Oprimidos pero no vencidos." Luchas del campesinado aymara y quechua de Bolivia, 1900–1980*, Geneva: UNRISD.

Rivera Farfán, Carolina et al. 2005. *Protestantismo en el Mundo Maya Contemporáneo*, Mexico City: UNAM and UAM.

Roberts, Kenneth M. 2008. "The Mobilization of Opposition to Economic Liberalization," *Annual Review of Political Science*, vol. 11.

Robertson, Graeme. 2007. "Strikes and Labor Organization in Hybrid Regimes," *American Political Science Review*, vol. 101, no. 4.

    2010. *The Politics of Protest in Hybrid Regimes: Managing Dissent in Post-Communist Russia*, Cambridge: Cambridge University Press.

Rosefsky Wickham, Carrie. 2002. *Mobilizing Islam: Religion, Activism, and Political Change in Egypt*, New York: Columbia University Press.

Rosero, Fernando. 1990. *Levantamiento indígena: tierra y precios*, Quito: CEDIS.

Rovira, Guimoar. 1994. *¡Zapata vive! La rebelión indígena de Chiapas contada por sus protagonistas*, Barcelona: Virus Editorial.

Rubin, Jeffrey. 1997. *Decentering the Regime: Ethnicity, Radicalism, and Democracy in Juchitán, Mexico*, Durham, NC: Duke University Press.

Rubio, Luis. 1998. "Coping with Political Change," in S. K. Purcell and L. Rubio (eds.) *Mexico Under Zedillo*, Boulder, CO: Lynne Rienner.

Rus, Jan. 1994. "La Comunidad Revolucionaria Institucional," in J. P. Viqueira and M. H. Ruz (eds.) *Chiapas: los rumbos de otra historia*, Mexico City: UNAM, CIESAS, CEMCA, UdeG.

Rus, Jan and R. Wasserstrom. 1984. "Evangelization and Political Control: The SIL in Mexico," in S. Hvalkof and P. Aaby (eds.) *Is God an American? An Anthropological Perspective on the Missionary Work of the Summer Institute of Linguistics*, Copenhague: IWGIA/SI.

Saavedra, Marco. 2008. *La Comunidad Rebelde*, Mexico City: COLMEX.

Saavedra, Marco and J.P. Viqueira (coords.). 2010. *Los indígenas de Chiapas y la rebelión zapatista: Microhistorias políticas*, Mexico City: COLMEX.

Salinas de Gortari, Carlos. 2000. *México. Un paso difícil a la modernidad*, Mexico City: Plaza y Janés.

Sambanis, Nicholas and A. Zinn. 2006. "From Protest to Violence: Conflict Escalation in Self-Determination Movements," Yale University, unpublished manuscript.

Sánchez, Consuelo. 1999. *Los pueblos indígenas: del indigenismo a la autonomía*, Mexico City: Siglo XXI.

Santana, Roberto. 1992. *Les Indiens d'Equateur, citoyens dans l'ethnicité?* Paris: CNRS.

Schatz, Edward. 2009. "Ethnographic Immersion and the Study of Politics," in E. Schatz (ed.) *Political Ethnography: What Immersion Contributes to the Study of Power*, Chicago: The University of Chicago Press.

Schedler, Andreas. 2002. "The Nested Game of Democratization," *Journal of Democracy*, vol. 23, no. 1.

2006. "The Logic of Electoral Authoritarianism," in A. Schedler (ed.) *Electoral Authoritarianism: The Dynamics of Unfree Competition*, Boulder, CO: Lynne Rienner.

Schock, Kurt. 2005. *Unarmed Insurrections. People Power Movements in Nondemocracies*, Minneapolis: University of Minnesota Press.

Seawright, Jason and J. Gerring. 2008. "Case Selection Techniques in Case Study Research: A Menu of Qualitative and Quantitative Options," *Political Research Quarterly*, vol. 6, no. 2.

SRA (Secretaria de la Reforma Agraria). 1992. "Reforma Agraria," Dirección General de Información y Documentación Agraria, Database.

Siegel, David A. 2009. "Social Networks and Collective Action," *American Journal of Political Science*, vol. 53, no. 1.

2011. "When Does Repression Work? Collective Action and Social Networks," *Journal of Politics*, vol. 73, no. 2.

Sierra Guzmán, Jorge Luis. 2003. *El enemigo interno. Contrainsurgencia y Fuerzas Armadas en México*, Mexico City: Plaza y Valdés Editores.

SNIM (Sistema Nacional de Información Municipal). 2003. *SNIM Cd-rom*, Mexico City. Secretaría de Gobernación.

Smith, Adam. 1776/1994. *The Wealth of Nations*, New York: Random House.

Smith, Christian. 1996. "Correcting a Curious Neglect, or Bringing Religion Back In," in Christian Smith (ed.) *Disruptive Religion: The Force of Faith in Social Movement Activism*, New York: Routledge.

Snyder, Richard. 2001a. *Politics after Neoliberalism: Reregulation in Mexico*, Cambridge: Cambridge University Press.

2001b. "Scaling Down: The Subnational Comparative Method," *Studies in International Comparative Development*, vol. 36, no. 1.

Sokoloff, Kenneth and E. Zolt. 2008. "Inequality and Taxation: Evidence from the Americas on How Inequality May Influence Taxing Institutions," *Tax Law Review*, vol 59, no. 2.

Sonnleitner, Willibald. 2001. *Los indígenas y la democratización electoral. Una década de cambio político entre los tzotziles y tzeltales de Los Altos de Chiapas, (1988–2000)*, Mexico City: COLMEX and IFE.

Stark, Rodney and Roger Finke. 2000. *Acts of Faith: Explaining the Human Side of Religion*, Berkeley, CA: University of California Press.

Stavenhagen, Rodolfo. 1992. "Challenging the Nation-State in Latin America," *Journal of International Affairs*, vol 34, no. 2.

Stepan, Alfred. 2000. "Religion, Democray, and the 'Twin Tolerations'," *Journal of Democracy*, vol. 11, no. 4.

Stokes, Susan. C. 1995. *Cultures in Conflict: Social Movements and the State in Peru*, Los Angeles: University of California Press.

Stoll, David. 1993. *Between Two Armies in the Ixil Towns of Guatemala*, New York: Columbia University Press.

Tarrow, Sidney.1998. *Power in Movement*, Cambridge: Cambridge University Press.

2007. "Inside Insurgencies: Politics and Violence in an Age of Civil War," *Perspectives on Politics*, vol. 5, no. 3.

Taylor, Michael. 1982. *Community, Anarchy and Liberty*, Cambridge: Cambridge University Press.

Tello Díaz, Carlos. 1995. *La rebelión de las Cañadas*, Mexico City: Cal y Arena.

Tilly, Charles. 1978. *From Mobilization to Revolution*, Reading, MA: Addison-Wesley.

2006. *Regimes and Repertoires*, Chicago: The University of Chicago Press.

Tocqueville, Alexis de. 1858/1983. *The Old Regime and the French Revolution*, New York: Anchor Books Doubleday.

Toledo, Sonia. 2002. *Fincas, poder y cultura en Simojovel, Chiapas*, Mexico City: UNAM.

Tomz, Michael et al. 2003. Clarify: Software for Interpreting and Presenting Statistical Results, http://gking.harvard.edu/stats.shtml

Trejo, Guillermo. 2009. "Religious Competition and Ethnic Mobilization in Latin America: Why the Catholic Church Promotes Indigenous Movements in Mexico," *American Political Science Review*, vol. 103, no. 3.

Van Cott, Donna Lee. 1995. "Indigenous Peoples and Democracy: Issues for Policymakers," in D. L. Van Cott (ed.) *Indigenous Peoples and Democracy in Latin America*, New York: St. Martin's Press.

2000. *The Friendly Liquidation of the Past: The Politics of Diversity in Latin America*, Pittsburgh, PA: Pittsburgh University Press.

2001. "Explaining Ethnic Autonomy Regimes in Latin America," *Studies in Comparative International Development*, vol. 25, no. 4.

2008. "Indigenous Peoples and the Left: Tentative Allies," *Global Dialogue*, vol. 10.

Várguez, Luis. 2008. "Construyendo y reconstruyendo las fronteras de la tradición y la modernidad. La Iglesia Católica y el Movimiento de Renovación Carismática en el Espíritu Santo," *Convergencia*, vol. 15, no. 46.

Villafuerte, Daniel et al. 1999. *La tierra en Chiapas. Viejos problemas nuevos*, Mexico City: Plaza y Janés.

Villarreal, Andrés. 2010. "Stratification by Skin Color in Contemporary Mexico," *American Sociological Review*, vol. 75, no. 5.

Viqueira, Juna Pedro. 1994. "Los Altos," in J. P. Viqueira and M. H. Ruz (eds.) *Chiapas: los rumbos de otra historia*, Mexico City: UNAM, CIESAS, CEMCA and UdeG.

Viterna, Jocelyn. 2006. "Pulled, Pushed and Persuaded: Explaining Women's Mobilization into the Salvadoran Guerrilla Army," *American Journal of Sociology*, vol. 112, no. 1.

Weber, Marx. 1956/1978. *Economy and Society*, vol. I, Berkeley: University of California Press.

1930/1993. The Protestant Ethic and the Spirit of Capitalism, London: Routledge.

Weinstein, Jeremy. 2006. *Inside Rebellion: The Politics of Insurgent Violence*, Cambridge: Cambridge University Press, 2006.

Wickham-Crowley, Timothy. 1992. *Guerrillas and Revolution in Latin America. A Comparative Study of Insurgents and Regimes since 1956*, Princeton, NJ: Princeton University Press.

Wolf, Eric. 1957. "Closed Corporate Peasant Communities in Mesoamerica and Central Java," *Southwestern Journal of Anthropology*, vol. 13, no. 1.

Womack Jr., John. 1999. *Rebellion in Chiapas. An Historical Reader*, New York: The New Press.

Wood, Elisabeth J. 2000. *Forging Democracy from Below: Insurgent Transitions in Southern Africa and El Salvador*, Cambridge: Cambridge University Press.

2003. *Insurgent Collective Action and Civil War in El Salvador*, Cambridge: Cambridge University Press.

Wright, Angus and W. Wolford. 2003. *To Inherit the Earth: The Landless Movement and the Struggle for a New Brazil*, Oakland, CA: Food First Books.

Yashar, Deborah. 1998. "Contesting Citizenship: Indigenous Movements and Democracy in Latin America," *Comparative Politics*, vol. 31, no. 1.

2005. *Contesting Citizenship in Latin America: The Rise of Indigenous Movements and the Post-Liberal Challenge*, Cambridge: Cambridge University Press.

Index

Alfaro, Roberto (CIOAC leader), 114, 119–22, 129, 187, 191–2, 284
ANCIEZ, 177–9
Archdiocese of Antequera, 88, 102–4
Archdiocese of Puebla, 88, 103–4
Archdiocese of Yucatán, 89, 108
Armed insurgencies
  armed rebel groups, 1–3, 10–13, 66, 69, 143–7, 150, 165, 167, 174–80, 223–9
Army
  Mexican army/military, 1, 66, 69–70, 75, 116, 119, 144–5, 165, 191, 195, 207, 233–4, 242
Autocracy
  closed autocracy, 31–3, 43, 45, 65–7, 114–16
  electoral autocracy, 8–10, 17, 42–50, 69–71, 73–4, 116–24, 130–1, 136–7, 259–63
  single-party autocracy/hegemony, 43, 70, 134–5, 210–11
  subnational autocracy, 151, 169–70, 240–2

Bias
  geographic, 275–6
  temporal, 273–5
Bible
  study groups (Catholic), 8, 122, 131, 133, 163–4
  study groups (Protestant), 37, 91, 102
  translation to indigenous languages, 7, 14, 37, 40–1, 91–2, 218–19, 229–30
Bolivia, 155, 258, 261, 268
Brazil, 258, 268

Case studies, 22–3, 186–7, 218–21
Castellanos, Absalón (Chiapas Governor), 75, 119–24

Castillo, Ramón (Father), 100, 117, 188–9, 194, 283
Castro, Manuel (Archbishop), 87, 89, 108–9
Catechists, 94–98, 98–102, 103, 104–7, 188–93, 195
Catholic Church, 7, 8, 12, 13, 14, 87–90, 93–7, 102–4, 105, 108, 116, 125, 135, 162, 218–21, 229
  and charismatic renewal, 108–9
  and decentralized social networks, 8, 13, 17–18, 19, 39–40, 100–2, 122–4, 136–7, 174, 180–2, 183–5, 188–93, 196–7, 257, 262–3, 267–8
  and economic and social cooperatives, 38–9, 94, 103, 105–7
  and ethnic identities, 14, 41, 218–21, 229–30, 258
  and human rights, 99–100, 162
  and rural indigenous movements, 8, 39, 98–100, 106–7, 131–4, 157–8, 162, 194, 258–9, 262–3
Chiapas (Mexico), 1–2, 12, 62–3, 75, 144–7, 156–64, 167–71, 178–80
  Altamirano, 2–3, 8, 13, 99, 178
  Amatenango del Valle, 193–4
  Chilón, 79–80, 95, 100, 132–3, 178, 218–21
  Lacandón jungle, 2, 144, 163, 178–9, 187–93
  Las Margaritas, 99, 112–30, 178, 187–93
  Ocotepec, 1, 3, 8, 10, 12, 79
  San Cristóbal de Las Casas, 117, 179, 181, 281
  Simojovel, 161–2, 179, 181, 194–6
  Tenejapa, 2–3, 8, 13
  Venustiano Carranza, 181, 195–6
Chile, 261, 264
Chol, 1, 93–100, 178–9, 181

CIOAC, 22–3, 99, 113–30, 135, 161–2,
    181, 187–91, 194–5, 221–2, 225,
    227, 242, 284
CNC, 82, 119, 164, 210–11
COCEI, 106–7, 130–1, 165–6, 168, 170, 284
Collective action (*see also* protest/
    mobilization), 17, 41, 54–5, 82–4,
    109–10, 122–4, 141–3, 261, 270–1
    independent, 29, 31–2, 35, 122–4, 172, 262
    insurgent, 141–3, 145–7, 253, 268–70
    popular, xv, 16, 54–5, 82–4, 109–10, 254–6,
    259–61
Compensatory policies, 12, 18, 164–7,
    171, 265
Concessions
    partial, 47–50, 74–5, 80–1, 120–4, 164–7
Controlled comparison, 23, 112–14, 156–9
    paired comparison, 23, 157
Co-optation (Government), 10, 23, 45–7,
    120–4, 165, 168, 261–3
Corporatism, 5, 45, 66–7, 76–7, 82, 108,
    119–20, 210–11, 215–16
Corripio, Ernesto (Cardinal), 87–8, 90,
    102–4, 109

Demobilization, 10, 128–30, 131–3, 137, 222,
    263–4
Democracy
    transition to democracy, 5, 19, 231, 251–2
Democratization, 5, 19, 231–2, 252–3, 268–70
    from below, 231–2, 252–3, 268–70
    of electoral institutions, 232, 234–9, 242–6,
    251–3, 268–71
Diocese of San Cristóbal de Las Casas, 69,
    86–8, 90–100, 113–14, 124–5, 127,
    135, 156–64, 167–8, 181–2, 185, 190–1,
    193–6
Diocese of Tehuantepec, 89, 104–7, 131,
    133–4, 156–9, 167

Ecuador, 258, 261, 268
Effective number of parties (ENP), 73–4,
    79–80, 169, 214
Effective number of religions (ENR), 72–3, 79,
    99, 107, 180, 183, 214, 215–17, 226–7
El Salvador, 176, 260, 263–4, 268, 270
Electoral competition, 8, 14, 43–5, 53, 73–4,
    79–80, 83–4, 125–30, 136–7, 151, 154–6,
    165–7, 182, 214, 217, 228, 239, 259–61,
    263–4
    competition for indigenous votes, 59,
    84, 255
Electoral fraud, 14, 43–4, 166, 217, 221,
    223–5, 230, 232, 240–2, 245, 259, 266

Endogeneity, 79, 80
EPR, 144–7, 167
Escalation
    of peasant demands into ethnic claims, 2–3,
    14–15, 50–3, 204–9, 211–13, 223–5, 230
    of protest into rebellion, 2–3, 10–13, 47–50,
    141–3, 150–1, 154–6, 170–1, 172–3,
    175–8, 181, 185, 197, 265–8
Ethnicity, 14, 50–3, 204
    ethnic identities, 40–1, 51–3, 209–13,
    218–21, 230, 271
    politicization of ethnicity, 13–15, 52–3,
    204–5, 207, 230
EZLN/Zapatistas/Zapatism, 1–3, 12, 14–15,
    24–5, 79, 88, 102, 126–30, 143–7, 157,
    161–4, 171, 174–180, 180–186, 186–196,
    208–9, 215–17, 221–223, 223–230,
    233–53

Framing, 16, 29, 54
    cognitive liberation, 96–7, 110
    ideas, 85, 109
    ideology, 29, 39, 54–5
Free and fair elections, 15, 44, 232, 234–40,
    245, 269

Globalization, 4–7, 13–15, 201, 229
González, Patrocinio (Chiapas Governor),
    159–64, 167–70
Government-controlled elections, 8, 23, 42–5,
    69–71, 73–6, 259
Guatemala, 258, 260, 263–4,
    267–8, 281
Guerrero (Mexico), 63, 75, 144–7, 222, 282

Hernández, Antonio (CIOAC leader), 113–15,
    117, 119–22, 125–7, 129, 161, 187,
    191–2, 221–2, 242, 284
Hidalgo (Mexico), 63, 75, 89, 104, 145–7, 283
    Huejutla, 89, 104, 283
Historical sequences, 233
Human rights *see also* (repression)
    Demands for human rights respect, 64, 132,
    207
    NGOs, 100, 107, 132

Indigenous claims/demands
    for autonomy and self-determination, 13,
    64, 206–9, 213, 223–5
    for free and fair elections, 64, 206–7
    for human rights , 64, 206–7
    for land redistribution, 64,
    206–7
Indigenous communities

closed corporate, 8–9, 12, 14, 33–6,
    100–2, 118
of cultural survivors, 4–7, 59, 76, 82–3,
    201–3, 217
pluralistic/heterogenous/diverse, 14, 36, 59,
    82–3, 100–2,
    201–3, 217
Indigenous languages, 1–4, 7, 14, 33–5, 37,
    40–1, 91–2, 204–5, 209–11, 218–19,
    229–30
Indigenous rights
    ILO Convention 2, 5, 6–7, 52, 166, 169,
        213, 225
    indigenous rights in Mexican states, 250–1
    indigenous rights in Mexico, 8, 105–6,
        219–21
    international indigenous rights 5–6, 13,
        212–13
    rights to autonomy and self-determination
        3, 64–5, 207, 208–9, 223–8, 246–50, 252,
        269
Inequality
    Income inequality 31, 38, 50–1, 54–5,
        152, 157
    Land inequality 31, 163–4, 182–6
Institutionalization
    (*see also* demobilization)44, 128–30, 136,
        252, 263–4

Jesuits/Jesuit Mission, 88–9, 94–5, 100, 132–3,
    190, 218–22, 283

Land
    end of land reform 5, 10–11, 76, 147–50,
        157–8, 163–4
    liberalization, 1, 5, 10–11, 13, 76, 81–2,
        147–50, 170–1, 211–13
    reform/redistribution, 4, 12, 66–9, 71, 75,
        81, 115, 159, 168–9, 206–8
Leftist opposition parties, 9, 70, 73, 135,
    221–3, 235–9, 242–6, 248–50
    and centralized social networks, 9, 17–18,
        117–18, 136–7, 191–3, 197, 262–3
    and demobilization, 10, 128–30, 131–3,
        137, 222, 263–4
    and ethnic identities, 203, 217, 221–3
    and rural indigenous mobilization, 9,
        117–18, 131–2
    and socio-electoral coalitions, 9–10, 125–8,
        131–2, 136, 195, 236–7, 245–6
Life histories, xvi, 21–2, 85–90, 109–10,
    187–93, 280–4
Lona, Arturo (Bishop), 87, 88–90, 104–7,
    165, 283

López, Eduardo (catechist and deacon),
    100–1, 114–15, 119–22, 130, 163–4,
    187–93, 283

Median voter, 14, 42, 247, 253, 264
Mexican Indigenous Insurgency Database
    (MII), 21, 60–5, 71, 75, 116, 151, 205–8,
    213, 273–7
Mixe, 102–3, 107, 134
Mobilizing structures (*see also* social
    networks)16–18, 29, 54, 256–9
    organizational infrastructure for collective
        action, 39, 41, 54–5, 83, 86, 88, 98–102,
        109–10, 196–7, 256–9

NAFTA, 1, 66, 76, 147–8, 158, 239
Nahua, 89, 144
Native pastors, 7, 37, 94, 104, 258
Natural experiments, 22, 86–7, 90
Negative binomial regression, 77–8,
    215–16, 278
Neoliberal agricultural reform, 1, 5, 6, 10, 11,
    147–50, 211–13
Nicaragua, 117, 176, 225

Oaxaca (Mexico), 12, 62–3, 75, 104–7, 133–4,
    145–7, 156–9, 164–71, 282
    Juchitán, 106, 130–1, 134, 165–6
    Mixe highlands, 102, 107, 133–4
    Tehuantepec Isthmus, 104–7, 133–4
Ordered probit regression, 152–3, 183–4

Padrón, Joel (Father), 162–3,
    194–5, 283
Paramilitaries
    paramilitary forces, 66, 225–8
Partially free and unfair elections, 8, 17,
    42–4, 259
Pentecostal churches, 90, 102, 194
    charismatic practices, 108–9
    Neo-Pentecostals, 108
Police
    subnational, 70–1, 75–6, 99, 116, 119–23,
        161–4, 207
Political process approach, 16–18, 29,
    54–5, 82–4, 111–13, 135–7, 170,
    259–61, 263–4
Popular movements, xv, 3, 54–5, 82–6, 254
    popular collective action/ mobilization,
        xv, 16, 19, 54–5, 82–4, 109–10, 254–6,
        259–61
    poor people's movements, xv, 3, 85–6, 254
Poverty, xv, 3, 31, 38, 50–1, 54–5, 77–8, 182,
    184–5, 215–16

PRD, 74, 80, 125–30, 131–5, 221–3, 235–40, 243–8, 250
PRI, 2, 9, 15, 34–5, 66–71, 74–5, 80–2, 119–20, 129, 131–5, 150, 155, 157, 159, 164, 170, 210–11, 235–42, 243–51
Private guards, 99, 114–16, 119–20
Protest/mobilization
 cycles of rural indigenous protest, 1, 4, 6, 8–9, 13, 14, 21, 54, 61–5, 83–4, 111–13, 133, 136–7, 256, 259–64
 independent protest, 3, 10, 44–7, 133–4, 136, 169, 256
 peaceful protest, 2, 54, 63, 169
 rural indigenous protest, 1–2, 3–6, 71–2, 77–84, 99–100, 107, 109–10, 122, 125–8, 151, 154–8, 160, 166, 178–9, 181, 183–5, 211–13, 255
 social protest, 44–7, 54–5, 83–4, 135, 254
Protestant/Protestantism, 8, 87, 90–3, 102, 104, 105
Protestant churches, 90–3, 102, 104, 202, 218–21
U.S. Protestant missionaries, 7, 90–3, 102, 104, 110, 183, 229, 258, 262
Puebla (Mexico), 62–3, 73, 75, 88, 103

Racial exclusion/discrimination, xv, 50–2, 168, 204, 210–11
Ramírez, Heladio (Oaxaca Governor), 164–70
Regime reversion threats, 12, 19, 48–9, 162–4, 186, 197, 230, 265–8
Religion, 41, 85, 109, 137, 196, 229–30, 256–7
 in autocracies, 32, 85, 257
 and dissident movements, 85, 109, 137, 196, 257
 and social identities, 229–30
Religious competition, 7–8, 17–18, 36–41, 72–3, 79, 85–6, 90, 93–7, 102–7, 108–10, 135, 157–8, 173, 180–1, 183, 197, 202, 226, 230, 256–8
 competition for souls, 7, 229, 255
 Neo-Pentecostal competition, 108–9
 Protestant competition, 7, 12, 90–3, 102, 104, 173, 180, 196–7
Religious monopoly, 32–3, 36
 Catholic monopoly, 33–6, 103, 104, 194
 monopoly clergy, 32–3

Repression (Government), 10–12, 14, 18, 31–2, 39, 42–4, 45–7, 48–50, 74–6, 80–1, 99–100, 115, 119–24, 131–2, 151–2, 156, 158, 159–64, 168, 171, 181–2, 185, 196–98
 moderate and targeted, 70–1
 lethal and random, 66
 massacre, 65–6, 225–6
Revolutionary coalition, 15, 235–9, 242–6, 252–3
Ruiz, Samuel (Bishop), 86–9, 93–102, 161–2, 180, 191, 282
Rural governance
 in autocracies, 66–8, 114–16
 in electoral autocracies, 69–71, 116–24

Salinas, Carlos (Mexican President), 232, 235–9, 240–2
SIL, 90–1, 93–4, 102, 104, 108, 218
Social movement theory, 16–19, 29, 54–5, 83–4, 111, 135–7, 170–1, 240, 256, 259–61, 263, 265
Social movements
 for free and fair elections, 9, 43–4, 126–7, 131–2
 independent, 3, 6, 43–7, 119–25, 176–7
 for indigenous rights, 7–8, 14, 40–1, 52–3, 100, 107, 132, 136, 211–13, 221–3, 230, 254, 258–9, 260
 for land redistribution, 7–8, 38–40, 99–100, 107, 114–19, 130, 132, 136, 176–7, 254, 258–60
Social networks
 centralized and hierarchical, 9, 17–18, 117–18, 136–7, 191–3, 197, 262–3
 decentralized and horizontal, 8, 13, 17–19, 39–40, 100–2, 122–4, 136–7, 174, 180–5, 188–93, 196–7, 257, 262–3, 267–8
Socio-electoral coalitions, 9–10, 43–5, 236–8, 260–1
Subcommander Marcos (rebel leader), 164, 175, 177

Tojolabal, 1, 22, 93–100, 113–30, 161, 163, 178–9, 181, 187–93, 221–2
Trejo, Humberto/Tacho (EZLN commander), 114, 187–93, 195
Tzeltal, 1–3, 8, 10, 93–100, 132–3, 178–9, 181, 194, 218–21
Tzotzil, 1, 93–100, 176, 178–9, 194–6

UCIRI, 107, 133–4
United States, 7, 90–3, 102, 104, 110, 183,
    229, 258, 262

Vazquez, Límbano (CIOAC leader), 114, 127,
    187–8, 190, 284
Veracruz (Mexico), 62–3, 75, 144–7, 281

Western Europe, 41, 229–30, 231, 252

Yomlej, 132–3, 284
Yucatán (Mexico), 62–3, 75,
    89, 108

Zapotec, 102–3, 107, 130–1
Zedillo, Ernesto (Mexican President), 209,
    232, 242–51
Zoque, 1, 3, 8, 10, 134–5, 179,
    181–2

Other Books in the Series (*continued from page iii*)

Michael Bratton, Robert Mattes, and E. Gyimah-Boadi, *Public Opinion, Democracy, and Market Reform in Africa*

Michael Bratton and Nicolas van de Walle, *Democratic Experiments in Africa: Regime Transitions in Comparative Perspective*

Valerie Bunce, *Leaving Socialism and Leaving the State: The End of Yugoslavia, the Soviet Union, and Czechoslovakia*

Daniele Caramani, *The Nationalization of Politics: The Formation of National Electorates and Party Systems in Europe*

John M. Carey, *Legislative Voting and Accountability*

Kanchan Chandra, *Why Ethnic Parties Succeed: Patronage and Ethnic Headcounts in India*

Eric C. C. Chang, Mark Andreas Kayser, Drew A. Linzer, and Ronald Rogowski, *Electoral Systems and the Balance of Consumer-Producer Power*

José Antonio Cheibub, *Presidentialism, Parliamentarism, and Democracy*

Ruth Berins Collier, *Paths toward Democracy: The Working Class and Elites in Western Europe and South America*

Christian Davenport, *State Repression and the Domestic Democratic Peace*

Donatella della Porta, *Social Movements, Political Violence, and the State*

Alberto Diaz-Cayeros, *Federalism, Fiscal Authority, and Centralization in Latin America*

Thad Dunning, *Crude Democracy: Natural Resource Wealth and Political Regimes*

Gerald Easter, *Reconstructing the State: Personal Networks and Elite Identity*

Margarita Estevez-Abe, *Welfare and Capitalism in Postwar Japan: Party, Bureaucracy, and Business*

Henry Farrell, *The Political Economy of Trust: Institutions, Interests, and Inter-Firm Cooperation in Italy and Germany*

Karen E. Ferree, *Framing the Race in South Africa: The Political Origins of Racial-Census Elections*

M. Steven Fish, *Democracy Derailed in Russia: The Failure of Open Politics*

Robert F. Franzese, *Macroeconomic Policies of Developed Democracies*

Roberto Franzosi, *The Puzzle of Strikes: Class and State Strategies in Postwar Italy*

Timothy Frye, *Building States and Markets after Communism: The Perils of Polarized Democracy*

Geoffrey Garrett, *Partisan Politics in the Global Economy*

Scott Gehlbach, *Representation through Taxation: Revenue, Politics, and Development in Postcommunist States*

Miriam Golden, *Heroic Defeats: The Politics of Job Loss*

Jeff Goodwin, *No Other Way Out: States and Revolutionary Movements*

Merilee Serrill Grindle, *Changing the State*

Anna Grzymala-Busse, *Rebuilding Leviathan: Party Competition and State Exploitation in Post-Communist Democracies*

Anna Grzymala-Busse, *Redeeming the Communist Past: The Regeneration of Communist Parties in East Central Europe*

Frances Hagopian, *Traditional Politics and Regime Change in Brazil*

Henry E. Hale, *The Foundations of Ethnic Politics: Separatism of States and Nations in Eurasia and the World*

Mark Hallerberg, Rolf Ranier Strauch, and Jürgen von Hagen, *Fiscal Governance in Europe*

Stephen E. Hanson, *Post-Imperial Democracies: Ideology and Party Formation in Third Republic France, Weimar Germany, and Post-Soviet Russia*

Gretchen Helmke, *Courts Under Constraints: Judges, Generals, and Presidents in Argentina*

Yoshiko Herrera, *Imagined Economies: The Sources of Russian Regionalism*

J. Rogers Hollingsworth and Robert Boyer, eds., *Contemporary Capitalism: The Embeddedness of Institutions*

John D. Huber and Charles R. Shipan, *Deliberate Discretion? The Institutional Foundations of Bureaucratic Autonomy*

Ellen Immergut, *Health Politics: Interests and Institutions in Western Europe*

Torben Iversen, *Capitalism, Democracy, and Welfare*

Torben Iversen, *Contested Economic Institutions*

Torben Iversen, Jonas Pontusson, and David Soskice, eds., *Unions, Employers, and Central Banks: Macroeconomic Coordination and Institutional Change in Social Market Economies*

Thomas Janoski and Alexander M. Hicks, eds., *The Comparative Political Economy of the Welfare State*

Joseph Jupille, *Procedural Politics: Issues, Influence, and Institutional Choice in the European Union*

Stathis Kalyvas, *The Logic of Violence in Civil War*

David C. Kang, *Crony Capitalism: Corruption and Capitalism in South Korea and the Philippines*

Junko Kato, *Regressive Taxation and the Welfare State*

Orit Kedar, *Voting for Policy, Not Parties: How Voters Compensate for Power Sharing*

Robert O. Keohane and Helen B. Milner, eds., *Internationalization and Domestic Politics*

Herbert Kitschelt, *The Transformation of European Social Democracy*

Herbert Kitschelt, Kirk A. Hawkins, Juan Pablo Luna, Guillermo Rosas, and Elizabeth J. Zechmeister, *Latin American Party Systems*

Herbert Kitschelt, Peter Lange, Gary Marks, and John D. Stephens, eds., *Continuity and Change in Contemporary Capitalism*

Herbert Kitschelt, Zdenka Mansfeldova, Radek Markowski, and Gabor Toka, *Post-Communist Party Systems*

David Knoke, Franz Urban Pappi, Jeffrey Broadbent, and Yutaka Tsujinaka, eds., *Comparing Policy Networks*

Allan Kornberg and Harold D. Clarke, *Citizens and Community: Political Support in a Representative Democracy*

Amie Kreppel, *The European Parliament and the Supranational Party System*

David D. Laitin, *Language Repertoires and State Construction in Africa*

Fabrice E. Lehoucq and Ivan Molina, *Stuffing the Ballot Box: Fraud, Electoral Reform, and Democratization in Costa Rica*

Mark Irving Lichbach and Alan S. Zuckerman, eds., *Comparative Politics: Rationality, Culture, and Structure, 2nd edition*

Evan Lieberman, *Race and Regionalism in the Politics of Taxation in Brazil and South Africa*

Pauline Jones Luong, *Institutional Change and Political Continuity in Post-Soviet Central Asia*

Pauline Jones Luong and Erika Weinthal, *Oil Is Not a Curse: Ownership Structure and Institutions in Soviet Successor States*

Julia Lynch, *Age in the Welfare State: The Origins of Social Spending on Pensioners, Workers, and Children*

Doug McAdam, John McCarthy, and Mayer Zald, eds., *Comparative Perspectives on Social Movements*

Lauren M. MacLean, *Informal Institutions and Citizenship in Rural Africa: Risk and Reciprocity in Ghana and Côte d'Ivoire*

Beatriz Magaloni, *Voting for Autocracy: Hegemonic Party Survival and Its Demise in Mexico*

James Mahoney, *Colonialism and Postcolonial Development: Spanish America in Comparative Perspective*

James Mahoney and Dietrich Rueschemeyer, eds., *Historical Analysis and the Social Sciences*

Scott Mainwaring and Matthew Soberg Shugart, eds., *Presidentialism and Democracy in Latin America*

Isabela Mares, *The Politics of Social Risk: Business and Welfare State Development*

Isabela Mares, *Taxation, Wage Bargaining, and Unemployment*

Anthony W. Marx, *Making Race and Nation: A Comparison of South Africa, the United States, and Brazil*

Bonnie M. Meguid, *Party Competition between Unequals: Strategies and Electoral Fortunes in Western Europe*

Joel S. Migdal, *State in Society: Studying How States and Societies Constitute One Another*

Joel S. Migdal, Atul Kohli, and Vivienne Shue, eds., *State Power and Social Forces: Domination and Transformation in the Third World*

Scott Morgenstern and Benito Nacif, eds., *Legislative Politics in Latin America*

Layna Mosley, *Global Capital and National Governments*

Layna Mosley, *Labor Rights and Multinational Production*

Wolfgang C. Müller and Kaare Strøm, *Policy, Office, or Votes?*

Maria Victoria Murillo, *Political Competition, Partisanship, and Policy Making in Latin American Public Utilities*

Maria Victoria Murillo, *Labor Unions, Partisan Coalitions, and Market Reforms in Latin America*

Monika Nalepa, *Skeletons in the Closet: Transitional Justice in Post-Communist Europe*

Ton Notermans, *Money, Markets, and the State: Social Democratic Economic Policies since 1918*

Aníbal Pérez-Liñán, *Presidential Impeachment and the New Political Instability in Latin America*

Roger D. Petersen, *Understanding Ethnic Violence: Fear, Hatred, and Resentment in Twentieth-Century Eastern Europe*

Roger D. Petersen, *Western Intervention in the Balkans: The Strategic Use of Emotion in Conflict*

Simona Piattoni, ed., *Clientelism, Interests, and Democratic Representation*

Paul Pierson, *Dismantling the Welfare State? Reagan, Thatcher, and the Politics of Retrenchment*

Marino Regini, *Uncertain Boundaries: The Social and Political Construction of European Economies*

Marc Howard Ross, *Cultural Contestation in Ethnic Conflict*

Lyle Scruggs, *Sustaining Abundance: Environmental Performance in Industrial Democracies*

Jefferey M. Sellers, *Governing from Below: Urban Regions and the Global Economy*

Yossi Shain and Juan Linz, eds., *Interim Governments and Democratic Transitions*

Beverly Silver, *Forces of Labor: Workers' Movements and Globalization since 1870*

Theda Skocpol, *Social Revolutions in the Modern World*

Regina Smyth, *Candidate Strategies and Electoral Competition in the Russian Federation: Democracy without Foundation*

Richard Snyder, *Politics after Neoliberalism: Reregulation in Mexico*

David Stark and László Bruszt, *Postsocialist Pathways: Transforming Politics and Property in East Central Europe*

Sven Steinmo, *The Evolution of Modern States: Sweden, Japan, and the United States*

Sven Steinmo, Kathleen Thelen, and Frank Longstreth, eds., *Structuring Politics: Historical Institutionalism in Comparative Analysis*

Susan C. Stokes, *Mandates and Democracy: Neoliberalism by Surprise in Latin America*

Susan C. Stokes, ed., *Public Support for Market Reforms in New Democracies*

Duane Swank, *Global Capital, Political Institutions, and Policy Change in Developed Welfare States*

Sidney Tarrow, *Power in Movement: Social Movements and Contentious Politics, Revised and Updated Third Edition*

Kathleen Thelen, *How Institutions Evolve: The Political Economy of Skills in Germany, Britain, the United States, and Japan*

Charles Tilly, *Trust and Rule*

Daniel Treisman, *The Architecture of Government: Rethinking Political Decentralization*

Lily Lee Tsai, *Accountability without Democracy: How Solidary Groups Provide Public Goods in Rural China*

Joshua Tucker, *Regional Economic Voting: Russia, Poland, Hungary, Slovakia and the Czech Republic, 1990–1999*

Ashutosh Varshney, *Democracy, Development, and the Countryside*

Jeremy M. Weinstein, *Inside Rebellion: The Politics of Insurgent Violence*

Stephen I. Wilkinson, *Votes and Violence: Electoral Competition and Ethnic Riots in India*

Jason Wittenberg, *Crucibles of Political Loyalty: Church Institutions and Electoral Continuity in Hungary*

Elisabeth J. Wood, *Forging Democracy from Below: Insurgent Transitions in South Africa and El Salvador*

Elisabeth J. Wood, *Insurgent Collective Action and Civil War in El Salvador*

30831623R10187

Made in the USA
San Bernardino, CA
24 February 2016